D0975539

By James Lacey

Moment of Battle

The First Clash

*Takedown: The 3rd Infantry Division's
Twenty-One Day Assault on Baghdad*

Pershing

Keep from All Thoughtful Men

By Williamson Murray

Moment of Battle

*The Change in the European Balance of Power, 1938–1939:
The Path to Ruin*

War in the Air 1914–1945

A War to Be Won: Fighting the Second World War
(with Allan R. Millett)

The Iraq War: A Military History
(with Major General Robert H. Scales, Jr.)

MOMENT *of* BATTLE

BANTAM BOOKS | NEW YORK

WITHDRAWN

MOMENT
of
BATTLE

*The Twenty Clashes
That Changed the World*

JAMES LACEY
and
WILLIAMSON MURRAY

Copyright © 2013 by James Lacey and Williamson Murray

All rights reserved.

Published in the United States by Bantam Books,
an imprint of The Random House Publishing Group,
a division of Random House, Inc., New York.

BANTAM BOOKS and the rooster colophon are registered trademarks
of Random House, Inc.

Maps by Dave Merrill

LIBRARY OF CONGRESS CATALOGING-IN-PUBLICATION DATA
Lacey, James.
Moment of battle: the twenty clashes that changed the world /
James Lacey and Williamson Murray.
p.   cm.
Includes bibliographical references.
ISBN 978-0-345-52697-7
eBook ISBN 978-0-345-52699-1
1. Battles. 2. Military history. 3. Military art and science—History.
I. Murray, Williamson. II. Title.
D25.5.L27 2013   355.0209—dc23   2012034481

Printed in the United States of America on acid-free paper

www.bantamdell.com

246897531

First Edition

Book design by Susan Turner

To
the two loves of our lives,
Sharon and Lee

CONTENTS

INTRODUCTION

LEON TROTSKY, ONE OF THE MORE COMPETENT PRACTITIONERS OF THE art of war, is reputed to have commented that "you may not be interested in war, but war is interested in you." Nevertheless, over the past several decades, the whole trend in American academic history seems to be moving in the opposite direction. Its fundamental mantra appears to be that wars and military and strategic history are irrelevant to the study of the past, which should instead involve the study of great sweeping social movements and factors other than military power. The adherents of this approach have their point, because the study of "pure" military history and battles, divorced from their political and social context, can perhaps seem not only arcane but unmoored from the very events that precipitated them and gave them meaning. Moreover, today's academics also argue that the so-called great men of history have in fact played minor roles in the ultimate flow of pivotal events. In other words, battles, wars, generals, and statesmen are simply the colorful but materially insignificant blips on the radar screen of any serious analysis of historical change. Yet it is the contention of the authors of this volume, who have seen war all too closely, that wars and battles have had a direct and massive impact on the course of history, one that is essential to understanding the world in which we live. We suspect the reader may agree with us.

For all of the intriguing insights of the wider academic analysis of the deep and complex currents that run through history, wars and battles *have* turned the course of human events in fundamentally new directions. In fact, the impact of military factors has changed the course of history not only in the short term, but in the long term as well. However, there are dangers when one removes war and battles from the cultural context in which they take place. The Battle of Cannae, the great clash between Hannibal's Carthage and the Roman Republic, is a particularly good example. Few battles in history have attracted as much interest from a spectrum of individuals ranging from military historians to strategists. By the end of that gruesome day in 216 B.C., some fifty thousand Romans lay dead on a blood-soaked plain in southern Italy. Yet what did Hannibal's victory achieve? Rome did not collapse. Though seriously wounded, the Republic continued to produce legions one after another and to challenge the Carthaginians throughout the western Mediterranean as well as in Italy and eventually on their home ground.

The only significant result of Cannae was that it allowed Hannibal and his army to remain in Italy for another decade, a troublesome factor for the Romans but one that failed to shake their resolve. In the end, Scipio's legions invaded North Africa and forced Carthage to recall Hannibal to defend his city. The resulting Battle of Zama then led to his defeat and the establishment of Roman hegemony over the Mediterranean that lasted for over half a millennium.

In deciding what battles to include in this volume, the authors have followed the direction set out by Edward Creasy in his classic study, *Fifteen Decisive Battles of the World*: "There are some battles . . . which claim our attention . . . on account of their enduring importance, and by reason of their practical influence on our own social and political condition, which we can trace up to the results of those engagements. They have for us an abiding and actual interest . . . by which they have helped to make us what we are; and also while we speculate on what we probably should have been, if any one of those battles had come to a different termination." In other words, like

Creasy, we have selected our battles on the basis of their long-term impact on the course of history, not on the basis of their importance to the study of military art. Thus, Napoleon's most decisive victories, Austerlitz and Jena-Auerstedt, have no place in our volume, because they failed utterly to achieve Napoleon's aim of creating a French hegemony over the European Continent. So too neither Crécy nor Agincourt, despite the impressive killing power of the longbow, managed to achieve anything other than short periods of English domination in France.

Battles that have piqued our interest are particularly those that still reverberate down through the ages. And that in turn has forced us to delve into the precarious game of counterfactual history. In other words, had the outcome been different, would it have turned the course of the future in substantially different directions? The Battle of Hastings is a case in point, because William the Conqueror's victory tied England closely to the Latin West. Moreover, the subsequent amalgamation of the Saxon and Norman cultures resulted in the creation of the English language. Ironically, in strictly military terms King Harold's victory at Stamford Bridge a few weeks earlier than the Battle of Hastings was far more decisive. But Stamford Bridge remains a mere footnote in history, while the long-term impact of Hastings continues to reverberate in the current world. That, of course, did not stop the British Labour Party in 1933 from passing a resolution, the thrust of which was that "war had never changed anything in human history," despite the fact that its annual conference was meeting near the site of the battle.

As with much of history that attempts to ask the larger questions, our choices of those battles that we believe to have been decisive are idiosyncratic. Yet, for example, the first five battles in our list provide a clear indication of what we mean by decisive:

1. MARATHON—Made possible the continued existence of a distinct Greek civilization and culture, exemplified by Periclean Athens in succeeding decades.
2. GAUGAMELA—Led to the creation of the Hellenistic world, which in turn proved crucial to the spread of Christianity.
3. ZAMA—Broke the economic and political power of Carthage

forever and made Rome the dominant power in the Mediterranean for the next five centuries.

4. TEUTOBURGER WALD—Placed a limit on Roman expansion and created the Latin-German divide that has plagued European peace over the course of the past two millennia.

5. ADRIANOPLE—Marked the beginning of the collapse of the western half of the Roman Empire and ended a five-hundred-year period of the military and strategic domination by the Roman army.

There will be those who object to our selection of decisive battles, an inevitable reality for those who write military history. In fact, the authors are more than willing to admit that a number of important battles are deserving of consideration. Certainly Lepanto was in serious contention, but in the end we decided against it. While the Ottomans indeed represented a terrible threat to the Christian lands of the western Mediterranean, in the late sixteenth century history was already moving away from them. In fact, because of the explosion of the Europeans on the global stage in that century, the Mediterranean world was losing its position as the dominant focus of the European powers in political, economic, and cultural terms.

Part of our interest in the subject of decisive battles was sparked by the bizarre claims of defense analysts in Washington in the late 1990s who posited the idea that America's military was on the verge of creating capabilities that would allow its military forces to conduct rapid decisive operations against any power that dared to stand against the United States. In effect, they were pursuing the mirage of battle for battle's sake—the myth of an overwhelming decisive battle that is won at little cost to the victors. What they missed was the fact that all too many battles are not decisive in the long run, that victory on the day of battle is all too often followed by dark days of defeat, death, and brutal sacrifice.

In the end, the battles that we have discussed in this volume were wretched, miserable, and bloody affairs even for those on the victorious side. But what marks them as special, we believe, is the fact that they changed the flow of history in profoundly fundamental ways that still echo through our world. The fact that there are 350 million fluent

English speakers in India today who live in a democratic nation that functions under the rule of law is a direct reflection of two battles fought an ocean apart in 1759, what the British at the time termed "the annus mirabilis"—"the year of miracles."

It is to those battles that continue to reverberate through to the present that we have addressed this volume.

MOMENT *of* BATTLE

MARATHON

Athens Saves Western Civilization

490 B.C.

TWENTY-FIVE HUNDRED YEARS AGO, TEN THOUSAND ATHENIAN HOP-lites stood against the full might of the Persian Empire. But rather than meekly await the approach of the Persian horde, the Athenians attacked. As they surged forward, they shouted their fierce war cry: *Alleee!* To the vast host of waiting Persians, the Athenian charge was reckless to the point of insanity. How could a mere ten thousand foot soldiers hope to defeat more than three times their number of Persian veterans? But still they came on, first at a trot and then at a sprint. In another instant, the Persian line reeled under the crushing impact of Athenian heavy infantry, on whose prowess this day rested the survival of Western civilization.

The Persian Empire, founded by Cyrus the Great in mid–sixth century B.C., was the greatest empire in the ancient world until the rise of Rome. It stretched from the Indus River to the Mediterranean Sea and from the shores of the Black Sea to Egypt. Created in war, Persia maintained its empire for over two hundred years only through the mighty exertions of its powerful army. Nevertheless, just over twenty years before Marathon, a Persian army came close to disaster when the Great King, Darius, led it north of the Danube into the empty vastness of Scythia. Drawn deep into the steppes, Darius's army was tormented by hit-and-run attacks by highly mobile foes who withdrew before any serious engagement could begin. Unable to bring the Scythians to battle, Darius wisely retreated before his army was decimated by a thousand small cuts. While Darius's losses in the Scythian campaign were probably not as disastrous as the ancient Greek historian Herodotus claims, they were certainly substantial.

The mostly Greek cities of Ionia, which had been conquered decades before by Cyrus, witnessed the return of the defeated Persian army. Sensing weakness, they revolted. Herodotus describes the conflict as an ill-considered enterprise doomed to failure from its inception. However, as it took the Persians six years of near maximum effort to crush the revolt, one may question Herodotus's judgment that the outcome was preordained. Still, Persian power was formidable. To meet it, Ionian envoys were sent to enlist Spartan and Athenian support. The Spartans, always reluctant to send their army far from home, refused. Athens, with closer ties to Ionia, along with Eretria sent a small force. In conjunction with its Ionian allies, this force marched on, captured, and then burned Sardis, the western capital of the Persian Empire. But when the Persians brought the full extent of their military power to bear, the Athenians beat a hasty retreat across the Aegean. The retreat came too late to avoid Darius's undying enmity. Informed that the Athenians had participated in the burning of one of his cities, Darius inquired about them. According to Herodotus, who likely inserted the name of a god familiar to his Greek audience, after being told, Darius

> took a bow, set the arrow on its string, and shot the arrow towards the heavens. As it flew high into the air, he said, "Zeus let it be granted to me to punish the Athenians." After saying this, he appointed one of his attendants to repeat to him three times whenever his dinner was served: "My lord, remember the Athenians."

After half a dozen years of war, Ionia succumbed. Darius, ostensibly having dined nightly contemplating revenge, was now free to turn

Darius I (550–486 B.C.), king of Persia and founder of Achaemenid dynasty; on throne, relief, Achaemenid era, sixth–fifth century B.C., Persepolis, Iran *Gianni Dagli Orti/The Art Archive at Art Resource, NY*

his full attention to Greece. All along the empire's coasts, ports were alive with shipbuilding activities, for Darius had ordered the construction of a great fleet, including special transports for his cavalry. In tandem with this construction, Persia's greatest general, Datis, began gathering the battle-hardened veterans of the Ionian revolt. As this irresistible force assembled, the Great King sent envoys to demand tokens of submission from the Greeks.

Many submitted and sent back earth and water—the sign of submission. Sparta and Athens killed the Persian envoys. For them, it would be war.

THE PERSIAN ONSLAUGHT

After subduing a number of Aegean islands, including Eretria, the Persian army landed at Marathon in August 490 B.C. Datis chose the site for a number of reasons. Probably the most important was the

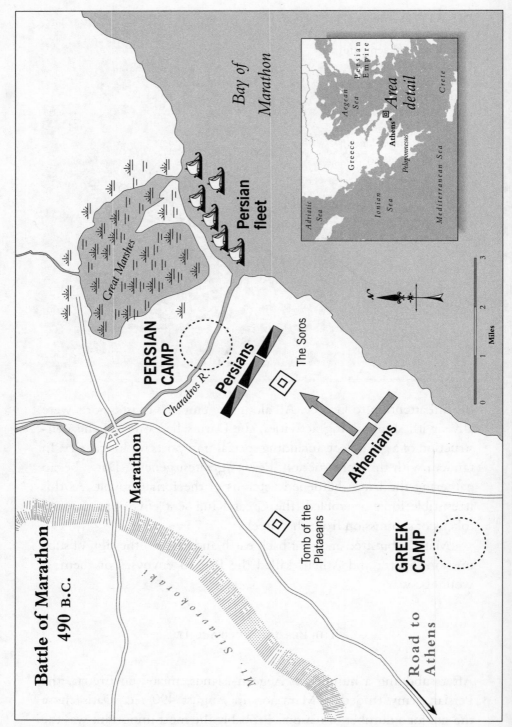

**Battle of Marathon
490 B.C.**

advice of Hippias, a deposed Athenian tyrant. Hippias was now near eighty and making a final bid to regain power. He surely had memories of landing on this same coast when his father, Pisistratus, made a similar military bid for power in Athens. At that time, the hill people had rallied to his father's cause and joined him on his triumphal march into Athens. No doubt Hippias expected a comparable welcome on this occasion and promised as much to the Persians.

The plain of Marathon may have seemed a safe landing site, and it did provide a secure harbor. However, it had one serious disadvantage. There was only one exit from the plain suitable for an army's rapid movement. Moreover, rather than seizing that exit and marching immediately on Athens, the Persians tarried on the coastal plain for an extended period. How long they lingered is uncertain, but it was long enough to allow the Athenians to mass their hoplites on the only practicable outlet from the plain. It is almost inconceivable that the Athenians would have not strongly outposted this exit, as it had been the road used by the last successful invader of Attica—Pisistratus. The most likely reason the Persians did not march off the Marathon plain, therefore, was that there were several hundred determined Athenian hoplites standing behind a fortified wall across the southern road. They could not have held this Thermopylae-like position indefinitely, but they did not have to. By the time the Persians had assembled sufficient forces to be certain of overrunning the Greek position, the rest of the Athenian army had arrived.

At the same time the main Athenian army was marching to Marathon, the Athenians had sent one of their runners, Pheidippides, to Sparta to enlist the support of the finest army in Greece. The Spartans would have been under no illusion as to their eventual fate if Athens fell, so they resolved to help. Unfortunately for Athens, however, they were celebrating one of their many religious festivals and refused to march until the full moon.

The Athenian vanguard would have arrived at Marathon in less than half a day after setting out and was probably there before sunset. From the hills, they watched over thirty-five thousand Persians deploy across the plain, with tens of thousands more sailors lounging near the shore, preparing an evening meal. One wonders if the clever old commander of the Athenian army, Callimachus, was pleased as he surveyed the ground. He had reason to be, as the Persians had placed themselves in a bottle, and he and his army were the cork.

Datis's lack of energy remains inexplicable, as he needed to make relatively quick work of the Athenians before dwindling supplies forced an ignominious Persian withdrawal. Callimachus knew this, of course, so one may reasonably picture him smiling as he considered the advantages with which Datis had presented him. If the Persians advanced for a decisive fight, they would find his army arrayed in a fortified position, on ground of his choosing. If Datis ordered a with-drawal, there would be a moment when they would have some troops loaded and others milling on shore. In that moment of vulnerability, Callimachus would order the Athenian phalanx forward. In the meantime, the Athenians could train, prepare, and await the Spartans.

Upon arrival at the base of the plain, the Athenians made camp within the Sanctuary of Herakles. Here one thousand Plataean hop-lites joined them. The site the Athenians had chosen was a strong defensive position. The sanctuary possessed an extensive grove, and at the time the surrounding area was still heavily wooded. Taken as a whole, the site provided excellent protection against cavalry and was easily defensible against infantry. Before the Athenians stretched the Marathon plain and the Persian army. All around the plain were hills of sufficient size to hem the Persians in, even if they were not strongly outposted with Athenian hoplites. The Chardra River (actually a large stream) bisected the plain, while the northern half was domi-nated by a great marsh, almost impassable by any significant force. At the northern edge of the marsh, the Kynosoura Peninsula extended at ninety degrees from the beach, providing a perfect shelter for the Per-sian fleet beached along a narrow strip of sand between the sea and the great marsh. Between the marsh and the Athenian positions the bal-ance of the plain was almost barren, with some sparse tree growth at scattered points.

Herodotus tells us of the Athenians' arrival at Marathon but leaves us guessing as to what transpired immediately afterward. We do know that several days went by without either side engaging in combat. It would seem that the only notable event during this initial period was a debate among the ten tribal generals and Callimachus, the overall Athenian commander, or *polemarch,* on the advisability of attacking.

In Herodotus's account, each of the ten Athenian generals held command for one day on a rotating basis. As far as he was concerned, Callimachus's role as *polemarch* was mostly honorary and he had no more authority than any of the other generals.

Herodotus relates the dispute among these generals, stating: "The Athenian generals were divided in their opinions: some against joining battle, thinking their numbers were too few to engage the forces of the Medes, while others, including Miltiades, urged that they fight." The ten generals remained evenly divided, so Miltiades asked Callimachus to make the tie-breaking vote. Herodotus has him do this through a fine piece of oratory that convinced Callimachus to vote for battle:

> It is now up to you, Callimachus, whether you will reduce Athens to slavery or ensure its freedom. . . . If you add your vote for my proposal, your ancestral land can be free and your city the first of Greek cities.

After this, the four generals who had supported Miltiades handed over to him the days they were to command the army so he could attack when he pleased. Miltiades accepted the extra command days, but Herodotus reports that he refused to attack until it was his day to command.

As for Datis, he could not wait any longer. After five days he was out of food, and the stench of rotting animal flesh and the waste of more than sixty thousand men were making conditions within the camp intolerable. Datis no doubt considered attacking the Greek position, but it must have been a daunting prospect. Every day he could see the hoplites assembled in front of their camp, their shields glistening and spears bristling, daring him to attack. But as he studied the ten thousand disciplined hoplites arrayed with thousands of light troops crowded behind them, he always thought better of it. Without a large body of reliable heavy infantry, he simply had no way of pushing the Greeks out of their fortifications.

With no other options, Datis gave the orders for the next day—prepare to break camp and return to the ships. It was the most dangerous operation conceivable, one that invited attack. It would take all night to break camp and move the ships into place. The job was made more difficult by the necessity of hiding these preparations from the Athenians. From past experience, Datis knew that getting the cavalry on board ship was the most difficult task ahead, so they would have to board before daybreak, as the rest of the army stood guard. If that went well, he would collapse his perimeter back toward the narrow strip of beach where the marsh protected one flank and the ocean the other. Here his elite Persians and Saka (elite Scythian troops, usually cavalry) could hold the line, protected by thousands of archers, while the rest of the army boarded ship. As Datis studied the Athenian line that the Great King had ordered destroyed, he must have thought one more time, If only the Athenians would attack. One must always be careful what one asks for.

That night, the Athenians heard unusual sounds coming from the Persian camp. Callimachus and Miltiades must have guessed what was happening, but they needed to be sure. They sent out spies, and soon

Procession of archers; glazed bricks from the palace of Darius I, sixth century B.C., Susa, Iran
Erich Lessing/ Art Resource, NY

enough confirmation came back: The Persians were preparing to depart. The Greek generals understood that they must not allow the Persians to leave with their strength intact. The next actions of such a force would be unpredictable and dangerous, as the Persians had a number of options available to them, none of them pleasant from the Athenian perspective. They might sail north to Thebes, never a friend to Athens, which had offered the requisite pledges of submission to Darius. From there, they could have enlisted Theban hoplites to provide the heavy infantry they lacked and together march on Athens. Alternatively, they could land elsewhere and march on Athens before the Athenian army could assemble to counter them; or they could attack any number of vulnerable points along the coast to scour Attica with damaging raids. Even more dangerous, they might find common cause with Aegina, Athens's perennial nearby enemy, and winter on that island, recouping their strength for another descent on Attica the following year. Even joining with Argos and removing the Spartan threat was a possibility. Considering all these scenarios, it was clear to Callimachus that if Athens was ultimately to survive, the Persian force needed to be severely damaged while still on the shores of Marathon. Athens could not keep its men under arms forever. It was now or never.

Callimachus called together the ten tribal generals and gave the orders, which he had previously reviewed with them. His novel plan for victory was based on his observation that the elite of the Persian army was always placed in the center of their battle line. This was the force that Callimachus aimed to destroy, for it alone was irreplaceable. To do so, the Athenian hoplites would need to stretch their line as far as possible to avoid being outflanked by the more numerous Persians, but they could use even this to advantage. The Athenian line would be eight deep on each flank and only four deep in the center. Callimachus's plan called for the flanks to win, while the center drew the elite Persians deep into a trap. It was a tremendous risk, for if the center broke before the flanks had done their job, disaster was all but certain.

Before sunrise, the Greeks mustered.
Dawn broke.

The holy paean was sung.
The order came—επιτίθεμαι ["advance"].

In the vital center was the Leontis tribe, commanded by its general, Themistocles, later to become the savior of Greece when Darius's successor, Xerxes, returned to finish what Darius had begun. Next to Themistocles stood the general of the Antiochis tribe, Aristides. The two despised each other, and Themistocles would soon have Aristides ostracized from Athens, only to see him recalled just in time to command the Athenian army at the Battle of Plataea in 479 B.C. But for that day, their tribes stood arrayed together; both tasked with the day's most difficult and dangerous mission. Any chance the Athenians had for victory rested on the valor of both men. On the far right, with their flank on the ocean, stood the Aiantis tribe. Here, Stesileos stood beside his father, Thrasylaos, the tribe's general. Stesileos would not survive the day, dying within arm's reach of his father. With the men of Aiantis marched the Athenian commander, Callimachus, who was one of them and by right of his position stood on the far right of the phalanx. He too was fighting his last battle, as he would die at its climax, pierced by so many spears that his body did not fall. Also standing in the ranks of the Aiantis men was Greece's greatest dramatist, Aeschylus. Today he would fight bravely but also witness the savage death of his brother Cynegeirus, struck down just as the final victory was won.

Datis was an experienced commander. He must have seen that the Athenian lines were tighter today, more disciplined. Possibly he could see that the shields and body armor were polished to a higher shine than before. Did that mean anything? If he or any of the other Persians actually sensed anything was different, it did not cause them to change their daily routine, which they had maintained to camouflage their imminent departure. As they had done every morning since landing at Marathon, they formed up to face the Greeks. There seemed no reason for haste. After all, they still had three times the Athenian numbers. Even the Greeks were not crazy enough to attack against such odds.

The Athenian ranks stepped off. For the first few steps they walked, but then the pace picked up, first to a fast walk and then to a trot. The hoplites crushed together, shoulder to shoulder and shield to shield, as each covered as much of his exposed right side behind his neighbor's shield as possible. Dread and fear melted away now that the army was advancing. Men who had soiled themselves in the line drew strength from the surging tide surrounding them. At six hundred yards' distance, the mass of hoplites began to scream their fierce and nerve-shattering battle cry—*Alleeee!*

The Persians could not believe what they were seeing. The Athenians had no cavalry or archers. This attack was madness. But the Athenians were coming on, and they were coming fast.

Hastily, the Persian commanders aligned their troops. Men holding wicker shields went to the front, as thousands of archers arrayed themselves in the rear. In another moment, these archers would release tens of thousands of deadly bolts into the sky, and that would be the end of the Athenians. Despite the speed of the Athenian attack, the Persian army showed no panic. They too were professionals, victors of dozens of bloody battles. True, none of them had ever faced an onrushing phalanx, but none of them doubted they would make short work of the charging hoplites.

The Persian spearmen were on line now. Patiently they waited for the hail of arrows that would darken the sky and surely decimate their foe. That done, the infantry would advance to slaughter the shattered remnant.

But a different kind of war was charging down on them. And it was arriving at almost incomprehensible speed, for at two hundred yards' distance the Athenian trot became a sprint. Athenian hoplites had learned the art of war against other hoplites, a brand of war that was not decided by a hail of arrows. A collision of wooden shields and deadly iron-tipped spears wielded by heavily armored warriors settled matters: a horrific and terrifying melee of pushing, screaming, half-mad men who gouged, stabbed, and kicked at their opponents until one side could bear the agony no longer and broke. Then the true slaughter would begin, as men freed of fear felt the surge of bloodlust propelling them forward in murderous pursuit of the fleeing foe.

Finally, the Persian archers let fly—but to no effect. Never having seen such a rapid advance, many of the archers mistimed their shots, and masses of arrows missed their targets entirely. Most of those that did strike the Athenians bounced off shields and heavy armor. Hastily the archers reloaded, as the shield bearers and protecting infantry, seeing that ten thousand metal-encased killers were almost upon them, uneasily began inching backward.

The screams of *Alleeee!* were earsplitting now, but even that could not compare with the incredible noise of thousands of shields clanging off one another as the compressed Greek ranks came within striking distance.

In a shuddering instant, the hoplites smashed into the lightly protected Persians, convulsing their defensive line. Wicker shields were trampled down and the first rank of Persian infantry died in an instant. Unusual for a hoplite battle, most of the spears did not shatter on impact, for the Persians were without serious armor. Again and again, Athenian spears lunged forward, more often than not finding targets. Men screamed, fought, and died. But soon enough the hoplites passed through the protecting infantry to rampage amid the archers.

Now the real killing began.

The flanks, where Callimachus had massed his hoplites eight deep, made rapid progress. In a very short time, the Persians facing the men of Aiantis on the Greek right and the Plataeans on the left lost their cohesion and will to resist. In packets, unprotected archers drew their short swords and daggers to make a stand. But they made little impact on the locked shields of the Greeks. Like a heavily armored tank, killing as it came on, the phalanx rolled over the opposition. Some Persians fell, only wounded. The front line of Greeks stepped over them, intent on killing or maiming those still standing before them. Other hoplites, coming behind them, would dispatch the wounded men by raising spear points high and then plunging the metal spikes at their spear's base into their prostrate victims. Any Persian who survived would be stabbed to death by the swarm of light troops following in the phalanx's wake. When the Persian flanks could no longer stand the horror of hoplite warfare, they broke and ran desperately to the rear, attempting to reach the safety of the ships.

In ancient battles, this was where the bulk of the casualties were inflicted on the losing side. Panicked men on the run are incapable of any defense. In turn, their pursuers, propelled forward by an instinctual bloodlust, would almost always lose their formation as they rushed

Bust of Miltiades
(d. 489 B.C.), marble,
480–336 B.C.
*The Art Gallery
Collection/Alamy*

to cut down the fleeing enemy from behind. And for approximately a hundred yards this was just what the Athenians did.

But then they did the impossible. At least it would have been impossible had the Athenian army actually been the mass of unprofessional rustics tradition posits.

Callimachus, seeing the Persian left routed, ordered the bugle blown. Instantly the Athenian right flank halted. For a moment the killing stopped, as the Athenians reordered their ranks and turned ninety degrees. Behind them swept a mass of light troops, armed similarly to the Persians but with the inestimable advantage of being in pursuit rather than in panic. These light troops would not be decisive, but they would keep the pressure on and protect the Athenian flank while Callimachus closed the jaws of his trap. For on the other flank another bugle was also blown, and here too Greeks and Plataeans instantly began re-forming their ranks and turning toward the center of the battlefield. The skill required to achieve these maneuvers cannot be passed over too easily. What the Athenian army had just accomplished, only a professional force operating as part of a preset plan could have accomplished. Moreover, such a maneuver required that the Athenians possess an iron combat discipline found only in veteran units, again strongly suggesting the Greeks were not the amateurs at war that historians often claim.

While the Athenian flanks swept all before them, things had not gone as well in the center. Here, the hoplite array was only four deep and the men of the Leontis and Antiochis tribes lacked the mass to overwhelm their opponents. They were also facing the more heavily armored and disciplined elite core of the enemy army, the Persians and Saka. The first impact had sent the Persians reeling, but after that, numbers told. After an exhausting charge, there was a limit to how long the front rank of Athenians could fight. To keep the pressure on, the Greeks did what they could to move fresher hoplites forward, but the press of the Persian counterattack made that difficult. The only advantage the Greeks in the center had was that Callimachus expected them simply to hold, not to go forward. Even that was proving difficult.

Despite the exhortations of the intrepid Aristides and Themistocles, the Athenians were nearly fought out. Nearing exhaustion, they could no longer resist the weight of Persian numbers and began slowly stepping back. Under normal conditions, for a line as thin as the Athenian center, stepping back presaged disaster. But the Greek veterans did not rout. Rather, they fell back with deliberate slowness, still killing their enemies even in retreat. They were somewhat protected by a mass of Athenian *thetes,* men too poor to purchase hoplite armor, who ranged behind the thin Athenian line, throwing javelins and slinging stones into the Persian host.

As the Greeks bowed back, they entered the woods near their camp. The broken terrain caused the phalanx to lose its cohesion. Gaps opened between the shields, and hoplites began to fall. The men of Antiochus suffered heavily, and Aristides must have known his men were close to breaking. In another moment, the Athenians would be swept aside and the Persians would win the day.

And then, salvation.

Having reset their lines, the flanks of the Athenian army stepped off again. This time they were aimed at the exposed flanks of the Persian center. An ancient battlefield was a confusing melee, filled with screaming, horror, and blinding dust. So it is unlikely that the Persians and Saka, locked in mortal combat with the hoplites to their front and sensing imminent victory, even saw the looming threat until it was upon them.

When the crash came, it must have been a complete shock. Two steamrolling, disciplined, and murderous killing machines bore down on the exposed Persian center, snatching away the victory the Persians had glimpsed only a moment before. Any Persians who could, ran. Many, however, were trapped and died where they stood.

Datis could see what was happening to his center and must have cursed that he did not have enough organized troops to launch a counterattack. But it was all he could do to rally stragglers with enough fight left in them to hold back still pursuing Athenian light troops. Datis also knew that when the Athenian troops finished massacring the Persians and Saka, they would re-form and come at him again. He must have worried over how long his wavering men could hold the line against another phalanx charge. Behind him, thousands of panicked men were wading into the water, looking for any ship that could take them aboard. Datis needed to buy these men time. If he could get enough of them away, there might still be a chance to launch one more daring strike for victory.

The phalanx came on again. This time the shine of the Athenian shields was obscured by collected grime and dust, and the gleam of the spear points was dulled by drying blood. As for the men holding those spears, they were dirty, drenched in sweat, and splattered with blood. Despite their exhaustion, they knew they had the advantage and advanced with fresh determination. For Datis's men, given what they had just been through, the sight must have been horrifying. But they knew there was no place to which to retreat, and Datis through personal example held them to their duty.

This time the tired Greeks came on with deliberate slowness. Spared the crashing shock of a phalanx impacting at a run, the Persian line did not immediately break. The battle near the ships became fierce as desperate men grappled at close quarters. Here is where Callimachus fell, mortally wounded, and Aeschylus saw his brother's hand chopped off as he grabbed hold of a Persian ship. After a long, hard fight, the Persians gave way, and the Athenians swept across the narrow beach. But Datis's line had held just long enough for most of his ships and surviving soldiers to escape. In the end, the Athenians were able to capture only seven ships, as the surviving Persians moved out to sea.

As the Persians sailed into the Aegean, the Athenian hoplites rested, while the light troops hunted down and killed Persian stragglers, particularly the mass of men hiding in the great marsh. When the Athenian generals took stock, they found that 192 Athenian hoplites lay dead. Most of these losses had been from among the men of the Antiochis tribe, who had been pressed hard in the center, and from the men of Aiantis, who had suffered serious losses in the desperate fighting near the ships. Still, it had been a great victory, for more than 6,000 Persian dead littered the battlefield.

With the victory won, a messenger was dispatched to Athens. According to the traditional story, he ran the entire distance in full armor, shouted, "Hail, we are victorious!" and promptly fell over dead.

As the messenger winged his way to Athens, exultant hoplites

Helmet of Miltiades, given by Miltiades as an offering to the Temple of Zeus at Olympia. Inscription on the helmet: MILTIAΔES *Archaeological Museum of Olympia*

looked out to sea in dismay. The Persian ships were heading south, and everyone realized the battle was not over yet. Athens was undefended, and the Persians would be landing on the beaches of Phaleron, just a couple of miles from the city, before the sun had set. For a few dazed moments, the hoplites wondered if the battle had been for nothing. Soon, though, a new leader, possibly Miltiades, took over for the dead Callimachus and began issuing orders.

All along the beach, exhausted hoplites steeled themselves for one more great effort. They hefted spears, shouldered their *hoplon* shields, and re-formed their regiments. The bloodied Antiochus regiment was left to secure the battlefield and the tremendous booty found in the wrecked Persian camp. The other nine tribal regiments set off on a race against time, for it was almost twenty-six miles to Athens and the Persians had a head start.

When Datis eventually arrived off the coast of Phaleron, he saw that through an almost superhuman effort, the Athenian hoplites had beaten him there. All along the ridge overlooking the beach were arrayed thousands of determined warriors ready to contest his landing. After suffering more than six thousand losses and with his force still disorganized, Datis had had enough. The Persian ships turned back out to sea.

Athens had won.

The next morning, two thousand Spartans arrived. They had missed the fighting but still wanted to see the battlefield, probably wanting to confirm that the victory was as great as the Athenians claimed. Later in the day, after touring the battlefield, they praised the victors and marched for home.

SOME HAVE PROPOSED that Marathon made little difference in the creation and development of a unique Western civilization. After all, the argument goes, Pericles, Aristotle, Plato, and Socrates still would have been born. They still would have been brilliant, and their achievements would have been as great. One is hard-pressed, however, to think how these great minds and independent spirits would have soared as slaves in a despotic Persian Empire. In truth, Western civilization owes its existence to a thin line of bronze-encased "men as hard as oak" who bravely went forward against overwhelming odds to victory and never-ending glory.

An Athenian defeat would have been only the first step along the Persian road of conquest. With all of Greece subdued and placed under Persian rule, the political climate necessary for the birth, rooting, and advancement of the ideas on which democracy, free markets, and other defining attributes of Western civilization rest would have ceased to exist. In short, the fundamental ideas of what we consider crucial to the idea of "the West" would likely never have come into existence. As a result of Athens's victory, the concept of democracy flourished long enough for the idea of popular government to root itself so deeply that it never vanished from the West's collective memory. Moreover, the new concepts of art and philosophy that were already emerging throughout Greece continued to prosper. This cultural explosion, which the Persians surely would have extinguished, underpins much of the great art and literature the West has produced in the past two aeons.

Rescuing Western civilization would typically be enough to ask of any single battle. However, Marathon also holds a special distinction for military historians. For it was not only a duel between two diametrically opposed political and social systems. It was also the first trial of radically different modes of combat. At Marathon, the heavily armored Athenians, inured by long familiarity with hoplite warfare to the horrors of shock assaults and close-quarters carnage, engaged and decimated a Persian army that relied on the long-distance firepower of its archers. At Marathon, what Victor Davis Hanson has termed "the Western Way of War" had faced its first test against an Eastern army and had won decisively.

GAUGAMELA

Alexander Creates a New World

311 B.C.

DESPITE THE VICTORY AT MARATHON, FOR THE NEXT 150 YEARS PERSIA loomed over the West, an ever-present and powerful empire waiting for the moment to strike and put an end to Greek independence. Only a decade after its defeat at Marathon, Persia, now ruled by Xerxes, made one more mighty attempt to conquer Greece. This invasion force, many times larger than the one the Athenians faced at Marathon, was crushed at Salamis and Plataea, demonstrating to all that Greece was a tough nut to crack. How tough is probably more apparent to modern scholars than it was to contemporaries. Despite these defeats, Persia soon regained its strength, while Greece settled into a long series of debilitating internecine conflicts that first saw Athens humbled by Sparta in the Peloponnesian War and then Sparta, in turn, humbled by Thebes. In the end, these draining internal squabbles weakened Greece to the point that Philip of Macedon, assisted by his son Alexander, was able to march south and conquer most of Greece.

Although Persia remained a great empire after Xerxes's invasion was turned back, it never again inspired the level of existential fear among the Greeks that it had before it lost the test of arms against Greek hoplites. The trio of victories at Marathon, Salamis, and Plataea stunned the whole world, not least the Greeks themselves. Afterward, Greek attitudes toward Persia began to change. National pride soared, and the men who fought at Marathon became Athens's "greatest generation," who had beaten back the Great King's Asiatic horde. This well-deserved pride was displayed on the gravestone of the great dramatist Aeschylus: "Beneath this stone lies Aeschylus. . . . Of his noble prowess the grove of Marathon can speak, or the long-haired Persians who know it well." There was not a word about what the world still remembers him for, his plays. Aeschylus may fairly also be credited with starting the process that converted the Persians from terrible and feared warriors in the Greek mind into "those soft sons of luxury," as they are referred to in his great play *The Persians.* As one noted historian stated, Aeschylus "created a lasting stereotype, whereby the civilized Persians were reduced to cringing, ostentatious, arrogant, cruel, effeminate, and lawless aliens." But Aeschylus was not alone. Others of Greece's great playwrights, such as Aristophanes, often denigrated the Persians as weak, pampered, and effete.

As far as the Greeks could see, there was only one explanation for their apparently miraculous victory over the Persians. The Persians must be of poor stock. Over succeeding decades, the idea that the Persians were weak and effeminate became ingrained in the Greek outlook. It was during this time the meaning of the word *barbarian* changed from someone speaking an incomprehensible language (ba ba ba) to someone who was uncivilized and inferior—namely, Persians.

Great Greek orators in the years before Alexander never had a problem finding willing audiences waiting to feed on stories of Asiatic effeminacy, and the notion that the Persians were "bred for slavery" was widely accepted. But Persian degeneracy was not only a staple for the masses to consume. The greatest minds in Greece also accepted and promulgated the stereotype. In *Politics,* Aristotle wrote: "The Asiatic races have both brains and skill but are lacking in courage and will-power; so they have remained enslaved and subject." Later he declared that the Persians were barely human and fit only for slavery. One can only wonder how this viewpoint affected Aristotle's most

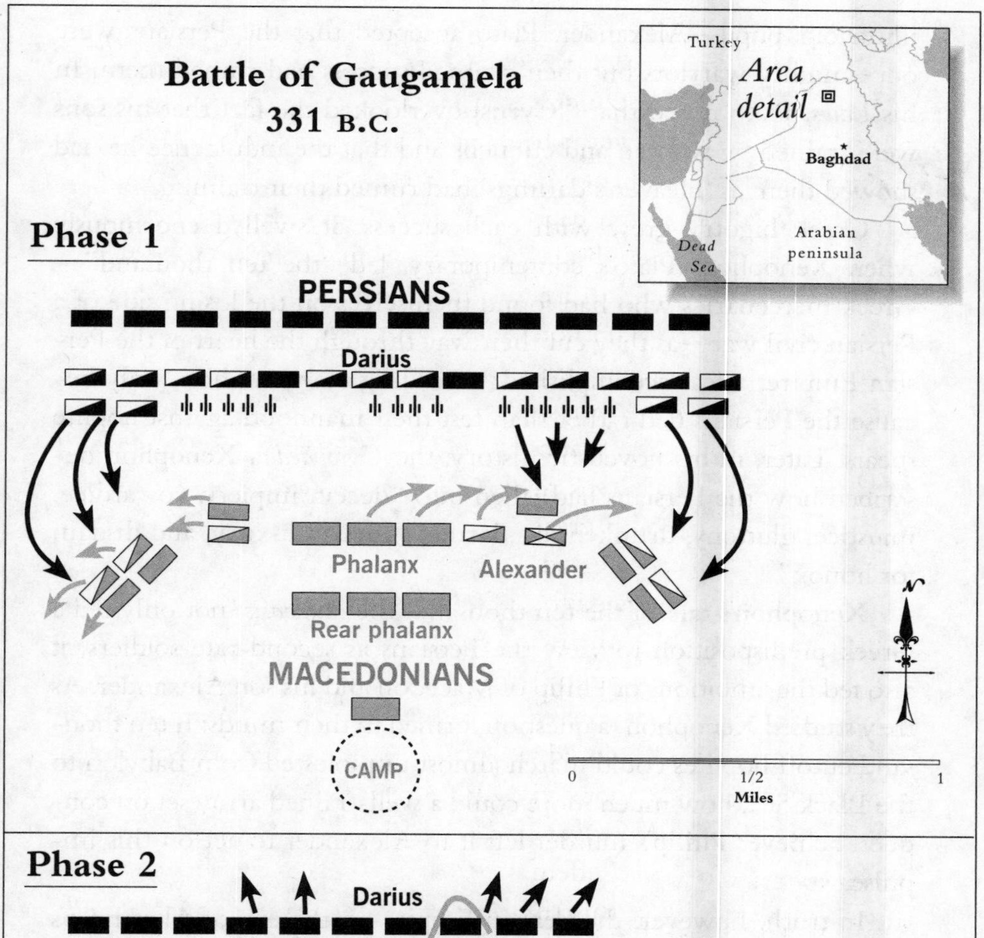

Battle of Gaugamela
331 B.C.

Area detail

Turkey

Baghdad

Dead Sea

Arabian peninsula

Phase 1

PERSIANS

Darius

Phalanx

Alexander

Rear phalanx

MACEDONIANS

CAMP

0   1/2   1
Miles

Phase 2

Darius

PERSIANS

Alexander

Rear phalanx

MACEDONIANS

CAMP

0   1/2   1
Miles

illustrious pupil—Alexander. Plato accepted that the Persians were once mighty warriors but then claimed success had ruined them. In his *Laws,* Plato noted that "[Cyrus] overlooked the fact that his sons were trained by women and eunuchs and that the indulgence he had showed them as 'Heaven's darlings' had ruined their training."

Greek bigotry grew with each success. It swelled enormously when Xenophon, Plato's contemporary, led "the ten thousand"— Greek mercenaries who had found themselves on the losing side of a Persian civil war—as they cut their way through the heart of the Persian Empire, a feat accomplished, according to Xenophon, only because the Persians fled rather than test their manhood against hoplite spears. Later, in his novelistic history, the *Cyropaedia,* Xenophon described how the Persians had fallen into "deceit, impiety, cowardice, injustice, gluttony, drunkenness, laziness, love of luxury, and disdain for honor."

Xenophon's tale of the ten thousand, the *Anabasis,* not only fed a Greek predisposition to view the Persians as second-rate soldiers, it also fed the ambitions of Philip of Macedon and his son Alexander. As they studied Xenophon, a question formed in their minds: If ten thousand cutoff hoplites could march almost unmolested from Babylon to the Black Sea, how much more could a well-trained army set on conquest achieve? Philip's murder left it to Alexander to act on this impulse.

In truth, however, the Persian Empire on the eve of Alexander's assault was probably at or near the zenith of its power. In the fourth century B.C., Persia remained the world's sole superpower. Its landmass covered 7.5 million square miles, stretching from the Aegean to India, and its population was probably in excess of forty million. Besides its vast size, it possessed the largest military force the ancient world had yet known, along with stored riches beyond even Alexander's powers of imagination.

Alexander, on the other hand, while nominally ruling a Greece unified by his father's conquest, remained uncertain of his base. For many Greeks, Alexander's home, Macedonia, represented a crude, uncultured place, little above what one might expect to find among barbarians. Alexander himself, despite his supposed refinement and tutoring by Aristotle, was to sophisticated Greeks still a savage. Most of Greece chafed under Macedonian rule, and Sparta remained defiant. In fact, when Alexander's father, Philip II, was conquering Greece, he had sent a warning to the Spartans: "If I enter Laconia, I will raze Sparta to the ground." The terse Spartan reply was: "If." The unsettled state of Greek politics forced Alexander to leave a sizable force behind when he marched into Persia, so as to stifle any attempts at revolt. Alexander's word was law in Greece, but it was Macedonian spear points that enforced that law.

Starting his Persian expedition in 334 B.C., Alexander crossed the Hellespont into Asia. Here he met a hastily raised Persian army arrayed along the Granicus River. In a hard-fought contest that nearly cost Alexander his life, the Macedonians smashed the Persian force, opening large swaths of Anatolia to conquest. The following months were absorbed in campaigns to solidify Alexander's hold on western reaches of the Persian Empire. It was not until the following spring that Alexander was able to march through the Cilician Gates and enter the Levant. Here, at Issus, he met the main Persian army, commanded by Darius—the Great King—himself.

In the fierce battle that ensued, the issue was long in doubt until Alexander, at the head of his elite Companion cavalry, charged and broke the Persian right flank. Although some of the hardest fighting took place between Alexander's phalanxes and the Greek mercenaries in Darius's service, the Persians also acquitted themselves well, with repeated cavalry assaults that came close to caving in one of the Macedonian flanks. Only Alexander's daring and risky assault at the head of his elite Companion cavalry turned the tide. Spotting a small gap in the Persian line, Alexander and the Companions plunged into it. Then, turning to the left, they smashed into the flank and rear of Darius's Greek mercenaries, rolling up the Persian center and right. After witnessing the butchering of his bodyguard, Darius fled the battlefield, with Alexander in close but fruitless pursuit. In his haste to reach safety, Darius left behind a sizable treasury, which funded much of Alexander's expedition over the next several years. Darius also abandoned his wife, his two daughters, and his mother.

Many have used Darius's escape, just as Alexander approached his position, as further evidence of Persian cowardice. The ancient historian Diodorus, however, gives an account that is very different from popular legend:

> The horses which were harnessed to the yoke of Darius's chariot were covered with wounds and terrified by the piles of dead about them. They refused to answer to their bridles, and came close to carrying off Darius into the midst of the enemy, but the king himself, in extreme peril, caught up the reins, being forced to throw away the dignity of his position and to violate the ancient custom of the Persian kings.

If Darius did run, he did so only at the very last moment and long after the fight had reached his position. One of the best sources we have for the life of Alexander, Curtius Rufus, relates what the scene around Darius's chariot looked like when Alexander examined it the following day:

> Around Darius' chariot lay his most famous generals who had succumbed to a glorious death before the eyes of their king, and who now all lay face-down where they had fallen fighting, their wounds on the front of their body. Among them could be recognized Atizyes, Rheomithres and Sabaces, satrap of Egypt—all generals of mighty armies—and heaped around these were a crowd of lesser-known infantrymen and cavalrymen.

Hardly what one would expect from a ruling class or an army that had been overtaken by effeteness or degeneracy.

THE BATTLE OF ISSUS saw off Darius and the main Persian army, but it still took Alexander all of 333 and 332 B.C. to reduce the Levant, most of that time spent besieging Tyre and Gaza. The siege of Tyre so delayed Alexander that once it fell, he was without pity. He ordered all men of military age crucified and the women and children sold into slavery. As for Gaza, it withstood several assaults before falling, but not before one of its defenders inflicted a severe shoulder wound on Alexander. Once again, Alexander had the men put to the sword, while the women and children met the same fate as those of Tyre. After Gaza's fall, Jerusalem, opting not to become a third example of Alexander's merciless resolve, threw open its gates. Upon entering the city, Alexander was shown the book of Daniel, which prophesied that a great Greek king would overthrow the Persian Empire. Evidently pleased by the prophecy, Alexander spared Jerusalem further tribulations and marched into Egypt. Here, he was greeted as a liberator and declared a god.

By early 331 B.C., after consolidating Macedonian rule in Egypt and founding the city of Alexandria, Alexander was ready to strike out into the heart of the Persian Empire. Almost inexplicably, Darius allowed Alexander to cross both the Euphrates and Tigris Rivers uncontested. The only explanations offered are that either Alexander fooled him by taking an approach route far to the north of what Darius expected or that the Great King was supremely confident in the huge army he had mobilized to face Alexander. It was likely some combination of both. Darius would probably have welcomed a chance to bloody Alexander's army on its approach, but he was also eager for a decisive battle at the earliest possible moment. As the Great King's hold on power must have been somewhat shaken by the severe humiliations the Macedonian upstart had already inflicted, the sooner Alexander was permanently vanquished, the sooner Darius could begin the painstaking job of rebuilding the prestige of the royal house and enforcing his divine right to rule. The stage was thus set for what was probably the greatest and most decisive battle in the history of the ancient world.

The arena was Gaugamela, an open plain about fifty miles northwest of the city of Arbail (present-day Irbil), a stronghold where the great Persian Royal Road joined the roads to Armenia and the Eastern satrapies and, therefore, an excellent spot to mobilize the scattered Persian host. Here, a worried Darius, concerned that the crafty Alexander would launch a surprise night attack, kept his huge army standing under arms throughout the hours of darkness. To keep up their morale, the Great King quit his own comforts and spent the night riding along the lines, encouraging his soldiers to great deeds. Unfortunately, he succeeded only in exhausting both himself and his army as the Macedonians rested. Alexander had already rejected a suggestion from Parmenio, his most trusted general, to attack at night, saying, "I will not demean myself by stealing victory like a thief." In truth, Alexander probably fully understood the perils of a night attack, where the cohesion of his finely tuned army might disintegrate in an instant. Rather than risk an unpredictable brawl, Alexander opted for a contest where Macedonian training along with his leadership could be fully exploited.

The well-rested Macedonians began assembling just before dawn. But there was no sign of their commander. Worried that something was wrong, Parmenio steeled himself to disturb Alexander in his tent. He found his king sleeping so deeply that it took some time to rouse him. Noting the bemusement of his officers, Alexander told them "that Darius had freed him from anxiety by assembling all of his forces in one place."

After summoning his officers, delivering words of encouragement, and issuing last minute instructions, Alexander ordered the army to advance. With his cavalry leading, the massed Macedonian phalanxes began their approach march to Gaugamela and the waiting Persians. Riding at the forefront was Alexander, wearing a Sicilian-made breastplate, over which he had laid a quilt of closely woven linen that had been part of the booty after the Battle of Issus. His iron helmet, inlaid with gems, was so highly polished that it shone brighter than the most refined silver. He carried with him a sword, his weapon of choice in a close fight, given to him by the king of the Citieans and much prized for its temper and lightness. Behind him, servants led Alexander's mount, Bucephalas. Bucephalas was getting old now, and Alexander rested him before battle. When the time came for the climactic charge to break the Persian line, Bucephalas, the ancient world's greatest warhorse, would be called forward.

As the Macedonian army crested a hill on the edge of the battlefield, its soldiers viewed, for the first time, the vast Persian array. Exactly how many of the enemy they saw is lost in the mists of history, but two hundred thousand would not be outside the realm of probability. We do know that Darius was making a supreme effort to rid Persia of the Macedonian threat, and one can assume he called forth every available soldier. After the battle, Alexander captured a copy of the Persian order of battle, confirming that Darius had indeed recruited his army from every corner of the empire.

In the center of the Persian army stood Darius himself, surrounded by his Immortals, the best infantry in the empire, easily recognized by the golden apples on their spear butts. Arrayed on both sides of these elite troops were Greek mercenaries (the only troops in the Persian army capable of meeting the Macedonian phalanx head-on) and a host of Indians, Babylonians, and assorted other infantry, formed in two great echelons. To their front lay Darius's secret weapons, fifteen elephants and approximately one hundred chariots with razor-sharp scythes extending out from each wheel hub. To increase the impact of these murderous weapons, Darius had the ground to their front laboriously leveled so the chariots would face no hindrances as they hurtled toward the Macedonian phalanx. The left flank of the Persian army was led by Bessus, Darius's most reliable commander. His main line consisted mostly of second-rate infantry from his own Bactrian satrapy. To their front, however, the best of the Persian cavalry was deployed, including one thousand Bactrians, several thousand Scythians (Saka), and possibly another one hundred chariots. On the Persian right flank stood Mazaeus, commanding a hodgepodge of infantry from a number of nationalities. Although Bessus controlled the army's best cavalry, the Cappadocian and Armenian horsemen Mazaeus placed along his front echelon were nearly their equal.

As huge as Darius's army was, it suffered from a number of defects. Foremost was the fact that although there were elite units within the Persian force, most of the army was of inferior quality. Unfortunately for Darius, many of the empire's best troops had already fallen fighting Alexander at Granicus and Issus. Moreover, in combat diversity is not usually a positive advantage. An army as large as Darius's presented a command-and-control challenge under the best of circumstances. With a non-veteran army that spoke a dozen or more languages, it was a nightmare. And as Stalin reputedly noted, while quantity has a quality all its own, there are any number of cases where such a belief is proved fanciful. As the American-led Coalition clearly demonstrated in Iraq in 2003, when a large but inferior force finds itself pit-ted against a well-trained, better-led, and technologically superior army, there is a strong likelihood the larger force will rapidly degenerate into a chaotic mob.

Against this immense force, Alexander brought a relatively puny seven thousand cavalry and forty thousand infantry. This, however, was no ordinary army. Rather, it was a well-integrated, combined-arms force that was light-years ahead of the phalanx that had fought at Marathon. Still, the first sight of the huge Persian army must have caused a moment of trepidation in every Macedonian heart. Undeterred, though, Alexander's veterans came on in steady columns; with clockwork precision, the Macedonian troops occupied their assigned positions in the battle line. For this encounter, Alexander had his army adopt a novel formation. Realizing that by virtue of their sheer numbers the Persians would easily overlap the flanks of the Macedonian army, Alexander ordered them bent back at a forty-five-degree angle from the center. Moreover, instead of marching directly at the Persians, the Macedonians advanced on an oblique angle to the right, which if left unchecked would allow Alexander to bring the bulk of his army against a single wing of the Persians.

Understanding that the decisive engagement would take place on the Macedonian right, Alexander took command of that flank. Stationing himself with the Companions, Macedon's elite heavy cavalry, Alexander watched as contingents of mercenary infantry and cavalry ordered themselves on an angle to his right. To Alexander's left, linking the Companion cavalry to the solid ranks of the Macedonian phalanx battalions, stood Nicanor's Hypaspists, Macedon's handpicked, heavily armored, elite shock infantry. Next in line came the bulwark of the Macedon army, the irresistible phalanx, arrayed in six battalions along the front. Upon the shoulders of these solid veterans rested Alexander's hopes, for it fell to them to wear down and grind away at the Persian will until Alexander spotted a weakness in the Persian line and thrust a dagger, in the form of his Companion cavalry, into it. At the far left of the phalanx battalions, where Parmenio commanded, stood the superb Thessalian cavalry, second in quality only to the Companions. Bent back at an angle from the Thessalians were the Thracians, along with other mercenary and allied cavalry. Behind the center of Alexander's deployment stood the phalanxes of his Greek allies and mercenaries. These units would support and add weight to the Macedon phalanx. Moreover, if the Persian cavalry did sweep around Alexander's flanks and into the rear of his army, these units were instructed to face about and create another defensive front. Finally, in the front of the army ranged the Agrianians. Armed with javelins (and sometimes slings), the Agrianians were the finest light infantry in the world. At Gaugamela, these skirmishers would prove crucial in wrecking Darius's plans.

Alexander's army advanced slowly but inexorably. By moving it at an oblique, Alexander hoped the Persians would remain inactive long enough for him to crush their left flank before they could do the same to his own left. Realizing the Macedonians were marching away from the ground he had ordered leveled for the chariot attack, Darius determined to stop the Macedonian march while the bulk of Alexander's army was still to his immediate front. He ordered his left flank cavalry forward to check and encircle Alexander's right. Bessus promptly ordered a thousand of his Bactrian cavalry and probably another thousand from the Dahae contingent into a headlong assault against the shifting Macedonian right flank.

Probably surprised by the Persian initiative and needing to buy time, Alexander ordered the reliable Menidas to lead a countercharge with Grecian mercenary cavalry units. With only four hundred recently arrived and untested horsemen, the countercharge never had a chance. Sheer weight of numbers told, and Menidas's force was soon reeling backward. But they had served their purpose. They had bought Alexander precious moments to organize a more effective counterattack. As Menidas's troopers fled, Alexander launched the heavier *prodromoi* and Paeonian cavalry into their wake. Supported by Cleander's heavy infantry, this formidable force checked the Persians. Temporarily nonplussed by the check, Bessus sought to turn the tide by releasing the rest of his Bactrian and Scythian cavalry. Thousands of fresh, heavy cavalry thundered forward, threatening to swamp and sweep away Alexander's heavily engaged right flank. It was here that training came to the fore and the professional Macedonians proved their mettle. Steady infantry blunted the Persian charge, for when it comes to breaking a line of spearmen rooted in place, the bravery of the rider counts for nothing. It is the bravery of the horse that decides, and no horse will ever willfully impale itself on a spear for the greater good of any cause. With the impetus of the Persian charge broken, the Macedonian cavalry began a series of attacks by squadron, hammering continually at the more numerous Persian horses. The Persians were not immediately repulsed, but they were halted. For the next few hours Alexander's right flank was a maelstrom of death, as charge met countercharge and thousands of men speared and hacked at one another in a frenzied, murderous bloodlust. At this point in the story, our sources become strangely silent about events on this flank. It is clear that some fighting continued in this sector at least until after Darius fled the battlefield. At some point after this, Bessus managed to draw off the disorganized remnants of his force.

Darius must have been dumbfounded. One might even trace the start of his later moral collapse to this moment. He had placed the best cavalry in the empire on this flank and had invested great hopes in Bessus's attack. It came as a shock to see his cavalry first halted and then finally repulsed in disarray. Worse, a relatively puny number of Macedonians were thwarting his plans. Still, Darius was not without resources. And as he watched the Macedonian phalanxes' slow advance, he judged the time right to send forward his secret weapon. On his signal, hundreds of horses, arrayed opposite the Macedonian center, strained and began dragging the deadly scythed chariots across the leveled field.

They were met by showers of arrows, javelins, and stones, shot and hurled by Agrianians. Specially trained for skirmishing and habituated to fighting alongside cavalry, the Agrianians rushed the disorganized chariot line. With murderous intent, they went about the business they knew best—exterminating Alexander's enemies. Horses were killed and charioteers dragged from their vehicles to have their throats cut. Some wounded horses, crazed by pain, turned back toward the Persian lines, where they caused horrendous damage. Those chariots that made it to the phalanxes shied away from the bristling spears in favor of the seemingly safe lanes the Macedonians opened up for them. When they passed through, they found themselves beset by the Royal Guard and slaughtered. The chariot assault, Darius's great hope, proved a miserable failure. All it had accomplished was a momentary disordering of the phalanxes, soon put right by the

The Alexander sarcophagus shows Alexander the Great on his horse, lion skin on his head, with raised spear   *Erich Lessing/Art Resource, NY*

disciplined Macedonian troops. After a few moments' pause, the phalanxes stepped off again. In another minute they would impact the Persian line and begin their ruthless grinding.

Now appeared Alexander's great chance. Bessus's advance of the Persian left flank created a gap with the center, which the Persian second rank failed to occupy. At that moment, an empire stood in the balance. For Darius, the battle, if not exactly won, appeared to be shifting in his favor. His troops were pressing hard on the Macedonian left, where Parmenio was doing his best to stem an overwhelming tide. Although Bessus's attack was stalemated, Darius remained confident that the Persians' numerical superiority would eventually wear down stubborn Macedonian resistance on that flank as well. The failure of the chariot charge and the steady advance of the phalanxes were worrisome, but Darius was confident his Immortals and his Greek mercenaries could hold long enough for one flank or the other to sweep aside the Macedonians and ride to victory.

Alexander's experienced eye must have seen the battle in much the same way. Dust and distance probably hid the fact that Parmenio was in trouble. But what was happening on the right was all too visible. There, his men were holding, and successive charges by Macedonian cavalry squadrons were still blunting the Persian assault. But the Persians had thousands of fresh troops left to commit, while losses and exhaustion were taking a toll on Alexander's cavalry. Each succeeding Macedonian charge was a bit weaker and pressed with less vigor than the one before. Alexander must have glanced anxiously toward the advancing phalanx, willing them forward. They had admirably withstood the chariot charge. Still, reordering their ranks took more time than he would have liked, and precious moments were lost before the phalanx could restart its advance. Alexander was far from beaten, but he had cause for concern.

Everything changed in an instant. A gap formed in the Persian line. More miraculous, it opened directly in front of Alexander, who had at his immediate disposal the perfect weapon for exploiting any fleeting opportunity—his Companion cavalry. Seizing the opportunity, Alexander ordered the Companions to form a wedge and wheeled them toward the gap. Seeing that Alexander was beginning his decisive charge, Nicanor ordered his elite Hypaspists infantry forward at the double-quick. Alongside them were four battalions of the phalanx, once again marching forward after stopping the Persian chariot charge. Pulled along by the Hypaspists' advance, they started forward at a trot.

Led by Alexander, probably now mounted on his fierce warhorse, Bucephalas, the Companions crashed into the gap. Some Persian troops moved on their own initiative to intercept the Companions, but their resistance was feeble. Unable to stand up to the terror inspired by the charge of the murderous Companions, the Persian line ruptured. At that moment, Alexander spotted Darius and changed direction, directly toward the Great King himself. Darius, still aboard his royal chariot, was surrounded by the closely massed ranks of his horseguards. However, if he placed much faith in their ability to hold back the Companions, he was mistaken. As Plutarch relates, "The horseguards were seized with panic at the terrible sight of Alexander bearing down upon them and driving the fugitives before him against those who still held their ground." Still, despite their terror and the disorganization caused by fugitives fleeing through their ranks, the horseguards stood fast. They were slaughtered.

Worse, Darius could receive no succor from his elite Immortals, as the Hypaspists and adjoining phalanxes had already crashed into them. Just as at Marathon, the wicker shields and light armor protecting the Immortals proved no match for the heavily armored Macedonian infantry. Likewise, Darius's own phalanx of Greek mercenaries found itself overmatched by the extra-long Macedonian *sarissas* (spears). Bravery now worked to the Persians' disadvantage. What they needed to do was find some way to maneuver. What they did do, however, was stand toe-to-toe against an invincible juggernaut. Darius stood in mute horrified witness as the best of Persia's infantry was pulverized.

The full horror of hoplite warfare was now on display, with all its brutal gore, only yards from Darius's chariot. Unremarkably, the Great King's nerve failed. Terror-stricken, Darius turned his chariot to flee. But his charioteer, encumbered by heaps of dead piled around the chariot's wheels and unable to manage the panicked and rearing horses, could not turn the huge vehicle. When a Macedonian spear

Alexander and Darius meet in battle
Lebrecht Music and Arts Photo Library/Alamy

impaled his charioteer, Darius abandoned the chariot, threw off his armor, bolted to a nearby horse, and fled.

Alexander's impetuous charge into the gap in the Persian lines had opened a hole in his own formation. Although the greater portion of the Macedonian phalanxes had followed Alexander into the gap, the battalions commanded by Simmias and Craterus were forced to stand their ground in support of Parmenio and the hard-pressed Macedonian left flank. Eyeing an opportunity, a mass of Persian and Indian cavalry plunged into the break in the Macedonian lines. If only this cavalry had been better led, Persian victory would have been assured, for once through the gap, they were presented with a number of opportunities. By sweeping left or right, they could have ridden into the rear of either Macedonian flank or smashed into the unprotected sides of the Macedonian phalanxes and rolled them up. The one thing they could not do, if the Persian cause was to retain any hope of success, was take themselves out of the fight. But that was exactly what they did: riding forward instead, toward the Macedonian camp. Opportunities to plunder an enemy camp were almost always an irresistible lure, particularly for undisciplined troops, and here too the Persian cavalry force continued on to loot the Macedonian camp rather than turn in a battle-winning charge.

It was the rare army that remained capable of staying in the fight when it saw its camp being looted and thousands of enemy cavalry in its rear. But Alexander's soldiers were not just any army. Rather, they made up the best-trained and -prepared force the ancient world would see until the advent of the legions at the height of Roman power. There was no panic in Macedonian ranks. Frontline soldiers, already engaged, ignored the new threat and continued driving forward against the collapsing Persian formations. To their immediate rear, the reserve phalanx that Alexander had posted for just such an eventuality turned about and marched on its own camp. There, the Thracians, whom Alexander had left to defend the camp, put up a stout fight, waiting for help to arrive before the entire camp was looted. Surprised by the approach of the unbroken reserve phalanx, the looting Persians were not prepared to meet the crushing Macedonian counterattack. Many were quickly killed, while the disordered survivors fled back in the same direction they had come.

The Persians still had one remaining chance of victory. From almost the start of the fight, Parmenio and the Macedonian left flank had been hard-pressed. Now, at the climax of the battle, the Persian right flank commander, Mazaeus, played his trump and unleashed his Armenian and Cappadocian cavalry. As with Bessus's attack on the opposite flank, thousands of horsemen thundered across the plain, threatening to overwhelm Alexander's tired infantry. But the always steady Parmenio also had one strong card to play—the Thessalian cavalry. These intrepid horsemen, no less proud than the Companions, countercharged the Persians. The two forces met with a thunderclap of clashing steel and in a welter of gore and death. The Persian advance was stopped, but Parmenio's position remained precarious. If his line gave way, the Persian cavalry could turn the Macedonian flank and sweep into Alexander's rear.

Parmenio sent a messenger to Alexander, either to ask for support or to warn him of impending disaster. By the time the messenger caught up with Alexander, the Persian center had already been torn asunder. It was the climactic point of the battle, and Alexander confronted three choices: chase after Darius, turn to the right in support of his beleaguered flank, or wreck the Persian army by going to the left and rolling it up on his way to save Parmenio. Through the dust, he was only just able to make out that Bessus's troops were faltering. They had seen their center disintegrate and were possibly aware that Darius had fled. Demoralized by the center's collapse, the Persian left flank started to fall apart under the renewed hammer blows of the Macedonian cavalry squadrons. Seizing their opportunity, the Macedonian infantry on that flank advanced, sealing the Persian rout. If Alexander had any doubts about how the battle to his right was going, they were put to rest when Menidas joined him with his tired but jubilant cavalry.

Knowing that his right was secure, and informed by Parmenio's messenger that his left was heavily engaged, Alexander had only one option—turn to his left and roll up the Persian line. After hastily re-forming his cavalry, Alexander renewed his attack, this time to his left. Seeing the Companions turn, the Hypaspists and the advancing phalanxes also pivoted to their left, killing as they came on. When the phalanxes changed their angle of advance, Alexander grasped the chance to destroy the entire Persian army. Rather than roll up the flank, as he planned, he led the Companions into the Persian rear, destroying all hope of escape. During this move, Alexander and the Companions first encountered the Persian and Indian cavalry returning from their raid on the baggage train, joined soon thereafter by the strongest and finest cavalry units of Persia.

Here, according to the Roman historian Arrian, ensued the hardest fighting of the day: "For the barbarians, posted many rows deep, encountered Alexander's troops face-to-face and resorted neither to javelin throwing nor to the countermarching of horses, which are common in cavalry actions. Instead, each man strove on his own to force a breakout, as this was their only hope of rescue. They eagerly struck and were struck without mercy, as they were no longer contending for another's victory, but each for his own survival." This ferocious struggle likely ended only when the phalanxes marched into the rear of the fleeing Persians. With Alexander's cavalry to their front and the grinding phalanxes behind them, the slaughter must have been fearsome. One can gain an idea of the fight's ferociousness by the fact that sixty—an unprecedented number—of Alexander's precious, select Companions died and many more received wounds, including Menidas, whose injuries were mortal.

Pressing on, Alexander and the re-formed Companions rode into the flank and rear of the Persians assaulting Parmenio. But here the Thessalians, who had "fought gloriously" and had proved themselves to be not "inferior to Alexander in action," had already turned the tide. Parmenio had his part of the battle well in hand, and it was now his turn to press the retreating Persians hard. Seeing that the battle was won, Alexander barely paused before turning his Companions to pursue Darius. The chase went on until nightfall, while Parmenio finished the destruction of the Persian army.

Darius escaped the battlefield with a small core of his force, including about two thousand Greek mercenaries. Later, Bessus and the remains of the Bactrian cavalry joined the Great King. Whatever plans Darius had of forming a new army and continuing the contest were ended when Bessus, his own kinsman, seized him and declared himself Artaxerxes V. With Alexander close behind, Bessus murdered Darius and retreated east to fight a guerrilla war against the invader and raise a new army. However, Alexander's pursuit was relentless and covered much of central Asia. Eventually, another satrap, Spitamenes, betrayed Bessus and turned him over to the Macedonians for execution. As the executioner of a regicide, Alexander was able to claim the loyalty of most of the other Persian satraps.

Alexander still had several years of fighting ahead of him, reaching the farthest extent of his conquests in India. But the Battle of Gaugamela effectively put an end to two hundred years of Achaemenid rule in Persia. The demise of the Persian ruling dynasty also ended the Persian threat to the continuance of Western civilization. As part of the greater empire of Alexander, the former Persian domains became the center of a Hellenized world, which combined the cultures of East and West to a degree never achieved before or since. Crucially, it was a Western conqueror who imposed this cultural combination on the East, ensuring that the Western or Greek civilization dominated much of the region. Although soon after his death Alexander's successors, the Diadochi, tore his empire into three warring segments, each segment remained sufficiently powerful to give Rome a hard fight during its rise. Egypt, ruled by a descendant of one of Alexander's generals, Ptolemy, did not finally succumb until Augustus's defeat of Mark Antony and Cleopatra in 31 B.C., almost three centuries after Alexander's death.

If Alexander had lost at Gaugamela, it is unlikely that he or any part of his army would have survived. Darius III, having had a near death experience, would surely have mobilized the full might of the empire to end the Greek menace forever. With Alexander's army wrecked, Greece would have been almost defenseless against a Persian counterattack. Undoubtedly the vengeful Persians would have done their utmost to erase all traces of a unique Greek civilization, likely through the use of mass deportations of Greeks into the vastness of the empire.

Instead, it was Persia that fell to the Greeks. Moreover, if Alexander was not well-disposed to the Persians on the eve of his invasion, by the time he entered their great cities his attitude had changed. There was much in Persia that Alexander liked, and he was not hesitant about melding large elements of Persia's cultural life and beliefs with those of the West. This cultural merging had effects that persist into the present. Primarily, this is found in the transmission of Rome's Latin culture, which in many ways proved no match for and was eventually overwhelmed by the post-Alexander Hellenistic Greeks. As the Roman poet Horace commented: *"Graecia capta ferum victorim cepit et artis intulit agresti Latio"* ("Conquered Greece has conquered the savage victor and brought her arts into rustic Latium"). And it was not only the arts that the Greeks brought to Rome. They also conveyed a long philosophical tradition that first infected and then inundated the Roman Empire, echoes of which are still heard today. In every important respect, much of Western culture and civilization is a result of the creation, survival, and later the spread of Hellenism throughout the Roman Empire.

Just as crucial, evidence indicates that Jesus was a Hellenized Jew (Jews who preferred Greek to Hebrew or Aramaic). How this affected his ministry and the early development of Christianity is still hotly debated. Still, there is little doubt that Christianity first took root among the Hellenized segments of the Jewish population in Judea. From there, it inserted itself among the various Hellenized Jewish colonies that were spread throughout the Roman Empire for the conduct of their widespread commercial activities. There is no debate that Hellenism had a profound influence on the writers of the New Testament. In large measure, the development of the philosophical edifice that underpins Christian beliefs is a Hellenistic interpretation of the life and traditions of Jesus, coming to us through a prism of cultural beliefs first established by Alexander's victory at Gaugamela. It is too much to claim that if Alexander had been defeated, Christianity would never have appeared, but it is clear that the trajectory and traditions of Christianity would have been radically altered if Alexander had been vanquished.

ZAMA

An Empire in the Balance

202 B.C.

Over the eight hundred years of Roman ascendancy, as both a republic and an empire, Rome confronted innumerable threats, but none as dire as when the great Carthaginian general Hannibal marched his mercenary army over the Alps to confront the Romans on their own soil. By doing so, he reignited the contest for control of the western Mediterranean between Rome and its mortal enemy Carthage, the first phase of which had ended a generation before, in 241 B.C., at the conclusion of the First Punic War (so called as a reference to the language of ancient Carthage, a form of late Phoenician). When that war started, Rome was merely a local power whose authority did not extend much beyond southern Italy. By the end of the Third Punic War in 146 B.C., Carthage was destroyed and Rome had become an imperial power. Rome's final victory left it in possession of a large swath of northern Africa, Sicily, Sardinia, Corsica, much of coastal Spain, and Macedonia. Moreover, as the Punic Wars took Roman armies far from Italian shores, Rome became accustomed to the long-term commitment of men and resources required to maintain prolonged overseas campaigns. In addition, the Punic Wars forced Rome to mobilize resources on a vast scale, and in doing so, it established the base upon which the Roman Empire was built. The struggle with Carthage was not the only element that propelled Rome toward empire, but it was probably the decisive one. For once Carthage was destroyed, there was no other power in the Mediterranean capable of long withstanding the might of *Senatus Populusque Romanus*—the "Senate and People of Rome" (SPQR).

If Carthage had won, the world would be a vastly different place, as victory could be accomplished only by destroying Rome and exterminating its population. For Rome possessed a view of war distinctly different from that of any other power in the Western world. When a state found itself at war with Rome, it was making a serious statement about its future, since for the Romans war was an all-or-nothing affair. Surrender or even compromise was alien to Roman nature. Carthage could not defeat Rome by winning one battle or even a dozen. With its vast reserves of manpower, Rome could and did generate new armies after defeats that would have left a less determined state begging for terms. This more than anything else probably accounts for Hannibal's failure to march directly on Rome after he virtually annihilated two full consular armies at the Battle of Cannae. In all likelihood, after inflicting such a crushing defeat on Roman arms, Hannibal expected Rome to sue for peace. Not for the last time, he had misjudged his enemy's tenacity, and he must have been astounded when he realized the war would continue. Hannibal lacked either the capability or the will to *erase* Rome and eradicate its people. Eventually Rome would demonstrate to Carthage that it lacked neither.

Had Carthage prevailed and pursued Rome's extermination, as Rome would later do to Carthage, it would have eliminated any possibility of the Roman Empire coming into existence. It is hard to overestimate the almost incalculable shift such an event would have had on the patterns of history. Rome ruled the greater part of the Western world for five hundred years. During that time it transmitted its language, culture, civilizational tenets, legal system, and even military methods to its conquered territories. Despite the near extinction of the remaining vestiges of Roman civilization during the Dark

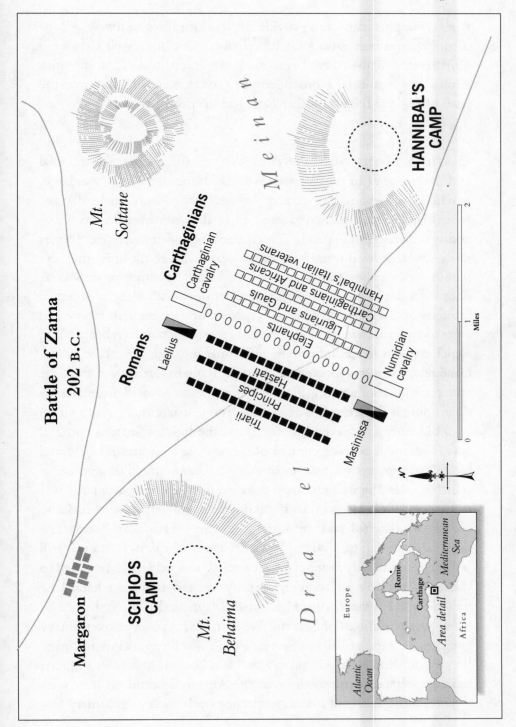

Battle of Zama
202 B.C.

Margaron

SCIPIO'S CAMP

Mt. Behaima

Mt. Soltane

M e i n a n

HANNIBAL'S CAMP

D r a a   e l

Carthaginians

Carthaginian cavalry

Carthaginians and Africans
Ligurians and Gauls
Hannibal's Italian veterans

Elephants

Numidian cavalry

Romans

Laelius

Triarii
Principes
Hastati

Masinissa

0   1   2
Miles

Europe
Rome
Carthage
Mediterranean Sea
Area detail
Africa
Atlantic Ocean

Ages, enough survived to provide the basis for most of the West's institutions and later cultural achievements. One may well wonder if Christianity, whose spread was made possible through the mobility afforded by a unified Roman Empire, could ever have achieved the level of a world religion if Carthage had been victorious.

CARTHAGE IN THE THIRD CENTURY B.C. was the greatest commercial and naval power in the Western world. Although its navy was large, it relied on mercenaries, mostly Numidians, to fight its land wars. Rome by 264 B.C. had conquered all of Italy south of the Po River and was looking to expand. The collision between these two powers of the western Mediterranean was the inevitable result of Rome's expansionist impulse. The Republic's voracious appetite for new conquests soon placed it in direct competition with the commercial interests of Carthage. At first, it seemed an uneven contest. Rome had a powerful citizen army, but it lacked any significant naval capability, which made it nearly impossible for Rome to strike directly at its foe. Carthage, for its part, could descend on Roman territory at the time and place of its choosing. Rome overcame its naval deficiencies by developing a navy capable of meeting the Carthaginians on the high seas, but only after several disasters and the building of several fleets was Rome able to take control of the seas, at least around Italy and Sicily. After over two decades of war, Carthage agreed to a peace, in which it ceded Sicily to Roman control and agreed to pay a large war indemnity. Unbeknownst to the Romans, however, the war had also created a powerful and unforgiving enemy—Hamilcar Barca. The one Carthaginian general the Romans had not beaten, Barca was still holding out in Sicily when the peace treaty was made. He returned to Carthage bearing an undying enmity toward Rome, a hatred he passed on to his three sons, Hasdrubal, Mago, and Hannibal.

It was Hannibal, one of the Western's world's foremost military geniuses, who provoked the Second Punic War by attacking the Spanish city of Saguntum, a Roman ally. He followed this up, in 218 B.C., with a spectacular march through the Alps to descend on Italy with twenty-eight thousand infantry, six thousand cavalry, and thirty ele-

Bust of Hannibal
Peter Horree/Alamy

phants. In two major battles at the Trebbia River and Lake Trasimene, Hannibal crushed two Roman armies.

Needing time to regroup, Rome appointed Quintus Fabius Maximus as military dictator. Fabius eschewed the normal Roman policy of seeking decisive battle at the earliest opportunity in favor of a defensive, guerrilla-style conflict. Roman troops would fight hundreds of small engagements to hinder Hannibal's plans, but they refused to meet his army in pitched battle. What became known as "Fabian tactics" were not well received by the legionnaires, who nicknamed Fabius the Cunctator—the Delayer. When the Romans could no longer tolerate Hannibal's pillaging, it elected two consuls, Gaius Terentius Varro and Lucius Aemilius Paullus, who favored offering Hannibal a pitched battle.

At the Battle of Cannae, Hannibal virtually annihilated two consular armies in an engagement that historians still consider a tactical masterpiece. After driving off the Roman cavalry, always their weakest arm, Hannibal allowed the Romans to cave in his center, while his flanks held firm. Eventually the armies found themselves fighting it out in a large concave formation. The Romans were on the verge of splitting the Carthaginian army in half when Hannibal ordered his flanks to turn inward on the Romans. Simultaneously, Hannibal's cavalry returned and smashed into the Roman rear, sealing the army's fate. Approximately ten thousand of the eighty thousand Romans present escaped. One of them was the man who would save Rome and become Hannibal's nemesis—Scipio. The young Scipio distinguished himself during the battle, and particularly in its immediate aftermath, when he was instrumental in rallying many of the survivors.

In Cannae's wake, Hannibal, who was without a siege train capable of breaching Rome's walls, opted not to press his luck. This led one of his senior officers, Maharbal, to lament, "You know how to win a victory Hannibal, but not how to profit from it." After the battle, Hannibal was nevertheless able to secure allies, establish a base in southern Italy, and even set up an independent kingdom of Gauls in northern Italy. His biggest gain came when Capua, Italy's second largest city, came over to the Carthaginian side. The Capuans were unable to resist the temptation to become Italy's leading city, which seemed an inevitable consequence of so many Roman disasters. They paid a heavy price for their treachery at Rome's most dire hour. When the Romans finally retook the city in 211 B.C., they crucified every male citizen—one every few yards along the road from Capua to Rome. For Hannibal, gaining allies proved easy. Protecting them was nearly impossible, as Rome continued to field new armies, each larger than Hannibal's.

Hannibal fought a number of battles over the next several years and won a few great victories. But he was increasingly bottled up in southern Italy with ever larger and more capable Roman forces closing in. If he was to turn the tide, he needed significant reinforcements. By this time, however, Rome controlled the seas, making it impossible to send a large force into Italy except through the Alps. Hannibal's brother Hasdrubal Barca did precisely that in 207 B.C., leading a new army out of Spain and into northern Italy.

This time, the Roman army and its leaders were up to the task.

The consul Nero led his army away from a position from which it had been monitoring Hannibal and force marched it to the north, where it joined the army of consul Marcus Livius. Together they wiped out Hasdrubal's army at the Battle of the Metaurus. Nero immediately force marched his troops back to the south and was in his original defensive positions before Hannibal was aware of his departure. Hannibal learned of his brother's fate when a Roman cavalryman rode up to his barricades and flung Hasdrubal's head into the Carthaginian camp. Numerous histories, including Creasy's *Fifteen Decisive Battles,* name the Metaurus as the decisive battle of the Second Punic War. Although there is much to commend this opinion, the authors believe that while the Metaurus was crucial to securing Rome's survival, it was the later Battle of Zama that ensured Carthage would one day be destroyed.

WHILE HANNIBAL WAS ravaging Italy, Rome was also attacking Carthaginian power in Spain. And it was in Spain that the brash young Roman commander Publius Cornelius Scipio was continuing to make a name for himself. After winning several major victories and capturing a substantial number of Punic cities and towns, Scipio confronted a major Carthaginian army at Illipa in 207 B.C. For several days, Scipio lined up with his legions in the center and his Iberian allies on the flanks. The Carthaginian commanders assumed this would be his formation on the day of battle. It was a fatal assumption.

On the day of battle, Scipio marched his troops out with his forces repositioned. The Iberians were in the center, while the legions were moved to the flanks. Before the Carthaginian commanders recognized the change, the Romans charged. The legions tore the inferior troops in front of them to pieces before turning on the better-trained forces in the center. Under pressure from Scipio's Iberians and with their flanks giving way, the Carthaginians attempted to retreat. Their withdrawal soon turned into a rout and a general massacre ensued, brought to an end only by a sudden downpour. Illipa broke Carthaginian power in Spain, while Rome had a new hero of the hour.

Scipio soon made his way back to Rome to put himself on the path to the ultimate confrontation with Hannibal.

IN RECOGNITION of Scipio's Spanish victories, the people of Rome elected him consul in 205 B.C., and he was given Sicily as his province. More important, Scipio was also given permission to cross over into Africa, the Carthaginian homeland, if he found it in Rome's interest. Upon arriving in Sicily, Scipio took command of two disgraced legions—the reconstituted remnants of the legions slaughtered at Cannae. After that crushing defeat, the Roman Senate had refused these legionnaires permission to leave the army and instead assembled them into two new legions, the V and the VI, and sent them to serve in exile in Sicily—a degradation that stood in contrast with the praise and honors bestowed on those Cannae survivors who were of noble birth, including Scipio. The exiled legionnaires keenly felt the stain of their dishonor, and every year they petitioned the Senate to return to Italy, where they might prove their valor against Hannibal and earn redemption. Every year, the Senate ignored their petition. When Scipio's powerful enemies in the Senate engineered his assignment to command these disgraced legions, that ever-calculating assemblage was aware it was doing him no great service.

Above all else, what made Scipio one of history's great captains was his ability to get close to and understand the men who served under him. It is doubtful that any other Roman of the patrician class would have understood the deep psychological need the men of the V and VI Legions had to prove themselves. In his eyes they were not disgraced; rather, they were men who by dint of sheer hard fighting had cut their way out of an encirclement that saw two consular armies nearly wiped out in an afternoon. Moreover, they had not just saved themselves, they had also rapidly re-formed to do their part in protecting the Republic in its most dire hour. Upon his arrival in Sicily, Scipio praised them and honored their long service. In return, they gave him their last measure of devotion.

Scipio's new legions may have been motivated, but they were far from ready. Although there had been some fighting in Sicily, there had been no pitched battles. Many years had passed since Cannae, and

Scipio found that as much as half his force was too old or unfit for combat. Fortunately, thousands of volunteers, including veterans from the fighting in Spain, flocked to Sicily, lured by the fame of their commander and the prospect of rich African plunder. Over the next year, Scipio drilled his soldiers until they were as effective as those forces he had led to victory in Spain. While his army trained, Scipio looked to those often neglected but crucial elements that in many cases meant the difference between victory and defeat: intelligence, logistics, and diplomacy.

Scipio made use of trusted spies and the other time-tested methods of gathering intelligence, but he took the added step of launching a sea raid against the North African coast. Thirty warships, commanded by Scipio's second in command, Gaius Laelius, were sent to inflict as much damage as possible on Carthage's African territories.

Bust of Publius
Cornelius Scipio
*The Art Gallery
Collection/Alamy*

Scipio never expected this attack to be anything more than an irritant. Its real value lay in what it told Scipio about Carthaginian readiness and reaction times. Even more vital, the fleet allowed Scipio to make contact with a Numidian king, Masinissa, who had previously served the Carthaginian cause well in Spain. Seeing which way the winds were blowing, Masinissa was ready to transfer his loyalty to Rome, but first he had to win a civil war against a Numidian rival—Syphax. Scipio pledged that Rome's legions would help him win that war. In return, Masinissa would provide Scipio with the one element Roman armies had always lacked when facing Hannibal: a numerous and effective cavalry force.

In 204 B.C., Scipio judged that all was in readiness. Under his command, a Roman invasion fleet of four hundred transports and approximately forty warships left for North Africa. After a small skirmish with Carthaginian cavalry, the Romans firmly established themselves near Utica. Masinissa, with a paltry two hundred cavalrymen, soon joined them. Scipio, who was expecting thousands of Numidian cavalry, must have been chagrined to discover that his Numidian ally, Masinissa, had recently been defeated in battle by his rival. After his victory, Syphax declared himself king of a united Numidian nation, and Masinissa fled with a small band of loyalists. Syphax, who was married to a Carthaginian princess, Sophonisba, daughter of the Carthaginian general Hasdrubal Gisco, promptly transferred Numidia's allegiance back to Carthage.

Word of the Roman army's landing sent Carthage into a panic. Despite numerous warnings of Scipio's impending descent on their coastline, the Carthaginians had done little to prepare their city's defenses. Rather than march directly on Carthage, however, Scipio chose to besiege the nearby city of Utica, which he hoped to use as a base for further operations. This decision has been roundly condemned by generations of historians, who believe Scipio could have taken Carthage with an immediate assault on its walls. However, given that the equally unprepared Utica withstood assault and then months of siege, it is unlikely Scipio would have fared any better against Carthage's stout defenses. Moreover, if he had been repulsed, Scipio would likely have been left with a demoralized force and without a base to fall back on. In the face of a gathering enemy army, failure before the walls of Carthage could easily have spelled doom for the Romans.

As Scipio besieged Utica, Hasdrubal (not to be confused with the brother of Hannibal who was killed at the Metaurus) and Syphax gathered an army in his rear. The ancient historians Polybius and Livy agree that the combined Carthaginian force numbered close to eighty thousand infantry and thirteen thousand cavalry. These numbers, as is common in many troop estimates presented by ancient writers, seem highly dubious. Given the difficulties involved in supplying such a concentration during the winter, it is unlikely that the Carthaginians had even half that number. Moreover, whatever force they had raised must have consisted of large numbers of poorly trained rabble, who would have fared poorly in a contest with Scipio's well-trained legionnaires. Although the Carthaginians greatly outnumbered the Romans, their commanders, Syphax and Hasdrubal, were content to wait in their respective camps, apparently in the belief that Scipio's penned-up army would either surrender, withdraw, or starve.

Over the next several months, Scipio first tried to lure Syphax over to the Roman side. When that effort failed, he pretended to go along with Syphax's attempts to mediate a peace between Carthage and Rome. Centurions disguised as slaves accompanied the officers Scipio sent to conduct the negotiations. Several of these centurions, proud men and veterans of decades of hard fighting, even allowed themselves to be beaten and otherwise degraded in order to sell the illusion that they were slaves and therefore not worthy of attention. As the talks progressed, the centurion-slaves wandered throughout the enemy camp, noting its strengths and particularly its weaknesses.

After allowing Syphax to believe he had accepted their peace overtures, and at the same time tightening the siege of Utica to ensure no sudden sally could interfere with his plans, Scipio called his tribunes together to discuss his plans. At the end of each day, the Romans sounded a series of bugle calls to mark the end of daily activities and to call the troops to dinner. That night, however, the bugle calls would instead signal the time for the Roman army, which had eaten an early dinner, to march out of its encampment. Unobserved, Scipio's two columns, one led by Scipio himself and the other commanded by his most competent subordinate general, Laelius, joined by Masinissa, would advance on the two enemy camps. Under cover of darkness, Laelius attacked first, taking Syphax's camp by surprise. The Romans set fire to the camp, while Masinissa's men along with some Roman reinforcements blocked the exits. The wooden camp was soon burning furiously. Believing the fire accidental and lacking the resources to fight it, most of the Numidians fled the flames, many of them unarmed. Once outside the camp, the Numidians were caught by surprise by the battle-ready Roman formations. Syphax's panicked Numidians were slaughtered mercilessly. As related by Polybius:

> Thinking that it was a mere accidental conflagration of the rampart, some of them started unsuspiciously out of bed, others sprang out of their tents in the midst of a carouse and with the cup actually at their lips. The result was that numbers of them got trampled to death by their own friends at the exits from the camp; many were caught by the flames and burnt to death; while all those who escaped the flame fell into the hands of the enemy, and were killed, without knowing what was happening to them or what they were doing.

The Carthaginians in the second camp, a little over a mile distant, witnessed the conflagration but discerned no sign of fighting. Also believing the fire accidental, many of Hasdrubal's men rushed to assist their allies in fighting the fire. Like the Numidians, they were cut down by cohorts Scipio had placed between the two camps. As for the remainder, "[They] hurried outside their own camp unarmed, and stood there gazing in astonishment at the spectacle. Everything having thus succeeded to his best wishes, Scipio fell upon these men outside their camp, and either put them to the sword, or, driving them back into the camp, set fire to their huts." Thrown into a state of confused panic, Hasdrubal's men offered little resistance to the Roman assault. Men, horses, and beasts of burden either met a pitiable death from fire or, if they escaped, were ignominiously "cut down defenseless and naked, not only without arms, but without clothing to cover them."

Understanding the devastating totality of the Roman victory, Hasdrubal made no attempt to rally his forces or to save the doomed camps. Rather, joined by Syphax, he fled with fewer than twenty-five hundred survivors to the fortified town of Anda. From there, Hasdrubal went on to Carthage, hoping to put some steel into their post-debacle deliberations, while Syphax built a new fortified camp at Abba. For the Romans, the battle had been an overwhelming success. For a trifling cost, they had destroyed an army of more than forty thousand men, including the capture of five thousand soldiers, a large number of whom were Carthaginian nobles.

There was panic in Carthage, but the city's Senate acted with the same resolution the Romans had displayed in the wake of the disaster at Cannae. After considering proposals to either recall Hannibal and his army or send an embassy to Scipio to treat for peace, the Carthaginians decided to leave Hannibal in place and continue the war. The Carthaginians transported four thousand Spanish mercenaries to North Africa, and local recruiting took on a new urgency. At the same time, they sent messages to Syphax entreating him to remain loyal to the Carthaginian cause. Still under the spell of his wife and buoyed by Carthaginian reinforcements, Syphax remained loyal. Within thirty days, Carthage once again fielded an army of thirty thousand troops, positioned to threaten Scipio's ongoing siege of Utica.

Alerted to the new enemy concentration, Scipio moved immediately to counter it. Leaving a minimal force to continue the siege of Utica, he marched the rest to meet Hasdrubal's new army on "the Great Plains." After a slow five-day march, Scipio came face-to-face with his opponent and established a camp approximately four miles distant. For the next three days, the two armies seemed content to size each other up. Each morning the Romans massed in a valley near the Carthaginian camp, but Hasdrubal refused to take the bait. On the fourth day, Hasdrubal, probably running short of supplies, could delay no longer. Each army formed up and advanced upon the other.

Hasdrubal placed his best and most reliable troops, newly arrived Spanish mercenaries, in the center. Arrayed to their right were the infantry forces salvaged from the most recent disaster. On either side of these troops were the new levies, who were flanked by the cavalry, with Syphax's Numidians on the left. Facing them was a Roman army arranged in its typical fashion. The two legions were in the center with the two auxiliary formations (who were little different from a legion at this point) on either side of them. The Roman cavalry was on the right flank, and Masinissa's cavalry was on the left.

It was a short battle. The Numidian horsemen, most of them hastily raised, untrained peasants, broke on the first charge. On the other flank, the raw Carthaginian levies, demoralized by the recent string of defeats, also crumbled under the impact of Masinissa's cavalry. Only the Spanish fought on. They had little choice, as they were not familiar with the territory, and with Roman cavalry already in their rear, they had little hope of escape. If caught, they expected no mercy, for in Scipio's eyes they were traitors, as their tribes had sworn loyalty to Rome during his campaigns in Spain. The Roman heavy infantry advanced in its standard three-line formation, with the maniples of the *hastati,* the first line, leading, followed by the more heavily armed and experienced *principes,* and finally the grizzled veterans of the *triarii.* Rather than feed in each line in succession, Scipio waited until the *hastati,* his most inexperienced troops but still veterans of several engagements, had pinned the Spaniards in place. He then marched the other two lines to the left and right. On signal, the Roman columns crashed into the flank and rear of the Spanish line, cutting down the Spaniards almost to a man. However, their sacrifice bought enough time for Hasdrubal and Syphax to escape.

The ancient sources make no mention of it, but Scipio, who had seen a Roman army destroyed at Cannae when the Carthaginian cavalry smashed into its rear, must have observed how much easier his fight against the Spaniards would have been if his cavalry had returned once it had driven the enemy cavalry off the field. It was a lesson he would make good use of at Zama. But that was for the future. For the moment, Scipio needed to decide his next move. While his men plundered the Carthaginian camp, Scipio met with his senior commanders. After listening to their advice, he decided to split his army in two. Laelius and Masinissa would head off into the Numidian heartland to destroy Syphax and restore Masinissa to the Numidian throne. Scipio kept the main body with him to secure the towns surrounding Carthage and demonstrate against the city itself. After taking Tunis and establishing a camp near Carthage, Scipio noted the still powerful Carthaginian fleet preparing to leave port. Realizing that his own fleet was imperiled, Scipio broke camp and force marched his army back to Utica. He arrived in time to save most of the Roman fleet, but the Carthaginians were able to make off with sixty Roman transports.

In the meantime, Laelius and Masinissa marched fifteen days into the heart of Syphax's own territory. By the time they caught up to him, Syphax had raised a new Numidian army, mostly from his own tribe—the Maesulli. For a time, Syphax's more numerous cavalry had the better of it, but as Laelius's Roman infantry came up, the tide turned. Steadily, the Romans advanced until Syphax's line broke. He himself fell into Roman hands while making a vain attempt to rally his fleeing soldiers. Soon thereafter, his Carthaginian wife, Sophonisba, surrendered herself and immediately started working her charms on Masinissa, who impetuously married her. Laelius was furious, as he and the rest of the Romans believed Numidian loyalty fickle and did not trust that Masinissa could resist Sophonisba's wiles. Still, Laelius agreed to leave her fate for Scipio to decide. All of Numidia was not conquered, but enough was won over so that Carthage could expect only minor aid from that corner.

When Laelius and Masinissa returned to the main Roman army, Scipio ruled that both Syphax and Sophonisba were captives of Rome and their fates lay in his hands. Masinissa, realizing that his hold on the Numidian throne rested on Roman power, did not contest the decision. But, unwilling to see Sophonisba led in chains before the Roman mob prior to a ritual strangulation, he sent his new bride a wedding gift of poison. Sophonisba, equally unwilling to serve as a Roman pawn or trophy, drank it without hesitation. The next day, as consolation, Scipio held a public ceremony honoring Masinissa and declaring him king of Numidia.

Scipio's next moves were disrupted when the Carthaginian Senate sent thirty of its most respected senior members to the Roman camp to treat for peace. Scipio imposed hard terms, including the handing over of most of the Punic fleet to Rome, the renunciation of all territorial claims to the Mediterranean islands, and the recall of Hannibal and his army. Moreover, while the Roman Senate decided on the final peace terms, Scipio demanded five thousand tons of food for his men and animals to see them through the winter. Throughout the winter, a tense truce held, even as Hannibal returned with his veterans. But when storms scattered a fleet of Roman supply transports, the Carthaginians sent out fifty warships to seize them. Scipio, claiming a violation of the truce, indignantly demanded the return of the transports and their contents. Buoyed by the return of Hannibal and his veteran army, the Carthaginian Senate refused to return the transports and even had the temerity to try to murder the Roman envoys on their return to Scipio's camp. There could be only one response from Rome. Scipio prepared for battle.

The Romans renewed the war with a vengeance, attacking and plundering cities and towns throughout North Africa. This time they spared no one. Even cities that surrendered without putting up resistance saw their menfolk killed and the women and children sold into slavery. This was the Roman way of war, which Tacitus, the great historian of ancient Rome, accurately described as "they make a desert and call it peace." Scipio's obvious strategy was to force Hannibal to march out and offer battle before his army was prepared. At the same time, Scipio sent messengers for Masinissa, who was off securing his hold on power, to raise a large cavalry force and make haste to join him.

Hannibal, ignoring the clamor for action coming from the Carthaginian Senate, refused to rush. However, when two thousand Numidian horsemen under Tychaeus, a close relative of Syphax's, arrived in Carthage, he judged the moment right. As he advanced from his forward base at Hadrumetum toward Zama, five days' march from Carthage, Hannibal sent out scouts to locate and assess Scipio's strength. The Romans captured three of these scouts. Rather than subject them to a gruesome execution, Scipio ordered them to be given a guided tour of the Roman camp and then sent on their way. Numerous historians have claimed that this was nothing more than a statement of confidence on Scipio's part. However, as Masinissa and his thousands of Numidian cavalry did not join Scipio until the day after he released the Carthaginian scouts, another motive suggests itself. These scouts, totally unaware of the pending arrival of Masinissa, reported to Hannibal that Scipio possessed only a limited number of cavalry at his disposal.

Hoping to take advantage of his apparent position of strength,

Hannibal advanced west from Zama and established a camp four miles from Scipio. There he asked for a parley, probably hoping to secure easy peace terms while he still had an unbroken army at his back. Both Livy and Polybius present lengthy accounts of the two generals' discussion, which are probably not to be believed. In any event, whatever Hannibal had wished to accomplish, short of meeting and sizing up his opponent, he failed. As Livy recounts, "[Both commanders] reported that their discussion had been fruitless, that the matter must be now decided by arms, and the results left to the gods."

The following morning, the Romans marched out to give battle. Although the legions advanced in their standard three lines, Scipio had ordered one major alteration. Instead of the second line filling the space between the maniples of the first line, in a checkerboard pattern, Scipio ordered the *principes* to line up directly behind the maniples of the *hastati,* with the *triarii* lining up behind them. Thus, he created wide lanes that would give Hannibal's elephants an avenue to rush through, assuming the animals opted not to be impaled on Roman spear points. For here, as with horses, the courage of the elephant decides and not that of his master. Of course, a wounded and therefore enraged elephant was likely to charge anything that presented itself. On the left wing the trusted Laelius commanded the Italian cavalry, while Masinissa led his four thousand Numidian horsemen on the right. In front of the Roman army and stationed in the gaps between the maniples was a swarm of light infantry skirmishers—the *velites*. It was their job to disrupt the Carthaginian elephant attack and harass Hannibal's first line.

Before them stood an army commanded by the greatest general of the age. Hannibal had also arranged his army in three lines. In the first were the elements of Hannibal's late brother Mago's army, recently returned from Liguria, where they had fought well in support of Hannibal's army in southern Italy. Behind them was a strong force of local Libyans accompanied by a number of Carthaginian volunteers, a rare display of personal valor by the Punic city dwellers. In the third line stood Hannibal's veterans, victors of a dozen major battles and countless smaller fights over a decade and a half. It was in these men, who had never before failed him, that Hannibal placed his and Carthage's final hope. We do not have an exact number, but as various sources attest that the Carthaginian final line was nearly as strong as the entire force of Roman infantry, they must have numbered between fifteen thousand and twenty thousand men, all of them probably outfitted in captured Roman uniforms and carrying Roman weapons. To support them, Hannibal placed his Numidian cavalry so it faced Masinissa, while the Carthaginian cavalry lined up against Laelius. To add menace to his formation, Hannibal posted eighty elephants to his front.

Hannibal's plan lacked the subtlety that had marked his great victories at Cannae and Trebia. Forgoing stratagems, Hannibal hoped to disorganize the first Roman line, the *hastati,* with his elephants and then use his own first line to take advantage of this disorganization. After that he planned to feed in troops from his other two lines, Roman style, to wear down the legions. His hope was that Scipio would be forced to commit and exhaust the *triarii* (his third line) before Hannibal sent in his tested veterans. As for his cavalry, the best

The Acts of Scipio: The Battle of Zama
© *RMN-Grand Palais/Art Resource, NY*

Hannibal could hope for was that it would hold its own until the Roman infantry was defeated.

Scipio, on the other hand, still remembered how Hannibal's cavalry had smashed huge Roman armies in the past and how he had very much wished for the return of his own cavalry at the Battle of the Great Plain. Outnumbered in infantry, typically the key element of any Roman success, he counted on his cavalry winning decisively and then returning to his aid before the legions were overrun.

It took several hours to arrange the respective forces, time each commander used to address his troops and build their courage. Notably, Hannibal decided to address only his veterans in the third line, deputizing subcommanders to address the first and second lines. Scipio, who possessed the marked advantage of commanding an army that knew him well after three years of campaigning, addressed his entire force. He made only one point, that there was nowhere to flee in the event of defeat, so they must go forth resolved to one of two fates—conquer or die!

After ineffectual cavalry skirmishing between the Numidian forces of each side, Hannibal gave the order for the elephants to charge. Unfortunately for the Carthaginians, the massive animals proved careless in selecting whom they considered an enemy. As they began to advance, Scipio ordered his trumpeters to sound loudly, which panicked many of the insufficiently battle-trained elephants. The elephants on the Carthaginian left were particularly affected, turning to charge into the mass of Numidian cavalry guarding Hannibal's flank. Masinissa did not miss the opportunity. He charged with his own four thousand Numidians, driving their opposites on Hannibal's side off the field, then, with the bit between his teeth, he led his troops off in wild pursuit.

In the meantime, the more intrepid of Hannibal's elephants continued forward into the ranks of the Roman *velites,* where they did some execution but suffered grievous wounds. Unwilling to crash into the solid walls of the Roman maniples, from which so many hurtful darts were pouring, many of the elephants opted for the path of least resistance and charged harmlessly down the paths Scipio had ordered opened for them. The remainder turned sideways to avoid the fusillade of missiles, then attempted to escape through the cavalry guarding Hannibal's right flank. Laelius, no slower in spotting an opportunity than was Masinissa, ordered an immediate charge. The Carthaginian cavalry fled with Laelius in pursuit.

The elephant attack had failed. But much to Scipio's chagrin and Hannibal's delight, the cavalry of both sides had ridden off the battlefield. The way was now open for the infantry contest that Hannibal hoped for. Before the cavalry was even off the field, Hannibal, well aware that time was not an ally, ordered his first two lines to advance, with his veterans in the third line fixed at their posts. The Romans waited in eerie stillness until the Carthaginians were almost on them. Then, at the last instant, they let loose a hail of spears and roared their war cry as they beat their swords on the metal of their shields. Momentarily unnerved, the Carthaginians hesitated.

The Romans charged.

The battle was ferocious. For a long time, neither side gained much of an advantage. The nimble warriors from Liguria were mercenaries and veterans of many hard fights. They gave a good account of themselves, but they were unsupported. Eventually, the *hastati* pushed forward, although their losses were heavy. In the next instant, the entire Carthaginian first line broke. Angry that the second line had not advanced to their support, the mercenaries began hacking at the Carthaginians and their Libyan allies. As this intramural conflict developed, the *hastati* continued to advance.

When they engaged the second line, their forward momentum ground to a halt. Exhausted after the hard fight against Mago's former army, the *hastati* initially made little impression on the citizens of Carthage. But they did not have to fight alone. Seeing that their legionary brothers were nearly fought out, the *principes* advanced to their aid. These fresh troops proved too much for the Carthaginians. As their experience in actual fighting was negligible, they must have found the spectacle unfolding around them horrifying. It is not difficult to imagine the terror the average Carthaginian merchant felt as armor-encased killers, brandishing bloody swords and screaming murderous war cries, slowly closed on him with only one intent—his destruction. It is a miracle that the would-be soldiers made any kind of a stand at all.

When they finally broke, the Carthaginians were cut down by the thousands by the closely pursuing Romans. With their bloodlust up, the *hastati* became a disorganized mob as they focused on only one thing—killing as many Carthaginians as possible. The terrified masses of Carthaginians found no succor from Hannibal's "Army of Italy." Ordered not to let the refugees disorder their ranks, these sturdy veterans lowered their spear points and refused the retreating second line entry, ordering them to move around the flanks and re-form to their rear. Some of them were able to do this, but a great many more were killed in the attempt.

According to Polybius:

> The space between the two armies was full of blood, wounded men, and dead corpses; and thus the rout of the enemy proved an impediment of a perplexing nature to the Roman general. Everything was calculated to make an advance in order difficult—the ground slippery with gore, the corpses lying piled up in bloody heaps, and with the corpses' arms flung about in every direction.

Scipio was not perplexed for long. At this point, Roman training and discipline counted most. At the sound of the trumpet, the *hastati* broke off their pursuit and re-formed. As they did so, Scipio had the Roman wounded evacuated and the Carthaginian wounded slaughtered. As the *hastati* re-formed, Scipio ordered the *principes* to move to one flank and the *triarii* to move to the other, creating a solid line of Roman infantry. Such a mid-battle reorganization is a feat of consummate skill and probably provided Hannibal his best chance to launch a counterblow. Inexplicably, the Carthaginian general held his position and allowed the Romans to form up unmolested.

When Scipio had completed his redeployment, the Romans again began beating their swords against their shields and shouting their nerve-racking war cry. With a crash of trumpets, they stepped off. It was to be a contest between phalanxes.

For some minutes, the issue was in doubt. "Being nearly equal in numbers, spirit, courage, and arms, the battle was for a long time undecided, the men in their obstinate valor falling dead without giving way a step, as two evenly matched veteran armies hacked away at each other." Rome's ultimate victory and Carthage's survival hung in the balance as twenty thousand men on each side went about the business of exterminating the other.

The tide turned in a sudden apocalyptic crash, for Laelius's and Masinissa's cavalries returned together and smashed into the unguarded Carthaginian rear. It was too much for Hannibal's veterans. The greater part of them, assailed in the front and rear, were cut down in their ranks. Those who fled were mercilessly pursued by the cavalry, and after finding no refuge on the desert expanse, they were slaughtered. When it was over, twenty thousand Carthaginian dead littered the battlefield, while a similar number were prisoners. Scipio had annihilated the last great Punic army at a cost of fifteen hundred Roman lives. Hannibal, joined by a few horsemen, made good his escape. As Polybius says, "For there are times when chance thwarts the plans of the brave; and there are others again, when a man 'though great and brave has met a greater still.' And this we might say was the case with Hannibal on this occasion."

SCIPIO IMPOSED a harsh peace on the prostrate Carthage. He deprived the city of its fleet except for ten triremes. According to Livy, as many as five hundred warships sailed out of Carthage's harbor to be burned. Moreover, Carthage had to pay an indemnity of ten thousand talents over a fifty-year period. The greatest indignity Carthage endured was that it was forbidden to wage war against anyone without Rome's permission. While the city could still govern itself internally according to its own laws and customs, the Romans now set Carthage's foreign policy.

The Second Punic War was the most difficult war in Rome's history, one in which the city faced multiple near death experiences. After enduring terrible defeats, some of which saw entire Roman armies nearly wiped out, the Romans in Scipio finally found a general whose genius rivaled Hannibal's. Slowly, almost imperceptibly, Roman doggedness coupled with Scipio's genius reversed the Carthaginian tide. Despite his victories on the battlefield, Hannibal eventually found himself bottled up in southern Italy, while his financial and recruiting bases in Spain were stripped away by Scipio's legions. When the Roman general at last led a Roman army into North Africa to threaten Carthage itself, the stage was set for the ultimate showdown between two of the ancient world's greatest generals. That battle, fought at Zama, placed more at stake than the reputation of Hannibal and Scipio. Both sides were staking the ultimate greatness and even the future existence of their cities.

If the Carthaginians had won, Zama might have resulted in Rome's ultimate ruin. A resurgent Carthage could have easily reclaimed gold-rich Spain and used it as a base for launching new armies against Italy and Rome. Even if Rome had managed to avert further calamitous defeats, it would have confronted a western Mediterranean rival with which it would have to contend possibly for centuries. With Carthage supporting Rome's many enemies and contesting its every move, it is impossible to envision any combination of circumstances that would have led to the creation of the Roman Empire. If Rome was to be the unchallenged master of the Western world, it first had to defeat the greatest maritime power and richest nation of the age—Carthage.

Given the enormity of Rome's victory at Zama, the speed with which Carthage regained its strength is remarkable and a testament to just how dangerous the city was to Roman ambitions. After paying off the Roman-imposed ten-thousand-talent indemnity, Carthage declared it was no longer bound by the other terms of the treaty. Then it did the one thing sure to draw Roman attention. Having been plagued by Numidian raids for decades, Carthage launched a war against Numidia without seeking Roman permission. Carthage lost that war, but its renewed militarism thoroughly alarmed the Romans. After a voyage to Carthage, a prominent Roman politician, Cato the Elder, began ending every one of his speeches, regardless of the topic, with: *"Ceterum censeo Carthaginem esse delendam"* ("Furthermore, I think Carthage must be destroyed"). In the end, Rome went to war. Scipio Aemilianus ended the Third Punic War after a three-year siege of Carthage. Afterward, the Romans razed the city and salted the ground on which the city had stood. A rebuilt *Roman* Carthage would remain an important city until its capture by the Vandals almost six hundred years later.

IT IS NO EXAGGERATION to claim that the fate of Rome and the West was decided at Zama. After this victory, Rome was free to unleash its legions in a two-hundred-year quest to conquer a Mediterranean empire, secure in the knowledge that it faced no significant threat to its own existence. Rome rose, relatively unimpeded, to become the greatest empire in Western history, while its rival, Carthage, disappeared into oblivion.

TEUTOBURGER WALD

The Division of Europe

A.D. 9

AFTER THE BATTLE OF ZAMA, THE ROMANS PURSUED THEIR IMPULSE for conquest almost without pause for another two centuries. Starting with a long series of wars, first with the Macedonians and then with Mithridates's Pontic kingdom, Rome went on to add all of Greece, Macedonia, Thrace, and Asia Minor to its dominions. By the time Caesar's legions had conquered Gaul, the already fraying fabric of the Republic dissolved as he and the other great general of the age, Pompey, went to war in a contest for control of Rome. This Roman civil war continued through uneasy, sporadic periods of peace long after Caesar and Pompey had perished, finally ending soon after Octavian Caesar, later called Augustus, defeated Mark Antony at the Battle of Actium in 31 B.C. Augustus's assumption of uncontested supreme power marked the end of the Republic and the start of the Roman Empire.

It did not, however, bring an end to Roman expansion. Many historians have taken Augustus's supposed final warning to his successors that they should "be satisfied with present possessions and in no way seek to increase the area of empire" as evidence that he did not favor further expansion. Whether or not Augustus actually bequeathed such policy advice is still a matter of historical debate. Certainly Augustus himself never followed such a policy. One look at the final testament he had written about his own reign, the *Res Gestae,* makes it clear that Augustus saw himself as conqueror in the same mold as his uncle and adopted father, Julius Caesar. Eight of the *Res Gestae's* thirty-five pages are dedicated to his conquests and military accomplishments. In fact, some historians believe that Augustus, based on a mistaken notion of geographic scope, was intent on conquering the entire world.

Everything changed in Germany's dark forest when in A.D. 9 a Roman army was destroyed at Teutoburger Wald.

ROME FIRST TOOK a serious military interest in Germany—Germania— during Caesar's Gallic campaign. In a remarkable engineering achievement, Caesar's legions bridged the Rhine and marched deep into the German forests. They remained only two weeks, but it was a prelude of things to come. For the next several decades, Rome's attention was absorbed by the conquest of Gaul and, after Caesar's murder, on the contest between Octavian Caesar and Mark Antony. The naval battle at Actium finally settled matters in Augustus's favor, and after a bit of cleaning up around the edges of the empire, Rome was ready to begin the conquest of Germania, at least as far as the Elbe. Unfortunately for the Romans, their German adversaries demonstrated a strong aversion to becoming Rome's next conquest.

In 15 B.C., Augustus, the final victor of the Roman civil war, traveled to Gaul. He remained for three years, overseeing preparations for the invasion of Germany. In keeping with his tradition of delegating crucial matters such as war and command of the legions only to family members, he entrusted the invasion to his twenty-five-year-old stepson, Drusus (brother of the future emperor Tiberius). By 12 B.C., Augustus judged that all was ready, and the army marched. The first objective was not conquest, but the punishment of the Sugambri, who had crossed the Rhine five years before and all but annihilated the V Legion. Learning of Roman intentions, the Sugambri launched a preemptive attack against Drusus's legions. They apparently met the

Roman army on an open field—never a wise move—and were crushed. Afterward the Romans devastated their territory, which corresponds roughly to the modern German state of Westphalia. Later in the year, Drusus led his forces on what amounted to a tour of northern Germania, which is better remembered for its engineering feats than for any major fighting. For the most part, the Romans overawed the locals with this demonstration of the legions' power. Before Drusus's army returned to the Rhine, the Chaukian, Frisian, and Batavian tribes had all entered into alliances with Rome.

In the following year, Drusus led a second invasion from the Roman camp at Vetera, east along the Lippe River, where the Romans constructed the great fortress of Xanten (Aliso). After a further advance to the Weser River failed to bring the Germans into the open, Drusus gave up and returned to the Rhine. As they marched, the Romans came under heavy attack and only narrowly escaped annihilation. They owed their salvation less to Roman valor than to German indiscipline. As the ancient Roman historian Dio relates:

> For the enemy harassed him everywhere by ambuscades, and once they shut him up in a narrow pass and all but destroyed his army; indeed, they would have annihilated them, had they not conceived a contempt for them, as if they were already captured and needed only the finishing stroke, and so came to close quarters with them in disorder. This led to their [the Germans] being worsted, after which they were no longer so bold, but kept up a petty annoyance of his troops from a distance, while refusing to come nearer.

This time, the discipline of Rome's legionnaires in close combat proved their deliverance. They would not always be so fortunate.

Drusus's bad luck continued in 10 B.C., when his attacks against the Chatti (near today's state of Hesse) met with little success. In his final campaign, Drusus reached the Elbe. However, soon afterward a lack of supplies forced him once again to retreat to the Rhine. During his return march, Drusus either had a serious accident or was stricken by disease. He died before reaching the great river boundary.

Undeterred by setback or the loss of his stepson, Augustus sent

Tiberius, who had been busy subduing Illyria, to replace his fallen brother. Over the course of 8 and 7 B.C., Tiberius waged two campaigns within Germania. Although his army marched throughout the area that lay between the Rhine and the Elbe, Tiberius met little resistance except from the still troublesome Sugambri. Adopting the tried-and-true Roman method of creating a desert and calling it peace, Tiberius came close to exterminating the Sugambri. The Romans transported those few who survived across the Rhine, where they could be watched more closely. After this, the intimidated German tribes offered no further resistance. Tiberius departed in 7 B.C. to enjoy a triumph in Rome and soon thereafter retired from public life for a decade.

Swift Roman marches through Germania and several successful battles had convinced Augustus and his advisers that Germania, in the words of the ancient historian Velleius Paterculus, who later fought with Tiberius, had been "reduced almost to the position of a tributary province." In truth, the Romans may have intimidated the tribes, but they had hardly defeated them. Despite several years of campaigning, much of Germany east of the Rhine had yet to experience the hard hand of a Roman army. The reality of the matter was that Drusus's and Tiberius's campaigns amounted to little more than raids. Except for the Sugambri, no tribe had been broken by Roman arms, while the slow process of permanent subjugation and assimilation had not even started.

For the next ten years, the sources are irritatingly silent on events along the Rhine and within Germania. We do know that in 6 B.C., the Roman legate Lucius Domitius Ahenobarbus received command of the legions in Germania. Four years later, he apparently got himself and a Roman army in trouble when he attempted to relocate the troublesome Cherusci in much the same manner that Tiberius had handled the Sugambri. As a result, Augustus relieved Ahenobarbus of command and replaced him with Marcus Vinicius. At about this time, many of the major tribes had risen in what the historian Velleius referred to as a "vast war." Unfortunately, no account of this war exists, but Vinicius must have at least held his own, for he was awarded a triumph on his return to Rome.

In A.D. 4, Tiberius returned to command the Rhine legions. The soldiers greeted him effusively. According to Velleius (who was present):

> Soldiers burst into joy at the sight of him, greeted him with enthusiasms, rushed with violence just to touch his hand and could not restrain themselves. "Are you with us again great general?" "I was with you great general in Armenia." "I was with you in Raetia." "I was rewarded by you at Vindelicia."

For the next two years, Tiberius campaigned in northern Germany. During the first year, he conquered the Canninefates, the Attuarii, and the Bructeri and subjugated the troublesome Cherusci. Soon thereafter, Tiberius had the Cherusci declared "friends of the Roman people." In A.D. 5, Tiberius launched a combined naval and land movement from the Roman camp at Anreuppen, in which several independent forces converged on the Elbe. The coordinated movement of large contingents was meant to intimidate those tribes that were still resisting Romanization. According to the historian and Tiberius's staff officer, Velleius, the assault was a great success, and afterward "nothing remained to be conquered in Germany."

From the Roman viewpoint, the only resistance still offered within the Elbe-Danube-Rhine triangle was the kingdom of Maroboduus, leader of the Macromanni in Bohemia. In A.D. 6, as part of a brilliantly conceived operation, twelve legions marched from Raetia, Germania, and Illyricum along separate routes that converged on central Bohemia. This crowning achievement in Augustan strategy was only days away from completion when Pannonia, a recently conquered portion of Illyricum, rose in a revolt that shook Rome to its foundation. It took Tiberius three years and the employment of ten legions, supported by nearly one hundred cohorts of auxiliaries, to crush the last embers of this rebellion. Doing so had pushed the empire to the limits of its economic and military endurance.

Throughout this period, Germania apparently remained tranquil. Its new governor, Publius Quinctilius Varus, had settled in without trouble and begun the long process of integrating the region into the empire. Over the past two millennia, an impression has taken hold that Varus was a dilettante, appointed by Augustus to a job for which by temperament and experience he was unsuited, and that he held his position because of family relations to Augustus, who remained loath to give anyone not part of the Julio-Claudian clan command of any of Rome's legions. This impression is based primarily on the image left to posterity by Velleius Paterculus—an enemy of Varus—who states: "Varus Quinctilius, descended from a famous rather than a high-born family, was a man of mild character and of a quiet disposition, somewhat slow in mind as he was in body, and more accustomed to the leisure of the camp than to actual service in war. That he was no despiser of money is demonstrated by his governorship of Syria: he entered the rich province a poor man, but left it a rich man and the province poor." That reputation, however, does not hold up to close scrutiny.

Varus, breaking his family's traditional position of supporting Republican ideals, was probably with Augustus at the Battle of Actium and was certainly with him during his tour of the eastern provinces after Antony's defeat. He then passed through a number of political and military posts, including commanding the XIX Legion in heavy fighting under Tiberius in modern Switzerland. In 8 B.C., Augustus appointed Varus governor of Africa, where he commanded the III Augusta Legion. This was one of the most important governorships in the empire, as Africa was a major source of Rome's food supply and the only Senate-ruled province in which Augustus stationed a legion. Varus's performance so impressed Augustus that he next assigned him to Syria. Here he commanded four legions and was responsible for keeping both the Parthian Empire at bay and an always troublesome region pacified. It was during this period that he led three legions in crushing a major Jewish revolt in the wake of King Herod's death. It was a significant operation that saw the cities of Sepphoris and Emmaus destroyed and two thousand Jews crucified. When it was over, Judea remained relatively quiescent for seventy years.

Despite Velleius's comments, one must credit Varus as an able administrator and a qualified general. His failure in Germania resulted from his acceptance of the widespread notion that Tiberius had crushed German resistance and that the country was ready for transformation into a Roman province, much as Gaul had been fifty years earlier. But the Germans had been defeated, not conquered. As the ancient Roman historian Florus writes, "Under the rule of Drusus they respected our manners rather than our arms. But when Drusus was dead, they began to detest the licentiousness and pride, no less than the cruelty, of Quintilius Varus." But what was the cruelty of Varus? As far as can be determined from the sources, his crime was to try to impress Roman civic order upon unruly Germans "as if he could restrain the violence of barbarians by the rods of a lictor and the voice of a crier." In German eyes, however, Varus's chief crime was his attempt to make Germany pay a portion of the cost of its occupation. In this, he was doing only what Augustus expected of every Roman governor in a "subdued" province—instituting a tax. As Dio notes, "[Varus] strove to change them more rapidly. Besides issuing orders to them as if they were actually slaves of the Romans, he exacted money as he would from subject nations. To this they were in no mood to submit, for the leaders longed for their former ascendancy and the masses preferred their accustomed condition to foreign domination." Be that as it may, the true seeds of the explosion that culminated in "the Varian disaster" were sown by what amounted to a tax revolt.

Unbeknownst to Varus, the German tribes were rallying around a compelling new leader, Arminius. His ascendancy and the timing of his revolt came at a time when Rome was least prepared to act. The bulk of the Roman army was still heavily involved in crushing the revolt in Pannonia. Thus, Varus's three legions were isolated in the heart of Germania, with little chance of immediate aid if they were to get into trouble. Despite their discontent, the German situation might have remained manageable if Arminius, a charismatic leader capable of uniting the various tribes for concerted action, had not appeared on the scene. He was the son of the Cheruscan war chief Segimerus, who had early thrown in his lot with the Romans. Because of these close family ties, Arminius and his brother were sent to Italy to train as Roman soldiers. While there, Arminius received Roman citizenship, still a rare honor at this point in Roman history, and membership in the equestrian order, the Roman petty nobility. In A.D. 4, Arminius assumed command of a Cheruscan force fighting as Roman auxiliaries in the Pannonian War under Tiberius. In A.D. 7, at the age of twenty-five, Arminius returned to Germany to serve as a chief aide to Varus. As Velleius relates:

> There appeared a young man of noble birth, brave in action and alert in mind, possessing an intelligence quite beyond the ordinary barbarian; he was, namely, Arminius, the son of Segimerus, a prince of that nation, and he showed in his countenance and in his eyes the fire of the mind within.

When word reached Varus that a small German tribe had risen in revolt, he reacted as would any Roman general. The playbook for stifling insurrections was clear: Move rapidly and massively at the first sign of trouble. The Romans knew from long experience that, left to fester, uprisings always grew worse and much more expensive in blood and treasure the longer one refrained from action. At the first sign of rebellion, the preferred Roman course of action was a rapid march with all troops available, followed by a short, bloody, decisive engagement, which concluded with a flurry of swift trials and slow executions. Well schooled in what was needed from his experiences in Palestine, Varus immediately set out with all of the troops at his disposal, three legions. Unfortunately for Varus, his opponent, Arminius, was Roman educated and trained, as familiar with the Roman playbook as was Varus.

Much has been made of Varus ignoring the warnings of Segestes, Arminius's father-in-law, that Arminius was organizing a major revolt and a second warning of the planned ambush in the Teutoburger Wald. In hindsight, Varus would have been wise to heed these warnings. At the time, the truth might not have been as easy to see. Arminius was a trusted soldier, trained in Rome, and had spent many years in Roman service. Although no one doubted Segestes's loyalty to Rome, Varus was well aware that Arminius had married Segestes's daughter against his wishes and that he had sworn perpetual enmity toward his son-in-law. From Varus's viewpoint, Segestes's warning was just part of a continuing family feud.

Putting aside Segestes's warning, the legions marched as if they had few concerns. Spread out over almost ten miles, the formation

Hermannsdenkmal monument, Teutoburg Forest, North Rhine, Westphalia, Germany (Arminius was also known as Armin or Hermann) *Imagebroker/Alamy*

became ragged and undisciplined. Many of the legionnaires walked unarmed among the baggage and camp followers. At no place was the tactical integrity of the legions or cohorts maintained. Worse, the German auxiliary force, commanded by Varus's "trusted" adviser, Arminius, had received permission to ride off to ensure the route ahead was clear of obstructions or threats. Confident that Arminius would alert him to trouble in sufficient time to form his legions into battle order, Varus marched unprepared—as Arminius and his fellow Germans prepared for a battle they trusted would obliterate Roman power east of the Rhine.

IN THE EARLY HOURS of the second day's march, a soft rain started. It grew worse as morning gave way to afternoon and lashing winds and pelting rain beat against the legionnaires. Soon, the soft ground turned to mud and the baggage train slowed to a crawl. The wretched Romans bundled themselves against the elements and doggedly trudged forward, unmindful of everything except their own misery. As they entered a narrow pass between the clumps of forests, they marched into a carefully laid trap.

Without warning, the Romans found themselves beset by missiles from all sides. The Roman ranks were thrown into chaos, their reaction uncharacteristically slow. Emboldened, German warriors edged closer, hurling ever more missiles and even overwhelming weaker parts of the line. Gradually but inexorably, legionary discipline asserted itself and battle-hardened centurions moved to the nearest standard, gathered nearby legionnaires, drew their swords, and counterattacked. After a ferocious fight, the legionnaires repulsed the first frenzied German attacks. As the Germans melted back into the woods, centurions moved along the line, slowly bringing pockets of order to the disarray. Hundreds of pierced, smashed, and mutilated men were already down. Wounded horses and mules kicked and thrashed in agony. Baggage carts were overturned and panicked camp followers clung to any legionnaire who could afford them protection.

But Varus still had the bulk of three veteran legions. They were shaken but recovering rapidly. At his direction, the survivors hastily constructed a fortified camp and burned their cumbersome baggage train. That night, Varus held a council of war and decided to break camp and march west in hopes of making it to the fortified Roman base at Xanten, over a hundred miles distant. After a sharp early morning fight, the Romans smashed open a gap in the German lines and broke into open country. All day they marched, as the continuing storm pelted them and the Germans harried their formations.

Varus doggedly led his legions forward. Eventually the battered Romans marched into the narrow Kalkrieser-Niederweder-Senke pass. Bordered by a high hill to the south and an impenetrable bog to the north, the pass stretched for almost four miles and was on average only three hundred feet wide. Here, Arminius and the bulk of the Germans waited behind a wall they had built at the hill's base.

Arminius could see that this time the legions were in full battle formation and ready to meet his assault. Fully aware that his forces could not defeat the Romans in a head-to-head fight with the Germans coming straight at the Roman lines, he opted for a different tactic. Keeping a tight rein on his troops' impulse to charge to their own destruction, Arminius held the warriors behind their protective barrier. From there they could assail the marching Roman column with thousands of arrows, stones, and rocks.

Some Roman cohorts, unwilling to remain passive targets, advanced on the wall at scattered points. The Germans repulsed most of these legionnaires with heavy losses, but at some spots the Romans broke through, only to be cut down by the thousands of Germans on the far side. As the German missile attacks continued, the Roman formations began to lose cohesion. Such a breakdown in legionary discipline spelled disaster, as the Romans would now have to meet any assault on German terms. When Arminius judged the moment right, he unleashed his warriors on the faltering legions. Thousands of Romans fell as both sides hacked at each other with sword and ax. German losses must have been greater, but they received fresh forces by the hour, while the nearest Roman help was at distant Xanten. Yet against all odds and despite heavy losses, the Romans somehow punched their way through the pass and onto open ground.

That night, the remaining legionnaires made camp. Too exhausted to build fortifications, many of them dropped where they stood. In the morning, they awoke to even worse weather and found themselves surrounded by ever growing German numbers. Their gloom increased when it became known that Varus's subordinate Vala had led the cavalry in a breakout. Tradition holds that this was a cowardly attempt to escape, which left the infantry exposed. However, in this kind of fight the cavalry was more of a hindrance than a help, making it just as likely that Varus ordered them to flee so as to salvage something from the disaster engulfing his army. In any case, they did not make it. German horsemen ran the Roman cavalry to ground and annihilated it.

Gloom turned to despair when word spread that the grievously wounded Varus had committed suicide. Knowing their doom was at hand, some legionnaires followed Varus's example, while others followed the lead of surviving senior commanders and surrendered. In a four-day running fight, the Germans had obliterated three entire Roman legions—XVII, XVIII, and XIX. Over the next days, the victors tortured Roman prisoners before hanging them or, in the case of senior commanders, burning them alive. They then nailed decapitated heads to trees or took the skulls home as souvenirs. Six years later, Germanicus, at the head of a new Roman army, revisited the battle site. Tacitus related the event:

> In the plain between were bleaching bones, scattered or in little heaps, as the men had fallen, fleeing or standing fast. Hard by lay splintered spears and limbs of horses, while human skulls were nailed prominently on the tree-trunks. In the neighboring groves stood the savage altars at which they had slaughtered the tribunes and chief centurions.

In the succeeding weeks after the destruction of Varus's army, German bands destroyed isolated Roman outposts and trading centers, and Roman power east of the Rhine disappeared. Two decades of Roman policy toward Germania lay in ruins. Although Rome was slow to accept that reality, Germania would never become an imperial

A battle mask found at
the site of the Battle of
Teutoburger Wald
Open Source

province. Distraught over the collapse of his strategy and the irreplaceable loss of three of the empire's twenty-eight legions, Augustus
rent his clothes, and during a long period of mourning he let his hair
and beard grow. Ancient sources claim that as he walked the halls of
his residence, he would often stop and hit his head against a wall,
wailing, "Varus, give me back my legions."

NEWS OF THE DISASTER caused panic in Rome and throughout the
western portions of the empire. The Romans expected a German
invasion of Gaul and northern Italy at any moment. In its hour of
distress, Rome called on its most reliable general, Tiberius.

With his nephew Germanicus, Tiberius restored calm to the
Rhine frontier. For the next two years, the two Roman generals conducted a number of bloody and vicious raids into Germania. These
assaults never penetrated far into barbarian–held territory and were
never meant to be part of a renewed war of conquest. Rather, they
aimed at impressing upon the Germans and the rest of the Roman
world that the legions remained invincible. For several years thereafter, Germanicus led major invasions of Germany. Twice more he
fought major but inconclusive battles against Arminius, and on two
other occasions he nearly lost the legions entrusted to him.

There is no profit to be had by a minute examination of Germanicus's invasions. In most ways they were a repeat of all that had
gone before. What is important is an acknowledgment of the fact that
the Germans repeatedly proved themselves capable of fighting Rome's
legions to a standstill. Tiberius, now the new emperor, had had
enough. Despite Germanicus's protestations that one more climactic
invasion would see German military power overthrown, Tiberius
called a halt. As far as he was concerned, the risks of future campaigns
in Germania far exceeded any benefit the empire might gain.

THE GERMAN AMBUSH and annihilation of Varus's three legions set the
world on a new course, one in which the power of Rome had limits.
During Rome's relentless drive of conquest, the legions had suffered
numerous setbacks, but they remained ever undeterred; after licking

their wounds, they always resumed the march to inevitable triumph. This inexorable process ended on the east bank of the Rhine. The legions continued to penetrate Germany almost until the final days of the empire, either as preventive measures or to punish its barbarian inhabitants. But after the Varian disaster at Teutoburger Wald, Rome gave up any idea of adding Germania as a Roman province. The effects on the empire were immediate. Having ceased to grow, Rome lost its primary driving force, its essential engine. For several centuries, the impulse to expand had relieved many of Rome's internal pressures. It made available new lands for settlement, filled the treasury with tribute, and provided slaves to power Rome's agriculture-based economy. Rome's great centuries of empire were still before it, but like the long-lived Egyptian kingdom, it had become an empire in stasis.

Furthermore, after Teutoburger Wald, although Rome would remain capable of lashing out against its enemies for centuries to come, the empire moved to the strategic defensive. From this point on, Rome was no longer master of its own fate. While the final outcome was still almost five hundred years off, the descendants of those Germans Rome failed to conquer eventually overran and brought an end to the Western Roman Empire. If Germany had been conquered during the reigns of the first emperors, Rome might never have faced a formidable challenge from German barbarians and would also have had a substantial buffer to meet the challenge that would eventually emerge from the Asiatic steppes to engulf the empire. The Roman Empire would not have lasted forever, but possibly it could have survived an additional five hundred years or more, as the Eastern portions of the empire did. How the world would differ if the Western Roman Empire had lasted another five hundred years can only be imagined. What is certain is that Rome's fall at the hands of German invaders set back the cause of learning and civilization for a millennium.

The more immediate concrete impact of Teutoburger Wald was that Germany remained outside the sphere of Roman civilization. Although there was considerable diplomatic and trading contact between both groups, neither Roman culture nor its civilizational tenets penetrated across the Rhine and Danube to a degree where they made a measurable impact on German societal development. Today, the effects of this separation remain easily apparent. On one side of the Rhine stand the Romance countries, bound together by a similarity of language and culture. On the other side stand the Teutonic civilizations, which despite five hundred years of continuous European integration still remain as alien in outlook and language as they did when Rome fell. In fact, German historians seemingly never tire of explaining that the countries that were once incorporated into the Roman Empire are part of a separate civilization, while their own nation is better described as a *Kultur*. This differentiation was idealized by both Hohenzollern and Nazi nationalists but fell into some disrepute after the Second World War. Today it is on the rise again, as even mainstream Germans begin to emphasize their distinct *Kultur*. The current German chancellor, Angela Merkel, recently made world news when she said Germany's *Leitkultur* (defining culture) needs to be accepted by Germany's seven million Turkish immigrants.

Rome's failure to conquer Germany both doomed its own long-term prospects and created one of the two major cultural divides in Europe, the other being the Slavic divide. As with the East–West divide brought about by the Battle of Marathon, this internal division of Europe has been the source of substantial tension within the West, particularly during the bloody first half of the last century. One may wonder if the twentieth century's two world wars would even have been fought had Germany been a Romance nation and shared a common culture with its neighbors. Today, despite Europe's postwar economic integration, Germany still appears to stand apart and many European nations remain fearful of unbridled German "differentness." They believe that the only way to contain a potential future German threat is to neuter it through continued political and economic assimilation, which has provided much of the rationale for the formation of the European Union. Even if this acculturation process meets with some success, there is little chance Germany will become culturally indistinguishable from the rest of the West in any foreseeable time frame.

THE WEST HAD MISSED its one chance to attain the goal of a united Continent. Varus's defeat at Teutoburger Wald marked an end to the opportunity to establish a unified Europe forevermore. From that point on, Germany would stand separate and apart from the rest of non-Slavic Europe. For most of those centuries thereafter, the German nation was too fragmented to present much of a threat to its neighbors. This, however, changed radically when Prussia by 1870 had united the German peoples into a colossus in the heart of Europe. From then on, much of Western history relates to the great effort required to fight, contain, or subsume German might—an effort that might not have been necessary if the Romans had not lost three legions at the hands of German barbarians almost two millennia before.

ADRIANOPLE

The End of Roman Supremacy

A.D. 378

FOR A FIVE-HUNDRED-YEAR PERIOD BEGINNING IN 100 B.C. WITH MAR-
ius's and Sulla's defeat of the massive tribal invasions of the Mediterranean world by the Teutons and the Cimbri, the Romans ruled the
northern frontier of their world, an empire that stretched across Europe from the mouth of the Rhine to that of the Danube. On the
other side of the Rhine lay fierce warrior tribes, which from time to
time posed serious threats to the empire's security. Yet for all their
fierceness, the tribes were consistently defeated by Rome's legions.
There were military defeats, of course, such as the massacre of Teutoburger Wald, but from the crushing of the Teutons and the Cimbri,
the Romans enjoyed an astonishing record of destroying the armed
mobs that characterized the German approach to war.

From the rise of Octavian Caesar, later titled Augustus, to supremacy over the Roman world in 32 B.C. with his defeat of Mark
Antony, a professional army of between twenty-five and thirty-three
legions (approximately 150,000 legionnaires and 150,000 auxiliaries)
defended the empire from Hadrian's Wall in northern Britain to the
upper Nile and from the Strait of Gibraltar to the Euphrates River in

Syria. This indeed was an extraordinary example of economy of force. What explains this stunning military effectiveness?

Above all, Roman military effectiveness depended on the discipline and training of the legionnaires, the hallmark of a professional military organization in the modern sense. Flavius Josephus, the great historian of the Roman-Jewish War of A.D. 66–70, described the Roman training regimen in the following terms:

> And indeed, if anyone does but attend to the other parts of [Roman] military discipline, he will be forced to confess, that their obtaining so large a dominion hath been the acquisition of their valor, and not the bare gift of fortune: for they do not begin to use their weapons first in time of war, nor do they put their hands first into motion, having been idle in times of peace; but as if their weapons were part of themselves, they never have any truce with warlike exercises; nor do they stay till times of war admonish them to use them; for their military exercises by no means fall short of the tension of real warfare, but every soldier is every day exercised, and that with real diligence, as if they were in time of war, which is why they bear the fatigue of battle so easily; . . . nor would he be mistaken [who] would call their exercises unbloody battles, and their battles bloody exercises.

In short, the Roman army with its legions and auxiliaries was the first true professional army in history, one that relied in battle on its discipline and training rather than on the psychological glue of culture and familial and social relations. In other words, it trained as it fought.

The resulting superiority allowed the Romans to dominate their world for two and a half centuries. But things fell apart in the first half of the third century. Unfortunately for historians, there are few written records for this crucial period. Between 31 B.C. and A.D. 211, excluding emperors killed in the two major civil wars, ten emperors died of natural causes and only three were assassinated by their officers or soldiers. However, in the forty-year period between A.D. 235 and 275, only one emperor died of natural causes, while no fewer than ten

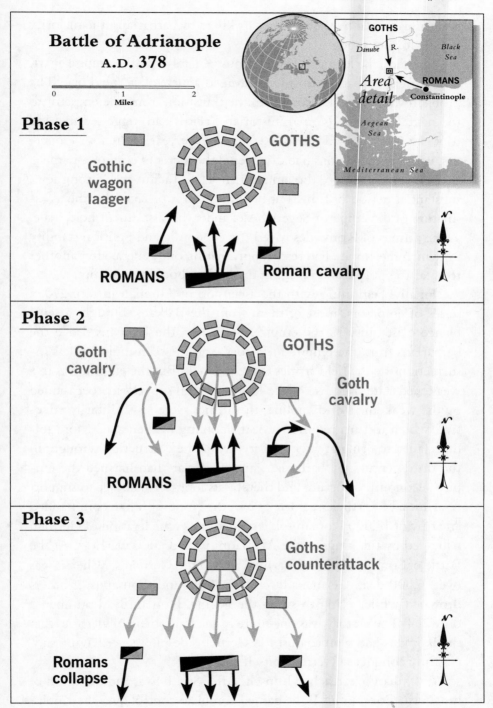

Battle of Adrianople
A.D. 378

0 — 1 — 2
Miles

GOTHS
Danube R.
Black Sea
Area detail
ROMANS
Constantinople
Aegean Sea
Mediterranean Sea

Phase 1

Gothic wagon laager

GOTHS

ROMANS

Roman cavalry

Phase 2

Goth cavalry

GOTHS

Goth cavalry

ROMANS

Phase 3

Goths counterattack

Romans collapse

were assassinated by their officers or killed by barbarians, the majority via the former mode.

In effect, the armies and ambitious generals tore the empire apart, while great barbarian invasions ravaged much of its territory. The problem was that of legitimacy in the transition from one emperor to the next. The great Roman historian Tacitus had suggested that the root cause of the civil war of A.D. 69–70, the year of the four emperors, was that the legions had discovered the secret of empire—namely, that *they* could choose the emperor. In fact, Tacitus was wrong for a substantial period of time, but beginning in A.D. 235 with the assassination of the emperor Severus Alexander, his assessment holds true, as the armies of Rome destroyed the economic and political stability on which the empire had rested, nominating one general after another to wear the purple and ravaging the broken body of the empire.

Finally, beginning with the ascension of Aurelian in A.D. 270, a series of emperors, most of them from the Balkans, brought a semblance of stability to the empire. Militarily, the Romans drove the barbarians from the empire's territory, and the seemingly endless insurrections by the field armies came to a halt. But the empire was in a weakened state. Because of the loss of tactical superiority, occasioned by the weakening of discipline, the armies were less militarily effective, which in turn required a near doubling in their size. More soldiers failed to bring greater security, while the destruction wrought in the third century by barbarians and civil wars had harmed the empire's economic structure and thereby its long-term ability to support its armies. Nevertheless, as late as 357, the emperor Julian commanded an army of 13,000 Roman soldiers against a confederation of German tribes led by the kings of the Alamanni with 35,000 warriors. At the Battle of Strasbourg, Julian's army crushed the Germans. When it was over, 6,000 dead Germans littered the field and thousands of others drowned while trying to swim the Rhine. Roman dead numbered only 264. The victory was one more in the long string of victories that the Romans had won against the Germans despite never having successfully conquered Germany itself.

But Julian overreached himself. After Strasbourg and the death of his cousin Constantius II, he gained complete control over the empire and determined to invade the Sassanid Persian Empire. In 363, he moved with a substantial portion of the empire's armies to the east, where the Romans advanced to the gates of Ctesiphon, the Sassanid capital. Thereafter matters did not go well, and in the midst of the campaign Julian was killed, probably by the Persians, although some ancient writers ascribed his death to a disaffected Christian, embittered by the emperor's apostasy. The empire then fell to one of Julian's generals, a certain Jovian, who patched together a humiliating peace with the Sassanids. Jovian promptly died, to be succeeded by one of Julian's more successful generals, Valentinian. Barely a month after acceding to the throne, he appointed his brother Valens co-emperor in charge of the Eastern Roman Empire, while Valentinian took charge of what appeared to be the more threatened provinces in the west. And here is where the troubles began, for although Valentinian had had considerable military experience, his brother had had little.

In the late fourth century, the empire confronted a number of major threats on its borders. On the eastern frontier were the Sassanid Persians, who for nearly 150 years had contested the frontier zone between the empires and who on occasion had even invaded Syria. To the north, a fearsome enemy had appeared in the third century—the Goths. For the past one hundred years, Gothic tribes had represented a significant threat to the empire's security. In the 260s, in the midst of Rome's most difficult period of civil wars among rival claimants to the purple, the Goths had launched a massive invasion of the Eastern Roman Empire. They had laid waste to most of the Balkans and reached all the way to the Aegean. The economic damage was such that confidence in the coinage collapsed under a massive wave of inflation, which turned the empire from a moneyed into a barter economy. Nevertheless, once the soldier-emperors of the late third century had returned stability to the empire, the Romans proved more than capable of handling the barbarians. Constantine the Great had smashed the Gothic tribes in an extensive campaign across the Danube in the last years of his life and imposed a harsh peace on the survivors. But the Goths had eventually recovered and again represented a latent threat to the empire's security.

If the threats posed by the Persians in the east and the Goths across the Danube were not sufficient to make Valens's life miserable, one of Julian's relatives, a certain Procopius, apparently with some connection to the army, proclaimed himself emperor, and Valens faced civil war in his portion of the empire. Within a year of his accession, Valens was able to crush the pretender, but the incident undoubtedly made him suspicious of the army's loyalty to his person and position. Yet at the same time, he needed his military forces, because the Eastern Roman Empire confronted threats almost immediately from the Goths in the north and the Persians in the east, although the latter appeared the greater threat for much of his reign.

Valens chose to deal with the Goths first for reasons that remain obscure. He launched two major campaigns in 367 and 369 against them on the northern side of the Danube in the area where much of modern-day Romania lies. The Romans laid waste to great swaths of the countryside, but unlike Constantine, Valens was never able to bring the Goths to battle. The tribes took the simple expedient of sheltering in the depths of the Carpathian Mountains and lived to fight another day. After the campaign of 369, Valens concluded peace with the Goths and turned his attention to the eastern provinces, where the kingdom of Armenia with Persian help was causing significant difficulties. Initially, the Romans, helped by tribal incursions into Persia's eastern domains, addressed the strategic problems associated with their client kingdom of Armenia without much difficulty. Still, the conflicts with the Persians kept Valens's attention firmly on the east and away from the Danubian frontier. In 375, the Persians returned from their own eastern conflicts to mix again in Armenian politics. Both sides began to prepare for a major war. To add to the complexities of the empire's politics and strategic situation, Valentinian died that year, leaving his young son Gratian as emperor in the west. Thus, Valans had to deal with a new opposite, young and untested, with whom he had only the relatively tenuous blood tie between uncle and nephew.

While Valens was dealing with the empire's eastern troubles, a serious threat was arising on the Danube. For millennia, difficulties deep on the steppes of central Asia, whether caused by overpopulation or by major climate changes, had resulted in great tribal migrations. Those migrations, like a row of dominoes, had pushed tribes one after the other farther to the west. Another great movement of tribes had

Barbarian fighting a
Roman legionnaire; stone
relief, early second
century A.D., Rome
*Erich Lessing/Art
Resource, NY*

begun in the middle of the fourth century. The appearance of the
Huns on the outer boundaries of Europe somewhere in what is now
the Ukraine during the last half of the fourth century had placed huge
pressure on the Goths. In 376, the Gothic tribes had appeared on the
Danube and requested asylum and protection within the Roman Empire's frontiers.

Deeply involved in his preparations for war with the Persians,
Valens found himself on the horns of a dilemma. On one side, the
Goths could provide substantial manpower to the empire's hard-
pressed military forces. On the other, much of the Eastern Roman
Empire's disposable military forces were concentrated on the Persian
frontier in preparation for war against the Sassanids. Thus, the question of who was going to control the Goths once they were admitted
to the empire and ensure they settled in depopulated areas and provided soldiers presented a major political and military problem.

The Romans, given the Gothic numbers and their own needs,
agreed to allow one of the major tribal groups, the Tervingi, but not
the other, the Greuthungi, to cross the Danube near its mouth—not
far from where Augustus had sent the poet Ovid to exile and eventual
death. Unfortunately, the Roman officials on the scene proved venal,
corrupt, and militarily incompetent. They stole much of the money

and grain provided to take care of the Goths. Moreover, those Goths remaining on the northern side of the Danube crossed to back up the Tervingi.

The Roman commander on the spot, Lupicinus, appears to have been an especially murderous, corrupt, and incompetent governor even by the standards of the time. He invited the Gothic leaders Alavivus and Fritigern to a banquet at his headquarters in the city of Marcianople, where he planned to murder them. But matters got out of hand. The Romans succeeded in murdering only the tribal chieftains' bodyguards before the barbarians at the gate rioted and attacked the Romans who were guarding them. Lupicinus panicked and let the barbarian chieftains go. To add to the political disaster, he then took what forces were available and attacked the Goths. For his troubles, the Goths massacred his soldiers, while Lupicinus escaped to the unhappy fate of having to answer to the emperor for the fact that a mass of enraged Goths and their even more furious leaders were now loose south of the Danube, not far from Constantinople.

The Romans now had a full-scale emergency on their hands, one that they were going to have to address as quickly as possible. In the meantime, the Romans in Thrace to the east of Constantinople had to hold off the Goths as best they could, while the armies of the Roman Empire east and west redeployed to meet the threat south of the Danube. To make the situation even more dangerous, other barbarians on the north side of the river crossed to join up with the Goths, hoping to participate in the looting of the Balkan provinces. Moving south from Marcianople in 377 all the way to Adrianople and the Aegean, the Goths took their measure of revenge for the extraordinary ill-treatment they had received from Roman officials. The only areas that remained outside the reach of the pillaging barbarians were the cities and fortified towns, which were preserved by the Goths' lack of tactical expertise in siege warfare. The invaders, mostly young warriors eager to make a reputation among their peers, wrecked, burned, murdered, and raped everything in their path.

One of the extraordinary trends in recent academic historiography is the argument that the invading tribes inflicted little systemic damage as they moved into the empire. Only academics who have spent their entire lives sequestered in school and with scant knowledge of the real world could gin up such nonsense. In fact, the rapine, murder, and pillaging that the Goths inflicted on the countryside of course represented an unbelievable catastrophe for their immediate victims and in the long run for the empire itself by destroying the infrastructure and rural base on which Roman urban life depended. The historian and soldier Ammianus Marcellinus recounts what befell the civilians in the path of the Gothic fury once the tribes broke through the Roman armies into the plains of Thrace:

> The moment that . . . the passage of these defiles was opened, the barbarians, in no regular order, but wherever each individual could find a passage, rushed forth without hindrance to spread confusion among us; and raging with a desire for devastation and plunder, spread themselves with impunity over the whole region of Thrace, from the districts watered by the Danube to Mount Rhodope and the strait which separates the Aegean from the Black Sea, spreading ravage, slaughter, bloodshed, and conflagration, and throwing everything into the foulest disorder by all sorts of acts of violence committed even against the freeborn. Then one might see, with grief, actions equally horrible to behold and to speak of. . . .

For Valens, the crisis put his other difficulties in the shade. He now had a full-scale war on his hands. The first order of business was to accept a humiliating peace with the Persians and move the bulk of the Eastern Roman Empire's military forces back to Constantinople to take on the Goths. But the speed of reaction of the Roman military forces in 377 depended entirely on how fast their armies could march and, equally important, how efficiently the empire's logistic system could supply them on the march—a time-consuming and difficult process in the best of times, and this was not the best of times. It would take the Romans much of 377 to reallocate their forces from Syria and Palestine to the Balkans. At the same time, Valens requested help from his nephew Gratian, who willingly promised to bring a substantial portion of the western armies to the Balkans to support the war against the Goths in 378.

Gratian would find that a difficult promise to keep. The barbarians on the other side of the Rhine discovered what was afoot, and, led by the Alamanni, a substantial number of them crossed the frozen river. The Romans stopped the initial thrust cold in February 378. But then Gratian and his military advisers decided that they needed to launch a preemptive campaign to eliminate the possibility of further incursions across the Rhine. This made it necessary for Gratian to recall troops that had already begun to move into Pannonia on their way to the Balkans and instead concentrate those forces for a thrust across the Rhine to block the Alamanni's plans to move into the empire. Gratian's campaign was successful, but it delayed the movement of Roman forces to the east until later in the summer at the earliest. Yet even with this major delay, the western army was well on the way to support Valens when he moved out to confront the Goths.

OVER SPRING 378, Roman forces recalled from Syria and the southern Caucasus, where most of them had been preparing for the war against Persia, began to flow into the area around Constantinople, the city

Battle between Romans and barbarians; relief, sarcophagus, marble, third century A.D.
Gianni Dagli Orti/ The Art Archive at Art Resource, NY

Constantine had founded and made co-capital with Rome. Their movement depended to a considerable extent on the onset of spring and the grass-growing season that fed their animals. Valens himself had remained in the east until the last moment and had not arrived in Constantinople to take charge of his gathering military forces until the end of May 378. The emperor was not popular with the populace, since he was an Arian Christian, while the city was largely Catholic. Thus, after remaining in the capital for barely a week, he established his headquarters outside of the city on the road to Adrianople, at one of his summer palaces.

Initially, the Romans followed a strategy of attacking the warrior bands that were still ravaging Thrace. Northwest of Adrianople, a Roman column under a general named Sebastianus caught sight of a party of barbarians. It is indicative of the fear and paranoia gripping the region, as well as the reputation that Rome's soldiers had acquired for their treatment of civilians, that the urban authorities at Adrianople refused to allow the Roman soldiers entrance to the city. Only after lengthy discussions did they finally permit Sebastianus to enter, but without his soldiers. Having wrangled a minimum of supplies out of the townspeople, Sebastianus then pursued and caught up with one of the pillaging column of Goths, who were heavily laden with booty, and slaughtered them. That small victory undoubtedly reinforced Roman confidence that once the army forced a battle on the Goths, it would win, as Roman armies had almost always done in the past.

In the short term, such Roman counterraiding parties achieved considerable success. But their successes, as well as intelligence that the Romans were gathering forces north of Constantinople, led the Gothic king Fritigern to concentrate the tribes in response. By early summer, Valens had moved much of his army up to Adrianople, where he planned to await the arrival of his nephew and the supporting army from the west. Fritigern then attempted to move his tribesmen between the Romans and their supply lines behind Adrianople, but the Romans preempted that move.

Considerable debate then took place among the Roman commanders and the high-ranking courtiers who surrounded the emperor. The debate appears to have centered on whether the army of the Eastern Roman Empire should remain on the defensive or march out and attack the Goths without waiting for Gratian and the army of the Western Empire to arrive. Here, the influence of Roman traditions, the failure to recognize the changes in the empire's strategic situation, and the lack of military experience in Valens's background all worked to undermine the more conservative but sensible choice to await Gratian's arrival. Aggressive, ruthless, offensive military action had marked Roman tradition throughout Rome's lengthy rise to dominance over the Mediterranean basin and its subsequent defense of that great territory. Traditionally, Roman generals sought out and then attacked their enemies. Only in desperate situations did they go over to the defensive. The fate of the consul Varro at the Battle of Cannae during the period of the Roman Republic is instructive, for it was his foolish, headlong attack that had led to disaster at Cannae. Yet the Romans did not punish him for the defeat, but rather honored him for his aggressiveness.

But a great deal had changed in the half a millennium between Cannae and Adrianople: Rome no longer had either a large surplus population or the martial traditions among its peasants that had made the legionnaires of the third century B.C. such fearsome soldiers. In other words, admittedly in retrospect, Rome's ultimate survival depended on the caution with which its emperors and generals husbanded the lives of their soldiers and the care they took to stack the odds in favor of their armies.

At a minimum, the strategic constraints that the late empire faced required competent, if not inspired, generalship. Unfortunately for the fate of his army, Valens was no general. With little military experience and even less skill, the emperor was unprepared to evaluate the advice his officers and courtiers provided as to whether immediately to attack the barbarians or await the arrival of his nephew. Thus, largely on his own, he made the decision that his army would march out from Adrianople and attack the Goths before Gratian arrived. Letters from Gratian about the success he and the western troops had had in attacking and then in short order defeating the Germans on both sides of the Rhine undoubtedly helped make up Valens's mind to seek action. Already, that success stood out in stark contrast with the failures in the east to stop the Goths.

The courtiers, of course, were only too ready to impress on the emperor how weak a figure he would cut if his nephew was to share the credit for defeating the Goths. Considerable argument took place among those in the court, but from the first the emperor leaned toward the more aggressive course of action. As related by the fourth-century historian Marcellinus: "The fatal obstinacy of the emperor prevailed, fortified by the flattery of some of the princes, who advised him to hasten with all speed, so that Gratian might have no share in a victory which, as they fancied, was almost already gained." Optimistic reports that the Goths barely numbered ten thousand men of the Tervingi further encouraged the emperor to seek victory before Gratian arrived. In fact, the Goths probably numbered twice that amount, because the Greuthungi had arrived to reinforce their fellow tribesmen.

Roman intelligence from terror-stricken fugitives and spies had indicated that the Goths had laagered somewhere to the north of Adrianople within easy reach of the Roman army. Since the main force of Goths traveled with their women and children in wagons and sent out cavalry raiding parties from the slow-moving central force, the Romans had a fairly good idea of their enemy's location, but obviously they had failed to pick up on the fact that the Goths had concentrated and represented a far larger and more dangerous force.

Thus, Valens ordered the army to march. Having chosen to attack, the emperor further demonstrated his unsuitability for command by the decisions taken immediately before battle. First of all, he ordered the troops to stand to before dawn without having made any provisions to feed them. To add to the difficulties his soldiers would confront on their march to battle, the emperor and his generals failed to make provision for adequate supplies of either water or food along their route. The lack of water undoubtedly represented a severe handicap, because summer temperatures in the Balkans hover close to ninety degrees Fahrenheit. Finally, without water and food the army marched north in full armor for a distance of approximately eight miles. Not surprisingly, they arrived in front of the Gothic encampment in the early afternoon largely exhausted and in considerable disarray.

The Goths, eager to ensure that the remainder of their troops could come up, had recalled their cavalry, which had been raiding and foraging in the area, raping and plundering whoever was unfortunate enough to lie in their path. As soon as the Goths saw the unmistakable sign that the Roman army was on the march from Adrianople—the huge dust cloud to the south created by thousands of Roman soldiers and animals on the march was an immediate indicator—they concentrated their forces and prepared for battle. To further hamper the Roman approach and to gain time for their horsemen to return, the Goths set fire to the brush and crops along the way, which served to exacerbate the Roman failure to supply water for their troops. The Goths then attempted to parley as the Romans approached. As Marcellinus relates:

> [The Goths] designedly delayed, in order that by fallacious truce which subsisted during the negotiation to give time for their cavalry to return, whom they looked upon as close at hand; and our soldiers already suffering from the summer heat, to become parched and exhausted by the conflagration of the vast plain[,] as the enemy had, with this object, set fire to the crops by means of burning faggots and fuel. To this evil was added that [the] men . . . were suffering from extreme hunger.

The Goths arrayed their warriors in front of their wagons, which formed a great circular formation, resembling the laagers of so many films about the American West. The women and children remained sheltered behind the wagons. In this case, the number of people protected by the laager was enormous, and there may well have been obstacles placed to the front of the wagons to make it more difficult for the Romans to fight their way through the mass of Gothic warriors. Moreover, the extent of the laager made it virtually impossible for Roman scouts to estimate the size of the enemy army, nor were the Romans when they arrived in front of the laager much better positioned to estimate the number of their enemies. Valens, since he believed he confronted only the Tervingi, erroneously thought he had superiority in numbers. Since in fact he was confronting both tribes, he was clearly outnumbered. From the outset of the battle, the Goths would enjoy substantial advantages, for their warriors had fed, drunk plenty of water, and spent the morning and early afternoon resting.

As the negotiations were taking place, the last Roman cavalry

Goths on the attack
against Roman troops
*The Art Archive/Museo
Nazionale, Palazzo
Altemps, Rome*

units straggled onto the battlefield to form up on the left flank. The most recent, and reasonable, calculation of numbers on the opposing sides suggests that had Valens waited for the troops from the west, the Romans would have enjoyed nearly a two-to-one advantage over the combined forces of the Goths. Valens, however, probably calculated that he had an advantage over the Tervingi of one and a half to one. In fact, he was outnumbered, since both Gothic tribes had arrived on the battlefield, but not to such an extent that Roman defeat was inevitable. Current estimates suggest a strength of fifteen thousand soldiers in the Roman army, with five thousand cavalry and the remainder in infantry formations. The forces available to the Goths probably approached twenty thousand men.

The Romans arrived on the battlefield exhausted and dehydrated from the trials of their march. They appear to have deployed in a higgledy-piggledy fashion. By their silence, our sources suggest that Valens and his generals had no clear plan of attack except that the infantry in the center, supported by archers, would smash ahead straight into the laager of the Gothic tribesmen, while the Roman cavalry deployed on the flanks would cut down those who attempted to escape. As Valens's last envoy was approaching the Goths drawn up in front of their wagons, a portion of the Roman army attacked without orders. The *sagittarii* (archers) and the *scutarii* (equivalent to the praetorian guard of the early empire) decided to charge the Goths, even though negotiations were still ongoing. Apparently they were supposed to intimidate the Goths but remain in a defensive stance. Nevertheless, they "yielded on their march, to an indiscreet impetuosity, and on approaching the enemy, first attacked them rashly, and then by a cowardly flight disgraced the beginning of the [battle]." Nothing better indicates the poor discipline of the late Roman army than this ill-considered and unplanned attack, one that immediately collapsed.

But for the moment, that was the least of the Roman troubles. Their front line held as the *sagittarii* and *scutarii* disappeared from the battlefield. But the very solidness of the infantry legions behind those units represented a weakness as control of the battle spun out of the hands of the Roman generals. With the decline in tactical discipline that had occurred since the beginning of the third century, Roman infantry had come to depend on the psychological bond of physical proximity to their fellow soldiers, rather than on the ruthless but tactically flexible discipline imposed by the centurions that had characterized the nearly invincible legions of earlier centuries. As such, the tactical formations of the late Roman armies were virtually solid blocks that were difficult to maneuver; nor did individual soldiers have much room to move. The very density of the infantry formations would redound significantly to the disadvantage of the soldiers, because as the pressure on the flanks increased, they had less and less area in which to use their weapons.

At the moment the *scutarii* and the *sagittarii* collapsed, the Gothic cavalry, led by their chieftains Alatheus and Saphrax, arrived on the scene with a group of Alani tribesmen, described by Marcellinus as "these descending from the mountains like a thunderbolt, spread confusion and slaughter among all whom in their rapid charge they came across." Our sources do not indicate upon which flank the Gothic cavalry fell, but obviously the barbarian cavalry shattered the Roman cavalry on one of the wings. The shock of their arrival must have rippled across the Roman lines, further exacerbating the disorder caused by the attack and the sudden collapse of the *sagittarii* and *scutarii*. In effect, Valens and his generals had lost control of the battle and could only hope their infantry could bail them out. Again our sources are silent as to what happened to the Roman cavalry on the other wing, but the most plausible explanation is that seeing the initial troubles, they embraced the ancient military principle that discretion is the better part of valor and took off on roads heading south away from the battle scene.

On the left, the Roman infantry had some success in fighting their way through the Goths to the wagons. But with the collapse of the cavalry on the two flanks, the Roman infantry, outnumbered as they were, had little chance of breaking the Gothic infantry. Instead, the fighting began to resemble what had occurred at Cannae, when the Roman soldiers, compressed into an ever smaller area, were eventually unable to use their weapons and even began to crush one another to death. Now, as Marcellinus has it, this battle, beginning in early afternoon, placed impossible demands on the Roman infantry,

> who were emaciated by hunger, worn out with toil, and scarcely able to support even the weight of their armor. . . .
>
> Many were slain without knowing who smote them; some were overwhelmed by the weight of the crowd which pressed upon them; and some were slain by wounds inflicted by their own comrades. The barbarians spared neither those who yielded nor those who resisted.

As we have seen on several occasions in European soccer matches or at rock concerts, when a panic ensues, the crush of bodies literally suffocates many. A similar situation occurred at Adrianople. As at Cannae, the Roman infantry with its cavalry cover chased off the battlefield fought and died in an enormous charnel house. The killing was not as terrible as that inflicted when the Carthaginians of Hannibal slaughtered upward of fifty thousand Romans. But it was dreadful enough. Adding to the horror of the scene were the gallons upon gallons of blood flowing onto the ground from the ferocious, brutal nature of the slaughter, mixed with the inevitable excrement, urine, and dust of the battlefield, all of which created a glutinous swamp of horror onto which the dying Romans fell.

> The ground, covered with streams of blood, made their feet slip, so that all they endeavored to do was to sell their lives as dearly as possible; and with such vehemence did they resist their enemies who pressed on them, that some were even killed by their own weapons. At last one black pool of blood disfigured everything, and wherever the eye turned, it could see nothing but piled up bodies of dead, and lifeless corpses trampled on without mercy.

It appears that Valens was caught up with the infantry and never had a chance to escape, so rapid was the collapse of the Roman cavalry. As a result, he died with the legions, but his body was never recovered, perhaps because by the next morning decomposition of the bodies, blood, and other desiderata in the Balkan heat made even the barbarians less than enthusiastic about digging through the mass of blackened, stinking flesh. And so perished much of the Eastern Roman Empire's infantry, a victim of gross incompetence and the arrogance of Roman military traditions.

IT WAS NOT NUMBERS that defeated the Romans, but rather the mistakes and overconfidence of their leaders that were responsible for the extent of the catastrophe. However, the fact that the Eastern Empire was at best able to bring barely fifteen thousand soldiers to the battlefield suggests the decline in Rome's ability to support its military forces. As with so much of history, there were considerable ironies accompanying the defeat. Adrianople did not spell the end of the Eastern Roman Empire. Instead, what historians term the Byzantine Empire struggled on for another millennium.

Yet the destruction of Valens's army was disastrous in the largest sense, because it destroyed the empire's reserve of military power.

Gratian had been able to move much of the Western Roman Empire's field army into the Balkans to aid Valens. Unfortunately for the fate of the empire as a whole, Valens decided to fight the Goths on his own. Thus, when the barbarian waves broke over the Western Empire in the fifth century, there was no reserve of troops in the east to come to the aid of the west, and without reinforcements, the Western Empire was no longer able to stem the barbarian invasions. Instead, in a great break with Rome's history, the barbarians overwhelmed not just the armies, but the provinces on which those armies depended and on which their reconstitution and rebuilding depended. Once the provinces fell into the hands of Rome's tribal enemies, there would be no recovery in the west.

Equally significant was the destruction of the remnants of the disciplined, trained troops that had characterized Rome's military power at the height of the empire. Those who made up the later armies of the Byzantine Empire gained their skill on the battlefield itself, where only the fiercest survived. Counted in their ranks were indeed fierce warriors, but not the expert, seasoned soldier of the legions. It would take over a thousand years before the Roman concept of trained, highly disciplined soldiers would reemerge in Europe in the early seventeenth century, first under Maurice of Orange, the great Dutch leader in the rebellion against the Spanish, and Gustavus Adolphus, the Swedish warrior-king. Significantly, the Swedish Articles of War promulgated by Gustavus would explicitly state that "soldiers must dig, when told to do so." No Roman legionnaire of Marius, or Caesar, or Trajan would have refused to dig when so ordered. For the armies of the Byzantines, or the Arabs, or the medieval Europeans, such orders were not to be taken seriously, if the soldiers were not inclined to dig.

Similarly, the Roman defeat was not the result of superior Gothic cavalry overrunning Roman infantry. Rather, the decisive role of the barbarian horsemen also reflected the mistakes of the Roman commanders. The Battle of Adrianople may have ushered in a period when cavalry dominated the battlefield, as the historian Charles Oman suggests, but that domination was the inevitable result of the lack of discipline among infantry that precluded their standing firm in the face of cavalry charges. Horses will not charge into a line of infantry that holds its ground. But once the cohesion of an infantry formation breaks, it becomes a mob of individuals, each fair game for charging horsemen.

Adrianople taught those who guided the policies of the Eastern Roman Empire the crucial lesson—the new reality—of the fragility of military power. And on that lesson the survival of the empire depended for the next millennium. Thus, the Byzantine strategic approach for the remainder of the Eastern Empire's existence emphasized the diplomatic and manipulative aspects of foreign policy. In fact, one might suggest that the Byzantine Empire invented the concept of strategy. Those who led the empire in succeeding centuries maintained their control over their territory by a mixture of diplomacy, outright bribery, and military power, but war was always their least preferred choice, a last resort, which they exercised only when no other option existed and the survival of the empire depended on military force alone. But in terms both of the resources available and their understanding of the relative strategic weakness of their power, they used force with the utmost discretion.

We might note in conclusion that the survival of the Byzantine Empire was, of course, essential to the future of Western civilization. For the military reformers of the seventeenth century, the Byzantines transmitted the fundamental secrets of Roman military power. In terms of developing military formations that marched in step and could maneuver fluidly on the battlefield, the military reformers of seventeenth-century Europe drew on ancient Roman military texts for the commands that still echo today on the parade grounds of Western armies and those trained in its traditions.

Of course, the transmission of Greek and Roman culture was the greater gift the Eastern Roman Empire provided Western civilization—that, and the fact that the Byzantine Empire served as the great bulwark that prevented the spread of Islamic conquests from the Middle East into a nascent and vulnerable European civilization just emerging from the Dark Ages. But it depended for survival on a combination of force, policy, and strategy very different from the raw military power of the legions that had gone down to their last defeat at Adrianople.

YARMUK

The Islamic Conquest Begins

636

IN 629, THE PROPHET MUHAMMAD, TAKING ADVANTAGE OF A TRUCE between himself and his mortal enemies, the Quraysh tribe, took the time to send a series of ultimatums to the kings of Persia, Yemen, and Ethiopia and the Byzantine emperor Heraclius. To Heraclius he wrote:

> Peace be upon him, he who follows the right path. Furthermore I invite thee to Islam; become a Muslim and thou shalt be safe, and God will double thy reward, and if thou reject this invitation, thou shalt bear the sins of persecuting Arians.

It is uncertain if Heraclius ever saw this ultimatum from an unknown desert upstart. But even if he had, it was unlikely to have made much of an impression on him. Desert raiders had plagued the Roman Empire since its founding. They remained a thorn in the side of the empire even after the Western Roman Empire collapsed and imperial power recentered itself on Byzantium. For Heraclius it was just one of many thorns, and far from the most dangerous he had encountered in the almost twenty years he had been on the throne.

Heraclius had seized the Byzantine throne just as the empire's fortunes approached a low ebb. The death of Justinian the Great in A.D. 565 left a leadership void that nearly destroyed all he had built. Faced with an empty treasury, his nephew and successor, Justin II, ended a tried-and-true Roman practice of buying off enemies that one was temporarily too weak to fight, leaving much of the empire open to invasion and ruin. Sensing weakness looming, barbarian tribes once again descended on the empire. The Lombards, who had been contained in the Balkans, immediately moved into northern Italy. Within a few years, they controlled almost the entire peninsula, wiping out territorial holdings that had taken Justinian's armies a generation to gain. The fierce Avars stayed in the Balkans, where they undertook a campaign of conquest that eventually led them to the walls of Constantinople. In 572, Justin's inept diplomacy, coupled with a refusal to pay tribute, led to a renewed war with Persia, a war Byzantium was ill prepared to fight. Justin's defeat in two campaigns cost the empire much of Mesopotamia and the fabulously rich province of Syria. It also cost Justin his sanity, and special rails had to be placed in the palace windows to keep the emperor from jumping out.

After the death of Justin in 578, his picked successor, Tiberius, rose to the throne. He managed to stop the Persian advance but then repeated the great Justinian's mistake of denuding the empire of troops, sending them off to regain distant portions of the lost Western Empire. For a while, Byzantine troops were able to reverse Lombard gains in Italy, but only at a high cost in treasure and the blood of veteran troops Byzantium could ill afford to lose. With the bulk of the Byzantine army either fighting in the west or guarding the Persian frontier, the Avars took the opportunity to continue stripping away the empire's Balkan provinces. Tiberius died, or more probably was murdered, in 582. He was succeeded by a Byzantine general, Maurice, who was having some success in a new round of fighting with Persia.

Upon his accession to the throne, Maurice launched a triumphal campaign against Persia. Taking advantage of political turmoil there, he decided to send an army to help the deposed Sassanid Persian ruler, Khosrau II, regain his throne. A combined Byzantine-Persian army defeated the usurpers at the Battle of Blarathon, restoring Khosrau to power and bringing an end to the Persian wars. To seal a lasting peace, Maurice married off his daughter Mariam to Khosrau. A grateful son-in-law not only returned all of Byzantium's lost territory, he also ceded Armenia to the empire.

In 591, with the Persian frontier secure, Maurice turned on the Avars with a vengeance. The Avars, who had been plundering the Balkans for over a decade and for a time even threatened the capital, had grown complacent. They were completely unprepared for the scale and ferocity of the Byzantine assault and were defeated south of the Danube. In 593, Byzantine troops advanced across the Danube into Wallachia. There, the Avars and their Gepid allies were roughly handled in their own homeland and sued for peace in 595. However, this peace was short-lived, and by 599 Byzantium and the Avars were again at war. In 602, the Avars suffered another crushing defeat in Wallachia, allowing the Byzantines to once again form their frontier defenses along the Danube. Behind these defenses, Maurice hoped to repopulate the devastated Balkans with an influx of Armenian settlers.

For a moment, it seemed that Byzantium had weathered the great storm and could focus on rebuilding. However, Maurice's treasury was empty, and in order to conserve money he made a number of unwise choices. First, he decided not to pay any ransom for the twelve thousand soldiers the Avars had captured during the years of war. The barbarian Avars, seeing no hope of profit, promptly slaughtered the captives rather than feed them through another long winter. Maurice's callous disregard for the lives of his soldiers unsettled his army. They selected one of their number, Phocas, to lead a delegation to Byzantium to place their grievances before the emperor. Maurice rejected these complaints and forced Phocas to endure the further insult of being publicly slapped about by court officials.

Phocas bore his humiliation silently and returned to the army to nurse his pride. Not long afterward, he and the rest of the army learned that Maurice, in another cost-cutting measure, had ordered their pay cut by a quarter. Thus, the army that Maurice ordered on a major punitive expedition across the Danube in 602 was seriously disgruntled. Despite the soldiers' anger, the campaign was successful, and the army was heading back across the Danube to occupy well-prepared and warm winter quarters when they were ordered to spend the winter on the far side of the river. Without prepared forts the army would not only freeze, it would be exposed to their enemies without any significant protection. At that point, the army, led by Phocas, understandably mutinied and crossed the Danube to march on Constantinople. Maurice fled to a nearby monastery.

Upon entering the city, Phocas was crowned emperor. His first act was to have Maurice dragged from the monastery and forced to witness the beheading of his six sons before his own execution. Well aware of the need to solidify his hold on power, Phocas played the part of populist. He immediately lowered taxes, for which his popularity with the masses soared—for a time, although that did little to help fill his empty treasury. Furthermore, all was not well outside the capital. King Khosrau, who had owed his Persian crown to his father-in-law, Maurice, took advantage of his benefactor's death to break the peace treaty and renew the Byzantine-Persian wars. Worse, the commander of the Byzantine army on the Persian frontier, Narses, remained loyal to Maurice and led his army into revolt. To deal with Narses, Phocas had to denude the Balkans of every available soldier.

Taking advantage of the Byzantine army's withdrawal, in 605 the Avars crossed the Danube in force. Before them lay the defenseless Balkan provinces for the taking. Meanwhile, the Persians marched from the east, ostensibly to save Narses, who was besieged in Edessa. So began a grinding war of attrition that lasted for twenty years. Moreover, in 608 the Byzantine commander in Africa, Heraclius the Elder, and his son, also named Heraclius, raised the banner of revolt. This caused rioting in many of the cities of Syria, which Phocas crushed with such severity that the region's enmity to Constantinople was reportedly still palpable centuries later. Of course, Byzantium's enemies took advantage of the civil war to renew their advances. The Persians took much of Anatolia, while at the same time Avar and Slav raiding parties were again daring to approach the northern walls of the capital.

It was at this low ebb in Byzantine fortunes that Heraclius the Younger entered the capital with a small force. The imperial guard, commanded by Phocas's son-in-law Priscus, threw in their lot with the new usurper. Phocas was brought before Heraclius, who became enraged by Phocas's answers to his questions, drew his sword, and beheaded Phocas on the spot. Heraclius's first attempts to restore the military situation failed, and Byzantium's enemies continued to advance. By 611, Persian campfires were visible from Constantinople's battlements. With no army and no money to raise a new one, Heraclius saw things go from bad to worse. First Antioch fell to the Persians in 611, followed by the collapse of Damascus two years later, and finally Jerusalem in 614. The loss of Jerusalem also meant the loss of "the True Cross," the most sacred relic in Christendom, which was taken to Ctesiphon, the Persian capital. In 617, Persian forces overran Egypt, thus stripping Constantinople of the province that supplied its food and a large portion of its tax revenues.

Heraclius remained behind Constantinople's impregnable walls, biding his time and preparing a great counterattack. By once again emptying the treasury, he was able to buy peace with the Persians, although when his cash on hand alone proved insufficient, he also promised the delivery of one thousand virgins. Through other inducements, Heraclius managed to achieve a temporary truce with the Avars in 619. This general peace bought the emperor time to reorganize the army and through extraordinary means, including melting down church treasures, raise a war chest. By 622, all was ready for Byzantium to take the offensive and regain its lost territory. Over the next five years, in a series of brilliant campaigns, Heraclius defeated the Persian armies and stood outside the gates of Ctesiphon. Khosrau's subjects believed that his defeats indicated the disfavor of the gods, and his son, Kavadh II, seized the throne, whereupon he immediately sued for peace. As a result, Persia withdrew from all occupied territories and returned the True Cross. After a triumphal march through the retaken provinces in 629, Heraclius returned the relic to Jerusalem.

Muhammad sent out his ultimatums soon afterward. These came at a time when the Byzantine Empire required rest above all else. The protracted wars had not only wrecked Persian power, but had exhausted Byzantium and devastated its richest provinces in Anatolia, Syria, and Palestine, all of which required many years to recover. And even though Persia lay prostrate, the Avars and Slavs still dominated the Balkans, depriving the empire's coffers of revenue. It would take a supreme effort for the empire to muster sufficient forces to fend off another invader. Moreover, any defeat would be catastrophic, as there were no reserves, either of treasure or of manpower.

This new threat facing the Byzantine Empire was unlike any that had come before it. The Byzantines had always had to deal with raiders coming out of the sands of Arabia, but what was about to break forth from the desert was much more than a pinprick raid by a rogue tribe set on gathering a bit of plunder before vanishing back into the wastelands. Rather, all of the desert tribes were now unified under the single banner of Islam, a highly expansionist faith that gloried in spreading its new creed through conquest.

When Muhammad died in 632, his unification of the Arab tribes remained unfinished. That job was completed by his successor, Abu Bakr, who quickly subdued apostatic tribes in the the Ridda Wars. When they were over in 633, Abu Bakr possessed a unified veteran army and a superb commander to lead it, Khalid ibn Walid, "the Sword of God." After securing his own position, Bakr sent eighteen thousand picked men, commanded by Khalid, into the Persian province of lower Mesopotamia (modern Iraq) in 633. The exhausted Persians put up the best opposition of which they were still capable, but by the end of the year most of the province was in Arab hands and the Persian capital was in danger. The final destruction of Persia's Sassanid dynasty was averted when Khalid received an urgent message to take his army to the aid of another Muslim invading force that Bakr had sent into Palestine.

The prelude to the Battle of Yarmuk begins with Khalid's arrival in Syria, where he immediately began raiding throughout the province. By this time, Heraclius learned of Arab victories over the Persians and realized he faced a much greater threat than mere raiding parties. He ordered his brother Theodore to assemble an army at Ajnadayn and prepare to meet the Arab army in the field. It took the Byzantines two months to concentrate local forces, a feat the fast-moving Arabs accomplished in a week. The Battle of Ajnadayn was long and hard-fought. Despite heavy losses on both sides, the Arabs held the field at the end of the day, as the Byzantine army scattered in three directions. In the aftermath of the battle, Khalid's warriors conquered most of Syria and Palestine, including the great city of Damascus. For his part, Heraclius ordered his brother arrested and had the reorganizing army retreat from the exposed city of Emesa to Antioch. Understanding that confronting the Arab threat was beyond local resources, Heraclius began assembling the imperial army for action.

In 637, the Byzantine army began to move. This army was a polyglot force of mercenary Slavs, Franks, Geogians, Armenians, and Christian Arabs (Ghassan tribe). This force was organized into five divisions each with its own commander and with Theodore Trithourios (not to be confused with the emperor's brother Theodore) in overall command, while Vahan, an Armenian, was expected to take command in the event of battle. Language barriers added to the problems of this impractical command structure, which was made worse by the simple fact that many of the commanders of the Byzantine divisions neither liked nor trusted one another.

There were also major command changes on the Arab side. By this time, Abu Bakr was dead, and the new caliph, Umar, promptly relieved Khalid and ordered Abu Ubaidah to assume command of the Arab armies in Palestine and Syria. Abu Ubaidah was a pious man and politically reliable, but although courageous, he was not on the same level as Khalid as a general. Remarkably, he was well aware of his own shortcomings and as Khalid remained with the army, Abu Ubaidah deferred to him in most military matters.

After the Battle of Ajnadayn, the Byzantine commanders were reluctant to face the Arabs in a major set-piece battle. Therefore, they

Gold denarius of Byzantine emperor Heraclius, c. 575–641
Alfredo Dagli Orti/The Art Archive at Art Resource, NY

began their advance hoping to surprise the Arabs and defeat each of their scattered forces before they could concentrate. Unfortunately, the Arabs had been watching the Byzantine buildup with some apprehension. Khalid advised Abu Ubaidah to abandon their gains, including Damascus, and concentrate the army farther south, nearer the friendly desert in case of a military reverse. As a result, the Arab army withdrew just before the Byzantines struck and began concentrating at Jibaya. Thus, the first and most powerful thrust of the Byzantine invasion struck open air.

Either because they were forced out by raiding Ghassanid Arabs (Christian Arabs in alliance with Byzantium) or because Khalid believed the ground near Yarmuk was a stronger defensive position, the Arabs retreated farther south and waited.

The Plain of Yarmuk lies about forty miles southeast of the Golan Heights. At the time, it was well watered and excellent for both grazing animal stock and maintaining an army for an extended period. It was fortunate for the Arabs that it was, as the Byzantines waited almost two months before advancing to attack the position. First, they tried to buy off the Arab invaders. When Khalid refused a final bribe offered by the Byzantine commander Vahan, the armies could no longer avoid battle. Some Christian sources state that the Byzantines were forced to attack as the caliph, Umar, was constantly sending reinforcements and the Byzantines feared they would soon find themselves outnumbered. Among these reinforcements were six thousand Yemenis, which included in their number one thousand elite Companions of the Prophet as well as one hundred veterans of the Battle of Badr—Islam's first battle.

According to a description given by the historian A. I. Akram, the battlefield consisted of the Plain of Yarmuk, which was fenced in along its western and southern borders by deep ravines. Also along its western side was the yawning Wadi-ur-Raqqad, which joined the Yarmuk River near Yaqusa. This steep-banked, deep ravine ran for almost a dozen miles from northeast to southwest. Although troops could cross the ravine at several places, there was only one main crossing.

Battle began on August 15, 636. Nothing is known of the Byzantine dispositions. Some sources claim the bulk of their infantry was on the right flank, with the Armenians in the center and their Arab allies (mostly Ghassanids) on the right. Others claim that the infantry extended along the entire front, with the Ghassanid cavalry stretched out in front and other cavalry formations dispersed evenly among the infantry line. Even less is known about the Arab battle formation, except that Khalid kept an elite cavalry formation in reserve and close to his person. Akram relates that, believing his men would be reluctant to abandon their wives and children to Byzantine mercy, he ordered them to pitch camp directly behind the Arab battle formation. As the women arrayed themselves, Abu Ubaidah visited the various camps, giving instructions to the women: "'Take tent poles in your hands and gather heaps of stones. If we win all is well. But if you see a Muslim running away from battle, strike him in the face with a tent pole, pelt him with stones . . .' The women prepared accordingly."

The first day opened with dueling champions. It appears that, by far, the Byzantines got the worst of these duels, and noon found their collection of champions much reduced. In fact, as many of these champions were senior commanders, their loss had a strong negative effect on Byzantine cohesion as the battle developed. To stop any further rot of Byzantine morale, Vahan ordered a large portion of his infantry to advance. The failure to rapidly replace commanders lost in the earlier duels probably accounts for the listlessness of this first attack. Although the fighting continued until sunset (at which time both sides separated for the night), it was not pressed home with any ferocity and casualties on both sides were minimal.

On the second day, the Byzantines attacked before dawn, hoping to strike while the Muslims were at morning prayers. They did manage to surprise the main Arab army, but a strong Arab outpost line slowed the advance and negated any Byzantine advantage. Although the Byzantines eventually overwhelmed the outpost line, the skirmishers held long enough for the Arab force to muster in battle formation and counterattack.

As the Byzantine center held the Arab center in place, successive heavy attacks, undertaken mostly by Slavs, hammered the Arab right. On the third Slavic charge, the Arab line broke. An Arab cavalry charge slowed the Byzantine pursuit just long enough to give the re-treating Arabs time to reach their camp. Here they encountered some-thing more fearsome than the Slavs—their own wives.

According to Akram, the women screamed curses in an attempt to shame the fleeing Arab force. When this failed to stem the Arab flight, the women assaulted them, as they had been instructed, with stones and tent poles. "This was more than the proud warriors could take. Indignant at their treatment, they turned back from the camp and advanced in blazing anger."

The same scene played out on the opposite flank. But here, the seventy-three-year-old Abu Sufyan, a respected warrior and father of the founder of the Umayyad dynasty, was the first to retreat. He there-fore was the first to encounter his wife, the formidable Hind. Hind was originally a strong opponent of Muhammad and was famous for supposedly eating the liver of Muhammad's uncle after he was killed in battle. According to Akram, "She struck at the head of his horse with a tent pole and shouted: 'Where to, O Son of Harb? Return to battle and show your courage so that you may be forgiven your sins against the Messenger of Allah.'" Abu Sufyan had experienced his wife's violent temper before and hastily turned back. With the help of Khalid's reserve cavalry, which attacked first on the right flank and then the left, the Arabs turned back the Byzantine tide. By the end of the second day, the toll in casualties had mounted, but no side had a clear advantage.

On the third day, Vahan decided to concentrate his assaults on the weakened Muslim right flank. To weight the attack, he reinforced his own left with Armenians from his center and right. As the assault began, the Byzantine center and right were expected to make enough of a demonstration to pin their opposite numbers and hopefully attract the attention of at least part of Khalid's reserve. They failed at both tasks.

At first, the Byzantine main assault made good progress. But as the rest of the army stood almost idle, Khalid was able to use his re-serve to strike at the exposed flank of the advancing Byzantines. At the same time, the Arab right-wing commander used his own cavalry to strike the other flank, threatening to trap over a third of the Byz-antine force in a deadly double envelopment. The Byzantines re-

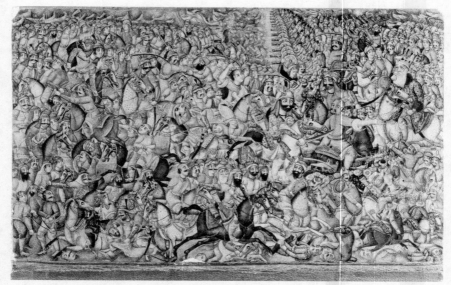

Battle of Yarmuk, from book cover, Persia, 1739
V&A Images/The Art Archive at Art Resource, NY

treated, suffering great loss without gaining much beyond forcing the Arab infantry to again suffer indignant insults from their wives. As one Muslim soldier exclaimed, "It is easier to face the Romans [Byzantines] than our women."

THE FOURTH DAY saw more hard fighting. Having witnessed Khalid commit his entire reserve against the Byzantine right flank the day before, Vahan planned to take advantage of a similar circumstance if one was offered or could be forced upon the Arabs. He once again sent his left flank against the seriously depleted Muslim right and waited for Khalid to commit his reserve. When he did, Vahan planned to order a general assault along his entire line.

Khalid had worried himself during the night about just such a stratagem. To counter it, he ordered his left flank and center to advance as soon as the Byzantine attack began. By doing so, he hoped to forestall a general Byzantine assault and to simultaneously force the Byzantine left flank away from the rest of the army so it could be enveloped and destroyed. As soon as the Byzantine assault on the Arab right flank opened, the Arab center and left went forward. When they came within range of the Byzantine archers, catastrophe struck. Hundreds of Muslims fell, and according to Akram, seven hundred Muslims lost at least one eye, including the aged Abu Sufyan. This calamity is still referred to in Arab lore as "the Day of the Lost Eyes." Unable to stand up to the intense arrow storm, the Arabs retreated.

While the Arabs were still reeling, the Byzantine right and center advanced. Under unrelenting pressure, the Arab line broke and the Byzantines came on with renewed fury. The day was saved only by a cavalry regiment commanded by the fearless Ikrimah, who refused to retreat and had his four hundred men join him in a blood oath. Ikrimah's cavalry struck hard at the advancing Byzantines and for a few moments halted their advance. But doing so came at great cost, as Ikrimah was killed and all four hundred of his regiment were seriously wounded or killed. Their sacrifice was not in vain. It bought time for the Arabs to form a ragged defensive line, which few thought could hold. For the Arabs, this was the crisis of the battle.

The women, who had been preparing to hurl insults at their retreating men, took up another plan when they saw the damaged Arab line turn and prepare to hold. They left the camp and went forward, armed with tent poles and swords. They pushed through the exhausted soldiers and took the first brunt of the Byzantine charge. As Akram tells the story: "The sight of their women fighting alongside, and some even ahead of them, turned the Muslims into raging demons. In blind fury they struck at the Romans [Byzantines] in an action in which there was now no maneuver and no generalship— only individual soldiers giving their superhuman best." This furious assault struck the Byzantine advance just as it was exhausting itself. In an instant, victory was snatched away, as the Byzantines, who fell back slowly at first, soon routed.

On the other flank, the day had gone much like the day before. The fighting had been brutal, costly, and inconclusive. There was, however, one bright spot for the Arabs. The Christian Arab Ghassanids had become separated from the main army during the battle. Rather than try to rejoin it during the night, the Ghassanids deserted the battlefield, depriving the Byzantines of their best cavalry formations.

The next morning, Vahan sent an emissary to ask for a truce to last a few days so that fresh negotiations could begin. Khalid, realizing that the Byzantines' offensive spirit was broken, had the emissary carry back his negative reply: "We are in a hurry to finish this business." There was no action that day, allowing Khalid to rest his men and reorganize his cavalry for an offensive the next day. He ordered all of his cavalry regiments formed into a single striking mass of eight thousand warriors. The only cavalry he detached was five hundred men, sent on a wide circle around the Byzantine left flank. There they occupied the only escape route the Romans would have come morning.

The following day began with another clash of champions. This time a Byzantine general, Gargas, demanded to fight the Arab commander. Khalid prepared to take up the challenge when Abu Ubaidah insisted that as he had been given command of the army by the caliph, it was his duty to take up the challenge. The fight between the two men went on for some minutes before Ubaidah dropped his opponent with a thrust to the neck.

As soon as Ubaidah reentered Muslim lines, Khalid ordered a general assault all along the line. Once the Byzantines were pinned in place, he took his cavalry on a wide, sweeping move around their left flank. As the cavalry approached the battle, Khalid broke it into two parts. One part attacked the Byzantine cavalry to keep it out of the battle. The other smashed into the exposed left flank and rear of the Byzantine infantry line. The Slavs holding this sector of the line fought fiercely, but, attacked from three directions, they were soon reeling toward the center. Their retreat disordered the already hard-pressed center, which began to come apart. Vahan saw what was happening and tried to gather his cavalry into a large striking arm so as to counter the Arab charge. It was the right idea, but Khalid did not allow him the time to complete this concentration. Successive Arab cavalry charges broke the Byzantine cavalry before it could form properly. Vahan, despite his desire to continue the fight, was swept away with his own cavalry as it retreated to the northwest.

As the Byzantine cavalry deserted the field, the Byzantine infantry was left to its fate. Khalid immediately re-formed the Arab cavalry and struck directly into the rear of the infantry, which promptly broke and ran in the only direction that appeared open, toward the imposing Wadi-ur-Raqqad, a ravine that could be crossed only at a single point. When the fleeing men arrived at the crossing, they found it held strongly by the five hundred horsemen Khalid had sent out the night before. Unable to break through and pushed hard from the rear, the Byzantines were herded into a compact mass. From that point on, the battle descended into a slaughter. Akram describes the end: "The screams of the Romans mingled with the shouts of the Muslims as the last resistance collapsed, and the battle turned into a butchery and a nightmare of horrors."

Khalid pursued the battered Byzantine remnants hard, catching up to them near Damascus. After a short fight, the Byzantine army was destroyed and Vahan killed. Khalid reoccupied Damascus without having to besiege it. As for Heraclius, he was enraged at news of the defeat. After consulting his advisers, he conceded that the loss was God's punishment for the sins of the Byzantines and his own transgressions, which included his marriage to his niece. Without money or troops to continue the war, Heraclius took a ship from Antioch back to Constantinople. He was able to create a buffer zone in Anatolia, but the Arab conquests went on without pause for another century. Constantinople itself went through many ups and downs before its final fall to a besieging Muslim Ottoman army over eight hundred years later, in 1453.

It is one of the quirks of history that the Muslim invasions struck at what may have been the only time they had the slightest chance of success. If they had come a decade before, they would have faced the full might of the Sassanid and Byzantine Empires before they had exhausted themselves in battle against each other. If they had come a decade later, the Muslims would have encountered two empires well along the road to economic and military recovery. In either case, the Arab invaders would likely have been torn to pieces by either empire or both. As it was, the initial Arab invasions were a near run thing, and they could have gone either way. However, in the end the Muslims prevailed and the Byzantines no longer had the wherewithal to create another field army. As a result, all of Syria and Palestine fell to the Arabs. This was merely the beginning of a century of Arab conquests that ended only when Charles Martel defeated an Arab invasion force at Tours in central France in 732. By that time, the Arabs controlled all of the southern Mediterranean, including most of Spain, and were pushing deep into India in the east.

It is one of the great what-ifs of history to ask what would have become of the Islamic faith if the Byzantines had won at Yarmuk. At the very least, they would have repelled the Islamic tide early, and the Arab-Islamic civilization that now dominates from the Bosporus to the Strait of Gibraltar would not exist. The entire Mediterranean would have remained culturally Greco-Roman and Christian, and if it survived at all, Islam itself would arguably have been relegated to the deserts of Arabia.

HASTINGS

The Remaking of Europe

1066

If any battle deserves to be imprinted on the Western consciousness, it is Hastings. For historians, the year 1066 and the Battle of Hastings are inextricably linked. Still, for most people the events that took place on that fateful battlefield remain shrouded in the mists of time. This is unfortunate, for that single day's combat nearly a thousand years ago created what eventually became the modern English state and later Great Britain. Prior to Hastings and the ensuing Norman Conquest, England was an inward-looking nation with only limited interests beyond its shores. In fact, Anglo-Saxon England's foremost concern was the forlorn hope that other Europeans would remain at home and desist from invading their island. In the centuries prior to Hastings, however, England was just too tempting a target to be left alone. First came the Romans, who extended their stay for centuries. Rome's retreat from empire opened the door for the barbaric Angles, Saxons, and Jute tribes, who pushed the original inhabitants into the inhospitable lands of Wales. Finally the Vikings came, first to steal the island's wealth and then to conquer. After Hastings, however, England departed from its insular ways and adopted a new outlook on the world, one that encouraged it to take a greater part in the activities of Europe and later the globe.

In 1066, the Normans, under William the Conqueror, were just the latest in a long line of invaders attracted by the island's natural wealth and apparent military weakness. What marked the Norman invasion as unique was that it was the *last* successful invasion of England. From the time of the Conquest, English armies were far more likely to tread on the Continent than the other way around. This was the natural result of the Norman lords taking over the estates of the defeated Anglo-Saxons while continuing to hold their own lands and castles back in France. In fact, since William the Conqueror also retained his extensive domains in Normandy, he became not only the king of England, but also the first ruler of what would someday become the base of the Angevin Empire, which included all of England and better than half of modern France. The English would not finally leave France until the fall of Calais in 1558—492 years later.

The infusion of Norman energy into the efficient political and economic structure of Anglo-Saxon England created a new power on the edge of Europe. That entity possessed the military and economic wherewithal to make itself felt in any matter in which it wished to become involved. With the exception of the years between the reign of Henry VI and Elizabeth I, English armies were the most feared on the Continent. While a later era of massed armies often caused Britain to recoil at the idea of putting large land forces on the Continent, at least until the twentieth century, it still found ways to manifest its power on a wider stage. For one, England never completely gave up the advantage of strong centralized control of the state and its inherent ability to mobilize resources. This ability allowed England to finance a powerful navy and to subsidize continental allies willing to do most of the land fighting involved in the conduct of any major war. Going from strength to strength, the English financial system adapted to the forces of change until it was able to finance the Industrial Revolution along with a simultaneous second hundred years' war with Napoleonic France. Only slowly, after the Treaty of Westphalia and proceeding through the post-Napoleonic era, did other nations begin to learn and adopt the secrets of England's economic vitality.

If the Normans had not come to England or if they had lost at

Hastings, the effects would have been immediate and profound. Anglo-Saxon success at Hastings would have seen off William and his Norman army but would have done little to encourage the Saxons to venture forth into the wider world. With the Norman lords retaining their strongholds in Normandy, the English would have lacked the foothold necessary for military operations on the Continent. Without a secure continental base, it is unlikely that any English army would have ever hazarded its chances in France or elsewhere, at least before the beginning of the modern era.

Another impediment to Norman-less England influencing the councils of Europe would have been the enhanced power of France. A Norman defeat at Hastings would likely have seen William's army trapped and exterminated. A disaster of that magnitude would have fatally undermined Norman power, which for centuries acted to stymie the spread of French royal authority. Undoubtedly, France's Capetian dynasty would have absorbed Normandy into its own domains soon after word reached it of the destruction of William's army. With such a powerful economic and military base, the rest of France could never have withstood royal expansion. Within a generation after 1066, France would have towered over Europe as a virtually uncontested colossus. From that point, the course history might have taken is guesswork. What is certain is that the ultimate path would bear little resemblance to the story we now know.

ONE OF THE LITTLE-REMEMBERED FACTS about the Conquest period is that Anglo-Saxon England was probably the most centralized and efficient state in Europe. Arguably, it was also one of the most militarily powerful states. This certainly was not the case in the generations prior to the Conquest, when Viking raiders were tearing England asunder. For a short period during, and in the immediate aftermath of, Alfred the Great's reign (A.D. 871–899), it seemed as if England would weather the Viking storm and in true Nietzschean fashion emerge stronger. For almost a hundred years after Alfred's rule, powerful Anglo-Saxon kings built on his achievements. In fact, during the reign of Edgar the Peaceful (959–975), areas of England controlled for well over a century by the Vikings (the Danelaw) were brought

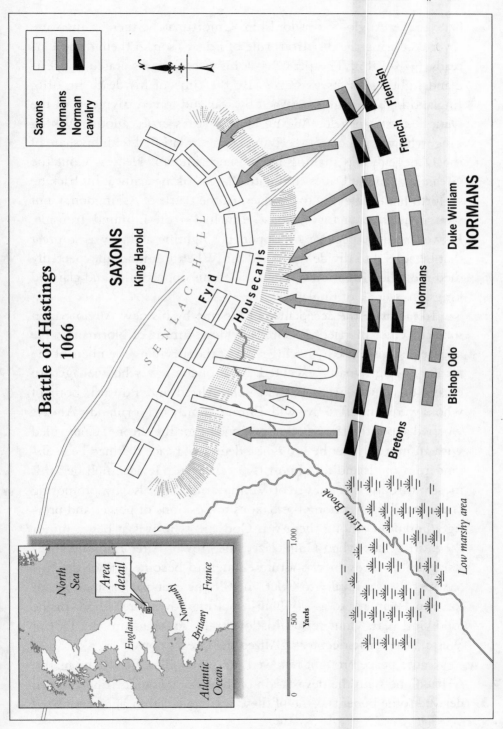

Battle of Hastings
1066

Saxons
Saxons
Normans
Norman cavalry

King Harold

SAXONS

SENLAC HILL

Fyrd

Housecarls

NORMANS
Duke William

Flemish
French
Normans
Bishop Odo
Bretons

Asten Brook

Low marshy area

North Sea
Area detail
Normandy
France
Brittany
England
Atlantic Ocean

Yards
0   500   1,000

back under Anglo-Saxon lordship. Unfortunately, these gains were reversed during the disastrous rule of Edgar's son, Æthelred the Un-ready (978–1016). The period saw his father's gains erased and England fighting for its existence. By the time of his death in 1016, England had been impoverished by war and forced payments to the Danes—the Danegeld. Adding to that year's crisis, another Viking king, who was either not receiving or was unsatisfied with his share of the Danegeld, was making his presence known. He was Cnut the Great, king of the Danes, and with a large Viking army at his back he set forth not to raid, but to conquer. At the Battle of Ashingdon, Cnut won a decisive victory against Æthelred's son Edmund Ironside. However, his respect for his opponent's fighting ability was so great that he agreed to divide the kingdom. When Edmund unexpectedly died the following month, Cnut seized his opportunity and claimed kingship over all of England.

To facilitate the acceptance of his rule by his new Anglo-Saxon subjects, Cnut married Æthelred's widow, Emma of Normandy. He also helped his cause by having most of the surviving members of the former ruling dynasty executed. Two of the few who managed to escape this purge were Emma's sons Alfred and Edward, both of whom were sent off to live with Emma's family in Normandy. Always worried about the rise of other contenders for the throne, Cnut ruled with an iron fist. But he brought a degree of peace that had been absent from the island for almost two centuries. He accomplished this mostly through the power of Viking arms, but also by promoting "new men" from among the Saxons to positions of power and prestige. Foremost among them was Godwin, who was at best a minor thegn in Sussex when Cnut seized the crown. After Edmund Ironside's death, Godwin was astute enough to become one of the first Saxons to swear loyalty to Cnut. In 1018, he even took a small Saxon force to Denmark to assist Cnut in putting down a rebellion. In the following year, Cnut repaid his loyalty by making him the Earl of Wessex, the former center of Alfred the Great's power.

Cnut's peace brought renewed prosperity. The fact of the matter is that along with the devastation of the Viking assaults, England had derived some benefits. One of these was the creation of a centralized government infrastructure and an efficient revenue collection system. Such a system was necessary, of course, if England was to have any chance of collecting the fantastic sums of Danegeld required to buy off Viking raiders. Now that England was free of the Danegeld, those resources remained at the crown's disposal. While the unified English state, as we think of it in the modern sense, was still some distance away, England by the early eleventh century was able to mobilize economic and military resources far exceeding those of any other European entity, with the possible exception of the papal domains.

These funds allowed Cnut and his successor to pay for a dedicated professional fighting force—the housecarls. Even after paying the costs of maintaining the housecarls year-round, a substantial amount remained. The evidence indicates that Cnut, following old Norse traditions, was not hesitant about distributing these funds to his supporters. In turn, they distributed gifts down the pecking order to buy loyalty or to acquire new domains from nobles who had fallen on hard times. Through it all, Cnut reigned supreme. But one rung below him was the grasping Godwin, who with his sons was spreading his tentacles throughout the realm.

On Cnut's death in 1035, there were multiple claimants to portions of his realm. His illegitimate son Harold Harefoot seized the English throne, while his legitimate son born of Emma of Normandy, Harthacnut, seized Denmark. But there was another claimant to the English throne, Emma of Normandy's son with Æthelred the Unready—Alfred. However, when Alfred traveled to England in an attempt to rally support, Godwin captured him and turned him over to Harold Harefoot, who had him blinded so as to make him ineligible to rule. He died soon thereafter. For his act of treachery, Godwin gained the support of his Danish overlord, as well as the undying enmity and mistrust of Emma and her last remaining son with Æthelred—Edward (known to history as Edward the Confessor). In 1040, Harold Harefoot died, and Godwin supported Harthacnut's claim to the English throne. But when the latter also died two years later, the male line of Cnut was extinguished. With no other acceptable choice available, Godwin threw his support behind Emma's remaining son, Edward the Confessor, thereby returning the royal

House of Wessex to the English throne. As Edward rightfully blamed Godwin for the blinding and death of his brother, their relations were strained from the start.

Despite the coolness of their relationship, Edward needed Godwin's support to maintain his hold on power. Taking advantage of the king's weakness, Godwin forced Edward to marry his daughter Edith. Godwin naturally assumed the marriage would yield a son, which would place his bloodline on the throne. Edward thwarted this ambition by refusing to take Edith to his bed. Edward also made the mistake of recruiting most of his advisers from Normandy, which caused a groundswell of opposition against further encroachments of Norman influence. Through either design or fate, Godwin found himself at the center of this anti-Norman cabal. Unwilling to give up advisers he was comfortable with, the king brought matters to a head in 1051, when the people of Dover—firmly within Godwin's territory—insulted the visiting Eustace II, Count of Boulogne. When Godwin refused the king's orders to punish them, he was declared an outlaw. With the support of several other earls who were fearful of Godwin's growing power, the king ordered Godwin and his sons banished and his lands forfeit. Edward had won the first round. Godwin, however, returned the following year with an army at his back. Growing popular support, not to mention Godwin's mercenaries, forced Edward to return Godwin's earldom. In 1053, Godwin died of a stroke. His son Harold Godwinson succeeded him.

Notwithstanding Edward's attempts to hold Harold and his brothers in check, by 1066 the Godwin clan controlled close to two thirds of England. By way of comparison, the two next strongest families, the Leofrics and the Siwards, controlled 31 percent and 3 percent, respectively. When Edward died childless in January 1066, the Saxon assembly of powerful lords, the witenagemot, selected Harold as king. There were only two problems with the selection. William, Duke of Normandy, was under the impression that Edward the Confessor had promised him the throne when he visited England in 1051. Worse, when Harold had been shipwrecked off Ponthieu in 1064, William rescued him from another noble intent on holding him for ransom. Harold then resided at William's court for a lengthy period, even joining William on campaign against Conan, Duke of Brittany. At some point during his stay, Harold apparently swore fealty to William and promised to support his bid for the English throne.

William, who was the grandnephew of Emma of Normandy, the mother of the last king—Edward the Confessor—considered his claim as good as anyone's. Moreover, he was not one to easily accept defeat. The bastard son of Duke Robert I of Normandy, he had been designated by his father as his heir despite the circumstance of his birth. When Duke Robert failed to return from a pilgrimage, William at the tender age of seven inherited his title. His survival to adulthood is enough to make one believe in miracles. In one memorable instance, William escaped one of the many plots on his life only because the assassin stabbed the child in the next bed and missed him. He grew up of average height (five feet eight inches), but powerfully built. Throughout his early life he had to struggle, first for survival and later to secure his inheritance. When William emerged from his minority, his Norman duchy was collapsing around him. Ducal authority had all but collapsed, and it would take many years of war to reassert it. William luckily found an early ally in Henry I, king of France (1031–1060). Together they defeated a gathering of Norman barons at the Battle of Val-ès-Dunes in 1047. While the barons remained strong, they lacked the ability to act in concert. Over the following years, William brought them fully under his control, until by 1053 King Henry began to feel threatened by his vassal's growing power. In 1054 and 1057, Henry along with Geoffrey II, Count of Anjou, invaded Normandy. Both times William repulsed them with heavy losses. Fortunately, William was spared further assaults by the death of both tormentors in 1060. By then Normandy was firmly within his grasp, and his wars now aimed at expanding his domains.

But these early trials taught him a number of lessons. First among them was ensuring that those close to him were fanatically loyal. He also learned the fine art of managing men who were nearly as powerful and cunning as he was. Still, for many years he had his hands full with the local Norman lords, who were an unruly and quarrelsome lot even during the best of times. Keeping them in line took a man with a strong arm, a ruthless nature, and a keen political sense. Respect was essential, but in those troubled times so was a streak of cruelty, for fear often worked wonders in aligning the nobles' interests with William's. Although his cruelty was not often on display, when it was William left a lasting impression. One notable episode involved the population of Alençon, who had the temerity to insult him publicly about his bastardy during a siege of their town. When the town fell, William had the leading citizens paraded out and their hands and feet cut off. After that, other besieged towns and castles typically surrendered upon his approach.

When Edward the Confessor died, William was the undisputed ruler of the most powerful and unified region on the Continent. Assisting him was a small group of a dozen nobles, including his two half-brothers, Robert of Mortain and Odo, bishop of Bayeux. These were men "inured to war," led by a man well equipped to be their leader, "bursting with confidence, [who] could make and take jokes, and accept or reject advice," as a recent history of Britain describes him. Above all he was a warrior, and one who had set his sights on the English crown.

Soon after Harold was declared king of England, William began preparations for an invasion. As a first step he sought the support of Pope Alexander II, who rewarded him with his blessing and a consecrated papal banner as a sign of God's favor. Even with the pope's blessing, recruiting an invasion army proved difficult. There was nothing in the feudal code that required vassal lords to invade a distant land. With so much to lose in Normandy, many were in no hurry to attack a country as strong as England, where the prospective gains might be great, but the risks were greater. William had to call three councils before he had worn down the resistance of his nobles sufficiently to gain their support.

By early August 1066, the invasion force had mostly mustered, including numerous mercenaries and adventurers who hoped to profit from victory. The army encamped near Dives-sur-Mer, where the fleet was also assembling. Here, William waited for over a month for the winds to turn. It was here also, as much as in battle, that William demonstrated his true genius for war, as a master of logistics. To centralize the distribution of food, he had a huge granary constructed. Moreover, he arranged for the shipment of supplies to feed at least twelve thousand men and perhaps as many as two thousand horses for over a month. The men alone consumed more than twenty tons of food daily, while the horses needed twenty-five tons of grain and hay a day. As no disease was reported in the camp, William appears to have devised procedures for getting rid of the thousands of tons of garbage and raw sewage an army creates daily—a substantial achievement for the era.

BACK IN ENGLAND, Harold was not idle. As William mustered his forces, Harold mobilized his army and navy along England's southern coast. But Harold was on the horns of a dilemma. William was not his only concern—his own brother Tostig had been deposed from the earldom of Northumbria in 1065, and since then he had been a constant thorn in Harold's side. In May 1066, Tostig, with sixty ships, ravaged much of England's southern coast. Forced to evacuate his base at Sandwich in Kent, Tostig retreated along the east coast, ravaging as he went. Repulsed by the two northern earls Morcar and Edwin, he took the remnants of his force—twelve ships—to Norway, where he allied himself with the formidable Harald Hardrada, the Viking king. Hardrada, who had been fighting since his teenage years, was one of the most renowned warriors of the Viking world. In what was likely his first pitched battle at Stiklestad in 1030, Hardrada had been seriously wounded. Afterward he made his way to Russia and eventually to Byzantium, where he became a member of the Varangian Guard—an elite force of Vikings in the service of the Byzantine emperor. By 1047, Hardrada was back in Norway, where he seized the throne as his birthright. In 1065, just before Tostig's arrival, Hardrada was at peace, but he still possessed a powerful army that was eager for booty and land. Tostig could not have arrived at a better time.

While Tostig plotted and William gathered his forces, Harold and the English army waited. All summer the fleet and probably at least a quarter of the *fyrd,* the equivalent of a national militia, stood in readiness. In early September, however, with the militia's food depleted and the two-month term of service its men owed their king fulfilled, Harold was forced to disband it. Soon thereafter, the fleet reached the end of its tether as well, and by September 10 it was back in London and starting to demobilize. With no fleet patrolling the English Channel and the coast denuded of troops, England lay wide open. William, probably informed by spies, began to stir. The Norman army left Dives-sur-Mer for the port of Saint-Valery-sur-Somme, about 160 miles up the coast and closer to his proposed landing sites at Pevensey and Hastings.

But the first strike did not come from William. On September 15, Harald Hardrada moved up the Humber River and landed at Riccall, ten miles south of York. The northern earls Edwin and Morcar had joined forces to oppose him, and the next day, at Fulford Gate, the two earls, with perhaps five thousand men, met the similarly sized Viking army. In a battle lacking in elegance but replete with savagery, two solid lines of men faced each other until the English finally charged. At first the English had the upper hand, pushing back the Viking flanks, where Hardrada had placed his least reliable men. At this crucial juncture, Hardrada unfurled his war banner, a white standard with a black raven, named Landeyda—Land Ravager. As the flag fluttered in the breeze, Hardrada ordered his personal guard forward. The Norse army took heart and attacked with renewed ferocity. Amid a great slaughter the English line broke, with many drowning in a nearby swamp as the Vikings pursued in a killing fury.

Hardrada entered York but withdrew later in the day, returning to his ships to celebrate his victory. From his perspective, he had just defeated the main English army and fully expected an immediate surrender. At the least, he assumed he would receive northern England to run as a new Danelaw. To ensure the defeated northern earls did not cause any further trouble, Hardrada demanded five hundred hostages. This was agreed to, and Stamford Bridge was selected for the surrender ceremony and the turning over of the hostages, which was scheduled for September 25. Until then, the Norse army sat idle. It was a fateful mistake.

Hardrada took two thirds of his men with him to Stamford Bridge, leaving the rest at Riccall to guard his ships. When he arrived there were no hostages. Instead, he found an army coming down the road—marching hard. His ally, Tostig, claimed it was his own supporters coming to greet him, and at first Hardrada believed him; but they were both soon disabused of that notion. Almost unbelievably, Harold had arrived on the scene from southern England and was now rushing to do battle with the Viking horde.

In the face of the Viking threat, Harold acted with decisive vigor. He had disbanded his army on September 8, the same day as Hardrada's arrival. When news of the invasion reached him, the only troops available were his professional housecarls. It took a full week to gather a force sufficient to make an impression on the Norsemen. But once his army was assembled, Harold set off on one of the great forced marches in history, covering over twenty-five miles a day. By September 24, Harold was at Tadcaster, only fifteen miles from York. Here, he learned of the disaster of Fulford Gate, but rather than halting to assess the damage, he went straight on to York. The next morning, Harold marched out with an army that had swelled with recruits all along its line of march.

As the English closed, Hardrada found himself in a weak position with a significant number of his men back at the ships. As for the several thousand he brought with him, most had left their armor behind. Moreover, Harold had caught him by surprise, and his Viking force had scant time to form for battle. According to tradition, the Vikings bought some time when Harold came forth to parley. He supposedly offered Tostig a third of the kingdom if he returned to the fold. When Tostig asked what Harold was offering Hardrada, Harold replied, "Six feet of fine English soil, or a bit more as he is such a big man." Tostig replied that he was unwilling to be seen by the Norsemen as the man who deserted their king in the face of a fight.

Immediately after talks ended, Harold ordered an assault. The English first struck the small force Hardrada had left behind on the far side of the Stamford Bridge. That force had but one purpose: to die hard and by so doing to delay the English long enough to allow Hardrada to set his lines. Once that intrepid band was exterminated, the English were further stymied by a massive Norseman in full armor, wielding a two-handed ax. Supposedly, this medieval Horatius killed forty men before an English warrior in a boat under the bridge thrust a spear through an opening in the planks, killing the Norse hero.

Harold's men swarmed across the bridge and fell on the Vikings. Hardrada had placed his men in a circle with his Land Ravager standard at the center. The battle was vicious. Strong men, their bloodlust raging, hacked at one another with ax and sword. The Vikings, without armor to protect them, fell by the hundreds. Finally, they were unable to withstand the onslaught and their line broke. Hardrada, realizing the battle was lost, went berserk. Flinging himself into the midst of his enemies, he swung his broadax in great, savage circles before an arrow through the throat finally felled him. Harold picked up the fallen Land Ravager and offered peace to Tostig and the remaining Norsemen. The offer was refused, songs were sung, and the Vikings came on in a final desperate charge.

By now, the rest of the Viking host was arriving from the ships at Riccall. They had double-timed the entire distance, carrying their shields and wearing chain mail. Some were so exhausted, they died on reaching the field; most were too tired to make the supreme effort required to break an English shield wall. Still, the slaughter went on until nightfall, when the surviving Vikings broke and ran for their ships. At some point during the struggle, an ax found its mark, killing Tostig. Harold took no time to mourn his brother as he led his army in pursuit of the fleeing Vikings. Realizing that the Norse threat was over for his lifetime, Harold allowed those Vikings still alive to return to Norway. They were able to man only twenty-four of their original three hundred ships.

It was a great victory, but Harold's army had also suffered grievous losses that he could ill afford. As his army recovered, word came that William's army had landed at Pevensey and was already busily ravaging the surrounding countryside. Harold gathered his housecarls and hastily marched south.

ON SEPTEMBER 28, the favorable winds for which William had been waiting finally arrived. The Norman army had first landed at Pevensey, a prosperous market town, but William soon moved his base to Hastings. Once there, his army began to lay waste to the surrounding country. As this region was part of Harold's personal holdings, William calculated that such depredations would bring his enemy to battle as rapidly as possible. William needed a quick and decisive battle; if Harold avoided fighting and opted instead to bottle up the Norman army at Hastings while using his seven hundred ships to cut off escape, William was doomed. Supplies would not last long, and the

Normans would find little in the countryside they had so recently devastated. It was a supreme gamble, but William knew his man.

After another forced march, Harold paused for five or six days in London to reorganize his tired army and gather new troops. His brother Gyrth advised Harold to wait until they had gathered an overwhelming force, while in the meantime burning the land between Hastings and London. If forced to advance across a wasteland devoid of food, the Norman army would find itself reduced to a miserable state and become easy prey for Harold's host. If Harold insisted on fighting, then Gyrth offered to lead the army. If he won, all would be well. If he lost, Harold would be free to raise another army and continue the struggle. Impatient for action, Harold ignored his brother's wise counsel and marched south with a fraction of the force he might have mustered if only he had tarried just a few weeks longer. William was already marching north to meet him.

On the morning of October 14, Harold positioned his army along the ridge in front of Battle Hill, astride the Roman road leading from Hastings to London. It was a strong position, only eight hundred yards long and flanked by heavily forested slopes that fell away rapidly on each flank, making flanking attacks impractical. To the front, the ground was wet and soggy, although not quite a marsh. If William wanted to march on London, he would have to march through Harold, and the only way to do that was by frontal assault.

Harold's army, probably numbering between six thousand and eight thousand men, formed their shield wall along the crest of the ridge. With locked shields, Harold's front line would have been approximately one thousand men long and six to eight men deep. This first line would have consisted of his housecarls and the most reliable troops of the other Anglo-Saxon lords, including those of his two brothers—Gyrth and Leofwine—and the best of the *fyrd*. Behind them, six or seven ranks deep, stood the remainder of the *fyrd,* possibly with some archers in the rear. Harold himself, surrounded by handpicked housecarls, set his standard behind the center of the English line.

William's army approached in column, swinging into battle formation almost within arrow shot of Harold's army. The Bretton division went to the left, William's Normans occupied the center, and

Franco-Flemish forces positioned themselves on the right. All three divisions assumed the same formation of three lines: archers to the front, followed by heavy infantry, with squadrons of cavalry in the rear.

As William's army assembled, the Anglo-Saxons started their unnerving war cry—*"Ut, ut!"* ("Out, out!")—as they beat their axes and swords against their shields. The din must have been frightful, as was the appearance of the bearded, battle-hardened Anglo-Saxon warriors. But William's army, seemingly unimpressed with the threat, spent two hours methodically moving from the column of march into battle formation.

When all was ready, a single man, possibly a minstrel named Taillefer, rode out in front of the Norman host and began juggling his sword. Both armies watched the display in silence. When his first act was over, he began singing *The Song of Roland,* that epic French story of battle and glory. Song completed, he charged the English line, supposedly killing three men before being struck down himself.

The preliminaries complete, William signaled the archers to advance. Instantly, the waiting Anglo-Saxon army doubled and locked their shields together, creating a human fortress. A thousand archers, possibly more, marked their targets, drew back their bowstrings, and

Bayeux Tapestry: William the Conqueror showing his troops that he lives
World History Archive/Alamy

released. The arrows hissed up the hill, some of them flying harm-lessly overhead, most of them striking a shield, but precious few doing any damage. So it went until the archers had expended roughly twenty-five thousand arrows.

Their arrows gone, the archers fell back. The Saxon line undou-bled. With one swipe of their axes, the thousand men in the front rank removed the arrows piercing the front of their shields. Then it came again, in a thunderous roar: *"Ut, ut!"* Thousands of men shouted and steel clanged on steel as the Anglo-Saxons defiantly announced to the Normans that their line held.

As the archers retreated, William's infantry slowly advanced. They were met by a fusillade of spears, rocks, and throwing axes. For a few moments they paused, shielding themselves from the deadly hail, but then they came on again. The fighting became a long and brutal slug-ging match. In places, a housecarl would step forward to swing his two-handed battleax with deadly effect. In other places, a Norman infantryman hooked the top of a shield and pulled it down, exposing the bearer to the sword and spear thrusts of other Normans. For a mo-ment there would be a gap in the Saxon front line, but it took a brave man to push into it. Any who did found the shield wall closing behind him as the rear Saxon ranks cut down the Norman before unceremo-niously throwing his body out of the formation, still shouting, *"Ut, ut!"*

Seeing that his infantry had failed to make an impression on the Anglo-Saxon line, William sent his cavalry forward. Riding through the infantry, they met the same hailstorm of missiles that had greeted the first Norman assault. Worse, because they had to advance uphill, the impetus of their charge was slowed. Moreover, much of William's infantry did not fall back to make room for the cavalry charge. No-where were the Saxons forced to endure the full shock of a Norman cavalry charge. So the battle continued much as before, only now some of those whacking swords and maces hammering against the shield wall were falling from those on horseback. Typical of the close-range battles of the ancient and medieval periods, the fighting and killing continued until one side could no longer stand the horror. This time it was the Bretons on William's left flank who broke first. As they streamed to the rear, the Saxons followed. Seeing the Bretons break caused the Normans in the center to start stepping back also, followed by the French on the right.

William, recognizing the danger to his line, advanced to the point of greatest danger. Before he could get there, his horse was killed and he was tossed to the ground. Rumors of his death spread, and an orderly retreat was soon on the edge of becoming a rout. Here was the crisis of the battle. If Harold had ordered a general attack along the whole line, something he could do only by advancing his own battle standard for all to see, there is little doubt the invaders would have been swept away. That he failed to do so is almost inexplicable.

William, on the other hand, acted decisively. After mounting another horse, he took off his helmet and rode along the line, roaring that he lived and that the army's only safety lay in victory. Through strenuous efforts, and assisted by his brother Odo, the ferocious bishop of Bayeux, William re-formed his center and right and got the Norman cavalry in hand.

Before him stood his first great opportunity. The Saxons from Harold's right were still chasing after the retreating Bretons. Without the protection of a formed shield wall, these men were easy prey for a Norman cavalry charge. William personally led the charge into their midst, unleashing a wholesale slaughter. It was during this fighting that Harold's brothers Gyrth and Leofwine fell. For the Normans, the crisis had passed.

BOTH SIDES PAUSED. William needed to re-form his shaken troops, while Harold had to thin out his left and center in order to re-form his right flank, which had suffered grievously as a result of its impetuous pursuit of the Bretons. That the Saxon shield wall had held against the initial Norman attacks must have given Harold pride and confidence. At the same time, the loss of his two brothers was of grave concern. As a large part of his army consisted of men sworn to support his brothers, Harold must have wondered how well and for how long they would fight with their lords dead. Moreover, Saxon losses had been heavy, particularly among the housecarls of the front rank. Unwilling to trust in the fighting qualities of the *fyrd,* Harold ordered his line shortened so that he could still man the front rank with housecarls. As the line shortened, the number of men in the rear ranks swelled, presenting an irresistible target for archers firing at a high angle, which William's archers soon proceeded to do.

William had problems of his own. It was getting late in the day, and night would end the fighting. He could not afford a draw, for his army would only get smaller, while Harold's would daily grow larger. Still, even though it seemed that a decisive victory was as far away as ever, he now had some advantages he had not possessed earlier in the day. His archers had been resupplied with arrows and were now inflicting severe damage on the rear ranks of the Saxon army. In addition, he had seen that significant portions of the Anglo-Saxon line could be tempted to break formation in pursuit of fleeing portions of his army. By attacking and then retreating, he could draw them out to be massacred by his heavy cavalry. Finally, the shortening of the Saxon line gave him a chance to work some of his forces around either flank or both, placing them on the ridgeline and avoiding the necessity of fighting uphill.

The fighting continued. By late afternoon, the Saxon line had contracted into a compact mass fighting in three directions, as the Normans gained the ridgeline. Almost surrounded, the *fyrd* lost morale, and for the first time men began to desert Harold's standard. Still, despite desertions and accumulating losses, especially from the steady barrage of arrows, the Saxon line held, and darkness was rapidly approaching. William, on the other hand, finally had a good position, but his men were exhausted and their horses blown. The situation called for one more supreme effort, but were the Normans capable of mounting it?

William gathered the best of his cavalry and ordered his archers to redouble their efforts. As the archers did their deadly work, the Breton, French, and Norman infantry renewed their assaults, and once again the terrible violence of strong men hacking at one another with deadly intent approached a crescendo. Unlike earlier in the day, however, this time William's men were pushing back the flanks. And thanks to a series of feigned retreats followed by vicious cavalry counterattacks, the Normans were inflicting enormous losses and beginning to open gaps in the Saxon front. Like Alexander at Gaugamela, William waited for his moment. Then, spotting a point of entry in the weak-

Bayeux Tapestry: King Harold dies from an arrow in the eye
GL Archive/Alamy

ening Saxon line, he led his Norman cavalry forward. This time the Normans smashed through the Saxon line and struck at the elite force of housecarls around Harold's standard. There, the king of England was found dead, either killed by an arrow through his eye or cut down during the vicious fighting around his standard soon after William's final charge.

With Harold's death, the remains of the shield wall crumbled away. William was victorious, but his army had suffered severe damage. He took it back to Hastings to rest and await reinforcements from the Continent. When no deputies arrived from London to surrender the country and give him homage, William set out again.

WILLIAM DID NOT march directly on London. Instead he proceeded along the coast toward the great port city of Dover, which opened its gates to him. His line of march is easily tracked in the *Domesday Book,* which recorded the devastation his army wrought along its path, much of which was still visible decades later. In all, William's march from Hastings covered 350 miles. When he finally arrived in London, the surviving Saxon earls surrendered the city without a fight.

William was crowned king of England on Christmas Day 1066. His coronation did not end the fighting. For the next several years, there were sporadic Saxon revolts against William's rule, which the Normans put down ferociously The most serious revolt took place in the north in 1068, prompting a destructive march known as "the harrying of the north," as William laid waste to large swaths of England's northern counties. By 1070, the Normans had crushed the worst of the opposition and Norman castles dotted the countryside, stifling further attempts at protest.

Saxon England was gone. In its place, a new country and people were forged, as Norman England slowly became just England. There is little doubt that the change had a profound effect on the future of Europe and the world. That England would give up its insular outlook and project itself out into the greater world was not a foregone conclusion. The great tides of history did not require that a small island on the fringes of the civilized world propel itself into the forefront of events. That it did so was a direct result of Norman dynamism. But that dynamism would have meant little without the well-developed political and economic structures established by the Anglo-Saxons. It was the centuries-long fusion of these two cultures into a single people that permitted English greatness, a greatness that would never have manifested itself if William had not conquered at Hastings.

THE SPANISH ARMADA

Miracle at Sea

1588

FOR OVER A CENTURY AFTER THE FALL OF CONSTANTINOPLE IN 1453, the borders of the Christian West faced nearly constant assault from the expansionary Ottoman Empire. Toward the middle of the sixteenth century, a combination of Christian victories in the defense of Vienna (1529), the defense of Malta (1565), and the Battle of Lepanto (1571) halted the Ottoman advance, at least for a time. In accordance with established European patterns, the Western states took advantage of the respite from Ottoman conquest to begin a new round of internecine warfare. Most of these wars were precipitated by Hapsburg Spain trying either to expand its control or to hold on to what it had. Using the wealth gathered from the New World, Spain launched its troops throughout much of Western Europe. Two nations were a constant drain on Spain's blood and treasure during this period. The first was the Netherlands, which fought the Eighty Years' War to free itself of Spanish rule. The second was tiny England, which since its retreat from the Continent in the wake of the Hundred Years' War had remained only a bit player in European affairs. By the middle of the sixteenth century, however, England was once again taking tentative steps to both commercially enrich itself and make its growing power felt on the world stage. In doing so, it could not help but come up against Spanish interests. By 1588, English interference with Spanish commerce and its involvement in the war with the Netherlands, combined with other long-simmering political and religious tensions, had pushed King Philip II of Spain to the limits of his endurance.

Philip's opportunity to deal with England came soon after the Battle of Lepanto. Victory at Lepanto not only halted Ottoman expansion, it also irrevocably changed the balance of power in the Mediterranean in favor of the Christian West. The Turkish threat had not vanished, but the Ottoman threat was reduced to such a degree that Spain's Philip was able to reallocate assets to other trouble spots throughout his far-flung empire. Foremost among his troubles was the Protestant revolt in the Netherlands. It was already three years old when the Christians halted the Turks at Lepanto. Thanks to English support, innovative financial methods that allowed the Netherlands to spend far beyond its means, and the tenacity of the Dutch themselves, the revolt had become a significant threat to Spanish rule. As the revolt wore on—and it was to continue for almost another eighty years—it was English aid to the Dutch that most annoyed Philip.

Determined to crush English power, not only because it was a burgeoning threat, but also because Philip despised the Protestant faith that held England in its grasp, Spain sent forth its mighty Armada. The Spanish Armada's objective was nothing less than the complete conquest of England. That done, the majority of the population would, through the "tender" ministrations of the Inquisition, be convinced to abandon their heretical Protestant ways and return to communion with the Roman Catholic Church. This was a great mission indeed, one that befitted Philip, Christianity's most powerful king. The great Armada was to have the assistance of the Duke of Parma's army, already assembled in Flanders, where it was taking a respite from the war with the Dutch and awaiting the Armada's arrival. If these battle-hardened veterans of the Netherlands war were able to link up with the Armada and cross into England, they would likely roll over the green, poorly trained, and barely equipped militias that formed the backbone of Queen Elizabeth's home guard, and England would be lost.

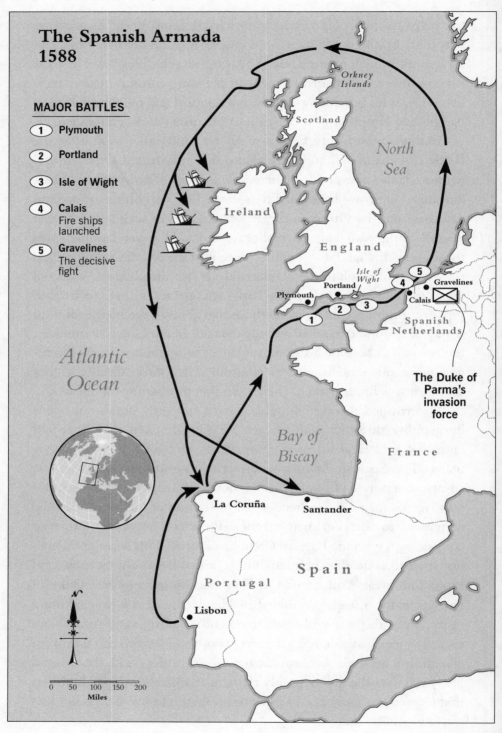

The Spanish Armada 1588

MAJOR BATTLES

1. **Plymouth**

2. **Portland**

3. **Isle of Wight**

4. **Calais**
   Fire ships launched

5. **Gravelines**
   The decisive fight

Orkney Islands

Scotland

North Sea

Ireland

England

Isle of Wight

Portland

Plymouth

Gravelines

Calais

Spanish Netherlands

The Duke of Parma's invasion force

Atlantic Ocean

Bay of Biscay

France

La Coruña

Santander

Spain

Portugal

Lisbon

0 50 100 150 200
Miles

* * *

THE GREAT CONTEST between England and Spain had been nearly averted years earlier when Philip married England's Queen Mary Tudor in 1554. For a short period afterward, Philip had lived in England with his new wife. Then, in 1555, his father, Charles V, renounced the Hapsburg throne and divided the empire between his son Philip and his brother, Ferdinand. Upon ascending the Spanish throne, Philip departed for his new kingdom, leaving the unpopular "Bloody Mary" alone in England. Their marriage failed to produce a male heir, which would have eventually led to the Catholic son of a Hapsburg ruling England. Fully occupied by the pressures of ruling a large and troublesome kingdom, Philip returned to England only once more, but not to produce an heir. Rather, he hoped to entice Mary into joining him in a war against France. She agreed to follow him into war, and as a result England lost the coastal port of Calais (1558), its last possession on the Continent. The loss destroyed whatever prestige Mary still possessed. But that was of limited consequence, as Mary, already in poor health, probably from uterine cancer, was struck down by an influenza epidemic in 1558. Upon her death, Philip ceased to be the king of England, and Elizabeth I, a Protestant, ascended the throne.

For some time, despite his religious differences with the English queen, Philip seemed willing to work with Elizabeth. His alternative was to support the claim of the Scottish queen, Mary Stuart, to the English throne. Many, including most English Catholics, considered her claim at least as strong as Elizabeth's. But Mary came with one terrible negative. She was a Guise, and that family was now acting as the power brokers for those contending for the French throne. In the worst-case but all-too-plausible scenario, a Guise would step out of the background to become king of France. As far as scenarios went, helping Mary gain the English throne only to see her ally herself with Spain's current mortal enemy, France, stood at the top of Philip's list of strategic dilemmas best avoided.

Also, after losing the English crown, Philip had much else to occupy his attention. Although the Ottoman threat had receded, Spain remained embroiled in France's civil war as well as incessant quarrels within its own Italian possessions. Moreover, a huge part of its military might was locked in a death embrace with the Dutch that had become a multigenerational quagmire. All of these conflicts were a constant drain on Philip's treasury, rarely on a sound footing at the best of times. Given its far-flung interests and commitments, Spain always outran its revenues. This was the natural result of a tax structure that almost killed off Spain's private industry, along with the fact that its empire, except for the Americas, always cost more than the revenues collected in taxes. Even the 350 tons of silver and several tons of gold that annually made their way across the Atlantic from America were typically pledged to the king's creditors before arrival. In fact, the king was entitled to only about 20 percent of the wealth coming out of America, and after that amount had passed through several layers of corrupt middlemen, little remained to finance the affairs of state. So the king found himself continually at the mercy of his bankers. At the start of Philip's reign, this meant the super-rich Fugger

Queen Elizabeth I   *Archivart/Alamy*

family, until successive Hapsburg defaults destroyed their wealth, after which Genoese bankers stepped forward.

Spain's financial weakness, coupled with its mortal fear that commercial competitors would muscle into its protected markets or, worse, make inroads into the highly profitable Americas, led the Spanish to limit the access of any other nation to their home markets as well as their colonial empire. This attempt at monopolizing Atlantic trade grated on an English nation grasping for its share of global riches. Foremost among those who hoped to gain at Spain's expense were the adventurers dubbed "the Sea Dogs," John Hawkins and Francis Drake. Hawkins's first two ventures were so profitable that even the queen invested in the third. For his 1567 voyage, Hawkins took ten ships, two of which belonged to the queen. This fleet, however, ran into a powerful Spanish squadron and was overwhelmed within the close confines of the port San Juan de Ulúa on the Mexican coast. Only two English ships limped home, one commanded by Hawkins, the other by Drake.

They arrived at a delicate moment in Anglo-Spanish relations. French Protestant privateers had recently attacked five Spanish ships carrying forty thousand pounds in gold and silver meant to pay Parma's Spanish armies in the Netherlands. The Spanish ships had run for the security of an English port and requested Elizabeth's protection. This she granted. Soon afterward, the queen learned of the destruction of her ships at San Juan de Ulúa. Realizing that the returns from the Hawkins expedition were forfeit, she ordered the Spanish gold seized and the ships secured. Spain, following the advice of its minister in England, ordered the seizure of all English property in the Netherlands and Spain. Furious, Elizabeth broke off diplomatic relations with Spain. For all practical purposes, Spain and England were at war from 1570 onward. Only Philip's preoccupation with other, more immediate crises kept him from striking immediately, although he never ceased looking for schemes to damage Elizabeth's interests.

Upon receiving intelligence detailing Philip's plans, Elizabeth took off the velvet gloves. She allowed thousands of refugees from Philip's domains to enter England and began sending money and later troops to aid the rebels in the Netherlands, as well as those Protestants working against Spanish interests in France. More troubling from the

Spanish perspective, Elizabeth unleashed her "Sea Dogs." Led by the likes of Hawkins and Drake, the English privateers made eleven major and enormously profitable expeditions against Spain's interests between 1572 and 1577. In one memorable raid, Drake took the *Golden Hind* around the world, returning in 1580 with one hundred tons of Spanish silver and one hundred pounds of gold.

In 1574, an incensed Philip ordered the assembly of a massive armada to strike at England. However, preparations were slow, and the Spanish abandoned the enterprise when the plague struck down most of the fleet's crews. Another expedition in 1580 aimed at setting off a major insurrection in Ireland. It achieved some minor success before descending into ignominy. A Spanish-papal force seized a small section of the Irish coast in Smerwick Bay, where they constructed the Castello del Oro and waited for reinforcements from Catholic Europe. Help never came. Instead, a naval force led by Sir William Winter, with six ships that would later see action against the great Spanish Armada, and a small army led by the intrepid Sir Walter Raleigh besieged the garrison. Following three days of intense bombardment, the defenders surrendered after being promised fair terms. Nevertheless, once they had vacated the fort, the English massacred all but fifteen, sparing those worth the most ransom.

Spain did have its own successes. In 1580, the last legitimate heir to the Portuguese crown died. Through his mother, a Portuguese princess, Philip had a claim to the crown. There were other claimants, but they did not possess the one thing that Philip had—an army. In a Renaissance forerunner of the Blitzkrieg, two Spanish armies, one led by the aging Duke of Alba and the other by the Duke of Medina Sidonia, smashed across Portugal. With the support of a Spanish fleet commanded by Álvaro de Bazán, the Marquis of Santa Cruz, hero of the Battle of Lepanto, the army captured Lisbon in late August. In less than two months, one of Europe's great powers ceased to exist as an independent state. By adding Portugal to its dominions, Spain not only gained a vast Atlantic empire, but also inherited Portugal's oceangoing navy. Until this point, Spain had been largely a Mediterranean power, but the galleys that dominated there were of minimal value in the Atlantic. Although Spain possessed a fleet of sail-powered galleons, they were no match for the fast racer-type warships produced by the English. With the addition of nearly a dozen sturdily built and heavily gunned Portuguese galleons, Spain became a true Atlantic naval power.

That was not the end of Spanish triumphs. Under the capable leadership of the Duke of Parma, whom Philip had sent to the Netherlands in 1578, Spanish armies had by 1580 captured most of Flanders and were set to invade the Dutch strongholds in Barbant. By 1585, Ypres, Bruges, and Ghent had fallen, and it seemed that Parma was unstoppable. Worse, in 1584 Spanish-paid assassins succeeded in killing William of Orange. Without his inspiring leadership, Dutch morale and prospects sank to a low ebb. Parma was not one to let an advantage slip away. In the following year, his army captured the great port of Antwerp. During the battle for that great city, the Spanish for the first time encountered a new and horrifying weapon—the hellburner—that was to have a tremendous effect on the outcome of the Armada battle.

Hellburners were a special type of fireship designed by an Italian engineer, Federigo Giambelli. Within their hulls, their builders emplaced two specially fitted oblong chambers filled with seven thousand pounds of high-quality gunpowder. All the space around these containers was filled with iron shards. Although they failed to save Antwerp, the explosion of one—the *Hoop*—killed eight hundred Spanish troops and was heard fifty miles away. The fact that the designer of these infernal weapons was in England when the Armada sailed terrified Spanish commanders. Fireships were always a danger to a fleet, but the hellburners brought a novel and horrifying dimension to this old threat, one that many thought might endanger the fleet's existence.

As the tide turned in Spain's favor in the Netherlands, the situation in France took a turn for the worse, at least from Elizabeth's perspective. Francis, Duke of Alençon and Anjou and heir to the throne, died unexpectedly in 1584, ending the direct male line. Henry of Navarre, a Protestant and the leader of the Huguenot cause, was next in line but was considered unfit by most of Catholic France owing to his religion. Rather than allow a Protestant to mount the throne, the Catholics formed "the League," with Guise at its head. The French Wars of Religion, which had appeared to be running out of steam, reignited with a new fury. Philip, unwilling to see France ruled by a Protestant, formed an alliance with the League and Guise. They signed a treaty at Joinville in which Spain promised to support Guise's uncle Charles, the cardinal of Bourbon, in his claim to the throne and provide the League with a huge cash subsidy every year.

When Philip added an embargo on all English ships to this list, it turned the tide of opinion among Elizabeth's councillors. For the first time, the majority of the queen's advisers were willing to risk all-out war. And they found the queen ready to heed their advice. Realizing that if England failed to stem the tide of Spanish success, Philip's power would be irresistible, Elizabeth prepared her countermoves. The Netherlands was placed under English protection, and the always parsimonious queen began releasing greater funds to the Dutch cause. But this time she went far beyond her previous hands-off support and promised to place an army on the Continent. Shortly before Christmas 1585, Robert Dudley, Earl of Leicester, landed at Flushing and began engaging in active operations against the Duke of Parma. Elizabeth also began supplying substantial financial aid to Henry of Navarre's French force, going so far as paying the cost of one of Henry's two major field armies.

For the first half of the 1580s, Spain and England drifted toward war without ever leaping off the precipice. Two events put them on a collision course that made all-out war inevitable. The first came in two parts. Elizabeth's highly effective secret service, led by her spymaster, Francis Walsingham, had cracked the Spanish codes and was reading a number of messages sent from Spain to Catholics in England. Through these, Walsingham thwarted a number of Spanish attempts on Elizabeth's life. These assassination attempts, in turn, unleashed Elizabeth's fury. In response, in late 1585 she dispatched Sir Francis Drake and twenty-five ships to attack the Spanish coast. As Drake took two of the queen's royal warships, Elizabeth clearly announced her support of the Sea Dogs. For almost two weeks Drake raided the coast, combining an insult to the Spanish crown with substantial destruction of Spanish property. Philip, feeling the sting of loss and insult, promptly began preparations for war.

When Philip decided for war, a part of his plan was to support a Catholic insurrection to depose Elizabeth and place her imprisoned rival, Mary, Queen of Scots, on the throne. This plan was ruined when Walsingham directly implicated Mary in the Babington Plot—another attempt on Elizabeth's life. After nineteen years of holding her cousin imprisoned in various castles and manors, the queen was convinced by her advisers that Mary was too dangerous to be allowed to live and was persuaded to sign Mary's execution warrant in February 1587. Mary's beheading enraged Catholic Europe and was particularly galling for the devout Philip, who always viewed himself as the defender of the faith. Her death also forced Philip to change his objective and strategy for the upcoming campaign. Unable to find another suitable claimant to the English throne, Philip decided on a full-scale invasion to depose Elizabeth, place his daughter Isabella on the throne, and bring England back into communion with the Roman Catholic Church.

PHILIP PLACED Santa Cruz in charge of assembling the fleet. Never one to think small, Santa Cruz told Philip that success would require 150 ships totaling 77,250 tons, supported by 400 smaller vessels. Of these, at least 40 would be the powerful Spanish and Portuguese fighting galleons. Once he had fought his way through the English naval defenses, Santa Cruz claimed, he would require fifty-five thousand frontline troops, most of them veterans, to conquer England. According to Santa Cruz, the whole enterprise would cost four million ducats, an estimate that was off by a wide margin.

Philip's other top military commander, the Duke of Parma, had a simpler plan in mind. He advocated detaching approximately thirty thousand men from the Army of Flanders and sneaking them across the English Channel on barges. Parma was sure that he could make the crossing in twelve hours, which would be followed by an immediate march on London. He did not expect any resistance that could long withstand his veterans. As most of England's experienced soldiers were already on the Continent with the Earl of Leicester, Parma's analysis appears correct, assuming the Spanish could maintain secrecy in assembling the barges and the army.

In the event, Philip decided on a combination of the two plans. A great fleet would set out from Iberia loaded with soldiers. However, while these soldiers would be available for operations onshore, their primary duty would be to board and seize English warships. This fleet would rendezvous with Parma's army on the Flanders coast and escort it across the English Channel. To ensure sufficient troops were on hand for a successful invasion, while simultaneously keeping the pressure on the Dutch, Philip recruited a new mercenary army in Italy and sent it north along the famous Spanish Road. Just how the fleet would coordinate its arrival with Parma's army, given the abysmal communications systems of the age, remained, as were so many things, "in the confident hope of a miracle." The miracle never came.

As the Spanish Armada assembled, preparations were hampered by the two great curses of Philip's reign: a constant shortage of funds and Sir Francis Drake. For most of 1586 and early the following year, Elizabeth was hopeful that a peace agreement with Spain could be hammered out. She was unaware that her ambassador in Paris was on Spain's payroll and feeding her a stream of false reports about Spain's peaceful intentions. Moreover, she failed to recognize that Parma was toying with her peace negotiators in Flanders so as to buy time for the Armada to complete its preparations. Then, inexplicably, in March 1587 she ordered Drake to sea with orders to do as much damage to the Spanish fleet as possible. Never one to lose time, Drake completed his preparations and immediately put to sea. It was not a minute too early. Soon after his ships set sail, Elizabeth had second thoughts. Fortunately for England, her messenger never caught up with Drake.

On April 29, 1587, Drake led sixteen warships and seven pinnaces into Cádiz. He found sixty large ships and a host of smaller ones. While beating off rather ineffectual defensive efforts, the English spent that night and the next day smashing up Spanish ships and supply stores. Upon the arrival of the Duke of Medina Sidonia with six thousand men and additional cannons, Drake made a leisurely retreat, but not before fully provisioning his fleet with captured Spanish stores. Behind him he left twenty-four wrecked Spanish ships and tons of destroyed supplies destined for the Armada. As Drake said of the exploit, he "had singed the king's beard." Adding further injury to those already inflicted, Drake sat off the coast, raiding and destroying any Spanish ship foolish enough to try running his blockade. Before heading back to England, he captured the *São Filipe,* returning from the Indies laden with treasure, 10 percent of which went to Drake.

Drake's two-month-long rampage cost Spain one hundred irreplaceable ships of all sizes and added incalculably to the Armada's cost. These costs were already running close to ten million ducats, while the delay caused by Drake was adding seven hundred thousand a month to that total. Despite record shipments of silver from Bolivia's Potosí silver mines, the treasury remained strained. Worse, when Philip turned to his Genoese bankers for loans to replace the supplies destroyed by Drake, they showed scant interest. Elizabeth's spymaster was demonstrating his true worth in England's hour of need. He had made it clear to the bankers that there would be a serious price to pay if they assisted the Spanish crown. Other sources of Spanish finance, such as trade, also dried up, as most of Spain's transatlantic fleet was conscripted into the Armada. The destruction caused by Drake and Philip's inability to raise sufficient funds to make good the damage delayed the Armada's departure for a year.

In the meantime, the Armada's commander, Santa Cruz, died. The king replaced him with the man who had come to the aid of Cádiz, the Duke of Medina Sidonia. Sidonia was smart, industrious, hardworking, tactful, and magnanimous. He was also one of the greatest grandees in Spain, an important factor in keeping his jealous subordinates in line. Simply put, even in times of dire emergency, many Spanish commanders would not follow the orders of anyone below them in social rank. Sidonia had all the qualities of a great naval commander except those he himself listed in a letter to the king asking to be excused from this duty. As he warned Philip, he lacked any naval experience, had no information about the enemy or the war plans, was in poor health, and was prone to seasickness. Nevertheless, he was an able administrator and made significant progress in reorganizing the fleet and preparing it to sail.

AT LAST, on May 30, 1588, the 117 ships and 18,973 soldiers of the Spanish Armada put to sea. Things went wrong right from the start. Tossed and scattered by storms, and finding most of his fleet's food stores rotten, Sidonia ordered the fleet to put in at La Coruña in the Bay of Biscay. A quick inspection revealed that many ships were severely battered, enough so that Sidonia asked the king to cancel the expedition. Refused permission to abandon his mission, he busied himself overseeing repairs and resupplying the fleet. On July 21, the fleet again set forth. It had not gone far before losing four galleys that proved unable to withstand the roughness of the open ocean and had to put back into port. Worse, one of his most powerful ships, the *Santa Ana,* lost a mast and had to drop out. By this time he was just one hundred miles from the British fleet.

Dawn broke on July 31, exposing the more than one hundred ships of the English fleet in Plymouth Bay. The English were led by Lord High Admiral Charles Howard aboard the *Ark Royal.* Howard was a forceful leader, possessed of tremendous administrative ability, but without practical experience at sea. During his three years as lord high admiral, he had remade the English fleet, turning it into a weapon ideally suited for the new form of naval warfare that was first displayed against the Spanish Armada. He made up for his lack of experience at sea with the greatest virtue of successful leaders: the ability to recruit talented subordinates and to then heed their advice. In command of the fleet's three squadrons were the nation's most feared Sea Dogs—Sir Francis Drake, John Hawkins, and Martin Frobisher, all men possessing considerable experience at sea as well as in fighting the Spanish.

The English sailed out of Plymouth and in a spectacular display of seamanship crossed in front of the Spanish Armada before swinging west to capture the weather gauge, an advantage they would not relinquish over the next several days. In "the Age of Sail," capturing the weather gauge—placing your ships upwind of the enemy—was usually a decisive advantage. Any downwind vessel trying to attack is forced to tack against the wind, while the upwind vessels can usually bring on an engagement at the time of their choosing. This was particularly true against the cumbersome vessels of the Armada. As they watched the English maneuver, the Spanish for the first time witnessed and envied the differences between their respective fleets. Although only a fifth of the English fleet consisted of royal warships, they were all built in the new racer design. These ships had a lower superstructure, making them faster and more maneuverable, and better gun platforms. The English racers could literally sail rings around the Spanish fleet at the time and place of their choosing. There were also well over one hundred converted merchant ships in the English fleet, most of them less than half the size of the fleet's warships. Individually, the converted merchantmen were useless against a Spanish warship. En masse, though, they provided a wall of fire on which the royal warships could maneuver in order to deliver their hammer blows.

That they could deliver these blows was due to the second great advantage the English possessed—firepower. The English had more and larger guns than the Spanish. More important, they had so rigged their guns that most could fire every few minutes. On the other hand, the Spanish, who relied on grappling and boarding as their decisive naval tactic, used a rigging system that made it difficult to fire their largest guns more than once a day. Those Spanish unfortunate enough to have previously faced an English warship in combat knew the danger:

Unless God helps us by a miracle the English, who have faster and handier ships than ours, and many more long range guns, and know their advantages as well as we do, will never close with us at all, but stand aloof and knock us to pieces with their culverins, without our being able to do them any serious harm.

The sailors in both fleets knew how to achieve victory. For the Spanish, it required getting close enough to grapple the English ships so that their overwhelming infantry might come into play. If they could close the distance, then the nearly twenty thousand soldiers crammed aboard the Spanish ships would make short work of the undermanned English vessels. If they failed to close, then English guns would tear their ships apart, slaughtering much of their fine soldiery in the process.

As the English maneuvered to seize the weather gauge, Sidonia signaled his ships to assume battle positions—the famous concave formation. On the right sailed the warships commanded by Don Alonso Martinez de Leiva, one of the king's favorites. Leiva was an experi-

English fleet gives chase   *Photos 12/Alamy*

enced commander with an enviable record of achievement both on land and at sea. Philip had placed him in charge of the Armada's infantry and expected him to play his main role once on English soil. Sidonia, impressed with Leiva's abilities, placed him in charge of one wing of the fleet. Unknown to Sidonia, Leiva sailed with secret orders to take command of the Armada if Sidonia was killed. He was fated never to return to Spain, drowning in a wreck off the Irish coast during the Armada's return voyage.

Two miles to the north stood twenty more ships commanded by Juan Martinez de Recalde, Spain's most experienced naval commander. Recalde had spent most of the last two decades at sea. In recent years, he had commanded a squadron in the Spanish assault on the Azores, fought the Dutch "Sea Beggars," and escorted the ill-fated Spanish expedition to Ireland. He was the best tactical commander in the Armada and was always found where the fighting was heaviest. He survived the battle but died two weeks after the Armada's return. In the center, with the remainder of the warships, was Sidonia, shepherding and guarding the Armada's supply ships.

With both fleets in formation, Howard ordered one of his smaller vessels, the *Distain,* to advance ahead of the fleet and fire a shot at the

Spanish flagship. The *Distain* lurched forward, fired an ineffective shot at the wrong ship, and then raced away. With the firing of the ceremonial shot, Sidonia unfurled his flags, and the battle commenced.

Howard signaled the first attack to begin. English ships surged forward in the first "line ahead" attack in naval warfare. One ship took the lead, followed in succession by each ship in the squadron. As each ship rode past an enemy, it fired its broadside, one carefully aimed gun at a time, into the enemy's stern. It would then sail on to the next target as the following ships, in turn, blasted an already reeling enemy a second, third, and fourth time. The English first fell upon Leiva's ships, which did not acquit themselves well. Although Leiva's own ship turned to fight, most of his squadron deserted their positions and crowded into the center of the Armada for greater protection.

The English swept on to engage Recalde on the opposite flank. This brave warrior turned his ship, the *San Juan,* to face the attack. He stood alone.

As the rest of the Armada continued eastward, the *San Juan* halted and cleared for action. Like dogs around a trapped beast, the English ships closed in for the kill. Five hundred years later, it is hard to read Recalde's intentions. Likely he thought the English would find the *San Juan* an irresistible prize and would be unable to resist the temptation to board and seize it. Recalde probably thought that if he could grapple two or more ships in this fashion, he could bring on the general melee on which the Spanish counted for victory. If that had been his intent, he was to be sorely disappointed. The English did swarm the *San Juan,* but they never closed, opting instead to stand off and use their long-range guns to turn it into splinters. Seeing the danger, Sidonia ordered several ships of the van to alter course and go to Recalde's aid. As they approached, the English retreated and the crisis passed.

Despite firing as much as three times as many shots as the Spanish, the English had failed to do any significant harm. Impressed with Spanish seamanship and their ability to maintain their close-order formation, the English were reluctant to get too close. Past experience told them they had to close to within two hundred yards before their most powerful guns could inflict significant damage. Still, as long as the Spanish stayed together, the English refused to sail closer than two hundred yards. As Lord Howard wrote in a letter to Walsingham that evening: "We durst not adventure to put in amongst them, their fleet being so strong." English wariness allowed the Spanish to avoid major losses in the first engagement. Then fate took a hand.

Around one thirty, as both fleets planned their next moves, approximately four miles distant from each other, a huge explosion ripped through the *San Salvador*. What happened remains uncertain. The best guess is that a German gunner, believing the *San Salvador's* captain was cuckolding him, threw a torch into one of the ship's powder magazines. The resulting explosion blew out two decks, killed or wounded hundreds, and damaged the ship's steering mechanism. Sidonia ordered a halt and rushed vessels to the aid of the stricken ship. The Spanish managed to extinguish the flames and tow the crippled *San Salvador* into the protective embrace of the Armada. But the next day, beyond repair, the *San Salvador* was abandoned. Fate, however, was not through with the Spanish yet.

The *Rosario,* rushing to Recalde's aid, had had a slight collision with another ship, damaging her steering. Before repairs could be made, the *Rosario* collided with the *Santa Catalina*. The damage was extensive, and the *Rosario* fell behind the Armada. Sidonia first proposed to stop and render assistance. But one of his other commanders, Diego Flores, reminded him that his highest duty was to the Armada and its mission and he could not put everything at risk for the sake of one ship—which, as it happened, was captained by Flores's hated cousin Don Pedro de Valdés. Sidonia was apparently unaware of the familial discord. The next morning, the crew of the *Rosario* awoke to find themselves abandoned and with Drake's *Revenge* positioned to blow her out of the water. Don Pedro surrendered the *Rosario* to Drake without a fight.

For Drake it was quite a haul, as the *Rosario* was carrying fifty thousand ducats from Philip's treasury. Still, it was odd that Drake was there to begin with. His assigned task was to follow the Armada closely, while maintaining a strong light in the *Revenge's* stern to guide the remainder of the fleet. Drake later claimed that he had seen several ships passing close to shore and had gone to investigate. He fooled no one. Drake had the soul of a pirate, and even in the hours of England's greatest peril he could not resist the chance to take such a rich prize.

The immediate effect was costly. With nothing to guide it, the English fleet scattered in the night. It took most of the next day to collect the stragglers, while the Armada continued down the English Channel unmolested. The long-term effects, however, proved catastrophic for the Spanish. The English removed over 250 barrels of powder and as much as 4,000 shot from the *Rosario* and the *San Salvador* and then distributed them to the English fleet, which was already beginning to run short of both. In total, captured Spanish powder and shot made up approximately a third of what the English expended in the fight against the Armada. One wonders if the English could have defeated the Spanish had it not been for the munitions taken off the two abandoned Spanish ships.

Toward evening, the reassembled English fleet caught up with the slow-moving Spanish. Once again, neither Howard nor any of his captains was in a hurry to try his luck against the solid Spanish formation. In the morning the wind changed, temporarily giving the Spanish the weather gauge. The English made for the coast in an attempt to sneak past the Spanish and recapture the weather gauge. This time they failed. With the wind behind them, the Spanish easily cut off the English and began closing the distance. For the next two hours, a fierce engagement ensued, with the Spanish continually closing the distance between the fleets.

For a moment, it looked as if the Spanish would achieve the decisive melee they sought. In fact, Elizabeth's mighty warship the *Triumph* almost found herself trapped between the coast and several onrushing Spanish galleasses (oar-powered warships). Fortunately, the *Triumph*'s captain, Martin Frobisher, was an old Sea Dog who knew how to handle a ship. He also knew how to handle galleasses, ordering his gunners to fire low and use chain shot rather than balls. Chain shot was incapable of making any impression on the Spanish ships' stout hulls. However, it was an excellent choice for shattering oars and men. Chain shot, entering through an oar opening, tore through swaths of oarsmen, turning the lower decks of the Spanish ships into charnel houses. Still, the Spanish came on, slowly but relentlessly. At the last moment, they were deprived of the prize they had paid so much to gain. The "Protestant wind" returned, and the *Triumph* skittered to safety along with the rest of the English squadron.

The English did not stay away long. Drake, taking full advantage of the wind change, charged Recalde's squadron, which Sidonia had left behind to guard his supply vessels as he tried to pin the English against the coast. As Drake approached, the Spanish vessels "flocked together like sheep." In effect, they masked one another's fire. Recalde, alone once again and facing an entire British squadron, was incensed: "[We] received no assistance from any other ship in the fleet, as they all wanted to take refuge . . . so they fled from the action and collided together. It is a disgrace to mention it." Sidonia, however, rallied several ships and went to Recalde's aid.

Lord High Admiral Howard considered Drake's attack to be ill-advised, but he still felt compelled to support his impetuous captain. He ordered the bulk of the English warships to turn toward the Spanish center and charged. Spotting Sidonia's flagship, the *San Martin,* rushing to Recalde's aid, Howard adjusted his direction and bore down on the mighty Spanish ship. Behind him came the rest of England's royal warships. Attacking in line, each English ship emptied her broadside into the *San Martin.* According to Spanish sources, for the next hour the *San Martin* was enveloped in smoke and invisible to the fleet. The *San Martin,* however, fought hard, firing eighty shots at her tormentors. She received five hundred in return. Still unwilling to close, the English ships moved off when a squadron led by Leiva came to Sidonia's aid. Leiva's ships escorted the damaged but still formidable *San Martin* back into the midst of the Armada to lick her wounds.

By this time, the English were seriously short of powder and shot. While they awaited resupply from the coastal towns and fortresses, the Armada re-formed and continued its passage down the English Channel. The English had proven they could outsail and outfight the Spanish, but they seemed incapable of inflicting decisive damage or stopping the Armada's forward progress. But the Armada's success was not being measured by its ability to bludgeon its way down the Channel. Its mission was to link up with Parma's Army of Flanders and escort it across the Channel to England. As of yet there had been no word from Parma, and Sidonia had no idea of the Spanish general's state of preparation.

Dawn brought the English a welcome sight. *El Gran Grifón,* a powerfully armed supply ship, had fallen behind the rest of the Armada. Drake pounced. Sailing in front of the Spanish ship, he blasted her with a broadside, brought his ship around to smash her with a second broadside, and finally circled around to the helpless *Grifón*'s rear to rake her a third time. It was a remarkable example of English seamanship, but before Drake's squadron could close in for the kill, Recalde and Leiva came to the *Grifón*'s rescue. As they towed the battered *Grifón* back into the center of the Armada, Recalde's and Leiva's squadrons engaged the English fleet and more than five thousand cannon rounds were expended. But the range was too great, and neither side reported any serious damage. When Sidonia signaled the Armada to turn and bring on the general melee he longed for, the English again drew off.

During the evening of August 3, Howard reorganized the English fleet. Instead of one single mass, all following behind the leader, he broke the fleet into four squadrons, under himself, Drake, Hawkins, and Frobisher. Each squadron commander was to use his own initiative to take advantage of any opportunities the Spanish offered. In effect, Howard created a pack of dogs to torment their quarry from multiple directions. His obvious strategy was to break up the Spanish fleet and keep it from moving into the Solent between the Isle of Wight and the English coastline. The English were well aware that if the Spanish reached that safe anchorage, they could remain there nearly invulnerable while waiting for Parma to announce his readiness.

The next morning, the English saw that two Spanish warships had fallen behind the Armada. Hawkins immediately ordered his squadron to attack, just as the wind failed. Undeterred, Hawkins ordered his small boats lowered so that they could tow him into firing range. Despite his efforts, the Spanish ships escaped when several galleasses arrived to take them under tow. Later in the day, the Spanish took advantage of a change of wind to mass against the becalmed *Triumph*. Once again, though, the "Protestant wind" returned, just in time for Frobisher to escape. However, Frobisher's retreat had uncovered the entrance to the Solent, offering Sidonia the chance to gain the protected anchorage and await further developments. He was thwarted in doing so by a vicious English attack from the south that threatened to push the Armada to its destruction against dangerous shoals. With no other choice, Sidonia ordered the Armada to reassemble and continue west. The Spanish had missed their chance to occupy the Solent. The next possible anchorage was the open harbor of Calais.

With their shot nearly exhausted, there was little the English could do to block or even harry the Armada's advance. For the next two days, the Spanish sailed west unmolested. On August 6, the Armada sailed into the exposed anchorage of Calais. At a council of war that evening, Sidonia and his chief lieutenants decided the best course was to lay anchored at Calais and await Parma.

The English had other ideas. Resupplied by convoy out of the Thames and reinforced by Lord Seymour Downs's squadron, the English now had 140 sail. Still, their anxiety was high, since they too remained as ignorant as Sidonia about Parma's readiness. For all they knew, Parma might already be at sea and ready to link up with the Armada, with fatal consequences for England. When an English captain suggested using fireships to break the tactical deadlock, Howard jumped at the idea. With the support of his squadron commanders, Howard ordered the fleet's carpenters to start turning eight small merchant vessels into fireships. On the night of August 7, there was a flood tide and a favorable wind. At midnight, the English loosed the fireships.

The Spanish managed to cast a line on two of the fireships and drag them away, but the other six continued on, heading into the heart of the Armada. Nerves there were already stretched thin. Fireships were always a terrible danger to a packed fleet at anchor. But the Spanish were also contemplating the horrors that awaited them if Giambelli had built new hellburners for the English. When fires set off several of the fireships' cannons, panic swept the Armada. Every ship cut her anchors and headed for open waters. There a swift current, a strong wind, and a lack of anchors made it impossible for the Spanish to hold their positions.

MORNING FOUND only five Spanish galleons, including Sidonia's *San Juan* and Recalde's *San Martin,* in position and ready to fight. The remainder of the Armada had scattered in some of the most dangerous waters in the world. About half the English ships moved to attack, but

Howard led the other half to seize a stranded galleass, the *San Lorenzo*. For two hours, half the fleet assaulted the *San Lorenzo,* which was eventually taken by the French while the main battle raged to the north. There, Sidonia had elected to stand and fight so as to give the rest of the Armada time to assemble. The ensuing Battle of Gravelines sealed the Armada's fate. There is little doubt that Sidonia and Recalde understood their stand represented a forlorn hope. As the English ships descended on them, they were sacrificing themselves to save the rest of the fleet. In Howard's absence, Drake led the attack, but Hawkins and Frobisher were not far behind. Moreover, the English now had the measure of the Spanish fleet, and they knew how to hurt it—get in close and pound it hard. For the next several hours, English warships moved to within musket range of the five Spanish galleons and unleashed their fury at close range. At one point, Sidonia's *San Martin* was surrounded and under fire from Drake's *Revenge,* Hawkins's *Victory,* and Frobisher's *Triumph.*

The five Spanish galleons fought valiantly, absorbing hundreds of

The Spanish Invincible Armada *intended to invade* ENGLAND *Defeated by the* English Fleet *Commanded by the Admirals.* Howard, Drake, Raleigh &c 1588.

English fleet closes for battle   *Picade LLC/Alamy*

rounds each. The *San Martin* was struck more than two hundred times, dropping masts, piercing the hull, and leaving her decks awash with blood. Still they gave no sign of yielding, and ever so slowly other warships came to Sidonia's aid, falling into a ragged formation around the flagship. For the next seven hours, a running battle raged. Drake and Hawkins, trying to break into the middle of the assembling Armada, moved away from the *San Martin*. Frobisher, however, did not follow, electing instead to stand off and make splinters of the *San Martin* and other nearby ships. This willingness, at least of Elizabeth's royal warships if not many of the private vessels, to close with the enemy had changed the nature of the fight. Until now, the Spanish vessels had mostly weathered the storm of shot unleashed by the English, who often fired at too great a distance to do much harm. Now, the Spanish ships were being torn apart. Worse, their crews were being slaughtered. Those Spanish ships that returned to Spain reported hundreds of killed and wounded.

Sir William Winter, on the *Vanguard,* later reported that his ship had fired more than five hundred shot, not one of them outside of musket range. For many of the Spanish, these new tactics were infuriating. Soldiers aboard one Spanish ship were close enough to taunt the British, calling on them to grapple their ships together and fight like men. When the English ship wisely refused the offer, the Spanish began calling them "Lutheran hens" among other things, all the while they were being massacred by English gunnery. No one ever doubted Spanish courage, but this was a new kind of war, one for which they were not prepared. Unable to either grapple or return the volume of fire they were receiving, the Spanish could only suffer. And suffer they did, particularly the powerful Spanish galleons, which stood firm to protect the Armada's weaker ships.

A little after noon, Howard and his large squadron rejoined the main fleet, which allowed the English to keep up the pressure. As one witness later wrote: "My Lord Admiral with the rest of the fleet came up and gave a very fresh onset." By late afternoon, though, a storm began to rise and a gathering darkness made it difficult to make out individual ships. By this time, the English had also spent most of their powder and shot. Howard, who needed little encouragement to break off the fight, soon signaled his fleet to bear away from the Spanish and re-form. Remarkably, it seems that Sidonia wanted the Armada to hold position and continue the fight in the morning. However, he was persuaded that the storm, strong currents, and condition of the fleet, which had close to two thousand men killed or incapacitated, were all conspiring to force the fleet to its destruction along the Flanders coast. Moreover, five ships, including two powerful galleons—the *San Filipe* and the *San Mateo*—were already lost. Reluctantly, Sidonia gave the order to head into the North Sea and return to Spain by way of Scotland and Ireland.

Few of the Spanish ships were prepared to face the gales of the North Atlantic. A number of them were barely holding together, and some needed to be bound with cables to keep from falling apart. Storms blew many ships up onto the rocks of Scotland and Ireland. Even ships that made it into a safe anchorage were often thrown ashore, as they had cut away their anchors when escaping the fireships at Calais. In the end, only 67 of the 130 ships eventually made it back to Spain. Philip, upon learning the extent of the disaster, said, "I sent the Armada against men, not God's winds and waves."

There were two further Spanish attempts to send an armada against England, both defeated by the weather. Despite Spain's grievous losses, the war dragged drearily on, even after Philip's death in 1598. However, Elizabeth's death in 1603 opened a window for peace, and a treaty was signed the following year.

The Armada represented the high-water mark of Spanish power. England, on the other hand, emerged as one of Europe's great powers and its foremost naval power. Over the succeeding centuries it was to have many challengers, but it would not relinquish its seat at the top until after the great wars of the twentieth century. None of this would have been possible if the Spanish Armada had succeeded in its mission. First, and arguably foremost, Spanish success would have ended any possibility of a future British Empire. At the time of the Armada, the English were just making their first forays deep into the Atlantic and had barely touched the Pacific. If England had fallen under Spanish domination, it is highly doubtful that Spain would ever have allowed it to colonize America's eastern seaboard. Even if such colonization had taken place, it would have been conducted under Spanish administration, rules, and laws, all informed by a suffocating structure of religion and the overbearing rights of the nobility. The ideas that gave birth to what historians describe as American exceptionalism would never have found fertile intellectual ground in which to take root. Although it is unlikely that a Spanish success would have stifled all the intellectual ferment that marked the era of the Enlightenment, it undoubtedly would have slowed and altered it.

A Spanish victory would also have surely meant an end to the Netherlands' independence. Without English support, the Netherlands after decades of draining war could not have withstood the combined might of the encircling Hapsburg domains. Finally clear of the strain and cost of fighting in the Netherlands, Spain would have tightened its stranglehold on Italy, leaving France surrounded and isolated. Regardless of how completely the Hapsburgs could have dominated the French, France surely would have had to forge a different path for itself. Beset on all sides by enemies, even an unconquered France could not have escaped a certain degree of vassalage that would have deprived it of future greatness.

Certainly the long-term prospects for the Protestant Reformation would have dwindled in the aftermath of a Spanish victory. With Protestantism extinguished or on the run in England and the Netherlands, it would have been difficult, if not impossible, for Protestants to stand against the Hapsburgs' royal power. Hapsburg power in Spain and the Holy Roman Empire, joined with the reforms of the Counter-Reformation emanating from papacy, would have presented a lethal challenge to Protestantism. In all likelihood, the Wars of Religion might still have taken place, but it is unlikely they would have matched the duration or intensity of the Thirty Years' War that devastated Germany from 1618 to 1648. Too, the victors would likely have been the forces of Catholicism.

It is hard to determine the extent to which a new era of papal power and Catholic stasis would have changed Europe. At a minimum, it would have set back (but not extinguished) the age of inquiry and free thought the Enlightenment was unleashing. Almost as bad, it would have wreaked havoc with the burgeoning economic progress that was just beginning to lift Europe out of the Malthusian trap it had been locked in since at least the fall of Rome. Much of the capital then being invested in the engines of progress, those harbingers of the Industrial Revolution and Europe's great leap forward, would have returned to "the dead hand of the church." Gold and silver from the New World, as well as new deposits in the Tyrol, might have kept the economic engines moving forward, but their pace would have gone from explosive to glacial.

On the other hand, England's victory not only changed the accepted power structure of Europe, but set that tiny island nation on its path to future greatness. Although there were challengers, the Dutch and the French in particular, the defeat of the Spanish Armada inaugurated the era of British naval dominance. With ever greater confidence and growing power, first British ships and then entire fleets ranged the globe, wresting commercial control from those Europeans who had gone before, while simultaneously keeping at bay new aspirants to global maritime power. For the next three hundred years, Britain built and maintained the empire on which the sun never set.

Unmolested by Spanish governors or the Inquisition, Tudor and then Stewart England blossomed. The age of superstition was not yet behind them, but new paths of learning and experiment were opening. The way was clearing for the eventual emergence of the Scottish Enlightenment, the adoption of new methods of scientific inquiry, and the germination of the political and economic seeds that led directly to the Industrial Revolution. It is no exaggeration to state that the defeat of the Spanish Armada made possible the modern era.

BREITENFELD

The Creation of Modern War

1631

IN 1631, THE THIRTY YEARS' WAR WAS IN ITS FOURTEENTH YEAR. IT had begun in 1618 as a rebellion by the Czechs against the rule of the Hapsburgs. Fearful that the future successor to the Austrian Hapsburg lands, Ferdinand—soon to become Ferdinand II, holy Roman emperor—would destroy their ancient liberties, the Czechs had thrown his representatives out of a Hradčany castle window, luckily to land in a manure cart. The incident has gone down in history as "the defenestration of Prague," an event that was to prove of enormous significance in European history, since it set off the Thirty Years' War. By their actions, the Czechs declared their independence from what they regarded as the officious rule of their Hapsburg Catholic sovereign and the threat that the Counter-Reformation of the Catholic Church presented to the Protestant religion throughout Bohemia and Moravia. They had reason to fear Ferdinand, who had received his education from the Jesuits and had already indicated that he was a fierce defender of the Roman Catholic faith.

The Czechs then invited Frederick, elector of the Palatinate, one of the more important principalities of the Holy Roman Empire lying to the west of the Rhine, to become the king of Bohemia. They thereby ignited the tinderbox that had been steadily growing in intensity since Martin Luther had begun the Protestant Reformation by supposedly nailing his "Ninety-five Theses" to the door of All Saints' Church in Wittenberg in 1517. The result of the revolution Luther had sparked had been religious and political turmoil throughout the Germanies, as they were then accurately described. The Peace of Augsburg, agreed to in 1555, allowed the German princes to choose the religion of their subjects, either Lutheranism or Roman Catholicism. By 1618, that peace had become increasingly frayed as the Counter-Reformation gained steam.

Nevertheless, the Catholic and Protestant princes had held on to a tenuous balance of power among themselves. Although they were often none too happy with the religious choices of their neighbors, at the same time they had no desire to see the Hapsburg emperor and his advisers establish a strong, centralized monarchy over the Germanies, one that would limit their freedom and independence. Thus the tensions in the principalities revolved around the pull of religion on the one hand and on the other the struggle of the princes to maintain their independence from the centralizing efforts of the Hapsburg emperors to create a unified Germany, similar in their endeavors to those of the monarchs in England, France, and Spain in the early seventeenth century to create powerful central governments.

By accepting the position of king of Bohemia, Frederick upset the balance of power between Catholics and Protestants and brought the power of Catholic Europe into play. That was bad enough, but there were few worse choices the Czechs could have made in choosing Frederick. The elector of the Palatinate was a supercilious young man who had no military background and was unable to persuade either his father-in-law, James I of England, or the Dutch Protestants to provide significant help. Marshaling the military forces available to the Holy Roman Empire, Ferdinand struck. At the Battle of the White Mountain in November 1620, the Hapsburg military forces utterly destroyed the Czech army, which comprised mostly nobles and mercenaries and was unsupported by any mobilization of the populace. Thus, one throw of the iron dice ended Frederick's rule. For the Czechs, the battle was a national disaster. Not only did they lose their religion, but Ferdinand placed the German nobility in charge of the Bohemian lands and Czech disappeared as a language of culture until it reemerged in the mid–nineteenth century.

From his success in crushing the Czech rebellion, Ferdinand moved against the Palatinate. He replaced Frederick with Maximilian of Bavaria as the elector, an unheard-of move in the politics of sixteenth- and seventeenth-century Germany. By 1625, Ferdinand, by now confirmed as emperor of the Holy Roman Empire, was well on the way to securing his position in central Germany. Ferdinand's military forces consisted largely of mercenaries, led by ruthless, extortionate leaders who ensured that they and their armies were well paid by both their employers and those whose territories their troops ravaged.

Foremost among these captains was Albrecht von Wallenstein, an outstanding general and soldier. But Wallenstein was also an ambitious, ruthless military leader with scarcely any scruples, who enriched himself at the expense of the defeated Czechs in the purge of Protestants and the seizure of their lands in Bohemia and Moravia after the Battle of the White Mountain. The other formidable commander of Ferdinand's mercenary armies was Johann Tserclaes, Count Tilly, who had first gained experience fighting for the Spanish in their war to suppress the Dutch rebellion. Both he and Wallenstein trained their forces in the *tercio* system the Spanish had developed, and both were highly competent field commanders, but neither of them was an innovator, willing to change the tactical or operational framework within which European armies had been fighting over the past century.

With the steady deterioration of the Protestant position in Germany, Christian IV of Denmark worried that the rise of Hapsburg power threatened the continued existence of Lutheranism in his own realm. Thus, at this point the Danes intervened to help the Protestant cause and redress the balance of power in the Germanies, which had now swung heavily in favor of the Catholics. For his trouble, Wallenstein and Tilly thoroughly thrashed the Danish army and its German allies in a swift, ruthless campaign. The former with his mercenaries drove all the way into Jutland, which Hapsburg mercenaries occupied. With no navy, however, Wallenstein could not cross

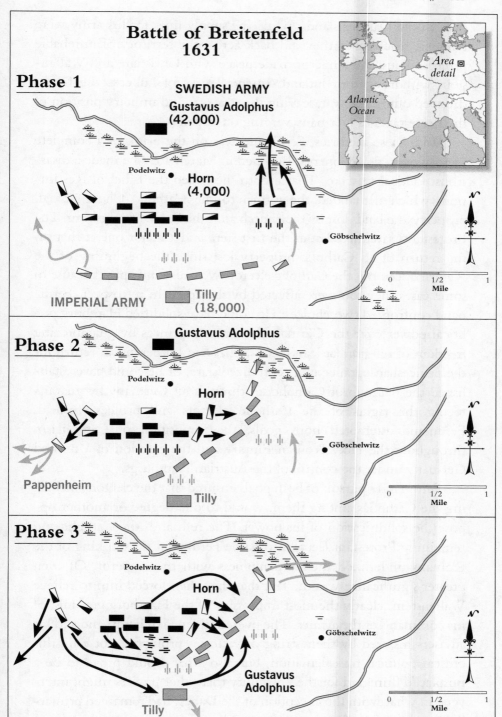

**Battle of Breitenfeld
1631**

Phase 1

SWEDISH ARMY
**Gustavus Adolphus
(42,000)**

*Area
detail*

*Atlantic
Ocean*

Podelwitz

**Horn
(4,000)**

Göbschelwitz

0   1/2   1
Mile

IMPERIAL ARMY   **Tilly
(18,000)**

Phase 2

Gustavus Adolphus

Podelwitz

Horn

Göbschelwitz

0   1/2   1
Mile

Pappenheim

Tilly

Phase 3

Podelwitz

Horn

Göbschelwitz

**Gustavus
Adolphus**

Tilly

0   1/2   1
Mile

over to the Danish islands, while the supply lines for his army were tenuous, reaching as they did back across the territory of unreliable princes. Thus, the emperor made peace with Christian, and Wallenstein withdrew from Jutland. In the Treaty of Lübeck, the Danes dropped out of the war, leaving the strategic and military position of the Protestants in Germany verging on hopeless.

With these victories, Ferdinand was on the brink of a complete victory over his opponents. But then in March 1629 he made a disastrous political mistake. That month, he issued the Edict of Restitution, which demanded the return to the Catholic Church of all property and lands lost by the church after the Peace of Augsburg. The Protestants saw the edict as the first step, and a major one at that, to the return of all Catholic property lost since the beginning of the Reformation. But the Catholic electors were also unhappy, because in some cases they too were affected by the edict. In retrospect, Ferdinand confronted two choices: He could have solidified Hapsburg political power over the German electors and princes by guaranteeing freedom of religion (at least to Catholics and Lutherans) in return for the princes' acceptance of a centralized state, or he could have established the triumph of Catholicism throughout Germany by guaranteeing the rights of the Catholic electors and princes. Instead, Ferdinand attempted both goals: the imposition of Catholicism throughout the Holy Roman Empire and the creation of a unified Germany under the control of the Austrian Hapsburgs.

Ferdinand's pursuit of both goals ensured that the electors, including the Catholics among them, would to one degree or another oppose the solidification of his power. The refusal of the Catholic and remaining Protestant electors to name Ferdinand II's son king of the Romans underlined their unhappiness with the emperor. Of even greater significance was the fact that they then forced him to relieve Wallenstein, clearly the most impressive of the Hapsburg generals, of his command of the armies. The overconfidence of Ferdinand and his advisers inspired by their string of victories prompted not only this critical political miscalculation, but also what would prove to be a misplaced disregard for the possibility that other powers might intervene in what, with the exception of the Danes, had remained primarily a matter of the Germanies.

While these events were transpiring in central Europe, profound developments were occurring in Sweden under the leadership of the young Swedish king Gustavus Adolphus. In the 1950s, the great British historian of Sweden in the seventeenth century, Michael Roberts, delivered a lecture in Belfast in which he argued that during the reign of the Swedish king, a military revolution had occurred that profoundly affected the manner in which not only Sweden but eventually the other European powers waged war. Although historians have modified and extended Roberts's thesis, they have confirmed its basic validity. Unlike too many historians who have focused on the technological developments, such as the supposed gunpowder revolution, Roberts emphasized the tactical, administrative, and logistical aspects of what Gustavus achieved during the span of his relatively short life.

The changes that Gustavus introduced into the Swedish army had an immediate impact on the battlefields of Germany, overturning the balance of military power entirely and eventually changing the course of German and European history. In effect, the Swedes revolutionized the tactics, discipline, and organization of their military forces in a fashion that Europe had not seen since the introduction of the English longbow in the fourteenth century or, more particularly, the highly disciplined and trained legions of the Roman army that had dominated Europe and the entire Mediterranean basin fourteen hundred years before.

The Swedish king did have the advantage of the efforts of other reformers, on which he was able to build his formidable military instrument. Maurice of Orange, stadtholder of the United Provinces (modern-day Holland), had already played a particularly important role in reforming the tactical framework within which European armies fought. In the last half of the sixteenth century, the primary tactical formation was the Spanish *tercio,* a mixed organization of pikemen and musketeers that numbered originally close to three thousand soldiers. By the early seventeenth century, the number of soldiers in a *tercio* had declined to approximately fifteen hundred men to increase their maneuverability on the battlefield. Much like the Greek phalanx, the *tercio* relied on the psychological dynamic of men in groups to maintain its cohesion in the midst of the terror of the battlefield. Even with its reduction in numbers, however, the *tercio* was not a truly maneuverable formation, but one that relied on mass and numbers to overwhelm its opponents.

Motivated by religion and group dynamics, the armies of fierce Spanish peasants, who made up its members, dominated Europe's tactical landscape with the fearsome military power that the *tercios* represented. Nevertheless, because its pikemen rimmed the outside of the *tercio* in a block resembling a square, many of its musketeers were buried within the confines of the formation, which minimized the potential of gunpowder weapons. Without a discipline imposed by officers and noncommissioned officers (NCOs), it had to rely on the cohesion provided by its breadth and depth. The very size and lack of systemic discipline in these formations also contributed to a lack of tactical responsiveness on the battlefield. The *tercios* could maneuver only within a rigid framework that aimed at keeping its mass of soldiers together. In effect, the *tercio* was not much more than a ferocious steamroller, which once pointed in a certain direction could smash nearly everything in its path. But it had little ability to meet threats coming from unexpected directions.

The basic tactical conundrum of the early seventeenth century lay in the fact that any increase in firepower required a thinning out of the formation. But such a thinning out would inevitably result in loosening the cohesion of the group. How to provide the glue to keep a more linear formation on the battlefield was the great tactical question that the generals and tacticians of the sixteenth century faced.

Confronting the Spanish in the Netherlands' interminable war of independence, Maurice of Orange had attempted to reintroduce the discipline and organization of the Roman legions to military affairs of the late sixteenth century. This demanded the continual training of units in a formalized syllabus and common doctrine. Maurice's reforms created a disciplined, thinner line of soldiers, held together by its training and the commands of its officers and eventually NCOs. In particular, he utilized the Roman marching and parade ground commands—translated from Latin—in order to develop more flexible tactical formations that would maximize the firepower of gunpowder weapons.

At first the Dutch had considerable difficulty making the Roman commands work on the parade ground, because they did not under-

Gustavus Adolphus (1594–1632), king of Sweden
Mediacolor's/Alamy

stand that the commands, such as "attention" and "left face," demanded a two-step approach: first the preparatory command and then an execution command, such as "atten" . . . "shun" and "right" . . . "face." But eventually, after considerable trial and error, they worked out the method that the Romans had used. In terms of the present echoing the past, it is worth noting that those very commands invented by the Romans in the first century B.C. to deploy and fight their legions and cohorts remain today the basis for the parades of all modern armies.

But it was Gustavus, one of the great geniuses in military history, who took Maurice's tactical innovations and placed them in a wider framework of tactical and operational reform. His reforms extended across a number of areas. Already in the early seventeenth century the Swedish army had moved away from the mercenary military forces of the time to establish a national system of conscription, which added both nationalism and religion to the army's cohesion. Moreover, by increasing the numbers of officers and NCOs, the Swedes were able to maintain the discipline of the drill field on the battlefield.

In 1621, Gustavus promulgated the Swedish Articles of War, which laid out the disciplinary framework of the "Swedish" army. Thus, the Swedish Articles of War came directly from the king, and the soldiers swore an oath of allegiance directly to their king, not to their captains, as was the case in mercenary armies. Gustavus demanded that his soldiers master and obey the articles, which were not window dressing. Among their many imperatives was one that ordered that soldiers must dig when ordered to dig, suggestive of the fact that for the previous millennium, since the collapse of legionary discipline in the third century A.D., soldiers had not necessarily dug when ordered to do so.

Included in Gustavus's reforms was the standardization of artillery as well as the creation of light artillery, the latter to accompany infantry formations on the battlefield even when they advanced. Two vital benefits accompanied these changes: First, artillery standardization led to the standardization of ammunition, which added considerably to the rate of fire; and second, the creation of light artillery pieces added to the firepower available to attacking infantry in breaking up enemy formations. Moreover, a stiff regimen of training ensured that Swedish artillery could maneuver and fire at a rate that no other armed force in the world could match.

In copying Maurice and the Romans, Gustavus adapted the structure of the cohort legion to the modern weapons of the early seventeenth century. The basic Swedish tactical formation became the battalion, with its 450 to 500 men corresponding almost exactly to the size of a Roman cohort. The four companies in each battalion again corresponded more or less to the maniples in a cohort. Two battalions formed a regiment, and two regiments formed a brigade. The nature of the systemic organization of the new model army allowed Gustavus and his senior officers to adjust tactically with great rapidity to the inevitable changes in any battle, much as the Romans had. Julius Caesar's defeat of the Nervii is a particularly good example of the tactical flexibility of the Roman system, which Swedish tactics now reflected with the addition of firepower.

The Swedish cavalry possessed a similar organization, but its tactical approach was considerably different from the general practice of the armies in Germany, as was that of the infantry. Interspersed among the troopers were units of infantry to add firepower and protection, while the horsemen relied far more on the cold steel of their sabers, an approach they had learned from the wars in Poland. The tactical reforms allowed the Swedes to deploy their infantry, supported by light artillery, in six lines, which allowed for a major increase in the firepower of their formations. At the same time, their cavalry possessed a steadfastness as well as a disciplined cohesion that the cavalry of the mercenary armies lacked. And these tactical formations were drilled intensively so that they could deliver salvos, either by alternative ranks or by alternative platoons. Finally, Gustavus dressed his soldiers in uniforms of the same colors—the famous blue-and-yellow brigades—for easy recognition on the battlefield, and officers and NCOs received distinguishing marks of rank to increase their ability to control and maneuver Swedish regiments on the field of battle. The same blue and yellow are now Sweden's national colors.

Gustavus rigorously trained Swedish infantry, artillery, and cavalry to work *together* on the battlefield. The Swedes also had the advantage of testing and adapting their new model army extensively on a number of battlefields against the Russians and Poles in the Baltic states and Finland before they arrived in Germany. The result of these major reforms, innovations, and combat experience was that Sweden, poor and small as it was, was able to deploy an army on the European Continent that was to enjoy a decisive advantage over the armies of mercenaries that the Hapsburgs deployed in northern Germany in the early 1630s.

Also deserving of emphasis is the fact that the Swedish king was an outstanding combat soldier, a general like Caesar and Alexander who led from the front. He was nearsighted and not particularly impressive at first glance, but in every sense of the term, he possessed command presence. When he spoke, his soldiers as well as his officers listened. His bravery and risk taking on the battlefield were legendary. In the end, that risk taking would lead to his death at the Battle of Lützen in 1632, but by then he had completely reversed the strategic and political situation in Germany. Equally important to the new Swedish system were the administrative reforms of Gustavus and his brilliant political adviser, Axel Oxenstierna, which created the first Admiralty in Europe and placed Sweden on a more coherent and equitable system of taxation. By 1630, the Swedish army that arrived in northern Germany was a finely tuned, murderous military force that was used to and expected victory. The Swedish soldiers had complete confidence in their system, their king, and their officers.

ON JUNE 26, 1630, Gustavus Adolphus landed in Pomerania. His aim was twofold: to prevent the destruction of Protestantism in Germany by the Counter-Reformation and to protect Sweden's interests along the southern shores of the Baltic. The Swedish king did not underestimate his opponents. He dared not commit his forces to battle against the mercenary armies of the emperor until he gained allies among the Protestant princes. The Swedes did receive a small subsidy from the French statesman Cardinal Richelieu, but at least in the early days of the Swedish intervention, it was barely sufficient to cover the cost of supporting a regiment over the course of a year, and the Swedes were bringing an army to the Germanies. For the moment, the Swedes were going to have to rely on what they could cobble together from the disputative and quarrelsome principalities of north Germany.

On the other side of the hill, the Catholics underestimated the danger that the Swedes and their new military system represented. After all, they had wrecked the Danish military without difficulty. What they failed to recognize was that Gustavus's army was an entirely different adversary in comparison with the armies fielded by their erstwhile opponents, having already honed its tactical and battlefield skills against the Poles and the Russians. For the immediate present, Gustavus had to firm up his logistic and political base along the Baltic, while reaching out to the Protestant princes. Given the run of success imperial arms had enjoyed, the Protestant princes and German city-states proved difficult to attract into an alliance with the Swedes against Ferdinand's swelling power. Despite the risk, the city of Magdeburg defied the emperor and joined the Swedes. Magdeburg's decision did nothing, however, to sway the crucially important Saxon elector John George, the most important of the Protestant princes, who displayed no willingness to jump off the diplomatic and strategic fence he had been straddling since the beginning of the conflict. In fact, when the Swedes landed, he was busily attempting to create a block of Protestant princes sworn to remain neutral. Above all, John George had not the slightest interest in things military; thus, Saxony and its military forces were hardly in any shape to engage in a major war.

By 1631, events consipired to force the Saxon elector's hand. In March of that year, Count Tilly, with the bulk of the empire's forces, laid siege to Magdeburg. In an attempt to divert Tilly from his siege, Gustavus struck at Frankfurt an der Oder, which was in the hands of the Imperialists. In an attack that was all too successful, the Swedes stormed Frankfurt an der Oder so quickly that it failed to divert Tilly. On May 10, Tilly captured Magdeburg and inflicted a terrible vengeance on the city and its twenty thousand to thirty thousand inhabitants, most of whom his soldiers raped and slaughtered in the chaos and fires that followed the city's fall. While the sack of Magdeburg was a severe political defeat for Gustavus, it was also a wake-up call for the Protestants in northern Germany. Nevertheless, for all Tilly's success in sacking Magdeburg, he discovered himself in a precarious logistical position. Gustavus and his Swedes had managed to establish themselves on the Elbe, thus preventing the movement of supplies up and down that river. Worse, the siege of Magdeburg had already cleared Tilly's area of operation of most of its foodstuffs.

In August, Tilly made a serious strategic and political mistake. On August 14, short of supplies, he moved his soldiers into a Saxony as yet untouched by the ravages of a war that had already destroyed much of the rest of Germany, forced by the failure of logistics and organization to violate Saxony's neutrality in order to feed his army. The Swedes responded by moving south into Saxony, leaving John George no choice but to conclude an alliance with Gustavus. At least the Saxon population, nearly wholly Lutheran in their beliefs, cheered delightedly at the arrival of the Swedes. Meanwhile, Tilly had captured the Saxon city of Leipzig by threatening its inhabitants with a fate similar to that of Magdeburg. In addition, the collapse of what little logistical system the Imperialists enjoyed meant that Tilly was going to have to remain in southern Saxony near Leipzig in order to feed his troops. His need to hold on to southern Saxony meant that the Imperialists would have to fight if the Swedes moved against them. And they did.

THUS, when the combined armies of Sweden and Saxony approached Leipzig in mid-September, Tilly had no choice but to meet them. Altogether Gustavus possessed approximately twenty-four thousand Swedes; John George had eighteen thousand soldiers in the Saxon forces. Tilly's force numbered close to thirty-five thousand troops, but the advantage clearly appeared to lie with the Imperialists, since the Saxon troops and their officers were neophytes to the business of war in every sense of the word. Both Gustavus and Tilly recognized the weaknesses of the Saxons and made their plans accordingly.

Tilly drew up his forces with his strongest cavalry on his left flank under the command of the dashing cavalier Gottfried Heinrich Pap-

Johann Tserclaes, Count Tilly (1559–1632); copper engraving by Pietter de Jode, seventeenth century
Interfoto/Alamy

ILLVST.ᵃᵛᵉ IOANNES. COM. DE TSERCLAES. DOM. TILLI BARO. DE MORBAYS, DOM. DE. BALLAST, MONTIG. HOLERS, HEESWYCK. DYNTER. ETC.

penheim. In the center, Tilly commanded the *tercios* with the heavy, almost immovable artillery out in front. On his right flank, facing the Saxons, Tilly stationed a strong force of cavalry and infantry aimed at breaking the Saxons at the start of the battle. In his deployment, Tilly established his *tercios* in a single line with none in reserve. It appears that if he had a plan, he was aiming to destroy the flanks of the forces opposed to him and then to crush the Swedes in the center. The Imperialists, given their run of successes over the previous decade, generally discounted the fighting abilities of their opponents, and they had not the slightest idea of the flexibility and firepower the Swedes were going to bring to the battle. At best, Tilly believed the lengthy experience of his infantry in war would allow the *tercios* to simply run over their inexperienced opponents.

On the other side, the Swedes understood that they could not rely on the fighting abilities of their Saxon and other German allies to hold up the Imperialists for even a short period of time. In fact, Gustavus may well have counted on the collapse of his allies to lure the Imperialists into an overhasty advance that would allow him to counterattack them in the flank and destroy the *tercios* as they pursued the defeated Saxons.

The Swedes and their German allies deployed their forces as follows: The Saxons and the other Germans advanced on the left flank. Next to them in the center, Gustavus placed his most outstanding general, Gustav Horn, in command of three squadrons of cavalry and at least two of the four brigades that made up the front line of Swedish infantry that moved forward. Behind those four brigades were two infantry brigades in immediate support, while a further three brigades were the general reserve available to Gustavus and Horn to use where the situation appeared to be the most dangerous. Finally, on the right flank, Gustavus commanded eleven squadrons of cavalry with their supporting musketeers.

It is clear from their conduct of the battle that Gustavus had carefully briefed Horn and his other senior commanders on how he expected them to act and especially what he expected the Swedish response to be if, as anticipated, their Saxon allies were to collapse. In many respects, the deployment of the Swedish infantry brigades followed the pattern of the standard Roman deployment of their legions.

The rationale was similar: to provide maximum flexibility to redeploy in order to meet expected or unexpected circumstances.

In the morning hours of September 17 (new calendar), the allied armies marched out and ran into the Imperialist forces deployed five miles north of Leipzig near the village of Breitenfeld. Over the first several hours, the artillery exchanged shots. At least in the center and on the allied right wing, where the Swedish artillery had deployed, Tilly's forces lost heavily. With standardized types of artillery pieces and ammunition and highly disciplined and trained troops, the Swedes with their thoroughly inculcated drill fired off three shots for each single one their opponents fired. Moreover, the very standardization of Swedish weaponry allowed for far greater accuracy. Not surprisingly, the Hapsburg artillery suffered heavily in the unequal exchange of fire.

The Swedish artillery fire also inflicted serious damage on the *tercios* both physically and especially on morale, as a cascade of shot smashed into the Imperial formations, pulverizing musketeers and pikemen in a terrible slaughter. Ironically, what kept the Imperialist soldiers together in their *tercios,* the psychological cohesion of men in groups, was precisely what maximized their casualties, as the Swedish cannonballs ripped through their crowded ranks. The damage from the fire was both galling and deadly, smashing bodies to pulp, severing limbs, and squashing heads like melons.

The artillery fire also galled Pappenheim to the point that without waiting for Tilly's instructions to advance, he ordered a charge. Accustomed to victorious combat against the German Protestants, Pappenheim's cavalry soon found themselves in considerable difficulties. First of all, instead of galloping out to fire their pistols, the Swedish troopers waited and allowed their musketeers to blast the Imperialist cavalry. Only then did they ride out to attack their disorganized opponents, while the musketeers had the time and cover to reload. The horsemen then fell back to let the Swedish musketeers fire another volley.

In response, Pappenheim attempted to feel his way around the Swedish flank, but at every step he found his troopers thwarted by the combination of firepower, discipline, and cold steel that the Swedish troopers brought to the battle as well as their tactics. Within a relatively short period of time, the morale of Pappenheim's individual riders began to collapse under the pressure of the entirely unfamiliar tactics used by the Swedes.

Meanwhile, on Tilly's right flank the cavalry, having seen Pappenheim's troopers charge, also charged. Their advance was followed almost immediately by the *tercios*. Tilly appears to have angled nearly the entire *tercio* line to the right to take advantage of what he expected to be the rapid collapse of the Saxon forces. The Saxons and other Germans lived up to his expectations. The combination of the attacks by Imperialist cavalry and the grim, tanklike advance of the masses of the *tercios* was too much for the supposed soldiers of John George's Saxon army.

In a matter of moments, the entire left flank of the allied armies dissolved in a mad, desperate flight to the rear led by their elector, John George, the whole of which perhaps resembling nothing so much as the modus operandi of Monty Python's knights: "Run away, run away . . ." But this was not a game; it was the terribly serious business of war.

However, while some of the Imperialist troops began to raise the chant of *"Victoria,"* their doom was already on the march, as the Swedes adapted to what appeared to be a desperate situation for the Protestant cause. Their tactical response came with a speed that had not been seen since the days of the Roman legions of the high empire.

As the Saxons and other Germans collapsed, Horn reacted and immediately swung his cavalry to cover the increasingly exposed flank of his forces. At the same time, he swung his left-most brigade and probably the two brigades that formed the immediate reserve of the Swedish front line to the left also to cover the collapse of the Saxon allies. He may further have requested that Gustavus release at least a portion of the main reserve, although he may have possessed that authority already.

But the crucial decision that Horn made, whether on his own or from prior instructions from Gustavus, was to attack as quickly as his brigades could change front. And because they were highly trained, the Swedish brigades with their constituent parts of regiments and battalions turned almost ninety degrees with an astonishing speed for the time, while maintaining their disciplined formations. They then advanced at a steady march directly into the flanks of the Imperialist troops. The Imperial *tercios,* for their part, were far too unmanageable to turn to meet the terrifying threat that emerged from the smoke-covered battlefield on their flanks.

Horn's counterattacking cavalry and then his combined-arms infantry brigades chewed up the *tercios* with smashing volleys of musketeers and light artillery, followed almost immediately with slashing attacks by the Swedish pikemen, who added to the confusion and psychological fear that the Swedish firepower had created. The first recognition that the soldiers of the various *tercios* had of their impending doom was the emergence out of the fog and smoke of blue-and-yellow-uniformed Swedish regiments on their flank. A deadly volley of muskets and light cannon followed hard on that perception, accompanied by a charge of pikemen out of the Swedish formation. The pikemen then pulled back so that the musketeers in the Swedish regiments could fire a second lethal volley.

It was all too much. As the *tercios* began to fall apart in panic and fear, the Swedish cavalry with its slashing sabers added to the terror infecting the Imperialists, who were now desperate to escape. It was a full-on slaughter of veteran troops who over the past decade had known nothing but success against their enemies.

Meanwhile, on the other side of the battlefield, Gustavus's highly honed cavalry had broken Pappenheim's cavalry and chased the Imperialist troopers off the field. Disciplined as they were, the Swedish troopers quickly returned to the battlefield and followed their king to capture the Imperialist artillery, which was almost immovable. But it was sufficiently movable for the Swedes, having sabered the artillerists, to turn the guns against the *tercios* that were moving toward the collapse of the Saxons on the allied left flank.

By now, the full weight of the Swedish brigades had shifted into an all-out assault on the *tercios.* One by one, the Swedish brigades smashed into and then chewed their way through their opponents, leaving the human wreckage of their brutal assault behind them. Those who survived the collapse of their individual *tercio* then added to the panic as they fled past the surviving Imperialist formations.

By late afternoon, it was over. The survivors of Tilly's army were in desperate flight toward Leipzig and other towns to the south. The

Period engraving of the Battle of Breitenfeld
Library of Congress, Washington, D.C.

Imperialist army left some seventy-six hundred dead on the field, such
was the destructive impact of Swedish firepower, with probably similar numbers wounded and soon to perish. The Swedes captured nine
thousand mercenaries, nearly all of whom were promptly incorporated into the Protestant armies. Barely fifteen thousand escaped the
rout, their commander one of the wounded fugitives. The disastrous
defeat of his military forces so terrified the emperor that he considered
fleeing from Saxony all the way to Graz in Austria. Altogether, the
Swedes lost slightly over two thousand men. It was as complete a victory as Europe had seen in centuries. As the great historian of Gustavus's reign, Michael Roberts, has noted, "Military men everywhere
were forced to rethink their precepts, for at Breitenfeld Europe witnessed the triumph of a tactical revolution. The art of war would not
be the same again."

Breitenfeld ended the emperor's presumption and that of his Jesuit
advisers that they could stamp out Protestantism in northern Germany and create a centralized German state. The question was
whether Ferdinand would manage to keep his hold on southern Germany. For the moment, Gustavus and the Swedes were calling the
tune, while the desperate emperor had no choice but to recall Wallenstein and hope that the great mercenary captain could restore the
suddenly catastrophic strategic situation.

Breitenfeld also put paid to any chance that the emperor and his
supporters would be able to create a great Catholic alliance with his
cousins the Spanish Hapsburgs in order to eradicate Protestantism on

the rest of the Continent. Nor would the emperor be able to use the power he would have acquired by the destruction of Protestantism in northern Germany to help the Spanish Hapsburgs destroy Dutch independence. Breitenfeld did not, however, end the Thirty Years' War. At the Battle of Lützen the next year, Gustavus Adolphus would win another smashing victory over the Hapsburg army, this time commanded by Wallenstein. But the Swedish king, as usual heedless of his own safety, was to die in a cavalry charge. Thus disappeared the possibility that the Protestants would overwhelm Catholic power in southern Germany.

Instead, the war dragged on for another seventeen years, a conflict in which the great French statesman Cardinal Richelieu would continue French support for the Swedes and the Protestants. Thereby he ensured that the Germanies remained divided along religious and political lines, preventing them from presenting a serious threat to the power of France. That policy would effectively keep the Germanies divided until 1870, when Napoleon's nephew Emperor Napoleon III misplayed France's strategic hand so badly that the Prussians under Otto von Bismarck succeeded in unifying the Germanies into a powerhouse that would come close to destroying European civilization in two great world wars in the first half of the twentieth century.

Had the Hapsburgs, with their strong support for the Counter-Reformation, been able to impose the harsh orthodoxy of the Roman Catholic Church and the Counter-Reformation on a unified Germany and Europe as a whole, they might have throttled the scientific revolution in its early stages. Only two short years after Breitenfeld, the Italian Inquisition tried the great scientist Galileo for heresy for daring to suggest that the earth revolved around the sun. The inquisitors found him guilty, forced him to recant, and kept him under house arrest for the remainder of his life. The message was clear: The Catholic Church would not tolerate serious scientific research that challenged what it regarded as its basic truths. Europe's scientists received the message loud and clear, and there was a wholesale migration of the Continent's brightest minds to the Protestant lands in northern Europe, now no longer threatened by the Counter-Reformation. Thus, the scientific revolution that had begun in the sixteenth century would continue its path into the future.

For the Swedes, Gustavus Adolphus's military successes proved to be a mixed blessing. Over the next century, they would find themselves deeply entwined in the affairs of the Germanies through their reward of a slice of the province of Pomerania. That involvement provided them with few strategic or operational advantages, while distracting them from the growing power of Russia, which in the eighteenth century would expel them first from the Baltic republics and then from Finland.

Nevertheless, Gustavus Adolphus and his "new model army" had changed the strategic, political, and intellectual face of Europe. In many ways, the king's greatest accomplishment was the creation of a revolutionary approach to war at several crucial levels. The most obvious was the reintroduction of Roman battlefield discipline to his army, which provided the Swedes with an enormous advantage in tactical flexibility and the utilization of firepower. Within a matter of decades, the French had copied the Swedish methods, followed shortly thereafter by the other major armies of Europe. The "new model armies" provided disciplined and responsive military instruments on the battlefield, while the imposition of civil discipline eventually ended the peacetime ravages of armies on their own territory.

Equally important was the fact that the Swedish administrative reforms led to the creation of admiralties and military bureaucracies that allowed for the maintenance of large peacetime forces. This also would lead to the projection of European military power via the great navies of the seventeenth and eighteenth centuries throughout the world. It would be not technological superiority, but organizational and tactical superiority that would allow the military forces of the West to dominate the military forces of civilizations on the other side of the world and lead to the creation of the great empires of the eighteenth and nineteenth centuries. Breitenfeld heralded the coming of this revolution in the power relationships among the world's civilizations.

ANNUS MIRABILIS

The Rise of British Supremacy

1759

IN THE OTHER CHAPTERS IN THIS WORK, WE HAVE FOCUSED ON SINGLE battles or campaigns where the issues of war have exercised a crucial impact on the trajectory of human events. In this chapter, however, we have chosen to examine two great battles, one on land and one at sea, the combined impact of which profoundly influenced the course of history and which still today are playing a role in determining the emerging strategic environment, the world's economy, and the cultural framework of globalization. These two battles were decisive in the outcome of the Seven Years' War (1756–1763), during which Great Britain and France contested for control of the world's seas and the empires that both nations were busily engaged in building.

The first of these battles occurred in Canada on the Plains of Abraham, which lay adjacent to the French citadel and town of Quebec; the second, the naval Battle of Quiberon Bay, occurred directly off the coast of the Breton peninsula. Thousands of miles separated these two battles, yet they were directly connected in terms of British strategy. They were to occur within approximately two months of each other, the Battle of Quebec on September 13, 1759, and the

Battle of Quiberon Bay on November 20, 1759. Together they brought to a close a year of such stunning successes for Great Britain in the war against France that the British public was soon to term that year "annus mirabilis," or "the year of miracles." In addition to these crucial battles, the British were making major military efforts elsewhere on the global stage, in the West Indies for control of the riches of the sugar islands and in India, both of which would also prove successful. But it would be the naval superiority gained at Quiberon Bay and the destruction of New France (Canada, including its then capital, Quebec) that would ensure Britain's almost total victory in the Seven Years' War.

The war between the British and the French represented the third great global war in history, the first being the War of the Spanish Succession (1702–1714) and the second the War of the Austrian Succession (1740–1748). In the War of the Spanish Succession (known as "Queen Anne's War" in North America), the British had played a key role in cobbling together an alliance with the Dutch and the Austrians to halt the advance of Louis XIV's France. Besides the stunning land victories of the Duke of Marlborough, without doubt the greatest general in British history, the Royal Navy had begun to establish a dominance at sea that would last for the next two centuries. It was during that conflict that the British captured Gibraltar, while the outlines of the Anglo-French struggle for control of North America, the Caribbean, and India had emerged. Similarly in the War of the Austrian Succession, the outlines of the struggle for global domination were clear, but the conflict had not settled matters. It would be a different story in the next great war that began eight years later.

The third great global war was the Seven Years' War (called "the French and Indian Wars" in North America). That conflict turned history in a direction that has influenced events down to our own time. Its initial skirmishes took place in 1754 on the far distant frontier between New France and the American colonies and involved no less a figure than the young George Washington, who was leading an ill-fated expedition to what is now Pittsburgh. However, war between France and Great Britain did not officially begin until 1756 and reflected a far larger war that involved all the major European powers.

Simply put, in an age where personal likes and dislikes among the

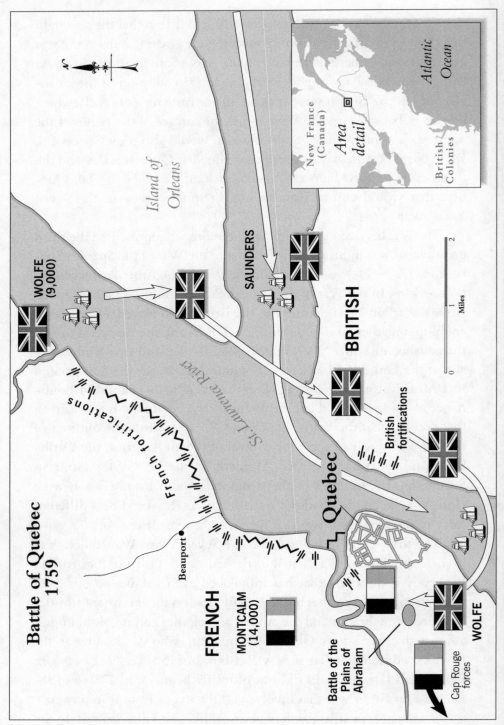

Battle of Quebec
1759

FRENCH

MONTCALM
(14,000)

Beauport

French fortifications

St. Lawrence River

Island of Orleans

WOLFE
(9,000)

SAUNDERS

BRITISH

British fortifications

Quebec

Battle of the
Plains of Abraham

Cap Rouge
forces

WOLFE

New France
(Canada)

British
Colonies

Atlantic
Ocean

Area
detail

0   1   2
Miles

rulers mattered, Frederick the Great of Prussia had managed to annoy the leaders of the other continental powers to an extent unusual even for the time. In the case of Austria, upon the accession of Maria Theresa to the Hapsburg lands in 1740, Frederick had announced that he was protecting the Austrian empress's territory from unnamed predatory powers and had promptly occupied the province of Silesia, which he would hold through two great wars and which would become a permanent province of Prussia and then Germany until 1945, when the Yalta Conference allocated it to Poland. Frederick's Machiavellian action had instigated the War of the Austrian Succession and, not surprisingly, made Maria Theresa a lifetime enemy of the Prussian king. In the case of France, Frederick referred to his hounds as his Marquises de Pompadour after Louis XV's mistress, an insult the two were not about to forget. With the French siding with Austria, the British joined Frederick in an alliance, following that basic principle of eighteenth-century politics that the enemy of my enemy is my friend.

The result had been a fundamental rearrangement of Europe's alliance system in the 1750s so that when war broke out in 1756 among the powers, France, Austria, and Russia had ranged themselves against Prussia and Great Britain. The initial British strategy, designed by the Duke of Newcastle's ministry, supported Frederick and mirrored that of the French. Thus the British attempted to pursue a strategy of fighting a war at sea against France's colonial possessions in the Caribbean and North America, while providing an army to support Prussia and the Electorate of Hanover in northern Germany, the latter a possession of Britain's King George II. In neither arena did the British achieve much success, but they certainly suffered significant defeats, including the loss of Minorca, which sealed the fate of the Newcastle ministry. British failures eventually brought William Pitt, clearly one of the greatest—and luckiest—strategists of all time, to form a new government. Pitt was to develop, articulate, and set in motion a grand strategy that overthrew the world order as it then existed and established Great Britain as the premier global power, the first in history. George II despised Pitt, which had for a while blocked him from office, but with the fall of the ministry of the Duke of Newcastle, the king had little choice but to grant Pitt real political power and the authority to determine Britain's strategy. It was to be the most important political appointment in British history until George VI confirmed Winston Churchill as prime minister on May 10, 1940.

Pitt proceeded to design and execute, to the extent possible for a single individual, a strategy aimed at overthrowing France's empire. Thus, unlike the strategy of his predecessor, in terms of British military power, Great Britain would not place equal emphasis on the struggle on the Continent. Instead the British would shower enormous subsidies on Frederick, providing him an amount each year eqivalent to what the Prussian government extracted from its subjects—an indication of just how wealthy Britain was becoming in the opening stages of its control over a world empire. Pitt's hope was that Frederick's military genius would enable Prussia to fend off the armies of Russia, France, and Austria. It was to be a close-run thing, and in the end, the Prussian king survived, but barely and at terrible cost to his realm and his health. Meanwhile, the British would steal the French Empire by deploying their superior naval and military forces on the global stage, a fact that did nothing to endear them to the Prussian king or the rest of Europe, for that matter. As Pitt accurately forecast, "We shall conquer America [and a lot more] through Germany."

By the end of 1757, Pitt, now in firm control of the government, had put together the various pieces of his grand strategy. In America, he moved to replace the arrogant and insensitive Lord Loudon, whose treatment of the colonists was akin to that of a drill sergeant, as he demanded they provide and pay for a substantial number of militia entirely out of their own resources. By mid-March 1758, matters had reached such an impasse between Loudon and the Massachusetts legislature that the delegates were on the point of refusing to vote either financial support or manpower for the war against New France.

However, on March 10, 1758, letters arrived in Boston informing the delegates that the British government had relieved Loudon and would pick up the tab for the recruitment, feeding, and equipping of the colonial militia for the war against the French in Canada. Not surprisingly, an ecstatic Massachusetts assembly, which had balked at supplying Loudon with 2,128 militia for military operations, voted to raise no fewer than 7,000 militia. Nevertheless, the operations that year in North America were not overly successful, but at least on the continent's periphery, the British were able to capture the great French naval base of Louisburg on the Cape Breton peninsula. One of the more outstanding brigadiers in that campaign was James Wolfe, who managed to inform a number of key figures back home in London of his role, somewhat exaggerated, in the campaign. The capture of that key fortress and base served to open up the St. Lawrence and New France to direct attack.

By 1758, the British effort under Pitt's imaginative and effective leadership had shifted into high gear. The first lord of the Admiralty, Lord George Anson, was a key player in Pitt's strategy and the success of British arms. Reappointed to the Admiralty in late 1757 by Pitt, Anson brought exceptional competence to his office with first-class ability as an administrator and a connoisseur of talent. His career at sea had been spectacular. Among his accomplishments was an epoch-making and enormously enriching journey around the world in the early 1740s that had seized enormous wealth from the Spanish, including one of their great treasure galleons off the Philippines. In every respect, his voyage had mirrored that of Drake nearly two centuries earlier.

But Anson was much more than a pirate. In late 1744, he had become the head of the Admiralty Board, from which position he introduced a broad variety of reforms, ranging from the introduction of uniforms for officers, to a fairer approach to discipline by revising the articles of war, to procedures that ensured the removal of captains and admirals who were either too old or incompetent, and to a thorough, honest, and efficient management of the Royal Navy's dockyards, at least by the standards of the time. He also succeeded in transferring the Royal Marines from the army to the navy, which would later have an impact on American practices.

In July 1746, Anson found himself promoted to vice admiral in command of the "permanent Western Squadron," stationed on the western approaches of the English Channel, another of his operational innovations. With a fleet at sea and home-ported at Plymouth or Portsmouth, the British were in a position to catch any French or Spanish fleet attempting to enter the Channel. In such a case, the Royal Navy would possess the advantage of wind, a crucial issue in the age of sail. In 1747, having told his ships' captains his desire that they display initiative rather than mindlessly follow the navy's "fighting instructions," Anson caught a French fleet as it sortied from Brest, the main French naval port on the Atlantic, in an attempt to reinforce France's position on Cape Breton Island in Canada. When the battle off Cape Finisterre was over, Anson had captured the entire covering fleet of six ships of the line.

Under Pitt, Anson now set in motion a shipbuilding program that steadily increased the Royal Navy's superiority over the French navy, a superiority that enabled the British to guard their trade, support the great expeditions issuing forth from Great Britain, and at the same time keep a watchful and effective eye on Brest and Toulon, the main French naval bases. In today's terms, it was all done on time and under budget.

In September 1758, Pitt appointed Jeffery Amherst to command in North America with instructions to carry the war into the heart of Quebec, and in November a great amphibious force left to attack the French islands in the West Indies. Then in December, for the final piece of British strategy for 1759, Pitt appointed James Wolfe to head a major assault up the St. Lawrence to seize Quebec City and its looming citadel. Wolfe had returned from the siege of Louisburg to London almost immediately after the conclusion of the campaign. Upon arriving back in the British capital, he had soon gained contact with Pitt and much impressed the great man. Nevertheless, it took all of Pitt's eloquence to persuade the aging king to promote Wolfe to major general. The great historian of the campaign has described Wolfe as possessing a "personality . . . as streaked by manic egotism as [Pitt's]," but that is perhaps why Pitt chose the young brigadier to lead such an important effort. For all the dysfunctional nature of Wolfe's personality, he was to provide the leadership and imagination that set the stage for the defeat of French forces in Quebec and British rule in Canada.

Pitt had designed a two-pronged invasion of Canada. Amherst would utilize the strength of British regulars supported by a major mobilization of the colonial militia to drive north from Albany up through Lakes George and Champlain and then down the Richelieu River to attack Montreal, while Wolfe was striking at Quebec. Although Amherst was in overall command in North America, given the tyranny of distance between Albany and Quebec, Wolfe had to all intents and purposes received an independent command. The great advantage that the British enjoyed lay in the fact that control of the Atlantic in 1759 by the Royal Navy allowed for a steady flow of supplies across that ocean to their forces in North America, while New France was largely isolated from support by its mother country.

Opposing Amherst and Wolfe was Louis-Joseph de Montcalm, a competent professional soldier but one who possessed little understanding of the difficulties as well as the possibilities that fighting with Indian allies in the wilderness of North America offered the French. The governor, the Marquis de Vaudreuil, *did* understand how different the circumstances of New France were from the mother country, but in spring 1759, the authorities in France ordered him to defer to Montcalm. While the British enjoyed a considerable superiority in numbers, the French had the advantage of interior lines and a better understanding of the terrain over which Amherst's drive would take place. The question of the hour was whether they could utilize those advantages.

The problem for the French was that Montcalm refused to use their greatest strength, their knowledge of the wilderness, a knowledge to which their Indian allies contributed considerably. As a European professional officer, Montcalm regarded the Indian approach to war as savagery. Given the collapse of communications with France, however, his regulars had lost considerable numbers whom he could not replace and whom he had had to augment with ill-trained, ill-disciplined Canadian militia. As a result, the French conventional forces stood little chance in a stand-up fight with the British. Finally, the relatively short campaigning season, which barely stretched from June through early October, did give the French an advantage. They had to hold off the British only until October, when the cold winds blowing south from the Arctic would freeze the St. Lawrence and force the British to shut down military operations until late the following spring.

WOLFE AT QUEBEC

Provided with eighty-five hundred troops and the support of the Royal Navy, Wolfe spent spring 1759 getting his expedition ready to drive the French out of Quebec. Like Amherst, Wolfe was late in starting and it was not until early June that his force sailed up the Gulf of St. Lawrence. Had the British moved earlier, they would have been in a position to prevent the last major French supply convoy of fourteen ships from slipping through to provide the Quebec garrison with the food and ammunition it desperately needed after a poor harvest the summer before. But instead of blockading the St. Lawrence, the Royal Navy had focused on readying the transports and ships of the line required to carry Wolfe and his expedition from Halifax to Quebec City.

The geography of Quebec City and the citadel that protected it was daunting. They sit on high bluffs, which cover approaches from the St. Lawrence River on the city's southern flank. Its northern flank rests on slightly lower bluffs, but formidable obstacles nevertheless. Moreover, the St. Charles River runs into the St. Lawrence from the

Portrait of Louis-Joseph de Montcalm (1712–1759) by Antoine-François Sergent-Marceau, oil on canvas, 1790
Library of Congress, Washington, D.C.

north, creating an additional obstacle to any attempt to approach the city from the north and northeast. Although the St. Lawrence is navigable for a considerable distance past the city, access to the plain lying behind Quebec City is limited to a number of steep footpaths up the bluffs, trails made more difficult by dense shrubbery.

From the moment of arrival on June 28, when the Royal Navy's transports began landing Wolfe and his soldiers down the St. Lawrence from Quebec, the British confronted the almost impossible task of getting at Montcalm. They soon realized that the French commander was more than content to sit behind his fortifications and wait the British out. It was during the following frustrating period that Wolfe coined his comment that "war is an option of difficulties." Despite his manic desire for fame and military glory, Wolfe possessed a weak constitution, which began to break down amid the pressures of campaigning. He was certainly suffering from kidney stones, which the medicine of the time could do little to relieve; his other health problems may have reflected a certain amount of hypochondria, but it is difficult to tell. Stymied in his desire to fight, Wolfe attempted to draw out Montcalm and the French from behind their fortifications by laying waste to the farms and villages that lay farther down the St. Lawrence—actions that to this day embitter the relations between the English-speaking and the French-speaking populations of Canada.

By late summer, it appeared that Wolfe was not going to be able to force Montcalm out of his defenses. As the British commander wrote home in late summer in a mood close to despair:

> My antagonist has wisely shut himself up in inaccessible entrenchments so that I can't get at him without spilling a torrent of blood, and that perhaps to little purpose. The Marquis de Montcalm is at the head of a great number of bad soldiers, and I am at the head of a small number of good ones, [who] wish for nothing so much as to fight him—but the wary old fellow avoids all action doubtful of the behaviour of his army.

Then, as so often happens in war, chance intervened. Captain Robert Stobo was one of the British officers who had accompanied George Washington in the disastrous expedition the future American leader had led into western Pennsylvania in 1754, which the French had soundly defeated. When Washington had surrendered Fort Necessity, he had given up Stobo as a hostage, and the French had then taken Stobo to Canada, where he had remained a prisoner at Quebec City. His captors had allowed him considerable freedom. By the time he escaped in early spring 1759, he knew the terrain surrounding the town and citadel inside and out. Stobo reached Louisburg before Wolfe, and he was able to pass along to Wolfe his extensive knowledge of Quebec City's geography as well as that of the surrounding terrain. Included in his intelligence was the fact that there was a trail at Fuller's Cove, several miles up the St. Lawrence, which ran up the bluffs to the Plains of Abraham west of the city.

Throughout the summer, Wolfe had not used that tidbit of information, undoubtedly because an effort to move the bulk of his forces up the steep trail might well place them in an impossible tactical situation. But by September Wolfe was desperate; everything that he had tried thus far had failed dismally. He determined to risk Stobo's trail in an attempt to get behind the French in Quebec City. To deceive the enemy, Wolfe moved most of his army upriver on transports so that it appeared the British were preparing to attack at Cap Rouge; but on the night of September 12/13, the British rowed down the St. Lawrence with French-speaking officers replying to the challenges they received from the shoreline. Wolfe was pessimistic as to the operation's chances but resolved to die a hero's death whatever happened. He got his wish.

Lieutenant Colonel William Howe, later to lead the British forces during the American Revolution, led the soldiers of the 58th Regiment as they scrambled up the cliff face. Howe's men overwhelmed a small French party at the top of the bluffs, but the French did get one of their number off to warn Montcalm that the British were up to something along Fuller's Cove. During the night, Montcalm and most of the French army had been preparing the city's defenses on its eastern side; an extensive British deception effort had convinced them that that was where the British were going to attack. Montcalm had also taken the precaution of sending two thousand soldiers and militia up the river in case the British indeed landed at Cap Rouge.

To add to the impact of Wolfe's move, Montcalm's aide refused to believe the warning from the picket at Fuller's Cove, declining to wake his commander and then going to bed himself. By the time other messengers had apprised Montcalm of the danger, Wolfe had nine battalions in line of battle on the Plains of Abraham, while another five were busily engaged in dragging cannons and ammunition up the bluffs from the river and broadening the path, which represented the army's lifeline to the river and the Royal Navy.

Montcalm was thunderstruck by the appearance of nearly the whole of Wolfe's army on the Plains of Abraham. It appears that he panicked, because instead of gathering his forces and recalling the two thousand soldiers from Cap Rouge, which would have provided him with a numerical advantage, Montcalm deployed the troops at his disposal in front of the city walls. He certainly did have the option of deploying them behind the walls and waiting for reinforcements, but he apparently feared that Wolfe might be able to begin a siege of the city, which would not last long, given that Montcalm had moved most of his supplies upriver in response to the British control of the lower river. Nevertheless, his decision to seek battle made little sense. There could not be much doubt as to the outcome.

And so the battle for Canada began. In spite of the galling fire of French and Indian snipers, the British line of regulars stood rock solid. In fact, Wolfe's troops were in a precarious position. If Montcalm managed to get messengers to the troops upriver, they would be in a position to attack the British in the rear. But at ten o'clock, with his troops deployed, the French commander made the disastrous mistake of ordering a general advance straight into the teeth of the long line of unwavering British regulars. Cheering enthusiastically, the French advanced. Almost immediately their discipline began to break down. At maximum range, they slowed their rush forward and fired a ragged volley. A few lucky shots hit their targets. One shot shattered Wolfe's wrist, but displaying the sangfroid expected of someone of his rank and class, he merely wrapped the wound in his handkerchief and continued to direct the battle. At this point the French troops, militia as well as regulars, lost all cohesion, with some running and others slowing to a trot as they approached the stolid redcoats.

Grim, unmoving, and utterly disciplined, the British line remained unfazed by the ragged firing of the advancing French. When the French were approximately fifty to sixty yards away, at Wolfe's command his officers and NCOs gave the order to fire. There was a single devastating blast. One of the officers present recorded the event: The result was as "close and heavy [a] discharge as I ever saw performed at a private field of exercise, insomuch that better troops than we encountered could not possibly withstand it: and, indeed, well might the French Officers say, that they never opposed such a shock as they received from the center of the line."

The French force collapsed almost immediately. Those not killed or wounded headed off as fast as they could run in the general direction of the city. Spurred on by the terrifying skirl of their bagpipes, the British regiments now pursued with bayonets, while the Highland Scots drew their claymores, all eager to get at those who had tormented and inflicted casualties on them throughout the summer. They took few prisoners.

A few French snipers on the left, north of the British line, extracted a measure of retribution by hitting Wolfe in the stomach and chest at the moment of victory. In moments he was dead. Montcalm too received a mortal wound in the wild French rout, but he lasted into the night.

The British officers were able to turn sufficient numbers of their disciplined regulars to intimidate the French soldiers Montcalm had sent upriver. Had any sort of leadership remained among the French, they might have held the city, but Vaudreuil, in charge after Montcalm was wounded, ordered the surviving French forces to pull out and left Quebec City in British hands.

Despite such serious shortages in supplies that some of the British soldiers came down with scurvy over the winter, the British held out until the spring. The question then was whose fleet would first arrive with reinforcements and supplies in the Gulf of St. Lawrence after the ice had broken up: that of the British or that of the French. Two months later, the Battle of Quiberon Bay off the coast of France would decide that question.

The Death of General Wolfe by Benjamin West, oil on panel, 1770 *The Bridgeman Art Library, New York*

QUIBERON BAY

In the naval sphere in 1759, Pitt's control of British strategy and the military appointments on which it depended was positioning Great Britain to overthrow the French Empire and its naval power lock, stock, and barrel. Not surprisingly, given the British tradition of muddling through in times of peace, under Newcastle the war at sea in 1756 had started off almost as badly as had the war on land in North America. The Royal Navy had not been ready for war; its funding had been set at too low a level over the previous decade of peace. In the Mediterranean, Britain's position on the strategically important island of Minorca had almost immediately come under attack by a French fleet. The defending fleet under Admiral Sir John Byng was both outnumbered and in considerably worse shape than that of the French. Nevertheless, the fleet action was indecisive. Byng, however, decided to return to Gibraltar to refit, and the British lost Minorca.

A furious British public demanded its pound of flesh for the defeat, and the ministry ordered that Byng be tried for cowardice. A court-martial found him guilty and sentenced him to death. However, its members undoubtedly believed George II would pardon the admiral. The king did not, and Byng went to his death—a death that Voltaire characterized as one motivated *"pour encourager les autres"* ("for the encouragement of the others [admirals]"). In fact, Voltaire's quip masked the reality that Great Britain expected little from its generals but a great deal from its admirals. Byng had failed to measure up to those standards.

Confronted by the naval difficulties at sea, and to cement his political ties to his predecessor and hold his new ministry together, Pitt relied heavily on Lord Anson, whom he had recalled to duty as first lord of the Admiralty in late 1757 and granted authorization to fix the problems. Among his many acts, Anson ensured that the commander of the Western Squadron (renamed the Channel Fleet)—the command that he had led to victory at what later came to be called the First Battle of Cape Finisterre—would remain Sir Edward Hawke, who matched Anson's record as a fighter. In 1746, Hawke had caught a French attempt to fight their merchant ships out of the blockade the British were maintaining off Brest. In the Second Battle of Cape Finisterre, only two out of eight French ships of the line guarding the convoy escaped. The British captured the rest, with three falling into the hands of Hawke. The British lost some 170 killed; the French, 4,000—which suggests how thoroughly Hawke had trained the gun crews of the ships under his command. Hawke was undoubtedly the greatest tactician and battle leader the Royal Navy would possess until Horatio Nelson. In fact, one might as much speak of "the Hawke touch" as of "the Nelson touch."

In 1756, Hawke still commanded the Channel Fleet, again carrying out a distant blockade of Brest. One of the major risks of Pitt's strategy was that it denuded the British Isles of troops in order to support the expeditions to destroy French power in Canada, the West Indies, Africa, and India. Thus, the one hope the French had to redress the looming disasters was to launch an invasion of the British Isles to destroy Britain's pretensions of being a great power. To that end, the French had gathered an invasion force at Quiberon Bay, which needed the cover of the Brest fleet to have any chance of reaching Great Britain. Therein lay the rub, because throughout the summer and into the fall, there patrolled, in the words of the great naval historian Alfred Thayer Mahan, "those far distant, storm-beaten ships" of the Channel Fleet. Mahan was, of course, speaking of the role of the Channel Fleet in guarding the British Isles during the wars of the French Revolution and Napoleon. Thus, between the French and world dominion lay the Channel Fleet guarding the British Isles.

Hawke maintained the blockade of Brest only by means of an innovative and difficult system of victualing his ships at sea via supply ships sent out from Great Britain. The medical profession of the time had yet to discover the causes of scurvy, but by shipping out fresh food, Hawke achieved the extraordinary record of having only twenty sailors out of fourteen thousand become ill over the six months his ships maintained their position off Brest. Moreover, the unbroken blockade of Brest had hardened the tough sailors of the British ships to handle the worst weather, while the gun crews' constant practice had turned the fleet into a murderous weapon of war.

By fall 1759, the blockade and their defeats had made the French desperate. Then, in mid-November, the waves and winds of a ferocious fall storm blew Hawke's ships all the way back to Torbay on the southwest coast of England. The French admiral, the Count de Conflans-Brienne, under pressure from his government, took advantage of the gale and sortied from Brest to sail south to Quiberon Bay to rendezvous with the invasion fleet. British frigates lying outside Brest immediately sailed up the English Channel to inform Hawke that the French were out, and of course the admiral knew where Conflans was headed. The weather mitigated, at least for a short time, and the British put to sea to beat down the Channel and then around Brittany with the same objective Conflans had in mind: Quiberon Bay. It was a race the British had spent the past six months preparing to make. The French, however, had spent the past six months in harbor in Brest and were hardly ready to face the Atlantic gales of November.

In the early morning hours of November 20, as the French were approaching Quiberon Bay, the weather again worsened. That alone would have presented Conflans with the challenge of shepherding his inexperienced fleet through the narrow channels that led through the reef-and-island-studded entrance into the bay itself. The first thing the French spied was a group of British frigates in front of the bay on watch for any movement by French ships to break out. Conflans initially moved to trap them, but suddenly a lookout cried out his sighting of a line of sails astern making straight for the French fleet. It was Hawke. As the British admiral later recalled, "At about half past eight on the morning of the 20th . . . the *Maidstone* made the signal for seeing the [enemy] fleet. I immediately spread about the signal for the line abreast, in order to draw all the ships of the squadron up with me."

In fact, while covering a greater distance, Hawke had arrived at Brest only a few hours after Conflans. Sailing with inexperienced crews unprepared to handle the roiling seas of fall in the Atlantic, the French were in a dire position. As in all wars, experience and discipline told. In the case of one French ship, the *Thésée,* the crew consisted almost entirely of peasants conscripted from their fields a few months earlier. The crews of the other French ships were not much better—and not just the sailors, but the gun crews too were distinctly inferior to those on Hawke's grim ships. Throughout the eighteenth century, the French never managed to bring the gun crews on their ships up to the standards of the Royal Navy. For every shot a French gun crew could get off, a British gun crew could fire two and sometimes three shots. Moreover, the British fired directly into an enemy's ship with the aim to destroy it; the French tended to fire into an enemy's rigging, the better to get away.

Conflans confronted the dilemma of whether to turn and fight in the midst of an Atlantic gale or to try to get his ships into Quiberon Bay, where, given the dangerous shoals and reefs, even the British would not dare to follow. He chose the latter course, but in the face of the howling winds, with his inexperienced crews, he dared not have his ships carry their full set of sails. Hawke, on the other hand, had his crews deploy every sail the masts of his ships could bear. Consequently, the British gained steadily on the fleeing French.

By two thirty, the van and the center of the French fleet were rounding Les Cardinaux, the rocky shoals that marked the end of the Quiberon peninsula and what Conflans believed to be safety. But Hawke's leading vessels had already caught up with the rear section of the French fleet and began ripping them apart with devastating broadsides. "Black Dick" Howe, captain of the *Magnanime,* later to command the British fleet off the American coast early in the revolution and then the Channel Fleet during the French Revolutionary Wars, laid his ship up close to the *Formidable* and had his gun crews blast the Frenchman's hull, "pierc[ing it] like a cullender."

Almost immediately, it was clear there was great danger in opening the lower gun ports, because the turbulent seas might flood a vessel and send it to its death. That was precisely what happened when the British warship *Torbay* engaged the *Thésée.* As the waves threatened to swamp both vessels, Augustus Keppel, captain of the *Torbay,* turned his ship into the wind, but the French crew of peasants failed to act as quickly. As had occurred with Henry VIII's *Mary Rose* two hundred years earlier, water flooded in through the lower gun ports, and the *Thésée* turned turtle and went straight to the bottom. The peasant crew, having undoubtedly already suffered enormously during their first experience at sea, now faced a few last moments of agonizing horror as their ship slipped beneath the raging Atlantic and its dark waters drowned their cries and their lives. Only nine sailors from the *Thésée* managed to swim ashore.

With the storm reaching its height, gigantic waves and ferocious winds made any kind of controlled course almost impossible, but British seamanship proved sterling. Hawke made the extraordinary decision to continue the pursuit over the unchartered reefs and shoals into Quiberon Bay. Leading the pack, the British admiral and his ship of the line went after Conflans's flagship. He ordered the ship's captain to lay the *Royal George* beside the *Soleil Royal,* and when the captain raised the possibility that they might smash into the rocks, Hawke shouted back: "You have now done your duty in apprising me of the dangers, let us now see how well you can comply with my orders."

As it became suddenly clear the British were following them into Quiberon Bay with murderous intent, the French gave way to wholesale panic. Like a flock of sheep fleeing a pack of wolves, they now thought only of escape. With the enemy having clearly abandoned any inclination to fight, Hawke's captains smelled blood and pounced. By the end of the afternoon as darkness settled, besides the *Thésée,* the French had lost the *Superbe,* with the *Formidable* and the *Héros* taken as prizes, the latter lost later when she ran aground. The British did lose two ships but saved most of the crews.

Only the early autumn night saved the French from losing their entire fleet. With the storm still raging and darkness rising, fighting halted as the ships of both fleets anchored. The next day, to avert its capture by the British, Conflans ordered his flagship burned. Eight French ships of the line had slipped out during the night, while seven escaped in the early morning hours by dumping their guns and everything not nailed down into the bay and then crossing the bar into the Vilaine River. There they remained, moldering and rotting, unable to get back out. Hawke had tried to catch them before they crossed the bar, but a fierce wind out of the northwest held his ships back. The French lost one other ship of the line when the *Juste* was wrecked in the Loire. All in all, Hawke had taken enormous risks in his remorseless pursuit of the French into Quiberon Bay in the midst of a ferocious gale, straight into a harbor for which the British had neither pilots nor charts. But he relied on the skill of his captains and his sailors, and they returned that trust fully in their performance. The Battle of Quiberon Bay was as complete a victory as any naval commander has ever won, and it destroyed French naval power for the remainder of the war. There would be no substantial reinforcements to support the French forces isolated in New France, the West Indies, or India.

ON MAY 12, 1760, as French engineers were laying out the siege lines to begin an attempt to regain Quebec City from the starving and disease-ridden remnants of Wolfe's army, they spied the first ships to sail up the St. Lawrence. The ships were flying the Union Jack, harbingers of the reinforcements and supplies that were on the way and that would complete the conquest of French Canada. As one of the French officers exclaimed, "A single ship of the line and the place would have been ours." But the French ships of the line either had been sunk, were rotting in the harbor, or were flying the white ensign as newly incorporated members of the Royal Navy's fleet, having been captured in combat at sea.

Great Britain's victory in the Seven Years' War created a period of oceanic dominance that would last for over the next century and a half. It was the stupendous victories of the annus mirabilis that set the seal for the great global empire the British would rule. The fruits of Pitt's strategy ended the century-long contest between the monarchies of France and England (and then Great Britain) for dominion over the world's oceans, as well as control over North America, India, and the Caribbean's sugar islands. The victory over France reflected the extraordinary political and strategic effectiveness of British leaders, particularly Pitt, admittedly helped by the abysmal incompetence of the French monarchy, which contributed mightily to its collapse a quarter of a century later.

Ironically, the British victory on the Plains of Abraham set the stage for the success of the American Revolution. The experience the colonial militia gained in fighting beside British regulars, an experience paid for by Pitt's government, would form the basis for the military effectiveness of the colonists in the Revolutionary War two decades later. But outside of that negative result—at least for the short term, since the United States that eventually emerged would play a crucial role in Great Britain's defense during the world wars and the Cold War—Britain's enormous victories in the Seven Years' War and its newly acquired position as the dominant world power would have a series of unintended effects that extended far beyond the riches that flowed into the new center of world trade. These included the fueling of the Industrial Revolution in Great Britain, which has had such an enormous and beneficial impact on the course of history and also ensured that the British rather than the French would control India, with huge political, economic, and strategic implications that still echo today in the twenty-first century.

Equally important would be the fact that English, not French, has become the dominant language of global intellectual and commercial exchange. The facts that India has the largest population of fluent English speakers in the world, remains a democratic state, and rests on the concept of the rule of law are all the unintended effects of the British Raj, which resulted from the events that occurred during the annus mirabilis. That reality bodes well for America's global interests and the course of history over the coming century.

SARATOGA

The Victory of Amateurs

1777

ON JULY 4, 1776, IN A MOOD OF IMMENSE ENTHUSIASM AND OPTIMISM, the representatives of the thirteen American colonies had signed the Declaration of Independence. Thirteen months earlier, the militia of New England, reinforced by volunteers from as far away as Virginia, had shot to pieces British regulars at the Battle of Bunker Hill; only the fact that the colonists ran out of ammunition had prevented them from winning a crushing victory. By spring 1776, the British had had to withdraw from Boston. But almost immediately after the Continental Congress declared the colonies' independence from Great Britain, the nascent nation's strategic situation collapsed in a welter of defeats. The British Army, under the command of General Sir William Howe, had badly battered the Americans in late summer and fall 1776, driving them from Brooklyn, then Manhattan and Westchester, and finally from what were then called the Jersies. At times, it seemed as if the British redcoats were going to entirely destroy the colonists' ill-equipped, ill-trained army of amateurs.

As 1777 dawned, the political and strategic situation of Britain's rebellious colonies appeared desperate. Admittedly, the Americans' leading general, George Washington, had won several small skirmishes at the turn of the year, but the victories at Trenton and Princeton were hardly sufficient to encourage Britain's European enemies to help the rebels. And now the British were concentrating their military power, intent on ending the rebellion that year. The major British force in North America, occupying New York City, could choose from a number of strategic options: It could move directly through the Jerseys to strike at the colonists' capital at Philadelphia; it could strike north along the Hudson River; or it could use the Royal Navy to transport it to virtually any point along the coasts of the rebellious colonies.

Equally threatening in spring 1777 was the large army that the British had built up in Canada, this one under the command of "Gentleman Johnny" Burgoyne, playwright and sometime general. For all his posturing, Burgoyne was a serious student of military affairs who had for his time an enlightened view about how officers should treat their soldiers. Not surprisingly, unlike most British officers, he had an excellent rapport with the common soldiers, who regarded him with both respect and admiration. Nevertheless, he also had a British aristocrat's contempt for the plebeian, common Americans, who had dared rebel against the crown. Burgoyne's army was now poised to drive up the Richelieu River from Montreal, cross Lake Champlain, and then drive down the Hudson from Lake George to Albany. A combined offensive by Burgoyne and Howe, with their two armies meeting at Albany, could thereby seize control of the Hudson River valley. Strategically, such a campaign, if successful, would split the New England colonies from the other colonies and allow the British to divide and conquer their rebellious subjects.

However, the British generals failed to cooperate in their efforts in 1777. Much of the confusion in British strategy had to do with personalities, both those in London and those in command of British forces in North America. The tyranny of distance was also a contributing factor. A crossing of the Atlantic took on average six to eight weeks, if one was lucky; important dispatches could take four to five months to reach their intended recipient. Under such circumstances, cobbling together and maintaining a coherent strategic approach between London and British forces in North America was next to im-

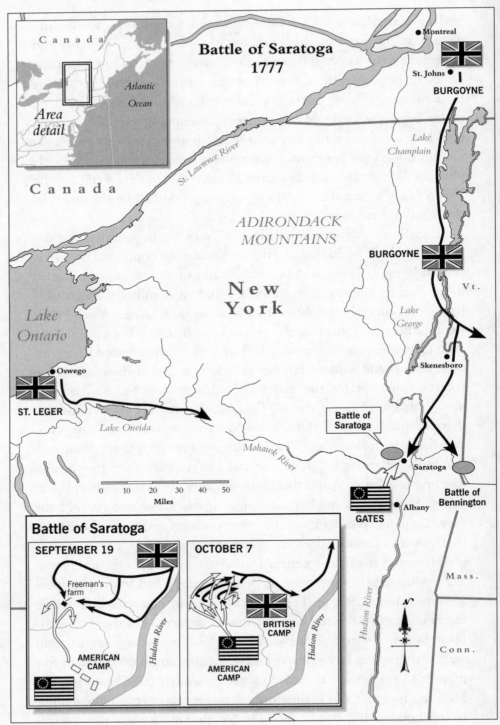

Area detail

Canada

Atlantic
Ocean

**Battle of Saratoga
1777**

Montreal

St. Johns

BURGOYNE

Canada

St. Lawrence River

*Lake
Champlain*

ADIRONDACK
MOUNTAINS

BURGOYNE

**New
York**

Vt.

*Lake
George*

*Lake
Ontario*

Oswego

Skenesboro

ST. LEGER

Lake Oneida

Mohawk River

Battle of
Saratoga

Saratoga

0   10   20   30   40   50
Miles

GATES

Albany

**Battle of
Bennington**

Battle of Saratoga

SEPTEMBER 19

Freeman's
farm

Hudson River

AMERICAN
CAMP

OCTOBER 7

BRITISH
CAMP

Hudson River

AMERICAN
CAMP

Mass.

Hudson River

N

Conn.

possible. In his last speech before the House of Commons, William Pitt, Britain's great strategist during the Seven Years' War and severe critic of George III's policy of intimidation toward the American colonies, had warned Lord North's government: "Three thousand miles of ocean lie between you and them. No contrivance can prevent the effect of this distance in weakening government. Seas roll, and months pass, between the order and the execution; and the want of a speedy explanation of a single point is enough to defeat the whole system."

Equally important in the failure of the British strategy was the fact that two of the principal actors in the development of that strategy—Lord Germain, secretary of state for the American Department, who was responsible for the running of the war among King George III's ministers; and "Gentleman Johnny" Burgoyne—had little understanding of the difficulties the American wilderness would pose, not only to the advance of a European-style army, but to its logistical support as well. Germain had never been to the colonies, while Burgoyne's experience had been limited to short periods in Boston, when the colonists had besieged the town in 1775, and in Canada after the British had abandoned that city and New England in 1776. Moreover, like most members of the British upper classes, both considerably underestimated the willingness and ability of the colonists to fight in defense of their recently proclaimed independence.

After the British withdrawal from Boston in April 1776, Burgoyne had moved to Canada to become the chief subordinate of General Sir Guy Carleton, the governor in chief, but had then returned to London at the end of the year. There he persuaded Germain to place him in command of an army in Canada that would drive south from Montreal to Albany and meet up with Howe's army moving north from New York City. Unfortunately for British fortunes, Burgoyne's underlying assumptions about his proposed campaign were to prove disastrously faulty. The logistical difficulties were by themselves daunting. The terrain through which the British would move would favor the colonists, a factor that anyone who had been involved in Jeffery Amherst's British and colonial efforts in the area during the Seven Years' War would have known. Moreover, Burgoyne and Germain believed, as was to be the case with virtually every British commander in the war, that only a small portion of the population supported the rebellion and that a substantial reservoir of Tory sentiment would rally to the British Army once it arrived.

Finally, and most disastrous, Burgoyne and Germain assumed Howe would move north to meet the invading force from Canada. It would not be until he reached Saratoga that "Gentleman Johnny" would learn that Howe had set off on an extended campaign to seize Philadelphia and destroy Washington's Continental army. In fact, Howe failed to support the move from Canada because Germain neglected to inform him that the government expected him to support Burgoyne. To get to Pennsylvania, Howe decided not to advance across the Jersies, because he believed the logistical difficulties of supporting a campaign from New York into Pennsylvania would prove too great. Instead he took his army all the way south by sea to the entrance to the Chesapeake before landing in Maryland and marching from that point on Philadelphia. British forces remaining in New York under Sir Henry Clinton were insufficient to mount a major campaign to support Burgoyne. At best they could launch a raiding force up the Hudson, which they were eventually to do. Although that force enjoyed some success, capturing West Point and reaching

Portrait of British general John Burgoyne (1722–1792) by Sir Joshua Reynolds, oil on canvas, c. 1766
The Frick Collection, New York

and burning Kingston, then the capital of the colony of New York, it could reach no farther and eventually had to fall back to New York City, then consisting only of a small portion of the island of Manhattan.

AND SO Burgoyne would end up going it alone. Although he was not informed that Howe planned to move against Philadelphia, it is doubtful Burgoyne would have changed his plans, such was his confidence in his army and contempt for the martial qualities of the colonists. Burgoyne arrived in Canada in early May 1777 to inform Carleton that he was not to command the army to invade the colonies, but rather would remain in Canada to command the troops Burgoyne, having chosen the best regiments, would leave behind.

The majority of Burgoyne's army consisted of British regulars, men who had enlisted for a number of reasons: for drink, to escape the boredom and poverty of their life, and in many cases to avoid the hangman's noose—in eighteenth-century Britain there were more than three hundred crimes for which one could be hanged. The discipline imposed on the enlisted ranks was savage, brutal, and swift for even the most minor offenses. The other portion of the army consisted of German mercenaries, recruited from the minor states of Brunswick and Hesse. Frederick the Great was so contemptuous of the minor princes hiring out their subjects to the British that he imposed a cattle tax on the troops that crossed his territory on their way to North America. The Germans were under the same harsh discipline as British soldiers. Whatever merciless regime they were subject to, the British and German soldiers formed highly trained, cohesive, and responsive combat units of the highest quality. But Burgoyne's soldiers had been trained to fight in the open, on relatively flat terrain. In such circumstances they would be virtually unbeatable—if they could find such locations in the wilderness of the northern colonies.

Burgoyne's plan to reach Albany had two major components. The main force, under his command and totaling approximately seven thousand British and German soldiers, with a sprinkling of Indians and Tories, would follow the route up the Richelieu River and then use Lakes Champlain and George and the Hudson River to reach

Albany. These numbers would begin to shrink before his troops engaged in serious combat with their American enemies, since as he moved south, he would have to garrison the major points his army captured, such as Forts Ticonderoga and Edwards. At the same time a second force, approximately one thousand men under Barry St. Leger consisting of a mixture of Tories, regulars (two hundred British and more than three hundred Germans), and Indians, moved from the west using Lake Ontario and the Mohawk River to join Burgoyne at Albany. Colonists under the future traitor and brilliant soldier Benedict Arnold defeated that arm of the British advance with relative ease.

In late spring, Burgoyne and his army began their march south. As his British and Germans proceeded, Burgoyne, displaying the qualities of a bad playwright rather than a general, issued a histrionic proclamation that announced his intention to liberate the colonists from "the unnatural rebellion" under which they were suffering. Nevertheless, if the colonists failed to greet their liberators with proper respect and affection, he continued, "I have but to give stretch to the Indian forces under my direction, and they amount to thousands, to overtake the hardened enemies of Great Britain and America. I consider them the same wherever they might lurk. The messengers of Justice and Wrath await them in the field; and devastation, famine, and every concomitant horror that a reluctant but indispensable prosecution of military duty must occasion, will bar the way to their return." Burgoyne could have produced no tract better calculated to stoke the anger as well as the fear of the Americans than to indicate that the British were unleashing the fury of an Indian war not only on the frontier, but deep into settled areas of the colonies as well. The reverberations of Burgoyne's missive echoed and reechoed deep into New York and New England, even reaching Maryland and Virginia.

The campaign opened with what appeared to be brilliant success. By late June, Burgoyne's forces, shielded by their Indian allies, had reached Fort Ticonderoga. The defenders were thoroughly ill prepared; the fort itself had been badly placed, so that if an enemy gained the heights of Sugar Loaf Mountain and placed artillery on those heights, the fort itself would become indefensible. The Americans failed to guard the mountain, the British pushed artillery to the heights, and Ticonderoga fell without a fight. Burgoyne then sent a detachment under Brigadier General Simon Fraser in pursuit of the routed rebels.

But in a nasty little fight at Hubbardton, the Americans put up stiff resistance against Fraser's troops. The fight was definitely not out of the Americans. While the colonials suffered heavier casualties, they inflicted losses on the British that in the long run Burgoyne could not afford. Moreover, again distance and the necessity to maintain contact with Canada had a significant impact on the British. Burgoyne had to leave four hundred soldiers to garrison Crown Point to guard his ammunition supplies and another nine hundred to ensure that Ticonderoga would remain in British hands to protect his lines of communication.

The question now confronting Burgoyne was how to conduct the next stage of the advance on Albany. There were two possible routes, both with their defects. Originally, he had planned to move from Lake Champlain across to the northern portion of Lake George and utilize that body of water to move south to the Hudson. This presented several difficulties. First, there was no road between the two lakes; second, the rough terrain between the two virtually precluded the timely construction of a road and the easy movement of the army and its supply train. The other option was the route that ran between Skenesborough and the Hudson. Several factors led Burgoyne to choose this route. First was the fact that the lead elements of his army had already reached Skenesborough. Choosing the Lake George route would have forced him to pull the army back a considerable distance. Second, it was only sixteen miles from Skenesborough to the Hudson, a much shorter distance than the first route. It seemed a simple matter of having the army cut its way through the forest and construct a road to ease the passage of artillery and supply wagons. Surely such a task would represent no great difficulty?

What looked straightforward on the maps turned out to be a nightmare born of Burgoyne's ignorance of American terrain. Those sixteen short miles consisted of pure, primeval wilderness. To add to the challenges involved in building a road in such trackless terrain, the Americans, as they retreated south, cut down huge trees into tangles of branches and trunks into which they rolled boulders, dammed up streams, and caused other mischief along the route the British had chosen. Nature with its insects, heat, humidity, rain, and dark, wild forests made its contribution to ensuring that the task of those cutting their way south with axes and saws was a dismal one indeed. While the British, now moving at a snail's pace, chopped their way through to the Hudson, the colonials were gathering their forces.

Nevertheless, when the British arrived on the Hudson, the troubles they had encountered thus far seemed to owe more to the terrain and distance than to the Americans. Matters were soon to change. War parties of Indians joined up with the British at Skenesborough on July 17, where Burgoyne unleashed them in the belief that his army could control them. In fact, the Indians waged war as they always had, scalping, killing, and raping anyone unfortunate enough to cross their path, including a certain Jane McCrea, the beautiful fiancée of a Tory officer in Burgoyne's army. Several Indians captured her and her companion and murdered, scalped, and stripped her. Jane's fiancé then recognized her scalp on the belt of one of the Indians. Burgoyne attempted to punish the murderers but met with little success. Outraged that the British chief wanted to subject them to the white man's laws, large numbers of the Indians proceeded to desert. On the other side, the incident was a windfall for colonial propagandists. Within a matter of weeks, the story had spread all the way to Virginia.

On August 3, Burgoyne at last received the extraordinary news of Howe's movements. According to a message smuggled through the lines, Howe was not advancing up the Hudson to meet the invading army from Canada in Albany. Instead, he was taking himself and his army off to Pennsylvania by way of the Chesapeake. Here was Burgoyne's opportunity to change his plan of campaign. Supplies were already running short as the logistical lines to Canada lengthened. The Americans were hastening reinforcements northward from as far away as Virginia. Nevertheless, Burgoyne resolved to proceed southward as if nothing had changed.

ENSCONCED IN HIS NEW POSITION at Fort Edwards on the Hudson, "Gentleman Johnny" decided to launch a foraging expedition eastward into Vermont and Massachusetts and then down the Connecticut River. His initial plan called for a jaunt that would have been almost two hundred miles in length. The purpose of the raid was twofold. First, it was to forage extensively to strengthen the army's supply base and capture horses for the German cavalrymen who had arrived in Canada with no mounts. Equally important in Burgoyne's calculations was the belief that a large number of Tories would rally to the British forces marching through the countryside. Nothing better illustrates the extent to which the British underestimated the colonists as well as their misconceptions about the political attitudes of the population they intended to bring to heel.

Piers Mackesy, the great historian of the British side of the war, acidly dissected the expedition's composition:

> The commander [whom Burgoyne] chose was a brave German dragoon called Colonel Baum who qualified for marching through a country of mixed friends and foes by speaking no English. His force was remarkable. He had 50 picked British marksmen and 100 German grenadiers and light infantry; 300 Tories, Canadians, and Indians; to preserve secrecy, a German band; to speed the column, 170 dismounted German dragoons in search of horses, marching in their huge top boots and trailing their sabers. They were reinforced on the march by 50 Brunswick Jäger and 90 local Tories.

The expedition was about to run into a buzz saw of opposition. New England and New York were up in arms at the threat of Indian massacres that Burgoyne had raised at the beginning of his march, fear and anger that the murder of Jane McCrea had served only to exacerbate.

Moreover, one of the most competent battlefield commanders the colonies were to throw up during the war, a certain John Stark, was leading a substantial number of New Hampshire militia toward Bennington as Baum moved out from the Hudson. Stark was hard-core indeed. He had been captured by the Indians before the outbreak of the Seven Years' War and then had so impressed the Iroquois by his bravery that they had made him a member of the tribe. Stark returned home, and with his knowledge of the Indians along with a natural talent for leadership, he subsequently became one of the most effective lieutenants in Rogers' Rangers during the Seven Years' War. At Bunker Hill, he led his militia regiment with exceptional skill in holding the far left of the line. At Trenton, it was his troops who broke the Hessians' last attempt to stand with several well-timed volleys. Yet the Continental Congress failed to promote Stark to brigadier general, instead advancing a politically connected individual from New Hampshire who had little military experience. An infuriated Stark resigned his commission and returned home to his farm. Burgoyne's threat to New England combined with his promise to unleash the Indians brought Stark back to lead the troops the state's legislature called up. The only requirement Stark levied on the legislature in accepting his commission was that he would be responsible only to New Hampshire and not to the Continental Congress or its officers. A hard man, John Stark.

Several thousand New Hampshire men promptly joined up with Stark to fight the invaders. The men Stark was leading represented an interesting military force. Although the young farmers among them were inexperienced in military affairs, their leaders were not. Eighteen years earlier, the British had mounted a major military effort up the Hudson River valley and on to Montreal to drive the French from Canada. Their regulars had borne the bulk of the fighting, but supporting them was a large force of militia units drawn from New England and upstate New York. The soldiers in the militia regiments had experienced the rigors of campaigning, observed the strengths and weaknesses of the "lobsterbacks," learned a modicum of drill, and occasionally fought short, sharp skirmishes with the French and Indians. Those men now served not only as the top leaders of the Revolutionary army, but as junior officers and sergeants buttressing the militia units that had begun to gather as soon as the colonists had received word of the British invasion from Canada. Thus, the militia facing Burgoyne's army was much more than a mob of hardscrabble farmers; they were made of tough, proud men led by individuals with considerable military experience.

The target for the British raid, selected by Burgoyne largely because it was the agricultural center of southern Vermont, was Bennington. As Baum advanced at a maddeningly slow pace, Stark and his New Hampshire militia arrived in the town to find a swelling number of militia units from the other New England states. Alarmed by his first contact with the colonists, who were gathering in larger numbers than expected, Baum requested reinforcements. Burgoyne then dispatched another contingent of Germans under the command of Lieutenant Colonel Heinrich Breymann, a military pedant of the worst sort. Constantly ordered by Breymann to order and reorder their ranks, his soldiers failed to reach Baum before the fighting began.

Meanwhile, Stark assumed de facto command of the colonial troops, and the two forces ran into each other in a pouring rain on August 15. As the weather cleared on August 16, Stark announced to his troops: "There are the redcoats and they are ours, or Molly Stark sleeps a widow tonight." A combination of superior numbers and broken, wooded terrain gave the Americans a distinct advantage. That afternoon, Stark struck. His militia units outflanked Baum's force after pinning the German grenadiers in their redoubt. Following some stiff fighting along the center of Baum's line, the German defenses collapsed under attack from both their flanks and front, with the remnants fleeing back the way they had come. The routed British and German soldiers then ran into Breymann's soldiers slowly approaching the battlefield. The colonials proceeded to maul that force badly, although darkness prevented them from destroying the second German force as they had Baum's. The Germans, Tories, and British scrambled through the darkness back to the safety of the main army.

Burgoyne now confronted a serious situation. Howe was not going to appear south of Albany to relieve the pressure on his army from the swelling numbers of colonial militia in their path. The losses to the army at the Battle of Bennington had been heavy, nearly one thousand men, or somewhere between 15 and 20 percent of the troops Burgoyne had available along the Hudson. Moreover, the defeat at Bennington had underlined that foraging for supplies would not be in the cards, since any unit engaged in such activities away from the army's main body was going to be gobbled up by American militia. And to cap it all off, Burgoyne's supply lines to Canada were tenuous and now open to attack by the Americans. Bennington had demonstrated clearly that the Americans were going to be tough fighters on their own ground. At that point, Burgoyne should have pulled back at the minimum to Ticonderoga, where logistical difficulties would have hampered the colonists from following him while his own supply problems would have eased.

But Burgoyne, ever the gambler, had no intention of withdrawing to Ticonderoga or Canada, since anything less than success would have ruined his military career. Instead, he remained confident that with his professional army he could fight his way through to Albany, where either the colonials would collapse or perhaps Major General Henry Clinton, now in command in New York, could get reinforcements up the Hudson River. Where Clinton was going to mobilize such a force with Howe's army off in Philadelphia never appears to have entered into Burgoyne's thinking. It is also likely that since the Bennington disaster had largely involved German troops, Burgoyne believed the Americans could not stand up to the cold steel and fire discipline of British regulars in an open fight.

What he did not realize, since his intelligence was weak, was that the American militia and Continentals defending Albany now numbered more than nine thousand, with their ranks growing daily as new units steadily joined the colonists' northern army. Their commander was General Horatio Gates, a former British officer who had served in the same British regiment with Burgoyne over thirty years earlier. Gates was a cautious, conservative general, who later in the war would suffer a stinging defeat at the Battle of Camden at the hands of Lord Cornwallis. He would display little initiative in the coming battles near the present-day town of Saratoga Springs. Throughout the Saratoga campaign he argued for a defensive strategy, despite his superiority in numbers, which increased as the days shortened into October. But Gates possessed several aggressive subordinates, most notably Benedict Arnold, perhaps the most competent battlefield commander the colonists would have during the war. These subordinates and Burgoyne's actions would force the American commander's hand during the upcoming battles.

On September 7, Gates ordered his troops to march north from their encampment near Albany. Upon reaching a set of bluffs that faced north ten miles from Saratoga, he had the army halt and construct a set of impressive fieldworks designed by the émigré Thaddeus

Portrait of Horatio Gates (1727–1806) by Gilbert Stuart, oil on canvas, c. 1793–1794 *Image copyright © The Metropolitan Museum of Art. Image source: Art Resource, NY*

Kosciusko. The position on what was known as Bemis Heights was close to impregnable, while to the west further bluffs and heavily forested terrain represented an almost impassable barrier to British advance in that direction. The position along the bluffs covered the only track leading south that ran along the Hudson's riverbank. Ten days later, the British had advanced just to the south of Saratoga within four miles of the American positions, but such was the denseness of the forests lying between that neither side had a clear idea about the location or strength of their opponents. By now, Burgoyne's forces had declined to barely seven thousand soldiers.

As the two armies prepared for battle, the fall colors of northern New York added a touch of brightness to the grim business of war. Whatever his sense of British superiority, or reports that the colonials were gathering in substantial numbers, Burgoyne knew he must act quickly before his supplies ran out. On September 19, he launched a major attack. His plan called for a feint toward the main American positions on Bemis Heights close to the Hudson, while the attack force swung out to the west and then moved toward the American left flank. Burgoyne's plan resembled what Howe had done against Washington's ill-prepared troops in the Battle of Brooklyn the year before. Lord Howe had fixed the Americans in front and then launched a devastating flank attack that had come close to destroying Washington's army of militiamen. But Howe's army had been far larger than the one Burgoyne possessed, while the terrain had been relatively open farmland, unlike the forestland of northern New York, which had few open spaces for soldiers to deploy. Moreover, ravines and small brooks cut up the landscape, which would make the movement of artillery pieces difficult.

Brigadier Simon Fraser commanded the attacking force, which consisted of Burgoyne's best regiments. Its mission was to outflank the Americans, while Burgoyne led the center division both to support Fraser and to provide the final punch, should the Americans come out and fight. Finally, General Friedrich Baron von Riedesel, commander of the German mercenaries, would feint at the main American positions along the river and then move west to support Burgoyne. It all looked clear on paper, but things began to fall apart almost from the moment the British moved into the woods and the trackless terrain inland from the Hudson.

Unfortunately for Burgoyne, the Americans were prepared to meet his effort to outflank their defenses along Bemis Heights. Arnold had persuaded Gates to deploy a portion of the American regiments on the western flank, where a British attack was likely. In fact, Arnold had wanted to push forward most of the American forces on the left wing and fight an attacking, aggressive battle against the British. There, deep in the forest, they could force the British to fight on terrain that would prove thoroughly disadvantageous to European tactics. Gates demurred, preferring to remain behind the fortifications his troops had constructed. In the end, the American commander partially relented and allowed Arnold to push Daniel Morgan's sharpshooters and Henry Dearborn's regiment of light infantry forward, where they might be expected to run into the British. Indicative of George Washington's more acute understanding of the war's strategic framework had been his willingness to send north a number of Continental regiments, including the two led by Morgan and Dearborn, even as Washington faced Howe's great army. Here in the northern woods, Morgan's riflemen pushed forward until they reached the southern outskirts of a centrally located farm belonging to John Freeman (a loyalist, supporting the British), which provided excellent cover to discern any British attempt to outflank the American positions.

The length of the barely cleared farmstead hardly reached one hundred yards from southern to northern edge. Morgan's men did not have long to wait. In the early afternoon, the skirmishers of Fraser's flanking troops emerged from the forest gloom into the northern side of Freeman's cleared acreage. There, they met the murderous fire of Morgan's sharpshooters, who with precise shots and little smoke at the battle's beginning picked off nearly every one of the British officers and sergeants. But Morgan's men then made the mistake of pursuing the routed British skirmishers and ran straight into the main body of Fraser's advancing troops. The intense firing on the American left led Gates to release a number of militia regiments to support those engaged. Arnold was already leading colonial soldiers in a rush to the front. There was a short pause while both sides reorganized their frontline troops and brought up reinforcements. Then an even fiercer

1777, Benedict Arnold leads charge against a Hessian emplacement
Pictorial Press Ltd./Alamy

fight exploded as militia regiments arrived on the colonial side, while Burgoyne brought up his main force from the center to reinforce Fraser.

There now ensued a violent struggle over the cleared areas of Freeman's farm. The center of attention on both sides proved to be the relatively few light artillery pieces the British had dragged through the forest. Always willing to set an example for his troops, Burgoyne, dressed in the spectacular full regalia of a British general, was far enough forward so that colonial sharpshooters were able to pick off his aide and narrowly miss the general. As an experienced soldier, he displayed not the slightest alarm and in fact kept his troops steady and firm in the furious firefight.

The battle lasted for somewhere between three and four hours, with heavy losses on both sides. With little generalship of the classic kind, what had begun as a skirmish devolved into a contest between individual soldiers and small-unit leaders. In the end, Burgoyne had to call on Riedesel to bring as many of his Germans forward as he dared onto the plateau where Freeman's farm lay, thereby exposing the main British and German camps to an American assault along the Hudson from Bemis Heights. True to form, Gates remained on the defensive while allowing Arnold to conduct the main fight. Later, however, he took most of the credit for the American success, which further exacerbated the tension between the American commander and his overly ambitious but highly competent subordinate.

At the end of the day, the Americans fell back in relatively good order from Freeman's farm, taking most of their wounded with them. Thus, Burgoyne could proclaim the initial encounter as a British victory, since his troops held the ground at the end of the day. But it was truly a Pyrrhic victory: the British had failed to break into the open and push the American army back on Albany. Their supply situation was now verging on desperate, since there was nothing but dark, forbidding forest in the neighborhood of the British camp. Moreover, combined British and German losses came close to seven hundred men, approximately 15 percent of Burgoyne's forces—soldiers he could not replace. Although the American losses were slightly heavier, they could be easily replaced, especially as news got around about how the colonial militia had stood up to and battered Burgoyne's best units.

For Burgoyne, the hard question was what next. His so-called victory had done nothing to improve his strategic position. Certainly the situation was clearer than in the days immediately after Bennington. His army was desperately short of supplies and had shrunk to barely five thousand soldiers. The Americans were far more numerous, with somewhere between nine thousand and twelve thousand available, while Freeman's farm had indicated that they were tough as well; if they were smart, they would soon use their numbers as well as their knowledge of the terrain to cut the British supply lines to Canada.

Finally, given the British officers' familiarity with one another, Burgoyne had to know that Clinton would not risk coming north with the minimal forces left to him in New York after Howe had taken the bulk of the army to Philadelphia. At best, Burgoyne could hope that a small raiding force might move up the Hudson to distract the Americans. In such circumstances, most commanders would prudently conclude that there was no other choice but to pull back to Ticonderoga and probably Canada. But "Gentleman Johnny" Burgoyne was not the sort to risk his reputation by retreating. Rather, he would attack and, if he lost, lose his reputation by way of the vagaries of war.

Matters were not entirely smooth on the American side. Gates and Arnold involved themselves in a fiery quarrel, driven largely by the former's envy and the latter's aggressive personality. Arnold was particularly furious that in his report to Congress Gates had taken credit for the fighting at Freeman's farm and had not even bothered to mention Arnold. In fact, Gates had sat in his tent while Arnold had commanded throughout the engagement. The upshot was that Gates removed Arnold from command and waited for Burgoyne, with whom he had served in the British Army, predictably to attack. Arnold then demanded permission to leave the army, but such was his reputation that every general, save Arnold's replacement, Benjamin Lincoln, signed a petition asking Gates to allow Arnold to remain.

On October 4, Burgoyne placed his army on short rations, underscoring the precariousness of the British position. He also held a council of war with his senior commanders. He proposed leaving a fifth of the army to guard the camp, while the remainder of the British and

German regiments moved out to the west once again to attack the Americans on their flank, a plan he quickly abandoned in the face of the objections raised by his subordinates and the reality of the situation—a situation in which his army had now declined in strength to barely five thousand men, while the American strength was swelling toward twelve thousand militia and Continental soldiers as more and more units arrived from New England and southern New York.

The next day, Riedesel suggested pulling back to the army's original position on the Hudson and, if relief did not appear from New York, retreating to Ticonderoga and eventually Canada, options Burgoyne had already rejected. That was certainly not to Burgoyne's liking. Instead, "Gentlemen Johnny" decided on a reconnaissance in force to feel out American positions directly to the south in front of his army. That force would consist of two thousand men—fifteen hundred British regulars and the rest Indians and Loyalists—including artillery, which the attackers would again drag through the woods. Riedsel did not like the proposed operation, arguing correctly that the force was too large to gather useful intelligence, while it was too small to make a successful stand if it came up against significant numbers of Americans. But Riedsel was not in command.

On the morning of October 7, Burgoyne launched his reconnaissance in force, leading it himself and again placing himself in great danger as an example to his soldiers. The movement issued on the far right flank, where the British and German troops had constructed two redoubts to cover the army's western flank. The redoubts were named for the commanders who had built them, Breymann and Balcarres, and would play major roles in the disaster that was about to enfold British arms. Once again, Fraser led the way. It was a crisp, clear day, with the northern fall foliage still out in all its glory. The combined force, slowed by the fact that it had to build small bridges for the cannons, dragged itself through the woods. It finally arrived at the north end of farmer Barber's wheat field in the early afternoon, while Burgoyne and his senior officers discussed what to do next.

American scouts had already picked up the movement. Gates then ordered Morgan and his Virginia riflemen, accompanied by Dearborn's light infantry, to advance north toward the British. Shortly thereafter, Arnold appeared at Gates's headquarters and asked permission to go forward to see what was occurring. Gates allowed him to do so, but only after extracting Arnold's promise that he would behave himself, not act rashly, and remain under the direction of General Lincoln. But when Arnold and Lincoln returned, Arnold coldly informed Gates that the riflemen and light infantry were not sufficient to hold the British. Gates exploded and informed Arnold that he had no business with the army and to leave it immediately. Lincoln, however, was able to persuade Gates to commit a larger force. The plan now was for Generals Enoch Poor and Ebenezer Learned to advance their brigades and attack the left (eastern) side of the British line, while Morgan and the light infantry circled around to the west and hit Burgoyne's right flank. Altogether, more than eight thousand Americans were to be engaged over the course of the fighting—a force far superior to what the British brought to the fight. Helping the Americans even more than their numbers was the fact that much of the fighting would take place in forested and semiforested areas where American tactical skills played to their advantage, while British artillery and close-order volleys lost much of their potency against an enemy that was hard to see and always moving.

The initial American attacks succeeded beyond expectations and quickly collapsed both flanks of Burgoyne's reconnaissance force. There matters would have remained, with Burgoyne rebuffed but no serious damage done. But then Arnold arrived on the field, having ignored Gates's order to leave the army. In fact, he had galloped off to the sound of guns as soon as the firing began. Gates sent an officer after Arnold with the order that he was to return immediately. That officer, however, was unwilling to catch Arnold, who had headed straight to the front lines, since, as he later commented, he had no desire to follow a general who was behaving "more like a madman than a cool and discreet officer."

On arriving at the front, Arnold once again displayed that innate ability that only great combat leaders possess to assess a situation and then act with a ruthless disregard for danger. He promptly grabbed Learned's brigade and led the militiamen in a smashing charge at the center of what was left of Burgoyne's line. In the confused fighting, "Gentleman Johnny" had his horse shot from underneath him, while two other bullets pierced his hat and coat. Fraser, the most inspirational of the British officers, went down with a stomach wound that proved mortal that night. The entire British line collapsed, with the survivors falling back on the redoubts, which under normal circumstances should have held against any American attack.

But these were not normal circumstances. Arnold was on the field. At this decisive moment, he first led a charge against the southernmost of the British defensive positions, the Balcarres redoubt. After perceiving that the Balcarres position was too strong, he galloped without suffering a scratch across the entire field in plain view of both sides. Upon reaching the Breymann redoubt, he led Learned's brigade in a charge that took the redoubt from the rear, while Morgan's men assaulted it from the front. The position collapsed, and Burgoyne's army was now in danger of being entirely swamped by the Americans. At last, however, one of the German soldiers managed to wound Arnold in the leg, while another shot his horse from underneath him. With Arnold's wounding, the impetus went out of the American attack. In every respect, Arnold had been the sole author of the greatest American success of the war. Burgoyne had suffered a devastating defeat. Considering the dwindling numbers left in his army, his casualty figures were dauntingly heavy—British: 184 killed, 264 wounded, 183 taken prisoner; Germans: 94 killed, 67 wounded, 102 taken prisoner—nearly 20 percent of the combined British-German force.

The next evening, the British and their German allies began a dismal retreat. They were in desperate straits, even leaving their wounded behind. Yet instead of speeding the retreat, Burgoyne dallied. For a while, he hoped to cross to the Hudson's east bank so that the army could retreat to Fort George. However, he soon discovered the colonists were on the east bank in strength. In the face of the American superiority, the fact that there was no clear route of retreat remaining, the lack of rations, and the arrival to the north of the British Army of John Stark and one thousand of his New Hampshire militiamen, where they seized a strong position north of the Batten Kill, the result was inevitable. On October 17, Burgoyne surrendered himself and his troops to their conquerors, the American colonists. As the British and German soldiers passed between the lines of grim-faced American militiamen, the more observant of the British officers noted that while their captors' clothes were an odd assortment of styles

The Surrender of General Burgoyne at Saratoga, October 1777, by John Trumbull, oil on canvas, 1820–1821   *National Archives*

and their bearing was anything but military, they were larger and better framed than their captives and they looked on the beaten with the eyes of hard, proud men.

THE SURRENDER of Burgoyne's army at Saratoga has echoed through American history. Its short-term impact was immediate and obvious. In terms of the strategic and political situation in North America, it ended whatever possibilities the British had to suppress the rebellion. For them, the strategic issue now was not whether they could regain control of their rebellious colonies, but whether they could hold on to the remainder of their empire, especially the sugar islands of the West Indies, which were already fueling the first stirrings of what historians now call the Industrial Revolution. In 1780, Lord Cornwallis would lead an army in the American South with considerable success. Yet it was all a hopeless venture that hardly touched on the strength of the rebellion.

For the Americans, Saratoga would mean immediate aid from France, the leaders of which welcomed the opportunity to pay back their ancient adversaries for the damage the British had inflicted on the French nation in the Seven Years' War. That aid and the French declaration of war allowed the Americans to place the British on the defensive throughout New England and the Middle American colonies. Moreover, substantial French ground forces in combination with the French fleet played a major role in the second great American victory at Yorktown, which finally forced George III and his ministers to recognize American independence.

The aftereffects of the American triumph would reverberate throughout the world. For France, the cost of a great world war against the British pushed the monarchy's finances over the brink into bankruptcy. That in turn forced Louis XVI and his ministers to convoke the Estates-General, which had not met for 175 years, exacerbating an increasingly revolutionary political situation that soon overthrew the monarchy and eventually led to a disastrous quarter century of war in Europe. Out of that terrible interlude would emerge the modern state system. Significantly, Ho Chi Minh, the child of both French and Vietnamese nationalism, would draw extensively from the American Declaration of Independence when he declared Vietnam's independence in 1945.

The long-term consequences of Yorktown would eventually dwarf those of the immediate present. But one should not underestimate the electrifying effect of the victory at Saratoga. Unlike the relative successes of the Concord and Lexington fights and the Battle of Bunker Hill, the victory at Saratoga was a success that involved soldiers and militia from New England, the Middle Atlantic states, and even Virginia. It was in fact the first *American* victory. And that success would help create a united nation, that great experiment that has now lasted for well over two centuries.

TRAFALGAR

Napoleon's Plans Thwarted

1805

ON MARCH 25, 1802, THE GUNS FELL SILENT. WITH THE SIGNING OF the Treaty of Amiens, Great Britain and the French Republic ended a decade of war. For the first time since the French Revolution in 1793, all of Europe was at peace. War-weary populations in both countries greeted the treaty with joyous celebration. All looked forward to lower taxes, increasing trade, and growing prosperity. But the peace was only a pause, an illusion that would be crushed over the next year as each side sought economic and military advantages over the other. France's refusal to open its ports to British trade and its strengthening of garrisons in Italy made the British wary of French intentions. A growing diplomatic crisis worsened when reports leaked that the French were active in the eastern Mediterranean and possibly considering another venture into Egypt. This in turn caused the British to retain their hold on Malta, in direct violation of the treaty's terms. By March 1803, England and France were again on the brink of war. When Napoleon formed an army under General Mortier at Nijmegen, clearly aimed at Hanover, the ancestral home of the British royal family, he threw down the gauntlet. Britain did not hesitate to pick it up. In mid–May, Parliament again declared a blockade of the French coast and on May 18, 1803, declared war on France.

For a time, Great Britain fought alone against the full might of Napoleonic France. Despite offers by British prime minister William Pitt of huge subsidies if they entered into another coalition against France, Russia, Prussia, and Austria remained aloof. But almost inexplicably, Napoleon throughout 1804 made a series of diplomatic blunders that accomplished what British gold could not—push the continental powers toward war. Instead of pursuing a policy of accommodation within Europe, Napoleon behaved almost as if he were daring the major countries of the Continent to oppose him, inflaming their smoldering hostility, alarming them all, and driving even the feeble Austrian monarch to desperation. By midsummer 1805, Russian and Austrian armies were on the march. The Third Coalition, resting on British gold, British sea power, and Austrian and Russian infantry, was formed.

For Napoleon, the surest route to ultimate victory was to remove Great Britain from the war. Without their cheerleader and paymaster, Napoleon believed the rest of the Third Coalition would be unable to sustain their war efforts for very long. Unfortunately for Napoleon's ambition, Britain's traditional protector, the English Channel, stood in his way. As *la perfide Albion* could be defeated only by an invasion and conquest, it was imperative that the British fleet be eliminated or at a minimum cleared from the Channel. Despite the fact that the French fleet had known little but repeated defeat at British hands for decades, Napoleon was convinced it could accomplish the task. He was so certain, in fact, that he began assembling his "Army of England"—the famous Grande Armée—in Boulogne, in preparation for a repetition of 1066. To some of his generals who did not share their master's confidence, Napoleon confidently declared, "The Channel is a ditch which one can jump whenever one is bold enough to try."

By September 1803, Napoleon's army stood in near readiness. For the invasion, he had collected 114,000 men (soon to grow to 160,000), 7,100 horses, and 432 cannon. To transport them, he had collected over 1,400 boats. On the other side of the English Channel, furious efforts were under way to fortify the coast and prepare Britain's small professional army and militia for war. Still, no one, least of all Great Britain, held out much hope of defeating the Grande Armée in open battle. With the army trained and in full readiness, all that was required was the arrival of the French fleet to protect the crossing. Without such protection, even a few British frigates would suffice to blow the French transports into oblivion. If the Grande Armée was ever to come to grips with its puny foe, it needed the French fleet to risk all in a mighty effort to sweep the sixty miles between France and England of British men-of-war.

As one can easily imagine, the Royal Navy was straining every nerve to ensure that never happened throughout the latter half of 1803 and 1804. A British fleet under Admiral William Cornwallis, the younger brother of General Charles Cornwallis of Yorktown fame, was maintaining a close blockade of French ships trapped in the ports of Ferrol, Rochefort, and Brest. Simultaneously, in the Mediterranean, Admiral Horatio Nelson, the man who had destroyed one French fleet in the Battle of the Nile in 1798 and forced the surrender of the powerful Danish fleet in the Battle of Copenhagen in 1801, was keeping a close eye on the French fleet at Toulon. This French fleet in Toulon was commanded by the experienced and dangerous admiral Louis-René Levassor de Latouche Tréville, but upon his untimely death, he was replaced by the hapless admiral Pierre-Charles de Villeneuve, who had survived the Battle of the Nile by beating a hasty retreat rather than engage with Admiral Nelson's closing fleet. Despite severe criticism of his actions within the French navy, Napoleon considered him a "lucky officer" and retained him on active service.

Spain's entry into the war on the side of the French in December 1804 upset all British calculations. With the powerful Spanish fleet now at his command, Napoleon possessed 102 ships of the line as compared with the British 83. But this preponderance of ships was useless if the fleet could not be brought together from the half-dozen ports over which it was currently spread. In early 1805, in conjunction with the start of his army's full-scale preparations for an invasion of Great Britain, Napoleon ordered Villeneuve to break out of Toulon and head for the East Indies, as part of an elaborate plan to unite France's scattered fleets. Along the way, he was to link up with the Spanish fleet sortieing out of Cádiz. Once in the Indies, Villeneuve

was to await the arrival of Admiral Honoré Joseph Antoine Ganteaume's Brest fleet, which had received similar breakout orders. In
the event the Brest fleet failed to break out, Villeneuve was to head for
Brest and assist in the breakout. Then, together the united Franco-
Spanish fleet would run down and defeat the Royal Navy and by
doing so make themselves masters of the English Channel. With that
done, Napoleon would be only a step away from fulfilling a boast he
had made to his admirals the previous spring to make himself "master
of the world."

Villeneuve managed to break out of Toulon thanks to a blun-
der on Nelson's part. Alerted by two of his watching frigates that
the French were exiting Toulon harbor, Nelson assumed they were
heading into the eastern Mediterranean and moved to cut them off.
After searching for the French fleet for a week, he learned Villeneuve
had gone west and had already passed through the Strait of Gibraltar. Nelson set off in furious pursuit, but the French had a huge head
start.

Nelson failed to catch Villeneuve in the Indies, as the French ad-

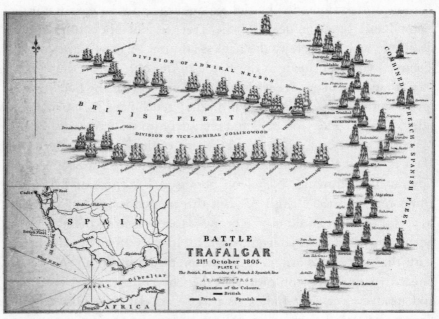

Period engraving of the battle's start
Atlas to Alison's History of Europe

miral, upon learning that Ganteaume was still trapped in Brest, determined to return to Europe and liberate him. The knowledge that Nelson was in the Indies searching for him helped to hasten his departure. Along the way, he was intercepted by British admiral Robert Calder's fifteen ships of the line. In the ensuing Third Battle of Cape Finisterre, Villeneuve lost two ships, but when Calder failed to press his advantage, Villeneuve was again able to escape. Thoroughly cowed by the near catastrophe, Villeneuve abandoned his plans to attack Cornwallis's Brest fleet and instead sailed for Ferrol in northwest Spain. Here he received orders from an enraged Napoleon to once again proceed toward Brest and link up with Ganteaume's fleet. Unsure where Calder's ships were, not knowing the size of Cornwallis's fleet, and fearing that Nelson would be on the scene at any moment, Villeneuve disobeyed orders and made for Cádiz. Here, on August 21, he was penned in by Admiral Cuthbert Collingwood's six ships. After a short rest in Great Britain, his first shore leave in two years, Nelson joined the Cádiz blockade on September 28. By this time, it had been strongly reinforced by a squadron of fifteen ships of the line Cornwallis had sent south under Calder's command. On Nelson's arrival, however, Calder departed for home, to face a court-martial after letting Villeneuve escape at Cape Finisterre. Although battle was imminent, Calder returned to Great Britain on the ninety-eight-gun *Prince of Wales,* a powerful ship Nelson could hardly spare.

The failure of his various fleets to break out and combine their forces convinced Napoleon that the opportunity to invade Great Britain had been lost. Besides, by this time the armies of the Third Coalition were on the march. Hoping to destroy the Austrians before the Russians arrived, Napoleon turned the Grande Armée south. To support this movement, Villeneuve was ordered to take his fleet back into the Mediterranean to assist in an assault on Naples. Napoleon, having lost what little confidence he had in Villeneuve, also ordered Admiral François Étienne de Rosily-Mesros to head for Cádiz and assume command of the fleet. Knowledge that his relief was en route goaded Villeneuve to action. On October 19, the combined French and Spanish fleet, consisting of thirty-three ships of the line, stood out to sea. Nelson, warned by his picketing frigates, ordered his twenty-seven ships of the line to intercept.

* * *

IT IS OFTEN assumed that the British captains at Trafalgar were a sea-soned group of veterans with long experience serving with Lord Nel-son. Nothing could be further from the truth. Only a third of the twenty-seven captains who fought that day had ever served with Nel-son before, and only five of them had ever fought in a major fleet ac-tion. The real battle-tested veterans of the British fleet were hundreds of miles north with Admiral Cornwallis, blockading the French port of Brest and guarding the English Channel. Yet all of them had full confidence in Nelson, and he returned that confidence in full mea-sure.

The effect Nelson had on a fleet is impossible to overestimate. His annihilation of the French Mediterranean fleet at Battle of the Nile in 1798 had made him a national hero, while his shattering of the Danish fleet at Copenhagen in 1801 had made him a legend. Among both officers and hard-bitten seamen, Nelson inspired a fervent loyalty. As a midshipman on the *Bellerophon* said, "Though we had no doubt of success in any action, yet the presence of such a man could not but inspire every individual in the fleet with additional confidence."

Outwardly, Nelson was far from impressive in appearance or manner. Exactly what it was about him that inspired such devotion is puzzling. He was a small, frail man with a weak constitution. He was prone to seasickness, often ravaged by disease, known to be petty and capricious, and given to suicidal fits of depression. He was also well-known for playing favorites. All of the captains at Trafalgar who had fought with him before were there because he had specifically re-quested them.

What did Nelson have on the plus side of the ledger that made men pray for the chance to follow him into battle? First and foremost, he was a fighter. When he was asked to present a testament of his ser-vice to the Admiralty in order to be given a pension, he wrote the following:

> Your memorialist has been in four actions with the fleets of the
> enemy, in three actions with frigates, in six engagements with
> batteries, in ten actions in boats employed in cutting out of har-

bours, in destroying vessels, and in taking three towns. He has assisted in the capture of seven sail of the line, six frigates, four corvettes, eleven privateers of different sizes, and taken or destroyed nearly fifty merchantmen. He has actually been engaged against the enemy upwards of 120 times and has lost his right eye and arm, and has been severely wounded and bruised in his body.

When this was written, he was just thirty-nine and his great battles at the Nile, Copenhagen, and Trafalgar were all before him. When he appeared off Cádiz, every British sailor was sure of two things: Decisive violent action would soon ensue; and victory was assured.

Nelson may have played favorites, but one became a favorite only when he proved to be supremely competent and abnormally brave. When Nelson admitted you into his "band of brothers," you were given his total trust in all things and his unquestioning loyalty. One example of this loyalty will have to suffice for many that could be mentioned. At an earlier point in his life, Nelson in a single ship was forced to flee before a sizable Spanish force. In his haste to escape, Nelson left Lieutenant Thomas Hardy and a shore party behind, intending to come back for him when it was safe. From his post on the quarterdeck, Nelson saw Hardy rowing hard to catch up to him while the Spanish fleet bore down. Exclaiming, "By God, I will not lose Hardy," Nelson swung his ship around to fight. The Spanish, sure they were walking into a trap, turned and fled. Hardy was saved, later to serve as Nelson's flag captain at Trafalgar and rise to become England's first sea lord. This devotion to his men was always returned to Nelson ten times over.

In his written instructions just before the battle, Nelson told his commanders, "No captain could do very wrong if he places his ship alongside that of an enemy." When the time came, this was exactly what most of them did.

But fleet engagements are not won by admirals or captains. Once they have done their part and put their ships in contact with the enemy, the decision lies in the hands of the men who man the guns. Under Nelson, these men thought themselves invincible. For the most

Portrait of Horatio
Nelson (1758–1805) by
Lemuel Abbott, oil on
canvas, 1800
*Pictorial Press
Ltd./Alamy*

part, the "iron men" at Trafalgar were long-serving veterans used to hardship and toil. In peacetime, they were a dangerous lot and often kept on board ship even when in port. In war, they were demons. They were not men easily impressed by rank or flash, but they loved Nelson.

The contrast with the Franco-Spanish fleet is stark. Napoleon's distrust of Admiral Villeneuve had already been made clear, with his relief, Admiral Rosily, arriving soon after he sailed out of Cádiz. Furthermore, Villeneuve was wholly pessimistic about his chances against Nelson, a fatalist infection that soon infused his entire fleet. His captains' feelings for him ran the gamut from mistrustful to overt loathing. In the midst of the battle, one Spanish captain read the orders coming from the flagship and announced that the fleet was doomed because "our admiral does not know his business." The Franco-Spanish fleet was also sorely undermanned, and quite a few of the seamen they had on board were untrained. In fact, many of the sailors were very new to their jobs, having recently been conscripted forcibly from local army garrisons. These men were no match for Nelson's "old salts."

Bravery was the single most common characteristic among the officers of Nelson's fleet, and it was present in equal measure among the seamen. Once a ship was engaged, captains had little to do except pace the quarterdeck under fire so as to be an inspiration to the crew. One captain, having seen every man on his quarterdeck killed or wounded, called the commander of the ship's marines to join him on that deck for some grapes and to converse about how gallantly the ship was fighting. At the time, his ship was being pounded by five enemy ships of the line. In another instance, the captain of marines aboard the *Bellerophon,* James Wemyss, did not leave the fighting deck until he had eight balls lodged in him and his right arm shot off. As he was passing the ship's commanding officer, on the way to the surgeon, he said, "'Tis only a mere scratch and I shall have to apologize to you for leaving the deck on so trifling an occasion."

Nelson's plan for victory was based on this courage. Forgoing the more usual and less decisive option of coming alongside the enemy fleet and exchanging broadsides, he opted to run straight at them in two columns, one commanded by him and the other by Admiral Collingwood. His simple plan called for a general melee brought about by each column penetrating at points close to the center of the Franco-Spanish line, after which each ship would seek out an enemy vessel and do its utmost to reduce it to splinters. Such a bold plan meant that the ships in the van of each British column would be subjected to multiple broadsides as they approached and could return fire only by dragging a single gun forward. This harrowing maneuver took nerves of steel, but Nelson's men did not let him down. In fact, every ship flew as much sail as could be tacked onto the masts, and several ships attempted to get ahead of Nelson and Admiral Collingwood (leading the second line) so that they could absorb some of the fire being directed at the flagships. For Nelson's captains, surrender was not an option. Many of them, in fact, had posted their flags in several places on the ships, making it impossible to "strike the colors" even if one wanted to. Even as British ships fought alone against three or four (and in once case eight) of the enemy ships of the line, there was never any thought of surrender. The very concept of striking their colors was alien to every man in the British fleet. They all knew that if they found themselves hard-pressed, the next ship in line would soon sail to their aid.

On the other hand, hard-pressed Franco-Spanish captains could not be sure any other ship would assist them, as all of their thoughts reliably turned to an early escape from the British onslaught. Failing that, many of them were ready to strike their colors as soon as they had convinced themselves that they had fought long enough to preserve their personal honor. Unfortunately, even a ten-minute close duel with a British ship could have devastating consequences.

To understand why this is so, one must analyze the final major element of British success—gunnery. The most important difference between the two fleets was doctrinal. British captains trained their gun crews to fire rapidly and not to worry much about accuracy since they counted on firing at ranges at which it was impossible to miss. French crews were trained to fire slowly and take proper aim, as befitted a navy that made it a practice to fight from a distance and retreat to safety whenever possible.

Moreover, as they had through most of their history, British crews fired much faster than their French or Spanish counterparts. Studies of rates of fire show that Franco-Spanish guns, in other engagements, fired on average one round every six minutes. This, however, pertained to well-trained crews, which Villeneuve did not have at Trafalgar. It would be optimistic to assume that the Franco-Spanish gun crews facing Nelson's ships were up to even this low rate of fire. British gun crews were markedly superior. Ships under Nelson's second in command—Admiral Collingwood, for instance—were known to fire their first three broadsides in a bit over three minutes, with a sustained rate of fire of one round every two minutes.

Assuming two one-hundred-gun ships met so they could exchange broadsides, at any given moment fifty guns were engaged on each ship. In a ten-minute engagement, the French would get off two broadsides (assuming the guns were preloaded). The British would get off six. Over the next hour, the French would be lucky to get off ten more broadsides, while the British would deliver thirty. In the first ten minutes, the French ship could expect to absorb into its hull three hundred rounds—more often six hundred to nine hundred, since the

British habitually double- and triple-shotted their guns—with the British enduring only one hundred rounds, most of those passing harmlessly through sails and rigging, reflecting the differing doctrines of the two navies. As we have seen, the longtime French policy was to aim for the masts and rigging on the theory that if you can do enough damage to the enemy's sailing ability, it will make your own escape that much easier. British doctrine, on the other hand, called for aiming into the hull of the ship to cause as much death and destruction as possible. One French captain complained after the battle, "An English shot would kill twenty of our men; a French shot in return would cut a hole in a sail." Franco-Spanish effectiveness was further hampered at Trafalgar because of the diminished accuracy of the poorly trained gun crews, which sent a significant number of rounds clear over the British fleet, while British rounds were killing men and wrecking guns, assuring that each successive French broadside would be weaker than the previous.

THE ACTUAL ENGAGEMENT was a long time coming. All morning on October 21, Nelson maneuvered his fleet on an interception course with the French. Progress was frustratingly slow, as there was barely any wind. Still, the British ships were flying every sail that they could tack on, and as far as the Franco-Spanish fleet was concerned, the damn English were closing with frightening speed. Bearing down on Velleneuve's thirty-three ships of the line were Nelson's twenty-seven, in two columns—Nelson in the *Victory* leading one, Collingwood in the *Royal Sovereign* commanding the other—aimed like arrows at the French line.

Nelson's flagship, HMS *Victory,* was one of three 100-gun first rates in the fleet, which also included four 98-gun vessels. The rest of the fleet consisted of sixteen 74-gun and one 80-gun second rates. The French fleet consisted of one 136-gun, two 112-gun, and one 100-gun first rates. The French fleet also counted on the fire of six 80-gun, twenty-two 74-gun, and one 64-gun third rates. Although the French had ten more capital ships, four of them carrying more guns than any of Nelson's ships, they were (as discussed earlier) totally outclassed. As Nelson began his approach, the French formation began to lose its coherence, a problem made much worse when Villeneuve ordered the fleet to wear (turn) together and head back for Cádiz. This turn reversed the order of the French fleet, with the rear now becoming the van. It also turned the French line ahead into something that resembled a confused mob.

At 11:45 A.M., the *Victory* flew the flag signal "England expects that every man will do his duty." Over the years, Nelson's message has become famous and figures prominently in the Trafalgar legend. At the time, though, Nelson's men were puzzled by it. More than one turned to a neighbor to say, "Ain't we always done our duty?" Collingwood grumbled, "I wish Nelson would stop signaling, we know well enough what to do."

Because of the slow British advance, their leading vessels were under fire from several Franco-Spanish vessels each for over an hour. Just before noon, Nelson flew his last signal: "Engage the enemy more closely." He then turned to his flag officer and said, "I can do no more."

Collingwood's *Royal Sovereign,* with a freshly cleaned hull, outran the rest of the British ships, and as she approached the French line she came under the close fire of six Franco-Spanish ships. Collingwood ordered his men to lie down, although he himself continued to pace the quarterdeck, seemingly oblivious to the fire. At the moment he broke the French line, several moments before Nelson did so with his line of ships, he turned to a junior officer and with a beaming smile said, "What would Nelson give to be here?" The *Royal Sovereign* broke the line directly behind the Spanish flagship, *Santa Ana,* which received a devastating double-shotted barrage as the British ship passed. Once through, Collingwood's vessel was set upon by every French and Spanish ship in the vicinity and fought alone for a considerable time before the next ship in line came to its aid.

Meanwhile, Nelson's *Victory* pushed through a similar hail of fire as it continued to bear down on the French line. One shot carried away the *Victory*'s primary steering mechanism. Another killed Nelson's long-serving (some say long-suffering) secretary. The marines tried to remove the body before Nelson was disturbed by it. However, Nelson saw them and asked, "Is that Scot?" Told it was, he said, "Poor fellow," and returned to pacing with *Victory*'s captain, Thomas Hardy.

When a shot struck the deck directly between the admiral and Hardy, Nelson turned to Hardy and said, "This is too warm work to last for long." Like Collingwood, both men ignored the blizzard of fire as they paced the deck.

At half-past noon, the *Victory* pierced the French battle line directly astern of the *Bucentaure,* Admiral Villeneuve's flagship. Hardy adjusted course to close the distance: fifty yards . . . forty . . . twenty . . . five. The French flag was close enough for the British gunners to reach out and grab it when, on his own initiative, Bosun William Willmet fired the massive sixty-eight-pounder carronade, which had been loaded with round shot and five hundred musket balls. In a shattering instant, virtually an entire deck's gun crews were swept away.

Then hell visited the French ship.

Belowdecks, the fifty thirty-two-pounder guns of the port broadside had been waiting for the carronade to fire. It was the signal for them to unleash their massive ordnance into the enemy. Before the echo of the carronade had died away, the first set of guns to bear on the *Bucentaure* belched out fire and deadly steel. As the *Victory* slowly sailed past the stricken French vessel, gun captains patiently awaited

HMS *Victory* breaches the French and Spanish line
Library of Congress, Washington, D.C.

their opportunity, aligned their guns, and fired. Most of the *Victory*'s one hundred guns were triple-shotted. Others were double-shotted, with musket balls poured in to increase the bloody carnage. As each gun came to bear, it unleashed seventy-five pounds of deadly steel into the unprotected French stern.

As the *Victory* turned to find a new victim, the screams of the French wounded could be clearly heard over the thunder of the guns. Hundreds of French sailors lay dead or dying, with torsos shattered and limbs ripped away. Dozens of the *Bucentaure*'s giant guns had been overturned, and the rear of the ship had been caved in by more than one hundred cannonballs. Despite this pounding, Admiral Villeneuve bravely ordered his ship to spin to starboard and fire a broadside with whatever guns he had left. But it was already too late.

Following close behind the *Victory* was Captain Thomas Fremantle's ninety-eight-gun HMS *Neptune*. With its band still on deck playing "Rule, Britannia!" and "Britons Strike Home!" the *Neptune* bore down on the crippled French flagship. Again, triple-shotted guns fired in succession as each came to bear. Like the *Victory,* the *Neptune* sailed on to engage other targets, but the *Bucentaure*'s agony was far from over.

Immediately behind the *Neptune* came the seventy-four-gun HMS *Conqueror,* which also unloaded her full triple-shotted broadside into the French flagship. But the *Conqueror* did not pass on to other targets. Instead she reloaded and swung around to fire again. There she lingered for over a half hour, battering the *Bucentaure* until it was a mere hulk. In the meantime, the French *Redoutable* had smashed hard into the *Victory* and driven Nelson's crew belowdecks with guns and grenades. It was a critical and dangerous moment for the *Victory,* as the French massed on their deck in preparation for boarding. The French captain was on the verge of ordering the assault when the British *Téméraire* approached from the starboard bow and blew the exposed French boarding party to pieces.

Before that happened, Britain lost its greatest admiral. A bullet fired by a sharpshooter on the *Redoutable* struck Nelson in the left shoulder, passed through his spine, and lodged two inches below his right scapula. As he fell, Nelson exclaimed, "They finally succeeded. I am dead." Hardy did his best to keep the news of Nelson's mortal wounding from the crew, and no signals were sent to the fleet. Later, when news of his death in the midst of battle spread among the fleet, men who would have killed their own mothers for a shilling broke down and wept unashamedly.

As Nelson was carried belowdecks, British ships continued to punch through the Franco–Spanish line, select targets, and blow them to pieces. The battle turned into the general melee Nelson had planned from the start.

The carnage inflicted by the first terrible broadsides of a passing British ship was often enough to decide the fight. Writing after the battle, the captain of the *Bellerophon* described his engagement with the French *Aigle:*

> Our fire was so hot that we soon drove them from the lower decks, after which our people took the quoins out and elevated their guns, so as to tear their decks and sides to pieces. When she got clear of us and did not return a single shot while we raked her; her starboard side was entirely beaten in.

The *Aigle* lost over two-thirds of her crew killed and wounded, and the ship was captured. This was a story repeated in many particular engagements throughout the Battle of Trafalgar. For instance, when the *Royal Sovereign* faced eight of the enemy alone, she inflicted double her own losses on the massive Spanish ship the *Santa Ana* and punished most of the other seven ships she faced equally hard. The *Colossus,* which engaged in a long fight against three enemy ships and suffered the highest rate of British losses that day, still managed to inflict almost three times as many losses on the enemy.

The battle itself was almost anticlimactic, the decision essentially made before the two fleets closed with each other. From the moment the *Victory* and the *Royal Sovereign* pierced the French line, the fight was decided. In the general melee that followed, the French could not match British confidence and gunnery. British captains would approach, fire a devastating broadside, and most often start peering through the smoke for another target. Then, as rapidly as possible, they would close on their new victim and unleash yet another withering broadside from only a few yards away. When they passed, all that

The Death of Nelson by Daniel Maclise, oil on canvas, 1859–1864
Classic Image/Alamy

was left behind was a near wreck filled with the dead and those waiting to die. Sometimes, however, a British ship would take a station alongside a French or Spanish ship, firing repeated broadsides until her prey was reduced almost to splinters.

There was no shortage of bravery within Villeneuve's command, but his ships were being battered to pieces by the overwhelming superiority of British gunnery. Although there were some tense moments in the opening stages of the battle as the lead British ships found themselves battling French and Spanish ships several times their number, successive British ships entering the fight quickly turned the tide. Over the next hour, the Franco-Spanish center and rear were overwhelmed. Ship after ship struck its colors, allowing their tormentors to move on to join the battle against whichever of Villeneuve's vessels were still fighting.

By six o'clock, the fighting was over and Nelson was dead. He had lived long enough to learn that a victory had been won and that no British ship had struck her colors. He died soon after, uttering, "Thank God I have done my duty."

In a single afternoon, the British navy had put a definitive end to Napoleon's plans to invade their country, while securing their dominance of the sea that would last another century.

Despite the Third Coalition's spectacular sea victory at Trafalgar, things did not go nearly as well on the Continent. In a brilliant campaign of maneuver and battle, Napoleon destroyed both the Austrian and Russian armies at the Battles of Ulm and Austerlitz. With that, the Third Coalition collapsed. Secure behind the wooden walls of its fleet, however, Great Britain continued the war against Napoleon to its ultimate conclusion ten years later at the Battle of Waterloo. During that decade, Napoleon continued to bleed France white in a series of progressively more costly wars aimed at keeping his hold on the Continent. Throughout this period, English gold helped subsidize any nation willing to fight Napoleon, while a small British army in Portugal and Spain helped create "the bleeding ulcer" that greatly diminished French military power just when Napoleon needed it most. All the while, Napoleon's continental enemies had studied his methods. In 1809, Napoleon had to stretch every resource at his disposal just to defeat Austria. Then in 1812 he finally overreached when he sent the Grande Armée into Russia. Out of an original force of over 600,000 men, only 110,000 frostbitten and starving survivors eventually made it out of Russia. The Grande Armée would never recover. Although it was still capable of fighting hard battles, such as Leipzig and Waterloo, the end was no longer in doubt.

The Battle of Trafalgar marks the rise of Great Britain as a global superpower. Its century-long control of the seas allowed it to maintain and grow its empire. Moreover, as the dominant naval and, thanks to its embrace of the Industrial Revolution, economic power of the era, Britain was, despite several notable exceptions (the Crimean War, the German wars of unification) able to maintain a general European peace—the Pax Britannica—from the fall of Napoleon until the start of World War I. During this time, Europe and its populations greatly outpaced much of the rest of the world in terms of wealth and living standards. While a Napoleonic victory over all of Europe might not have completely derailed Europe's economic and global expansion, it surely would have altered its course.

Why? Mainly because a powerful England, safely ensconced off the continental coast, never appeared as threatening to the other European powers as a powerful France would have seemed and as a strong Germany later proved to be. Other nations may have envied

Britain's wealth and power, but it was never an existential threat to their existence. On the other hand, an undefeated France surely would have gained the animosity of the other European powers, virtually guaranteeing decades of further debilitating wars.

In no small measure, the British victory at Trafalgar, by preserving Great Britain as a free and independent nation, ushered in the modern era.

VICKSBURG

Breaking the Confederacy

1863

ON JANUARY 29, 1863, ULYSSES SIMPSON GRANT ARRIVED DOWN THE Mississippi to resume command of the Army of the Tennessee from the senior officer present, the ambitious and overweening politician John McClernand. At the time, the overall situation for the Union's cause was as dismal as the rainy, cold, and dark weather. In the east, the Army of the Potomac had just suffered a disastrous defeat at the Battle of Fredericksburg at the hands of Robert E. Lee's Army of Northern Virginia. In central Tennessee, Braxton Bragg's Army of Tennessee had fought the Union Army of the Cumberland to a draw at the Battle of Stones River. Finally, along the Mississippi, Union efforts to capture the Confederate fortress citadel at Vicksburg had failed several times during 1862.

The difficulty was that Vicksburg was going to be a tough nut to crack in terms of both its geography and the fortifications with which the Confederates had ringed it. The town sits on high bluffs overlooking the Mississippi. In its terrain and positioning, it is similar to West Point, which had allowed the colonists to dominate the Hudson River and prevent the British from splitting the colonies in half during the

Revolutionary War. As long as Vicksburg remained in Confederate hands, the South could draw on the resources of the trans-Mississippi (Arkansas and Texas), while at the same time preventing the northwestern states of the Union from sending grain from their farms down the Mississippi to New Orleans for shipment to markets around the world.

Vicksburg itself presented a number of difficulties to any would-be attacker, with its naturally strong position commanding the bluffs towering over the river, and its draws and broken terrain on the landward side, while the terrain to its north was a nightmare of bayous and dense wilderness, mirroring the rugged terrain directly across the river from the town. The land to the south was less forbidding, but then any attacking Union force would have to move its troops and their supplies south of Vicksburg on the river's west bank, while Union gunboats and transports would have to run past the formidable guns on the town's bluffs in order to transport the army across the Mississippi.

GRANT IS THE GREAT ANOMALY of the Civil War. A West Point graduate, he had had an impressive combat record in the Mexican War but a dismal life thereafter. Binge drinking had ended his army career in Oregon; he had then tried farming and running a store, but by 1860 he was a clerk in his father's store in Galena, Illinois. Nevertheless, at the war's beginning the governor had appointed him colonel of the 21st Illinois, a unit that had a well-earned reputation for indiscipline. With the introduction of a "little regular army discipline," Grant quickly whipped it into shape. From that point, he was to rise spectacularly among the officers defending the Union. Small in size, light in weight, a man of few words, yet a master of clear, unambiguous prose, Grant proved himself a genius at the business of leading men from the war's first days. In his first command, he had experienced great trepidation about what his opponent might do to his small Union force. But when he arrived at the position the Confederates were holding, Grant discovered they had run away. As he recounted in his memoirs, "My heart resumed its place. It occurred to me that [the Confederate commander] had been as much afraid of me as I had

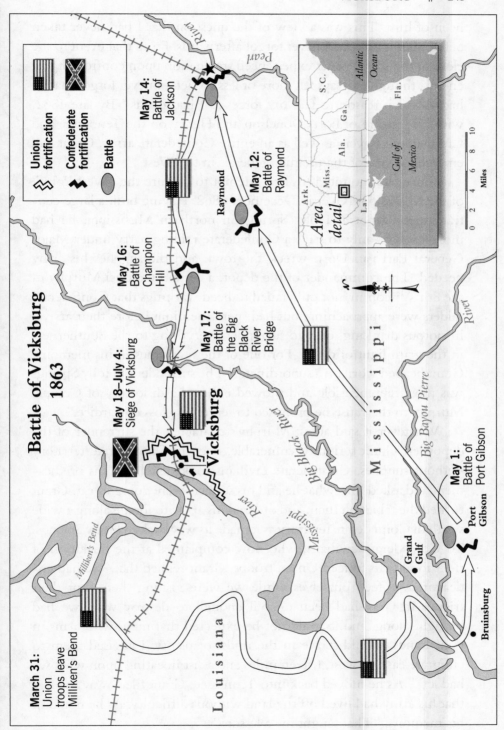

Battle of Vicksburg
1863

Union fortification ⌇⌇⌇
Confederate fortification ⌇⌇⌇
Battle ●

Union fortification
Confederate fortification

March 31:
Union
troops leave
Milliken's Bend

May 18–July 4:
Siege of Vicksburg

May 17:
Battle of the Big Black River Bridge

May 16:
Battle of Champion Hill

May 14:
Battle of Jackson

May 12:
Battle of Raymond

May 1:
Battle of Port Gibson

Vicksburg
Raymond
Port Gibson
Grand Gulf
Bruinsburg
Milliken's Bend

Mississippi River
Big Black River
Big Bayou Pierre
Pearl River

Louisiana
Mississippi

Area detail

Atlantic Ocean
Gulf of Mexico

S.C.
Ga.
Fla.
Ala.
Miss.
Ark.
La.

Miles
0 2 4 6 8 10

been of him. This was a view of the question that I had never taken before, but it was one I never forgot afterwards. From that event to the close of the war, I never experienced trepidation upon confronting an enemy, though I always felt more or less anxiety. I never forgot that he had as much reason to fear my forces as I had of his." By late 1862, with his capture of Forts Donelson and Henry on the Tennessee and Cumberland Rivers as well as an entire Confederate army, Grant had emerged as one of the premier generals in the West.

Grant had mounted his first attempt to capture the "West Point" of the Mississippi River in December 1862. Having built a large central supply depot at Holly Springs in northern Mississippi, he had moved south, only to have a Confederate raiding party under Major General Earl van Dorn wreck the town and the supplies his army needed. The commander of the depot, a certain Colonel Murphy of the 8th Wisconsin, not only failed to heed warnings that Confederate raiders were approaching, but had spent the night before their arrival in riotous drinking, only to surrender everything to the Southerners in the grim light of dawn. For one of the few times in his memoirs, Grant heaped scorn on a subordinate: "The surrender of Holly Springs was most reprehensible and showed either the disloyalty of Colonel Murphy to the cause he professed to serve, or gross cowardice."

Whatever it said about Murphy's character, the surrender of the depot left Grant seriously vulnerable, deep in Confederate territory without supplies. Confederate civilians took delight in his predicament and asked him what he and his soldiers were going to eat. Grant turned the tables on them and ordered his army to forage along a wide swath of Confederate territory as it made its way back to Holly Springs. To Confederate civilians, who now complained at the liberation of their foodstuffs to feed Union troops, Grant replied that "we had endeavored to feed ourselves while we were visiting them; but their friends in Gray had been uncivil enough to destroy what we had brought along, and it could not be expected that men, with arms in their hands, would starve in the midst of plenty. I advised them to emigrate east, or west, fifteen miles and assist in eating upon what we had left." As he moved back into Tennessee, Grant filed away the fact that his army had lived off the land without difficulty. As he noted in his memoirs: "That taught me a lesson."

Grant was already exhibiting strategic and political sensibilities that no other general, North or South, possessed. William Tecumseh Sherman would comment after the war, "While I see things in all their complexities, Grant sees them in their simplicity." Moreover, Grant was a learner, who observed and absorbed the war's harsh lessons. In the early days of the Civil War, virtually everyone on both sides had believed that one quick, decisive victory would settle matters between the states. Lee was to spend June and early July 1863 pursuing that mirage. But the breathtaking slaughter at the Battle of Shiloh in April 1862 had led Grant to recognize there would be no simple solution to the conflict. As he noted in his memoirs: "Up to the battle of Shiloh I, as well as thousands of other citizens, believed that the rebellion against the Government would collapse suddenly and soon, if a decisive victory could be gained over any of its armies. [The capture of Forts] Donelson and Henry were such victories. . . . But when Confederate armies were collected which not only attempted to hold the line farther south, but assumed the offensive and made such a gallant effort to regain what had been lost, then, indeed, I gave up all idea of saving the Union except by complete conquest."

One of Grant's strongest attributes was his ability to recognize talent among his subordinates. By early 1863, he was developing an outstanding team. Sherman had grown out of the difficulties, including almost a nervous breakdown, that had beset him in the early war years, helped enormously by the trust Grant had displayed in him on the first day at Shiloh. By the end of 1862, he was a competent, forceful corps commander. James McPherson had also shown outstanding competence and was ready to move into the position of corps commander. Finally, while John McClernand was often petulant, which would eventually lead to his being fired, he would make his contributions to the campaign. Like Lee in Virginia, Grant allowed his subordinates great latitude. He expected them to take initiative and seize opportunities as they arose and not await instructions. This command culture was the reverse of that which was entangling the operations of the Army of the Potomac in the East.

The effectiveness of the opposing armies and their commanders in the West stands in stark contrast with that of their respective counterparts in the East, in many ways almost their mirror image in military proficiency. Grant's Confederate opponents in the Army of Mississippi displayed none of the leadership qualities that defined their comrades in the Army of Northern Virginia. Exacerbating a less than impressive set of generals was a dysfunctional command structure. There were three individuals who guided the articulation of Southern efforts to hold Vicksburg. At the top was Jefferson Davis, who viewed himself as much the military as the political leader of the Confederacy. Admittedly, he had graduated from West Point and then had earned a splendid combat record in the Mexican War. But outside of his close relationship with Robert E. Lee, Davis's prickly personality produced constant friction with the better Confederate generals, while some of his choices for high command, like Braxton Bragg, were appallingly bad.

In late 1862, Davis had placed Joseph E. Johnston in overall command of the Confederacy's western theater of operations. Johnston had been one of the senior Confederate commanders at the First Battle of Bull Run, and then in spring 1862, he had led what would be called the Army of Northern Virginia at Seven Pines against Major General George McClellan and the Army of the Potomac, where he was badly wounded. Now partially recovered from his wounds, Johnston was supposed to supervise the Confederate defense of central Tennessee and Vicksburg—a considerable span of control, considering the dilapidated state of the Confederacy's railroad system. Attempting to guide armies that were hundreds of miles apart was virtually impossible under those circumstances. Over the course of the war, Johnston was to prove one of the more competent Southern generals, but he had a penchant for delaying rather than acting, which would prove particularly deleterious to the defense of Vicksburg. To add to his difficulties, he was still recovering from wounds suffered at the Battle of Seven Pines, while he and Davis never saw eye to eye on any matter.

The third player in Vicksburg's defense was Major General John Pemberton, a Northerner who had resigned his commission in the regular army and joined the Confederacy. Davis had rewarded him by appointing him to command the defenses of Charleston, where he had not particularly distinguished himself. In addition, the locals, the most rabid of the Confederates, had bridled at the thought of a "Yankee" commanding their defenses. Davis then transferred Pemberton to command Confederate forces from Grand Gulf, Louisiana, to northern Mississippi. There were few worse choices Davis would make. Pemberton possessed not the slightest ability to act decisively or display initiative; and he believed in obeying his orders exactly as they were written. After the Civil War, Grant recalled that during the Mexican War his Confederate opponent had refused to ride his horse as a junior officer because of an order issued months before that events had overtaken. Thus, while all the other junior officers were riding their horses, Pemberton walked, simply because an irrelevant order remained on the books.

Davis could not resist giving orders directly to Pemberton, something he never did with Lee's subordinates, while at the same time he neglected to inform Johnston of the orders he had issued. Moreover, there was a deep divide between Davis's view of how the Confederacy should defend the West and Johnston's view. The Confederate president believed that Pemberton should hold on to Grand Gulf and especially Vicksburg above all else. On the other hand, Johnston believed that the defense of Vicksburg rested on the Army of Mississippi, and therefore even if Vicksburg was lost but the army remained intact, the Confederates could regain the town and its crucial piece of terrain. Exacerbating those differences over strategy was a personal quarrel that had occurred in late 1861. The ability of the Confederacy to hold Vicksburg would turn on the relationships among these three men.

How, THEN, was the Army of the Tennessee to attack Vicksburg, given the geographic strength of the town's position and the strength of Confederate forces in the area? That was the strategic problem confronting Grant. His trusted subordinate William Tecumseh Sherman advised Grant to pull back to Nashville and move on Vicksburg from the route he had intended to employ in December—namely, through Holly Springs and south through central Mississippi, ultimately to attack from the north. But as Grant notes in his memoirs, he never liked to retrace his steps. As a result, the Army of the Tennessee would seek a new route. Even before he had linked up with his troops in January,

Grant had thought about a move south of Vicksburg to get at the town from that direction, but the weather and river conditions were not yet suitable for such a maneuver.

Throughout the remainder of the winter, Grant and the Army of the Tennessee searched for a means to get at or around Vicksburg. There were a number of potential avenues. On the Mississippi's western bank, Union efforts involved an attempt to cut a canal through the river's bend that swung by Vicksburg, which would have allowed Union ships to avoid most of the town's artillery. Nevertheless, the canal's southern opening would still have been within range of Vicksburg's guns. Enthusiastic digging ended in failure when the river broke the dam and flooded the evacuation efforts.

Another project on the west bank involved McPherson's corps attempting to dig a route leading from the river to Lake Providence, to the Red River, and on to its mouth, which opened above Port Hudson, a distance of nearly five hundred miles. Finally, on the eastern side of the river, one of the officers on Grant's staff, Lieutenant Colonel James Wilson, eventually to rise to the rank of major general by 1865, and Admiral David Porter attempted to work their way through the Yazoo River, its tributaries, and its bayous to strike at Vicksburg from the north. Like the efforts on the west side of the Mississippi, these efforts foundered in mud and a wilderness exacerbated by swampy, miserable terrain. Grant let the work continue through to the end of March, "believing employment was better than idleness for the men," but he had little confidence that any of the alternatives were going to work: "I, myself, never felt great confidence that any of the experiments resorted to would prove successful. Nevertheless, I was always prepared to take advantage of them in case they did."

By the beginning of April, Grant's efforts to get at Vicksburg appeared stymied. Instead, the winter's discouragements fortified his resolve to undertake a daring and unexpected move. It would involve having the three corps of the Army of the Tennessee, and the supplies necessary for a sustained campaign, move down the west bank of the Mississippi to a position south of Vicksburg. Meanwhile, Porter's gunboats and the army's transports would run Vicksburg's artillery defenses at night to meet up with the army south of the town, enabling Grant's troops to cross to the east bank of the Mississippi. The risk lay in the fact that the gunboats and transports would not be able to return upriver, because they would be exposed to Vicksburg's guns for too long, given the river's swift current. Any sustained campaign on the river's east bank south of Vicksburg would eventually depend on what the Union troops could forage, but here Grant's experience in the retreat back from northern Mississippi in December 1862 suggested they would have little difficulty in that regard. Finally, Grant believed such an offensive would require a significant distraction to divert Confederate attention from his main move south of Vicksburg.

At the beginning of April, Grant put the pieces together. He first had to persuade Porter to cooperate. The admiral immediately agreed. However, Grant's corps commanders were less than enthusiastic, none of them believing the proposed strategy was a good idea. Grant held firm, ending his meeting with them with the curt order "You will be ready to move at ten o'clock tomorrow morning." McClernand's XIII Corps led the move from Milliken's Bend on the western bank north

General Ulysses S. Grant
*Library of
Congress,
Washington, D.C.*

of Vicksburg to the wretched village of Hard Times south of the Confederate citadel. As the crow flies, the distance is approximately thirty miles, but the bends along the bayous and over the corduroy roads of tree trunks and bridges made the distance easily twice that. McPherson's XVII Corps followed while Sherman's corps remained in a threatening posture at Milliken's Bend, as if it were about to cross the river and attack Haynes Bluff on Vicksburg's northwest side. Sherman would remain in that posture until the crossing downriver had begun and then by a rapid march close up with his fellow corps commanders to cross the Mississippi last.

Meanwhile, two other crucial pieces of the puzzle fell into place. Porter and his sailors prepared the gunboats and transports for their journey past the bluffs. They covered the decks with bales of hay and cotton, lashed coal barges on the vulnerable sides of their ships, and concealed the fire issuing from the boilers so as not to prematurely telegraph the movement of the Union ships down the river. On the night of April 16, Porter made the first run under Grant's watchful eyes. The Confederates soon enough picked up the move and immediately began an intense bombardment as Porter's gunboats and the army transports sped down the river. The batteries mounted on the city's cliffs overlooking the Mississippi provided a spectacular show of noise and light, but in spite of a massive expenditure of shells, they managed to sink only one of the army's transports. All the gunboats got through. Six days later, Porter slipped six transports and twelve coal barges past Vicksburg's defenses. Again the Confederates provided a wonderful light show more impressive for its explosions and noise than for its effectiveness. The Confederates again sank only one transport; the others, though damaged, were all reparable.

By the time the second group of Union ships ran the batteries, Pemberton had other things on his mind. On April 18, Grant unleashed a major cavalry raid under Colonel Benjamin Grierson on Pemberton's rear. Of all the cavalry raids launched by the opposing sides during the conflict, Grierson's raid was to have the greatest strategic impact. Like Grant, Grierson had been a failure before the war. Moreover, a horse had kicked him in the head as a child, and not surprisingly, he had acquired an intense dislike for horses thereafter.

However, he had ended up in the cavalry when the war broke out and had done well enough to come to Grant's attention in 1862. In the postwar period, Grierson accepted a commission in the regular army and organized and commanded the 10th Cavalry Regiment, the famed "Buffalo Soldiers," consisting of black troopers.

Riding off from northern Mississippi with seventeen hundred troopers, Grierson headed south through the heart of the state. Hiving off raiding parties to confuse the Confederates as they proceeded, the Union raiders smashed up portions of the Mobile and Ohio Railroad, captured the town of Newton Station to the east of Jackson, destroyed two trains in the town, wrecked the main railroad from Jackson to the East, cut telegraph lines wherever they found them, and eventually, sixteen days after starting, arrived in Baton Rouge, which was in the hands of Union troops. By the time they reached the safety of Union lines, Grierson's raiders had thoroughly distracted Pemberton and the Southern high command from the threat posed by the movement of Grant's forces on the west bank of the Mississippi.

With the Confederates still picking up the pieces from Grierson's raid, Grant moved. On the night of April 29, he interviewed an escaped slave, who eventually indicated there were reasonable roads from the hamlet of Bruinsburg on the east side of the river that led inland toward Port Gibson and then into the interior of the state. Grant did not hesitate. He ordered Porter to move McClernand's corps across the river and Sherman to abandon his demonstration at Haynes Bluff on Vicksburg's north side and close up as quickly as possible with McPherson's corps.

Within a day, Porter had transported Grant's two advance corps across the Mississippi to the east side with all their horses, supplies, and artillery. Grant crossed with the leading troops, and as he was to recall twenty years later: "I felt a degree of relief scarcely ever equaled since. Vicksburg had not been taken it is true, nor were its defenders demoralized by any of our previous moves. But I was on dry ground on the same side of the river with the enemy. All the campaigns, labors, hardships, and exposures from the month of December previous to this time that had been made and endured, were for the accomplishment of this one objective." What followed was strategically the most important campaign in the Civil War. It was also a campaign that demonstrated the greatest operational virtuosity of any general in that conflict.

Admittedly, the Confederates in the theater possessed greater numbers, but they could bring that superiority to bear only if they could unite their forces, and from Grant's perspective that was unlikely. The Union move across the Mississippi caught his opponents in considerable disarray. Pemberton was more concerned about the aftermath of Grierson's raid, while Johnston was off in central Tennessee, since he believed that the main Union blow was going to come in that area. It took a direct order from the Confederacy's secretary of war, James Seddon, to get Johnston to move from Tennessee to Mississippi. Pemberton did request that he be allowed to abandon Port Hudson and use its garrison to supplement his forces farther north. However, Davis, exhibiting little understanding of the realities of the strategic situation in the West, rejected that request. The Confederate president ordered Pemberton to hold both Port Hudson and Vicksburg, come what may. With that explicit order, Davis ensured not only Vicksburg's fate, but that of Pemberton's army as well.

Grant's Army of the Tennessee immediately moved inland. Grant had first considered a move south to capture Port Hudson, with Major General Nathaniel Banks advancing north from Baton Rouge, but Banks reported his troops were not ready to move. Thus Grant, ever willing to adapt to the actual conditions that he confronted, determined to cut his lines of supply, a major break with the conventional wisdom of the time, and move to the northeast along the Big Black River. As Union troops advanced, he ordered his corps commanders to give Pemberton the impression they were looking to cross the Big Black and initiate a direct advance on Vicksburg. Grant's aim, however, was to move on Jackson, Mississippi, as quickly as possible to ensure that Confederate forces could not unite, and he could thereby defeat them separately, on his own timetable. In effect, Grant was using the same maneuver that Napoleon had attempted and failed at Waterloo—namely, to split his enemy and defeat them in detail. The key to Grant's generalship in the 1863 campaigns in the West was that he was always able to maneuver his forces so that they not only outnumbered their opponents, but maintained the advantage of surprise.

By May 9, the Army of the Tennessee was ready. Grant's quarter-masters had amassed sufficient ammunition and hardtack for the campaign; they had also seized from planters in the region every possible conveyance, while Porter had transported the army's wagons and supplies across the river. Once the army had consumed its last rations, Grant prepared to cut his lines of supply. At this point, he relayed his intentions to the general-in-chief of the Union army, Major General Henry Halleck, a mean-spirited bureaucrat thoroughly enwrapped in the minutiae of what passed for military doctrine at the time. As Grant noted in his memoirs, by the time the message reached Halleck and the reply came back, matters would have already been resolved. In fact, Halleck's message, ordering the Army of the Tennessee to return to the Mississippi and move south to cooperate with Banks in the seizure of Port Hudson, arrived just as Grant was in the process of shutting Pemberton into Vicksburg. To the horror of the major who brought the message, Grant crumpled up the message and paid it not the slightest heed.

The march inland proceeded rapidly. On May 12, McPherson's corps ran into a Confederate brigade under John Gregg at Raymond, Mississippi. Pemberton had ordered Gregg to attack the Union flank, since he believed Grant was still searching for a direct route across the Big Black River to Vicksburg. Confronting a whole corps, the Confederates had no chance, and after a fierce fight McPherson's lead division under "Black Jack" Logan, an outstanding combat commander and the most successful of the Union's political generals, drove Gregg's brigade off the field. At this point, it was beyond Pemberton's comprehension that Grant had abandoned his supply lines and was in fact advancing directly on Jackson, but that was precisely what the Yankee commander was doing. Sure now that Pemberton was out of the picture for the time being, Grant ordered Sherman and McPherson to drive directly on Jackson, while McClernand moved to the northeast to cover their rear.

As Grant's lead units approached Jackson, Johnston had finally arrived in the state capital. He had already ordered Pemberton to abandon Vicksburg and move with his entire army out of the town's defenses. But Pemberton, remaining true to Davis's orders, left behind a division of nine thousand soldiers to guard the city, while he moved uncertainly and slowly toward the west bank of the Big Black. While Pemberton dithered, Sherman's and McPherson's corps struggled toward Jackson under heavy rains. On May 14, Sherman and McPherson ran into Jackson's outer defenses. Johnston possessed Gregg's badly battered brigade and an assortment of reinforcements from the Gulf states. The two Union corps made short shrift of the Confederate forces and Jackson's defenses. The defenders retreated to the north of Mississippi's capital. Grant's seizure of Jackson denied Johnston the ability to interfere in his move against Pemberton.

Union soldiers then set about wrecking the railroads that ran north and south and east and west through the capital, as well as the manufacturing concerns scattered throughout the city. For their part, Grant and Sherman watched seamstresses sewing tent cloth on which the initials *CSA* were stitched. At that point, Grant records, "I told Sherman I thought they had done work enough. The operatives were told they could leave and take with them what cloth they could carry. In a few moments cotton and factory were in a blaze." That night, Grant slept in the same bed Johnston had used the night before. In the morning, as Grant and his staff departed, Charles Dana, the assistant secretary of war, who was accompanying Grant, paid the bill in Confederate dollars.

Dana's presence in army headquarters is an interesting and revealing story. Lincoln's secretary of war, Edwin Stanton, had sent Dana west to spy on Grant. Urged by many on his staff to give Dana the cold shoulder, Grant had instead welcomed the assistant secretary with open arms and included Dana in his headquarters group so that he could see everything Grant was doing. What the general understood was that Dana could, and would if well treated, act as a wonderful conduit to inform Washington not only of what was actually happening, but of Grant's view of the war.

At this point, with Johnston neutralized and the railroads radiating from Jackson wrecked, Grant changed the direction of the Army of the Tennessee. Now that he had destroyed Confederate communications through Jackson and given Johnston and the troops under his command a bloody nose, he turned to handle the Confederates defending Vicksburg. Grant ordered McPherson to take his XVII Corps and march his troops to the west, so that both he and McClernand could grapple with Pemberton's army. Meanwhile, Sherman was to complete the destruction of the rail lines to the north and east of Mississippi's capital and of whatever factories and supplies remained there. Grant's instructions to Sherman also made it clear he was to have his corps ready to move west in support of McClernand and McPherson if a battle with Pemberton should develop.

Meanwhile, Pemberton, with the seventeen thousand soldiers he had led out of Vicksburg, remained unclear as to what he should do. On the night of May 15, his army had crossed the Big Black and moved toward Jackson. That night, he held a council of war with his general officers, none of whom respected him. The advice his subordinates provided was anything but unified, some suggesting he move to link up with Johnston, others suggesting he drive south to cut off Grant's nonexistent supply lines. Johnston's memoirs best summed up Pemberton's inability to make a decision: "A majority of the members of the council voted for moving on Clinton in obedience to orders [that Johnston had given him]. A minority advocated a plan for seizing the enemy's communications by placing the army on the road from Jackson and Raymond to Port Gibson, to compel General Grant to attack it. Although averse to both opinions, General Pemberton adopted that of the minority of his council, and determined to execute a measure which he disapproved and which was in violation of the orders of his commander." The next morning, bewildered by the uncertainties and ambiguities of active campaigning, Pemberton instead ordered a withdrawal from the positions the Confederates held to the west of Champion Hill. They were to retreat toward the Big Black River, most probably as the first step to returning to the security of Vicksburg.

But before that withdrawal could make headway, McClernand's corps, leading the way with three of its divisions on separate roads, appeared. Champion Hill was a small hill that rose among a heavily forested flat area. Pemberton had one brigade up on the hill to watch for any Union approach from the east. Behind the hill lay a crossroad, with the rest of Pemberton's army deployed along the north–south road. One division already was in the act of marching east back toward the Big Black and eventually Vicksburg. In every respect, what now took place was an encounter battle.

McClernand, who was with the two southernmost Union divisions, hesitated to attack and would remain inactive for much of the rest of the day in spite of the fierce battle that developed to his north. However, his northernmost divisional commander, Major General Alvin Hovey, an Indiana lawyer in peacetime but a natural soldier who took to war the way a duck takes to water, acted aggressively. Initially he too held back, but as soon as Grant arrived on the scene, the midwesterner asked for and received permission to launch an attack. Upon hearing that Pemberton was to his front, Grant had ridden forward as fast as he could. On the way, he'd ordered McClernand's wagons off the road, to speed McPherson's troops forward to reinforce Hovey. Jauntily, Grant called out to one of McPherson's regimental commanders, whom he knew: "Colonel, we will fight the battle of Vicksburg today!"

Thus began the Battle of Champion Hill. Hovey's troops, driving the Confederates before them, quickly barreled over the hill and onto the broken ground beyond. By midday, after heavy fighting, they had seized the crucial crossroads on the far side of the hill. By that point, a portion of McPherson's corps had come up and joined in the fighting. Pemberton provided little overall guidance to the fight, focusing on the immediate battle and failing to concentrate his forces. The battle itself, taking place as it did in heavily forested woodlands, devolved into a number of smaller skirmishes. Pemberton's subordinates seemed more interested in quarreling than in fighting the Yankees. Finally, they managed to launch a counterattack, which regained the hill and drove Hovey's and McPherson's troops back to the positions from which they had started.

As Hovey's and McPherson's troops tumbled back over the hill, Grant refused to panic. He immediately took the two remaining fresh regiments available on that portion of the field and ordered them to drive the Confederates back off the hill. As he commented to a staff officer, "Hovey's division . . . are good troops and if the enemy has driven them, he is not in a good plight." The Union troops immediately recovered their morale, and the battle's momentum swung back entirely in favor of the Army of the Tennessee. The counterattack had come at precisely the right moment, and the entire Confederate position on the northern flank fell apart.

Union siege artillery   *Library of Congress, Washington, D.C.*

One last Confederate attempt to regain the day collapsed under the fire of a Union battery as the graybacks attempted to clamber over a fence to continue their charge. An observer noted that the guns "completely annihilated men and fence. . . . Such execution by a battery I never saw. It seemed as if every shell burst just as it reached the fence, and rebs and rails flew into the air together." It is the subtext of such descriptions that suggest the full horror of the Civil War battlefield. The damage that a double load of canister with its projectiles of lead and iron could do to human bodies remains entirely beyond our understanding, but at a minimum it suggests the detritus of a slaughterhouse run by a madman.

Had McClernand acted, the Army of the Tennessee would have put most of Pemberton's army in the bag at that point. Still, Grant's army had won a major victory. It had suffered 2,431 casualties, nearly half in Hovey's division, to an incomplete count of 3,801 casualties for the Confederates. But the crucial development was that Grant had put Pemberton in a position in which retreating into Vicksburg appeared to the Confederate general to be the only attractive route for his army to gain a measure of safety.

The prospects of the 1,844 wounded Union soldiers and 1,018 Confederate wounded had improved over the fate of those wounded in earlier battles. For the first time in the history of war—with the exception, perhaps, of the Roman armies—the medical profession, such as it was, saved more than its doctors and surgeons killed. The introduction of anesthetics (chloroform and ether) made a considerable difference in saving lives because it limited the lethal impact of shock. Unfortunately, Louis Pasteur's discovery of the lethality of germs would not come until shortly after the war, so there was no sterilization of wounds or operating instruments. One Confederate doctor noted in the 1890s that had he known during the war what he learned after it, he could have saved hundreds of thousands of Union and Confederate lives.

By this point in the war, the soldiers on both sides knew well the full horror of the battlefields on which they were fighting. The first truly literate army in history, they kept the folks back home informed of what they were doing but rarely described explicitly the horrors they were seeing. Compared with the European armies of the time, more often than not they appeared disheveled and undisciplined in their behavior, but most believed deeply in the cause for which they were fighting. The fact that over 60 percent of the Union soldiers, whose three-year enlistments were up in 1864, reenlisted to see the war through to the end suggests how deeply they believed in their cause. Nothing in the behavior of those in the Confederate armies indicates that they were any less committed, and the fact that they continued fighting in spite of the rags they were reduced to wearing, the lack even of shoes at times, and the wretched state of their rations underlines an extraordinary commitment to the Confederacy.

McClernand led the pursuit the next day. His troops, taking advantage of a badly planned defensive position, drove the Confederates back across the Big Black, thus ending whatever chance Pemberton had to pull out of Vicksburg entirely and prevent his army from being entrapped within the city. Their morale shattered, the Confederates raced for the security of Vicksburg, with Grant's soldiers in elated pursuit. Upon his arrival at Vicksburg, Grant ordered his corps commanders to assault the fortifications, which he correctly believed were being held by troops whose morale had been shattered by their defeats. But the engineering works that protected the town were simply too strong; the assault failed, as did a second assault two days later.

At this point, Grant settled down with the Army of the Tennessee for a prolonged siege. By bottling up the Confederates, Union troops were able to seize Haynes Bluff on the city's northern side and thus reopen lines of communication reaching back up the Mississippi to Memphis and Cairo, Illinois. Supplies flooded down the river to refresh and support the Army of the Tennessee, followed shortly by major reinforcements. Grant's former corps, the XVI, which had been guarding Union supply lines in western Tennessee, joined the besiegers, as did a division from the Department of Missouri and the IX Corps from the Department of Ohio. Thus, Grant was able to not only conduct the siege, but supply Sherman with thirty-four thousand troops to fend off any efforts that Johnston might make to relieve Pemberton. While Johnston received some reinforcements, they were not sufficient to challenge Grant and Sherman. And all the while Union forces were breaking down the Vicksburg defenses, Robert E. Lee was preparing to invade the North. As Lee had assured Seddon, "The climate in June will force the enemy to retire [from Vicksburg]."

Union trench lines around Vicksburg
Library of Congress, Washington, D.C.

* * *

PEMBERTON AND the Confederate quartermasters had made the Army of the Tennessee's task easier by their failure to lay in sufficient provisions and supplies for a prolonged siege. Vicksburg's soldiers and civilians were on half rations right from the very beginning of their entrapment. While the garrison hoped for relief from the outside, Grant's soldiers opened up a steady bombardment of the city and its fortifications. At the same time, Union troops began a series of parallel trenches and saps that slowly worked their way toward the Confederate fortifications. Meanwhile, miners in the Army of the Tennessee dug a number of mines under the main Confederate positions. By the end of June, they had finished the mines and filled them with gunpowder, waiting only for Grant's orders to explode them.

As he informed Charles Dana, Grant was ready to launch a massive attack on the Confederate positions on July 6. But Pemberton surrendered himself, his garrison of thirty thousand soldiers, and the city on July 4. That was one day after George Pickett's charge had collapsed before the murderous gunfire of George Meade's Army of the Potomac on the third day of the Battle of Gettysburg, thus handing the Army of Northern Virginia a resounding defeat. The Battle of Gettysburg was to garner greater glory than Vicksburg in the historical memory of the American people. Certainly, far more people each year visit the Gettysburg battle site in the beautiful forested hills of Pennsylvania than visit the run-down town of Vicksburg. Yet in retrospect, Grant's victory would seem to have been the more important. In every sense, the Confederate defeat at Vicksburg was the worst defeat ever suffered by either side during the war. It resulted in the total destruction of a Confederate army and cut off the Confederacy from Texas and Arkansas. But most important, as Abraham Lincoln noted: "The Father of Waters again goes unvexed to the sea."

GRANT'S CAMPAIGN against Vicksburg was the foremost example of operational art during the Civil War. He had ~~persuaded~~ CONVINCED his opponents that other threats were more dangerous. He took great risks in moving his troops past Vicksburg, while relying on the navy to run the batteries and thus provide him the transport to cross the river. He had then conducted a campaign of rapid maneuver, always leaving his opponents one step behind. By cutting his lines of communication and supply, he had gone against the conventional military wisdom of the time; and by supplying much of his army's needs from the local economy, he set an example that Sherman would repeat the following year when he marched across Georgia to the sea. And then at the conclusion of the campaign, Grant had neatly shut up Pemberton and his army within Vicksburg's defenses. Finally, he had conducted a masterful siege, while fending off relieving forces, and forced Pemberton to surrender the city and his army.

The fall of Vicksburg did not end the Civil War. But it did set in motion the events and circumstances that would result in the collapse of the Confederacy in the West. It severed the South from the food and resources of the trans-Mississippi; it opened up that great river for the movement of trade from the Midwest; it smashed a major Confederate army (the second that Grant was to capture); and perhaps most important, it established Grant as the premier military commander of the war. Grant himself saw the victory of Vicksburg as a stepping-stone to bigger things. He immediately suggested to Major General Halleck that the bulk of the Army of the Tennessee turn to the capture of Mobile, one of the key remaining Southern ports. Grant recognized that such a strike would also place tremendous pressure on the Confederates, which would ease the task that the Army of the Cumberland faced in southeastern Tennessee in driving toward Chattanooga.

Halleck, possessing neither imagination nor any sense of strategy, and always jealous of Grant's success, instead dispersed much of the Army of the Tennessee, while leaving Grant to molder with minimum forces along the Mississippi. But Halleck could not destroy the reputation for competence that Grant had acquired with the capture of Vicksburg. And when the Army of the Cumberland suffered a major defeat at the Battle of Chickamauga in September 1863, Grant was the obvious choice to repair the situation around Chattanooga, which he promptly did. The rest, as they say, is history. It was Vicksburg that opened up that path, a path that was to lead directly to the Union's triumph in the Civil War. Simply put, the word that describes the American nation is now a singular noun—the United States *is*—rather than a plural noun. And as a result of that victory, in which Vicksburg was the decisive turning point, the *United States* would come to dominate the world as no other power has done in history.

Yet there is still the mystery of Grant. This nobody from the American backcountry emerged to become the greatest general in American history. He had guided the Union armies in the West to their stunning victories in 1863. He would devise and then guide the Union's armies to victory in 1864 and 1865. He would be elected president in 1868; his reputation as one of the weakest presidents would rest largely on the vituperative assaults of Southern historians and their sympathizers in the North who attacked his efforts in Reconstruction to bring a modicum of decency to the treatment of the newly freed slaves. In fact, Grant was the only president between Lincoln and Franklin Roosevelt to do anything for that emancipated population. Finally, in the last years of his life, as he suffered excruciatingly from the pains of throat cancer, Grant wrote his memoirs, a work described by Mark Twain as the greatest work of English literature written in the nineteenth century. Grant wrote the last lines of his memoirs on one of the last days of his life.

THE MARNE

The End of Old Europe

1914

SOME EPISODES IN HISTORY ARE SO SHROUDED IN MYTH THAT REALITY and fiction merge. The Battle of the Marne, which launched the nightmare of the war on the western front in September 1914 with a bloodbath unequaled in history, is one of those episodes. Popular history as well as the conventional wisdom among historians both hold that the slaughter of the opening clashes resulted from the stupidity of generals and their military organizations, which were supposedly incapable of understanding that bullets and artillery shells were capable of killing masses of young men.

Nothing could be further from the truth. Both the Boer War at the turn of the century and the Russo-Japanese conflict of 1905 had underlined for contemporaries the lethality of the modern battlefield. The generals of 1914 recognized that reality. But the assumptions of political leaders and the so-called economic experts of the time presented military leaders with a strategic conundrum. The politicians believed the modern state was a fragile political entity, incapable of absorbing the terrible buffeting of war without dissolving into chaos and revolution. The revolution in Russia during the Russo-Japanese

War had seemingly confirmed that assumption. The economists argued that modern states were equally vulnerable to economic collapse. Thus, these ostensible experts agreed that the next war must be resolved rapidly if the contestants were to avoid the catastrophes of revolution and/or financial collapse. The experts could not have been more wrong. The economic and political basis of modern states has proven extraordinarily resilient—in fact, modern states have been able to mobilize their popular and economic power to an extent never before seen in history. In essence, by combining the popular enthusiasm of the French Revolution with the economic power of the Industrial Revolution, modern states could wage war on a scale never before seen in history *and* survive.

Except to a few Cassandras, none of this durability was clear before the war. For prewar military planners and leaders, the message was unambiguous: Win quickly or face economic and political collapse. Thus, the militaries of the major continental powers planned almost exclusively in terms of offensive operations. The cult of the offensive proved especially strong in France. Nevertheless, all of the European general staffs recognized that casualties in a future war were going to be horrific, but the political and economic mandate remained: Win quickly whatever the casualty bill.

A number of factors drove the powers to the brink of war in the early twentieth century, but the most telling might have been stated by the great historian of the Peloponnesian War and the greatest of all strategic historians, Thucydides, in the following terms: "The rise of Germany and the fear that rise occasioned in the other powers of Europe." The unification of the Germanies into a single powerful state through the statesmanship of Otto von Bismarck and the military genius of Field Marshal Helmuth von Moltke had created an economic and political powerhouse at the center of the Continent in the Seven Weeks' War of 1866 and the Franco-Prussian War of 1870. In spite of their success in those conflicts, both of these great men had come to realize by the 1880s that Germany had everything to lose and little to gain from another major European war.

But the very extent of the Prusso-German victory created new tensions in Europe. The peace that the new German Empire forced on a beaten France had included the incorporation into Germany of both

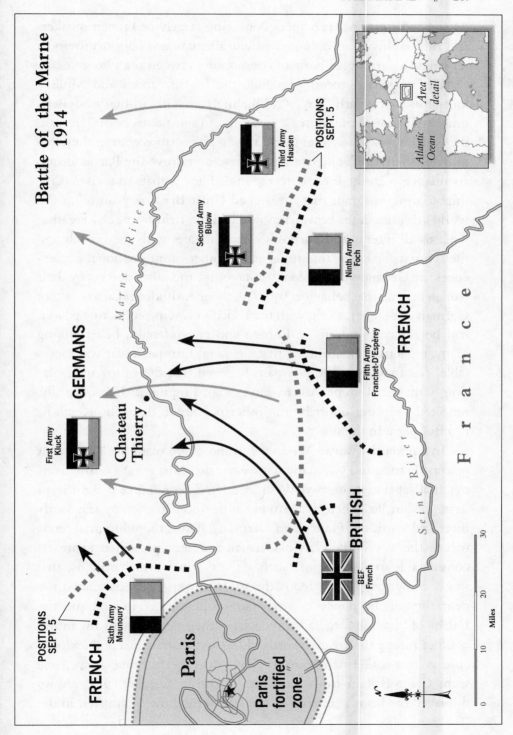

Battle of the Marne
1914

POSITIONS SEPT. 5

Third Army
Hausen

Second Army
Bülow

Ninth Army
Foch

FRENCH

Fifth Army
Franchet-D'Espèrey

GERMANS

Marne River

First Army
Kluck

Chateau Thierry

BRITISH

BEF
French

POSITIONS
SEPT. 5

FRENCH

Sixth Army
Maunoury

Paris

Paris
fortified
zone

Seine River

France

Miles
0   10   20   30

Area detail

Atlantic Ocean

Alsace and Lorraine, provinces consisting largely of French speakers and thoroughly Francophone in their allegiance. The lost provinces remained a permanent bone of contention between the two states.

Unfortunately, those who followed in Bismarck's and Molke's footsteps, particularly Kaiser Wilhelm II and his military advisers, inherited none of the strategic wisdom of their predecessors. Instead, the Reich's new leaders set Germany on a disastrous course: they terminated Germany's alliance with Russia and drove the Russians into an alliance with the French in response. They embarked on a massive shipbuilding program that threatened Great Britain's position as the world's dominant sea power and watched the British react by creating what to all intents and purposes were alliances with the French and the Russians. At the same time, at a number of international conferences the Germans proceeded to antagonize the other powers by their truculent, irascible behavior. By 1910, the ineptitude and arrogance of German diplomacy, along with the Reich's growing economic power, had heightened tensions in Europe and engendered a belief among many, especially the military, that a general European war was inevitable. For their part, the Germans believed that their growing isolation, with the decrepit Austro-Hungarian Empire as their only ally, reflected a sinister effort by the other powers to deny the Reich its rightful place in the sun.

In a potential war in Western Europe, there would be two major players: France and Germany. However, the short length of the frontier that separated the two Western powers represented a significant strategic hurdle. There was simply little room to deploy the vastly increased armies of France and Germany. Thus, the substantial territory to the west of the Franco-German frontier represented an area of considerable strategic significance, if the German army could use that space. However, in the 1830s the great powers had guaranteed the neutrality of the newly created state of Belgium. Holland and the Duchy of Luxembourg had also declared their neutrality in any future conflict among the great powers. Adding to the strategic complexity— at least from a German point of view—was the fact that, as we have seen, Great Britain from the time of Queen Elizabeth had always displayed the keenest interest in the fate of the Low Countries, in the belief that the occupation of that area by a major continental power would represent a significant strategic threat to the British Isles.

At the start of the twentieth century, German military leaders set out to resolve the problem of the lack of deployment space on their western frontier, in the belief that it was strictly a military problem they could solve while ignoring the strategic and diplomatic implications of their operations. Disastrously, the German military had come to believe that "military necessity" in the modern era of great armies and rapid movement trumped all political and strategic concerns. In other words, they dismissed the argument advanced in Carl von Clausewitz's classic *On War* that political aims and concerns must drive military operations. As one of the German generals wrote Basil Liddell Hart, the British military pundit, after the Second World War, *On War* was "a book to be read by professors."

The instigating institution in setting in motion the campaign that led to the Battle of the Marne was the German army's Grosser Generalstab ("Great General Staff"). The chief of that organization from 1891 through 1905, Count Alfred von Schlieffen, was the key player in the development of its plans for a future war. He posited that, given the length of time it would take czarist Russia to mobilize, Germany would possess a short window of opportunity during which its armies could defeat the French and then turn back to handle the Russians. Initially, he conceived of an invasion that would have encompassed only the Franco-German frontier, but the scale and growing sophistication of French defenses along that frontier led him to consider an alternative—namely, a massive drive of much of the Reich's active-duty and reserve military forces through the Low Countries. In a great wheeling advance, the bulk of the German army would outflank France's fortified zones and eventually destroy the French army east of Paris up against the Swiss frontier.

As for the international opprobrium that might accompany such a violation of neutral territory, Schlieffen gave the possibility no thought. After all, it was a matter of "military necessity." Whether or not Great Britain might find itself drawn into the conflict by a German invasion of the Low Countries, Schlieffen thought, as did his kaiser, that the British Army was a contemptible little force. As for the

Royal Navy, Schlieffen believed naval power to be an irrelevant factor in the short war his staff was planning.

The plan Schlieffen bequeathed in 1905 to his successor, Helmuth von Moltke, the nephew of the great Moltke, placed the weight of the German offensive on the right wing. Forces deployed on that wing were to invade Holland and Belgium, with minimal forces deployed along the Ardennes and Alsace-Lorraine. Similarly, Schlieffen left only minimal forces in East Prussia, Pomerania, and Silesia to fend off the Russians until the massive wheel through Belgium had crushed the French.

There were strictly military problems that Schlieffen never addressed in his planning efforts. How were the Germans going to supply this massive military force as it moved through Belgium and northern France? What if the Belgians and French destroyed their bridges, railroads, and tunnels in the affected areas? What then would be the logistical consequences? Finally, what if the Russians mobilized more quickly than expected and threatened to destroy German forces in East Prussia? All in all, the Schlieffen Plan represented an enormous gamble, which if it failed would pull Great Britain and the economic resources of its great empire into the struggle. As one historian has noted, "An ostrich-like refusal on Schlieffen's part to face even those problems which, after forty years of peace, could be foreseen" characterized the German planning effort.

To a considerable extent, Moltke accepted Schlieffen's plan, except that he decided the advance through Holland would not be necessary. In terms of the German deployment, the First, Second, and Third Armies would form the right wing, which would swing through Belgium and then advance into France. Thus, the right wing would deploy to the north and west of the other German armies. The German Fourth and Fifth Armies would form the center in the Ardennes, while the Sixth and Seventh Armies formed the left wing deployed in Alsace and Lorraine.

One of the assumptions of the German general staff planners that proved particularly damaging was that the Belgians would either cave in or put up minimal resistance. Therefore, they believed the two most powerful German armies on their right wing, the First and the Second, would have a relatively easy run through the Liège Gap into central and western Belgium, where they could then deploy for the great turning movement into northern France.

Unfortunately for the Germans, but fortunately for the fate of Europe, Moltke the younger was not a gambler. Instead he tinkered with Schlieffen's plan to make it less risky. First, East Prussia received a larger contingent of active-duty forces. But even more important, Moltke stripped the right wing that was to invade Belgium of a portion of its strength to bolster the forces scheduled to defend Alsace-Lorraine and the Ardennes. While Schlieffen had believed that it would not matter how deeply the French moved into those areas, Moltke refused to take the chance of a French success against those two provinces the Germans had seized in 1871.

The crucial point in French planning came in 1911, as relations among the great powers worsened and the possibility of war increased. The chief of the French general staff at the time, Victor Michel, had divined that the Germans were going to launch their main thrust deep into Belgium; to do so, he recognized they would utilize their reserves to an extent unmatched by the French. Consequently, he recommended that the French army take a page from the French revolutionary armies by combining regular and reserve forces into "demi-brigades" to meet what he believed would be the main German advance into Belgium. In taking such an action, the French would not only have considerably expanded the size of their army, but would also have the troops to cover their left flank that reached into Belgium. However, the response of the minister of war, as well as most of the other French generals, was that Michel was insane, and he was fired forthwith.

His replacement was General Joseph Joffre, whose most noteworthy characteristics seem to have been exceptional stubbornness and an imperturbable demeanor. Throughout the coming war, he was to insist on eating well and enjoying his daily naps. Not surprisingly, there was little imagination in his makeup. Above all, he was a reliable supporter of the Republic, which sat well with the politicians given the political troubles that had riven the army during the previous two decades and come close to destroying both the Republic and the army.

As the new chief of staff, Joffre developed the plan of campaign, Plan XVII, which rested on the assumption that the Germans would

General Joseph Joffre, commander of the French army from 1911 to 1916
Library of Congress, Washington, D.C.

not use their reserves and therefore would not mount an offensive that would drive deep into Belgium, but rather would remain to the east of the Meuse River. Joffre's Plan XVII aimed at driving French armies into Alsace-Lorraine, but the main emphasis was going to be on a major thrust by French forces into the southern portion of the Ardennes, which Joffre believed would be the weak point in the German deployment. Ironically, French intelligence, which was to prove so dismal in 1940, accurately depicted what would eventually turn out to be the German line of march.

The wild card in the correlation of forces was the British Army. The basic question was whether it would show up. Although there had been talks between the staffs of Great Britain and France, these had remained secret from public scrutiny and even all but a few of Britain's political leaders. The second major question mark had to do with the quality of British troops. In fact, British soldiers were to prove the best-trained combat infantrymen in all the European armies in 1914. The Germans were to discover that British infantry were exceedingly well prepared and capable of laying down a devastatingly accurate killing zone with their Lee-Enfield rifles.

The British generals were another matter; few would measure up to the challenges presented by the fighting in 1914. But the hard-nosed professionals of the old "contemptibles," as they called themselves in reference to the kaiser's dismissal of their abilities, were to prove adequate enough to throw a ratchet into the forward progress of the German war machine. As far as plans went, British generals expected to form up on the left of the French armies along the Belgian frontier, if—and that was a big if—Britain's leaders allowed them to go to the aid of the French. In fact, only the Germans could have made Britain's entrance into the continental war possible, and that possibility was precisely what their ruthless invasion of Belgium and Luxembourg succeeded in realizing.

In terms of weaponry, the opposing sides were equipped in much the same fashion. Infantry formations possessed bolt-action rifles. Although machine guns were making an increasing appearance, many senior officers still regarded them with suspicion since they might waste ammunition. But it was artillery that would prove the great killer in 1914 as well as during the remainder of the war. The French possessed the magnificent 75 mm cannon; weak in terms of its lack of range and hitting power, it earned the nickname "black butcher" from German troops when it was firing shrapnel. The fact that a four-gun battery of 75s could put down a rapid-fire barrage of ten thousand shrapnel balls in less than a minute suggests why the Germans feared it so much. On the other side, the Germans possessed a wider range of heavier artillery, including 105 mm and 150 mm howitzers. The Germans and British at least had the wit to provide their soldiers with dull-patterned uniforms, the former gray, the latter khaki. French soldiers still dressed in blue jackets and bright red pants. As one deputy proclaimed in a debate in the Chamber of Deputies in early 1914, to change the pattern of French uniforms to something that made a less obvious target was to attack the essence of being French: *"Le pantalon rouge c'est la France."*

* * *

ON JUNE 28, 1914, a Serbian high school student assassinated Franz Ferdinand, crown prince of Austria-Hungary, in Sarajevo. For the most part, Europeans paid little attention, but the leaders of Austria-Hungary, with the enthusiastic support of those of imperial Germany, escalated what should have been a manageable event into the spark that exploded Europe into a disastrous war. At the end of July 1914, the Austro-Hungarians declared war on Serbia. The Russians followed that declaration with a partial mobilization against Austria-Hungary and then hours later with a full one against Germany as well. The Germans promptly declared a "state of danger of war," and Moltke set his modified Schlieffen Plan into motion. As Winston Churchill commented in his brilliant if self-serving memoirs of the First World War, "Germany clanked obstinately, recklessly, awkwardly towards the crater and dragged us all in with her."

When Kaiser Wilhelm II suggested to the chief of the general staff that Germany might deploy its armies to the east against mobilizing Russia rather than to the west against France, Moltke informed his sovereign that the general staff had no plans for such a deployment. In fact, as recently as 1911 it had updated such a plan, which could have been dusted off and used to avoid invading France. But Moltke suffered virtually a nervous breakdown in front of the kaiser, and the German emperor relented. The invasion of France, and most important that of Belgium, would go forward. So on the occasion of a small war in the Balkans, the Germans launched a massive invasion of Western Europe.

The success of the German plans depended on moving the First Army under General Alexander von Kluck and the Second Army under General Karl von Bülow rapidly through the Liège Gap so that they could deploy into Belgium and then begin their great wheeling motion toward Paris. From the start, the frictions that Clausewitz had posited as the great inhibitors of successful military plans had an impact on the course of German operations.

In November 1913, during a state visit to Brussels, the kaiser and Moltke had explicitly warned King Albert of Belgium that his country had better side with Germany and its invincible forces or it would suffer terrible consequences. But Albert was made of stern stuff. Belgium would fight and fight hard. Already the chief of staff of the Belgian army had decided to deploy the bulk of his forces from the Dutch frontier south through Liège, with their southern wing anchored on Namur and the Meuse River. While the Belgian army was not particularly well trained, it possessed a formidable ring of fortresses and field fortifications that defended the approaches to Liège.

In keeping with their planners' longtime assumptions, neither Germany's military leaders nor the soldiers who initiated the attack expected that the Belgians would fight, much less put up sustained resistance. On August 2, German cavalry crossed into Belgium; initially they were uncontested. But on the morning of August 3 in the small town of Battice, the Belgians had the temerity to shoot at the invaders of their country. In reprisal for what the Germans regarded as attacks by *francs-tireurs*—guerrillas, as they termed them—the cavalrymen shot three civilians out of hand. So began a reign of terror as the Germans advanced through Belgium and northern France; by the end of the campaign, they had shot over six thousand civilian hostages, women as well as men, in response to such attacks, which for the most part were launched by either French or Belgian soldiers defending their homelands or even, in some cases, friendly fire incidents.

The initial German assaults on the Liège forts over August 5–6 underlined the lethal advantage possessed by soldiers, even second-class soldiers, dug in and armed with modern weapons, over troops attacking in the open. The Belgians slaughtered the attacking German troops. One piece of luck benefited the Germans. The deputy chief of the Second Army, General Erich von Ludendorff, who unlike most of the generals of the war was up with the advance troops, moved through the heavy fighting, commandeered a car, and drove to the Liège Citadel on August 7. With only his driver as backup, Ludendorff rapped on the citadel's main gate with his sword and demanded its surrender from several hundred astonished Belgian troops. They promptly complied, raising another of the great "what ifs" of history— for if they had either shot Ludendorff or taken him prisoner, subsequent events over the First World War would have taken a very different course. As a result of his heroics, Ludendorff found himself promoted to the position of chief of staff of the Eighth Army in East

Prussia, where he and General Paul von Hindenburg would win the Battle of Tannenberg, which launched the two on their disastrous political and military trajectories to supreme command.

Meanwhile, although the citadel had fallen, the Liège fortresses remained blocking the deployment of the First and Second Armies through the Liège Gap. Infantry attacks took two forts on the city's eastern side on August 8, but it was only after the monstrous siege guns produced by Krupp and the Škoda Works arrived on August 12 that the Germans were in a position to blast their way through the gap. The following day the Germans pierced the Liège defenses and drove deep into Belgian territory. Nevertheless, Belgian resistance had achieved two things: It had delayed the Germans by two to three days while inflicting heavy casualties; and most important, it had blackened the Reich's political standing among the neutrals, particularly the United States.

Retreating from Liège, the Belgians again refused to cooperate with the Germans. Instead of pulling back to the southwest to join up with the French, Albert ordered his army to retreat northwest toward Antwerp. With that action, the Belgian army presented a threat to the German right wing's lines of supply as it advanced deeper into France. As a result, Moltke had to deflect two corps from the First Army to protect the increasingly tenuous logistical lines reaching back into the Reich.

While the great German movement was taking place in Belgium, Joffre launched the French armies in a series of major attacks that began not far from the Swiss frontier and then followed in sequence one after the other to the northwest and the Belgian frontier. The French deployed their armies in opposite fashion to those of the Germans. Their First and Second Armies deployed on the right in Alsace and Lorraine, the Third and Fourth in the center along the Ardennes, and the Fifth on the left to the north of the Ardennes.

Underlying Joffre's operational concept was the assumption that the Germans would not use their reserve formations as frontline troops and hence could not deploy sufficient soldiers to support a drive west of the Meuse into central Belgium to outflank the French army on its left (western) flank. The first French attack came in the south and seized the Alsatian city of Mulhouse on August 8. But almost as quickly, the French lost the town in confused but fierce fighting. In a foretaste of what was to come, both sides suffered heavy losses. A second battle of Mulhouse eleven days later added to the losses as the French again failed to regain the city, while the Germans launched costly counterattacks.

The main French offensive came in Lorraine with their First and Second Armies. It began on August 14 with the aim of capturing Sarrebourg and driving the Germans back into the Rhineland. The Bavarians, under Crown Prince Rupprecht of Bavaria, one of the more competent generals in the war, shredded the massed French infantry attacks with artillery and machine guns. But instead of remaining on the defensive, as called for in German plans, Rupprecht argued that his army should counterattack the badly shaken French. Moltke, who was proving incapable of managing the uncertainties and ambiguities of a campaign that was already generating an unexpected number of surprises, allowed Rupprecht to launch a counterattack with his Bavarians. Molke apparently believed for the moment that his armies could achieve a double envelopment of the French. In fact, Rupprecht's attacking columns of Bavarian infantry, while pushing back the French, suffered huge casualties under the murderous blasts of the French 75s.

The third great French offensive of Plan XVII came with French Third and Fourth Armies attacking into the Ardennes, where they ran into Germany's Fourth and Fifth Armies. In this case, German reconnaissance had picked up the French advance, and the Germans dug in before the French attacked. Again German troops badly battered the French and forced them to retreat. One French division, the 13th Infantry Division, suffered eleven thousand casualties out of its frontline strength of fifteen thousand. But the Germans with their massed counterattacks also suffered heavily. Overall in terms of the Battle of the Frontiers, as these battles were eventually termed, the estimates are that each side suffered approximately a quarter of a million casualties from August 5 through August 21. In every case the French offensives had failed, but the Germans had gained neither a strategic nor an operational advantage over their opponents.

As the Battle of the Frontiers was occurring, the three German armies, constituting the right wing of the Schlieffen Plan, continued their march through Belgium. Along the way, they utterly destroyed the medieval university of Louvain, while executing 248 of the town's civilians, again supposedly in retaliation for guerrilla attacks, and deporting upward of 40,000 of the town's population to Germany. The Deuxième Bureau, the French intelligence service, reported fully on the growing danger, but Joffre remained unmoved. However, the commander of the Fifth Army on the left of the French forces, General Charles Lanrezac, recognized the German threat as well. Nevertheless, his warnings elicited not the slightest tremor of trepidation from Joffre, who still believed his armies were going to drive through the Ardennes into Germany. As he replied to reports of a German deployment into Belgium: "We are of the opinion that the Germans have not deployed there."

MEANWHILE, as the German invasion of Belgium and Luxembourg began, the British had declared war on Germany in response to its invasion of Belgium and its violation of a solemn treaty that the German chancellor had described to the British ambassador as "a mere scrap of paper," to the outrage of British public opinion. The British arrived in France with four of the six divisions they had originally planned to send; the cabinet, worried about the unlikely possibility of a German invasion of the home isles, held the other two divisions in Great Britain. The army mobilized its entire staff, including senior planning and administrative officers, making the subsequent expansion of the army that much more difficult when the war continued into the winter and beyond.

As the British Expeditionary Force (BEF) moved into place to the left of Lanrezac's Fifth Army, the commander of the BEF, Field Marshal Sir John French, met with his neighboring army commander. The meeting was a shambles. The British field marshal spoke hardly any French, while Lanrezac knew virtually no English. With their staffs no better prepared to speak their ally's language, the two generals used the approach that American tourists tend to use in similar circumstances: Each spoke very slowly and very loudly and understood virtually nothing of what the other was saying. This predictably resulted in minimal coordination, not to mention much less coordinated planning, between the armies of the two allies not only in the immediate battle, but through the remainder of the campaign. Still, the British at least formed a covering force of sorts on the French left flank.

What now occurred along the Franco–Belgian border was a series of encounter battles, all of which proved to be strategically inconclusive but hugely costly in terms of casualties to both sides. On August 22, two of Lanrezac's corps launched themselves straight into German attacks along the Sambre River. The Fifth Army had run into the German Second Army, commanded by General Karl von Bülow, which was now marching south. The French got much the worst of it. By the end of the day, attacking German troops had driven the French back ten miles and inflicted terrible casualties all along the way. On the next day, the German IX Corps of General Alexander von Kluck's First Army ran into the BEF's II Corps near Mons. While German artillery battered them, the British soldiers gave better than they received, slaughtering wave after wave of German infantry. One German officer described the battlefield: "Wherever I looked, right or left were dead and wounded, quivering in convulsions, groaning terribly, blood oozing from fresh wounds."

A British corporal noted that "the German tactics amazed us, and after the first shock of seeing men slowly and helplessly falling down as they were hit[, it] gave us a great sense of power and pleasure." Estimates suggest the Germans lost more than three men for every casualty the British suffered, but in the end German numbers told, and the British fell back on Le Cateau, where in a fierce engagement the Germans came close to trapping General Sir Horace Smith-Dorrien's II Corps. Yet again the Germans attacked straight ahead rather than using their superior numbers to outflank the BEF. The poor German tactics reflected a parade ground mentality that displayed little willingness to adapt to the actual conditions of war and even less imagination. But the fighting thus far in the early days of the war had already underlined that this was a problem common to all the European armies.

The British officers and soldiers at the sharp end had little doubt that they had bested the Germans, even though their superiors ordered them to retreat. Nevertheless, the sudden shock of the German attacks shattered BEF commander Sir John French's morale. He came close to losing his grip entirely, believing that he needed to pull the BEF back as fast as he could so that the overwhelming numbers of Germans would not destroy it entirely. Thus, the British retreat began with minimal coordination with their supposed French allies, which led the latter to believe they could not count on the BEF's commanders.

These initial encounter battles along the Franco-Belgian frontier signaled that the German right wing was now deployed and ready to drive forward to the victory to which Schlieffen had devoted his intellectual efforts for over a decade. But there were danger signs, the most obvious being the fact that no one central authority was monitoring, much less directing, the three German armies on the right wing, on which the success of the whole Schlieffen Plan depended. The younger Moltke was far removed from the battlefield, ensconced in Koblenz castle, partially to babysit the kaiser and partially to keep his eye on the battlefront in East Prussia, where major operations against the Russians were occurring.

Not until August 30 did Moltke and the German army's supreme

Field Marshal Sir John French, commander of the British Expeditionary Force, 1914 *Library of Congress, Washington, D.C.*

headquarters (Oberste Heeresleitung, OHL) move forward to Luxembourg, which nevertheless failed to improve communications with the forward-deployed armies driving deep into France. Moreover, Moltke allowed himself to be caught up in the euphoria of tactical victories. Still dreaming of a Cannae-like double envelopment of the whole French army, he refused to transfer troops from the left and center to buttress his right wing. Instead, he ordered Rupprecht's Sixth Army to storm the French fortress of Nancy and drive on through the Charmes Gap, an action that failed completely, with huge losses among the Bavarians. But perhaps the greatest indication of the sloppy thinking that occurred in the OHL during this period was Moltke's decision to ship two corps, one from the Third Army and one from the Second Army, to East Prussia to reinforce the German Eighth Army, which was maneuvering toward a pivotal engagement with an invading Russian army. He made this decision even though he knew that the corps would not arrive until after the looming Battle of Tannenberg had occurred.

To provide some control as well as guidance over the forward movement of the right wing, Moltke chose to place Kluck's First Army under Bülow's control. That proved a bad decision; the Second Army commander consistently placed the narrow interests of his own army above those of the right wing and the offensive as a whole. True to form, Bülow pulled the First Army in close to his own and refused to allow Kluck the latitude to outflank the BEF to the west and thus envelop the entire Allied position, thereby depriving the Germans of their greatest opportunity to outflank the Allied forces. Had Bülow allowed Kluck to follow his instincts, it is conceivable the Germans might have rolled up a substantial portion of the BEF and the French Fifth Army, winning the decisive victory the Schlieffen Plan was designed to achieve. As it was, Kluck's forces were able to gain only tactical victories and at considerable cost. Thus, on the right wing, as on the center and left, the Germans drove their opponents back in considerable disarray but failed to achieve a significant operational advantage over them.

★ ★ ★

WITH HIS OFFENSIVE DRIVES smashed and his armies in disarray, in a "come to Jesus" moment Joffre finally recognized the reality of what he had spent three weeks denying: The Germans were coming in great strength on his left and threatening to envelop the entire armed forces of France. Now, instead of seeking decisive, Napoleonic victories, Joffre informed the minister of war, Adolphe Messimy, that the army needed to prevent the Germans from occupying too much of France, inflict the maximum number of casualties on its opponent, and counterattack the Germans when the opportune moment occurred. The crucial operational decision was to pull back the French army's right wing to more defensible positions, while at the same time transferring the maximum number of divisions possible to the west and the left wing to meet the German drive. Finally, Joffre shredded the French army of those commanders who had failed, at least in his opinion. He fired no fewer than two army commanders, ten corps commanders, and thirty-eight division commanders during the first months of the war. Those who proved they could act and successfully incorporate the technological and tactical changes that had occurred in war found themselves rapidly promoted to replace the departed; among them, Colonel Henri-Philippe Pétain, a regimental commander on August 1, 1914, with few prospects for further advancement, would be an army commander within a year because of his innovative and adaptive employment of artillery.

While the movement to reinforce the Allied left occurred, the British and French on that front were going to have to fall back toward Paris, the Seine, and the Marne. Moreover, the British would have to be brought into some level of cooperation. What Joffre was unable to achieve with Field Marshal Sir John French, Field Marshal Lord Kitchener, Great Britain's secretary of war, achieved in a private tête-à-tête at the British embassy on September 1, where he informed the BEF commander that he must "remain conforming to the movements of the French Army."

The retreat was a nightmare for the British troops. Marches of twenty to thirty miles per day in the heat of the summer exhausted soldiers and horses alike, while clouds of dust coated everyone and everything. There was hardly time to sleep, much less to eat. And everywhere they marched, the malodorous scent of hundreds of thousands of young men who had not bathed for weeks accompanied them. Where serious fighting had occurred, the dreadful stench of the decaying flesh of tens of thousands of men and animals hung over a smashed-up landscape. But at least for the Allies, the retreat took them closer to their supply dumps and decent rations and eased the problems of supply.

For the Germans, the advance was equally debilitating. Admittedly the enemy was retreating, but as the Prussian war minister, General Erich von Falkenhayn, sarcastically asked Moltke: "Show me the trophies or the prisoners of war?" Moreover, there were two disturbing aspects to the German advance, the first obvious and the second not so clear at the time. The Germans were rapidly drawing away from their lines of supply; the massive demolitions the Belgians had carried out meant that the Germans would not have working railroads into central Belgium until the middle of September, and even then the difficulties in subsequently forwarding supplies by horse-drawn wagons to their troops deep in France represented a nightmare for supply officers. There would be no resupply of ammunition, much less rations, for the foreseeable future, nor did the rapid advance afford time to forage. Some officers took the dubious step of supplying their soldiers with champagne and wine to keep them going, an approach that had obvious consequences, few of them good.

The larger problem confronting German army commanders and the OHL was how they were going to complete their campaign. Already, decisions taken in late August without thought about their long-term consequences were troubling them. Certainly, Schlieffen's last warning not to weaken the right wing must have haunted a number of senior officers. The detailing of two corps to watch the Belgians in Antwerp and two corps to East Prussia, not to mention the heavy casualties suffered thus far in the initial battles along the Franco-Belgian frontier, meant the German numerical advantage over the French left had almost disappeared. In fact, the German left wing in Alsace-Lorraine in the south had as many troops as the right wing, while the center armies had approximately one hundred thousand more soldiers than those possessed by the three armies on the right.

★ ★ ★

IN EARLY SEPTEMBER, as German forces approached Paris and the Marne River to its east, the opening stages of what was to be called the Battle of the Marne unfolded. Kluck's First Army appeared to be marching directly on Paris. Now a major strategic question confronted the Germans, on which the success of their campaign rested: What were they to do with the French capital? In 1940, the French would declare Paris an open city and abandon it without a fight. In 1914, however, they intended to fight, and under the tough-minded colonial soldier General Joseph-Simon Gallieni, they had already undertaken extensive preparations to extend the capabilities of the fortresses and defense system ringing the capital. In addition, Joffre had been hustling units from his badly battered right flank from Alsace to his left flank, reinforcements that added steadily to Gallieni's troop strength.

For all the extensive effort that had gone into developing the Schlieffen Plan, the Germans had never properly addressed what they were going to do if the French chose to defend Paris, as they had done so successfully in 1870 when the Germans had had to surround and besiege the French capital over an extended period of time. And unlike the strategic situation in 1870, when the Prusso-German army had already destroyed the French army at Metz and Sedan, this time the Germans still faced a French army of considerable strength that remained in the field.

Thus, Paris raised major operational questions. Should the German armies assault or besiege Paris? How were they going to deal with the large French forces that remained in the field? What if the French had already amassed a major army in the city to launch a counterattack? Were the troops of the First Army going to fight their way into Paris? How many troops would it take to shield the German right wing if it bypassed Paris and moved off to the southeast in pursuit of the main body of the French army? In fact, in none of their operational planning or their decisions taken on the ground did the Germans address these essential questions.

Owing to the efforts of Gallieni and Joffre, the French had accumulated substantial forces in the capital. Admittedly, many of these units had suffered heavily in the fighting in Alsace and Lorraine, but the German troops in Kluck's First Army and Bülow's Second Army were hardly in better shape. At this point, in yet another demonstration of the extent to which the OHL had lost control of the campaign, Kluck acted without first seeking instructions from Moltke, who had moved to Luxembourg with the Kaiser. The First Army would handle the problem of Paris by ignoring it.

At midday on September 3, Kluck shifted the First Army's advance from the south, which would have eventually taken it to the outskirts of Paris, to a southeasterly direction, which allowed it to bypass the French capital to the east. That decision set in motion what historians today refer to as the Battle of the Marne. Almost immediately, French and British aerial reconnaissance reported to Gallieni the change in the direction of German troops. That night, the commander of the Paris garrison made the decision that if Kluck's advance continued to move away from the capital, his forces would move out from Paris and strike the Germans in the flank and rear. Joffre agreed, believing that the great opportunity for which he had been preparing was at hand, allowing the Paris garrison and the Sixth Army to attack Kluck's flank from the west out of Paris. And so began the Battle of the Marne.

The major issue from the French perspective was whether the British would participate. Here Lanrezac's replacement, General Louis Franchet d'Espèrey, and Joffre combined their efforts to successfully enlist Sir John French and the BEF to take part in the counterattack. On the morning of September 5, the Sixth Army under the command of General Michel-Joseph Maunoury moved out from the Paris defenses. Almost immediately, they ran into the corps Kluck had left to guard the First Army's western flank from just such an attack. The German IV Reserve Corps had lost heavily thus far in the advance, but it put up fierce and effective resistance despite being heavily outnumbered as the French attempted to move into the rear of Kluck's army. That defensive success ended the chance that the French Sixth Army could destroy the German First Army.

Nevertheless, the balance of forces between the contending armies in front of and to the east of Paris had tipped dramatically against the Germans. The three armies that made up the right wing of the

French firing line   *Library of Congress, Washington, D.C.*

Schlieffen Plan had already lost 265,000 of their soldiers killed in action, wounded, or missing. The number of divisions told a graphic
tale: Roughly 24½ weakened German divisions now confronted no
fewer than 41 Allied divisions, including the BEF.

Warned of the French threat and realizing the implications if the
enemy's Sixth Army got in his rear, Kluck reacted by changing the
entire front of his army to attack the forces marching out of Paris,
ordering: "Wheel First Army to the right at once, quickly form up on
the right, attack across the Ourcq." At midnight on September 5/6, he
ordered one of his corps to move as quickly as possible to the northwest to buttress the IV Reserve Corps protecting his western flank.
Half a day later, he ordered a second corps to move out to the northwest. In two days of incredible forced marches—thirty-five miles on
the first day, forty miles on the second—Kluck's reinforcements
reached the IV Reserve Corps and went over to the offensive. But to
achieve that concentration, Kluck had in effect not only split his First
Army, but created a yawning gap of nearly thirty miles between the
German First and Second Armies, covered only by two light cavalry
corps.

Directly in front of that gap was the BEF, which remained in relatively good shape, although battered in its earlier battles with the Germans. Yet Kluck persevered in his decision to attack the French Sixth Army. He ordered two more of his corps, which had temporarily been placed under Bülow's control, to detach themselves from the Second Army and move to reinforce the forces fighting the French Sixth to the east of Paris. That move in turn exacerbated the already huge gap between the German First and Second Armies.

By September 7, the Germans were in an astonishing position. Kluck's First Army had moved to face west with no direct contact with the Second Army. Bülow's Second Army, for its part, faced southeast with gaps on both its flanks. And both of those flanks were in serious difficulty. Particularly menacing to the positions of the German armies was the fact that the BEF was now advancing cautiously into the huge gap that Kluck's major wheel to his right and west had caused. Over a three-day period, the BEF advanced barely twenty-five miles into that gap against only the light resistance of the German cavalry units. Nevertheless, the BEF's movement forward proved sufficiently threatening to force the Germans to retreat, but the indecisiveness of its advance precluded the Allies from destroying one or both of the German armies and thereby winning a decisive tactical victory.

By September 8, Moltke had become deeply worried about the operational situation of the German right wing, as well he should have been. Instead of going forward from Luxembourg himself to examine the situation, however, he dispatched a senior general staff officer, Lieutenant Colonel Richard Hentsch, with full powers to decide what needed to be done. Moltke's mood is best summed up by a letter he wrote to his wife after Hentsch's departure: "It all goes badly. The battles east of Paris will not go in our favor." Moltke closed with a foreboding comment: "And we certainly will be made to pay for all that has been destroyed." Hentsch found real reasons for worry. Bülow and the staff at the Second Army painted a depressing picture of their operational and tactical situation with both flanks of the army up in the air. Moving over to Kluck's headquarters, Hentsch received a more optimistic briefing, albeit one based largely on the First Army's tactical successes against the French Sixth Army. But to meet the threat the BEF represented, Kluck would have to pull at least a corps, if not more, off his offensive against the French defending Paris, thereby ending the momentum of the First Army's drive to the west.

The most recent research on the Battle of the Marne by Professor Holger Herwig indicates that it was Bülow who bears the greatest responsibility for the German decision to retreat from the Marne. It was the tactical situation of his own Second Army that primarily pushed him to make that decision. To the east, d'Espèrey's Fifth Army was attacking the Second Army's right flank, which the French heavily outnumbered. French artillery with its 75s continued to kill vast numbers of Germans; although reserves of 75 ammunition had fallen from 465,000 shells to 33,000 in a mere five days.

Even more worrisome for the Germans remained the BEF movement into the gap between their First and Second Armies. Admittedly, at present this was more of a threat to Kluck's rear, but given the potential that a French attack on his left represented, Bülow had no reserves available to handle the British. He pulled back the Second Army, leaving Kluck's First Army no choice but to call off its attacks on the French Sixth Army and also retreat. At that point, the Battle of the Marne was over and the massive German offensive against the west had failed.

IN THE AFTERMATH of Germany's disastrous conduct of two world wars, a number of German nationalists clung to the belief that had Hentsch, Moltke's surrogate, acted aggressively, the German armies on the Marne and the Ourcq Rivers would have won a great victory and ended the First World War before it had barely begun. The weight of evidence suggests otherwise. Admittedly, Kluck's First Army was battering the French back toward Paris, but this augured at best a tactical success; Kluck's troops might have reached the outskirts of Paris's fortified zone, but there they would have stopped. Moreover, the threat posed by the BEF was real and any deeper British advance would have placed the German First Army in the utmost peril. Likewise, Bülow's Second Army was hardly in an advantageous position with both of its flanks exposed.

But the most perilous aspect of the German position lay in the fact that Kluck's and Bülow's armies were far removed from the railheads on which their supplies of ammunition and rations depended. Any prolonged battle along the Marne River and in front of Paris posed the possibility that the Germans would run out of ammunition. Finally, the Germans were outnumbered, with no prospect of receiving significant reinforcements, while the French, in full control of the rail lines from east to west, could expect a constant flow of additional troops. An extended fight on the Marne might well have led to the collapse and defeat of both the German First and Second Armies. In weighing these factors, Bülow and Hentsch came to the reasonable conclusion that the German army was going to have to pull back, regroup, resupply, and alter the balance of forces to create a more reasonable operational situation. So the decision was made, and the German armies began their retreat to defensible lines farther to the north along the Aisne River, guaranteeing that the war would continue for four more bloody years.

IN A TACTICAL and operational sense, there was little about the Battle of the Marne that was decisive. The German armies managed to retreat without difficulty, leaving their opponents as badly battered as they were. But it was in the strategic realm that Marne deserves to be termed a decisive battle. In effect, the Battle of the Marne ensured that the German Empire would not win the great conflict that would become known to history as the First World War. Germany's effort to achieve *Weltmacht* ("world power") and hegemony in Europe had failed in the war's first great campaign. What Europe would have looked like had the Germans won is difficult to say, but it would not have presented a pretty picture and would likely have led to a great conflict between the Reich and the United States at some later date.

At the time, some in Germany recognized the strategic significance of the defeat on the Marne. Moltke's successor as chief of the general staff, General Erich von Falkenhayn, would actually approach the German chancellor, Theobald von Bethmann Hollweg, in early November 1914 to warn that Germany could not win the war and should seek a compromise peace. Bethmann Hollweg turned him down cold. Like the other European statesmen, he could not envisage a compromise peace given the horrendous bloodletting that had occurred in the war's first four months. The attitudes on the other side of the hill were no different. There would be no peace.

The German failure on the Marne also meant that the great power of modern states, capable of mobilizing their industrial and popular resources, would fuel the continuation of a terrible war of attrition over the course of the next four years, running up a casualty bill never before equaled in human history. War in the industrial age was a horrendous experience for a generation of Europe's youth, while the war's pernicious effects—the unsatisfactory peace of Versailles, the rise of Fascist and Communist regimes that conspired to overthrow the entire world order, the collapse of the first period of globalization, and eventually the catastrophe of the Second World War—would reverberate until the Soviet Union's collapse in the early 1990s.

Germany could not win because it already had ranged itself against three of the other most powerful nations in Europe. Moreover, the emphasis of its leaders on "military necessity" would lead them to a series of steps, the most egregious being the declaration of unrestricted submarine war in January 1917, that would bring the United States and its immense economic power into the war. But such was the strength of the German Empire as well as the skill of its soldiers that the other great powers would require four blood-soaked years to encompass its defeat. During those four terrible years, the tactics and operational conceptions of modern war would begin to emerge. The Battle of the Marne was the watershed from which the future would flow. The French, with some slight help from their British allies, had brought the German flood to a halt, and history would turn on that success.

The net outcome of the Battle of the Marne was to ensure that the war would become a prolonged struggle that would have an impact on virtually every nation in Europe. The three great Eastern empires would eventually collapse. Czarist Russia would go first, sinking into the nightmare of Bolshevism that would last until 1991. In October 1918, Austria-Hungary would disappear into a welter of states whose very disunion would prove of enormous advantage in Nazi Germany's rise to power in the late 1930s. The collapse of the Ottoman Empire would remake the face of the Middle East, a process that reverberates to this day. And perhaps most disastrous, while imperial Germany would fall in November 1918, the war would not settle the German question, but lead to another great world war that would come close to destroying Western civilization.

THE BATTLE OF BRITAIN

The Nazis Stopped

1940

THE "WAR TO END WAR" HAD STOPPED ON THE ELEVENTH HOUR OF THE eleventh day of the eleventh month of 1918. A broken and defeated German army stood on the brink of complete collapse on the western front; Allied armies in Italy and the Balkans were surging into what was left of the Austro-Hungarian Empire, which was dissolving into political chaos and leaving the southern frontier of the Reich defenseless to a continued Allied advance from the south; and finally, Germany itself was collapsing into revolution with approximately seven hundred thousand deserters roaming its streets. The German surrender in 1918 represented a recognition that the Reich's military and strategic situation was hopeless. Given the irresponsible and appalling behavior of the Germans throughout the war, it is not surprising that the Treaty of Versailles imposed a harsh peace. By failing to address successfully the fact that Germany was the strongest nation on the Continent while simultaneously infuriating the Germans, the treaty fell between two stools.

Twenty years later, Adolf Hitler, leading a rapidly resurgent German nation, entirely overturned the peace settlement of 1919 at the

Munich Conference in late September 1938. At that Bavarian city, the government of Great Britain, led by Neville Chamberlain, and the government of France, led by Édouard Daladier, abandoned Czecho-slovakia to the none-too-tender mercies of the Nazis in the belief that there was nothing worse than war and that issues such as national security or preparing seriously for conflict were matters of the past and no longer operative in the modern age. When, upon his return, Chamberlain announced brightly to the crowds surrounding 10 Downing Street that he had brought back to London "peace in our time," Winston Churchill reportedly responded: "The government had to choose between war and shame. They chose shame and they will get war."

"Our time" lasted all of eleven months. On September 1, 1939, the armies of Nazi Germany invaded Poland. Despite a treaty of alliance to which the British government had agreed the previous spring, it took Chamberlain more than two days to honor Great Britain's obligations; it took the French even longer. And while the Wehrmacht dismembered Poland in a campaign that lasted less than a month, the French sat behind their fortifications and watched. For their part, the British government ordered its bombers not to attack German warships tied up to quays for fear of killing civilians.

The turn of the Western nations came in spring 1940: first Denmark and Norway, then Luxembourg, the Netherlands, Belgium, and France. Led by incompetent politicians and generals, the European powers fell one after the other. On June 17, 1940, the new French government of Marshal Philippe Pétain signed an armistice with Nazi Germany, recognizing the harsh military reality of the past six weeks: France had suffered a catastrophic military defeat. Hitler and his military, which had conquered Denmark, Norway, Luxembourg, Holland, Belgium, and France in less than three months, bestrode the European Continent as no power had since Napoleon. The remaining European nations hastened to make up to this newly emerged superpower. Typical was the response of the Soviet Union's foreign minister, Vyacheslav Molotov, who proffered the wholehearted congratulations of his government on the Wehrmacht's splendid victories.

Only Great Britain remained as an independent major power in Western Europe, and few military observers believed the British had

Battle of Britain 1940

Range of Radar
- · · · · · Low level
- — · — High level
- ⊗ Luftwaffe base
- ⊗ RAF base

SCOTLAND

UNITED KINGDOM

North Sea

✈ ✈ ✈

LUFTFLOTTE 5
From Norway and Denmark

Glasgow · Edinburgh

FIGHTER COMMAND GROUP 13

Sunderland

Leeds

Liverpool · Manchester

Dublin ★

IRELAND

Coventry

FIGHTER COMMAND GROUP 12

FIGHTER COMMAND GROUP 10

GROUP 11

Calais

BELGIUM

Atlantic Ocean

Plymouth

English Channel

LUFTFLOTTE 2

LUFTFLOTTE 3

0 20 40 60 80 100
Miles

FRANCE

much of a chance against Germany's military might. As the French general Maxime Weygand, who had commanded Allied armies for much of the debacle, commented derisively, Great Britain would soon have its neck rung like a chicken's. Certainly that was how American military leaders estimated the situation. Britain's chances were to prove far more favorable than the experts had calculated. Those chances rested on the competence of a number of extraordinary personalities, civilian as well as military.

In retrospect, the German military confronted a complex and difficult strategic and operational situation, one that their own incompetence and arrogance would significantly exacerbate. Yet one should not assume that the British success and German defeat were inevitable, because as Clausewitz suggests, no human activity rests as much on chance as does war. In 1931, Winston Churchill stepped off a sidewalk in New York City, looking the wrong way, and was hit a glancing blow by a taxi sufficient to put him in the hospital. Had Churchill been walking at a slightly faster pace, he might well not have been the prime minister of Great Britain in summer 1940. And without Churchill, it is doubtful that Britain would have remained in the war and risked all on a stand against the military power of the Third Reich. Similarly, for four years during the First World War, Adolf Hitler had served on the western front as a runner between the front lines and rear area headquarters, one of that conflict's most hazardous duties. Yet he had survived. Without his leadership, Germany would never have reached the heights of 1940 or the catastrophe of 1945.

IN THE 1930S, two key assumptions underlay Great Britain's foreign policy. The first was that Nazi Germany and Fascist Italy, for all their bluster and nationalistic and military buildup, possessed leaders with whom British statesmen could reach a reasonable accommodation, since both Adolf Hitler and Benito Mussolini supposedly recognized that their nations must not repeat the terrible experiences of the Great War. The second assumption was that Great Britain's geographic position made it increasingly vulnerable to enemy air attacks. As Stanley Baldwin, prime minister in the mid-1930s, declared to the House of

Commons, "The bomber will always get through." Not surprisingly, Baldwin's attitude, which reflected those of most of Britain's leading politicians, reinforced the efforts to seek an accommodation with Britain's potential enemies, particularly Nazi Germany.

But there were those who refused to accept the fear that there was no potential defense against air attack. Foremost among them was Air Marshal Hugh Dowding, who in 1936 had become the first head of the new Royal Air Force (RAF) Fighter Command. Dowding had served on the western front during the first two years of the First World War but had been returned after he had complained about what he believed were the needless loss in pilots caused by faulty operational concepts. His career thereafter had not suffered, and by the early 1930s he was the director of the RAF's research and development program. Dowding was never inspiring, but he was always competent. His persona inspired the sobriquet "Stuffy," but his performance in staff and command positions earned him considerable respect among his peers.

As the RAF's director of research and development, Dowding had set the specifications for the development of high-speed monoplane fighters, which by the late 1930s would lead to the production of the Spitfire and Hurricane fighters. In the mid-1930s, he supported the initial experiments run by scientist Robert Watson-Watt that had resulted in the discovery that radio waves could identify aircraft in flight as well as their paths. Here Dowding proved exceptionally capable in his ability to deal with civilian scientists. As historian Alan Beyerchen noted of the development of radar: "Dowding was indisputably the pivotal military figure, providing the pull toward new operational developments and innovation. He took a strong interest in radar research and development. He also insisted that military personnel be posted right with the 'Boffins,' as the civilian researchers became known. This insured that the RAF personnel actually understood what was happening and that the civilians could be kept aware of military constraints and needs."

Then, as the head of Fighter Command from 1936 to summer 1939, Dowding created an integrated air defense system into which he steadily incorporated the technological advances of radar and high-speed monoplane fighters. The fact that the British already possessed a systemic approach to air defense based on warnings provided by observers on the ground undoubtedly helped, but Dowding understood how useful it would be to integrate radar into the current system rather than create an independent one. He would then fight and win the Battle of Britain with the weapons and system of air defense that he had played a major role in developing. Ironically, given its record for making faulty decisions in defense and strategic matters, the Chamberlain government had emphasized the production of fighters rather than the RAF's preferred bombers. It had done so not because it believed in air defense, but rather because the former were cheaper than the latter. Still, that would prove to be the one correct strategic decision Chamberlain would make.

On the other side of the hill, the Nazis lavished vast resources on the creation of the Luftwaffe. Under the leadership of Hermann Göring, German airmen developed a wide range of capabilities that reflected a thorough study of the lessons of the First World War. While the leaders of the U.S. Army Air Corps and the British RAF had argued that the only capability that mattered was strategic bombing, the Germans had built a Luftwaffe that was able to perform a wide spectrum of missions, including reconnaissance, air superiority, interdiction, close air support, airborne assault, and strategic bombing. Thus, it had played a major role in supporting German ground and naval forces in the great victories of spring 1940.

Nevertheless, one of the myths that has grown up about the Luftwaffe is that the Germans had not interested themselves in preparing strategic bombing capabilities. In fact, by 1939 the Luftwaffe had developed blind bombing technologies (the Knickebein system, which used intersecting radio beams to identify targets at night and in cloudy weather) and pathfinder forces, capabilities that could be useful only in strategic bombing and terror attacks on enemy populations. What the Germans lacked, as did the American and British air forces of the time, was the productive base for building bombers and the intelligence resources that a strategic bombing offensive would require.

WINSTON CHURCHILL became prime minister of the United Kingdom on May 10, 1940, the day the Wehrmacht and its panzer divisions came west. Almost immediately, he confronted a number of desperate crises, any one of which would have daunted most political leaders. First was the fact that Allied armies on the Continent were in desperate straits from the opening shots of the campaign. Given Britain's sorry record of support for France during the interwar period, Churchill felt a moral responsibility for his nation to provide the maximum possible aid that it could afford to the beleaguered French nation. Included in that effort was the dispatch of four Hurricane squadrons to France to join the six squadrons already there.

Equally pressing was the substantial number of appeasers, led by Lord Halifax, who remained in the cabinet. As the situation on the Continent worsened, they increasingly gave voice to their belief that Great Britain needed to make peace with Hitler. Finally, as it became clear that Britain was going to have to fight on alone if it was to maintain its freedom, Churchill confronted the need to cement relations with a United States that still remained deep in the thrall of its love affair with isolationism.

On May 15, Dowding made clear in a cabinet meeting, chaired by the new prime minister, that Fighter Command could not afford to send any more Hurricanes to France without jeopardizing Britain's air defense. Dowding's advice was in direct opposition to Churchill's desire to help the desperate French. For all the prime minister's supposed unwillingness to tolerate dissent, in fact he did listen to and respect those who presented him with clear, well-argued positions, even if they ran counter to his hopes. The next morning, the commander of Fighter Command sent his written assessment to the Air Ministry, warning "that if an adequate fighter force is kept in this country, if the Fleet remains in being, and if the Home Forces are suitably organised to resist invasion, we should be able to carry on the war single-handed for some time, if not indefinitely. But if the Home Defence force [of fighters] is drained away in desperate attempts to remedy the situation in France, defeat in France will involve the final, complete and irremediable defeat of this country." No more Hurricanes would go to France.

Over the course of the six weeks between May 10, 1940, and the surrender of France, the British had a grandstand seat from which to watch the Wehrmacht's awesome military capabilities destroy their allies. At the end of May came the miracle of Dunkirk. Both the Luft-waffe and Fighter Command found themselves heavily engaged over the ever-shrinking beachhead as the withdrawal proceeded, and it was over the beaches of Dunkirk that Spitfires made their first major appearance in the air battles.

By the morning of June 3, Allied naval forces had succeeded in pulling approximately 350,000 British and French soldiers off the holiday resort's beaches; included in that number was virtually the whole British Expeditionary Force, although its abandoned equipment littered the fields and beaches of northern France and Belgium. The British escape reflected the fact that they regarded the sea as a highway, while the Germans believed that military operations terminated on the ocean's shore. But as Churchill warned the House of Commons, while lauding the bravery and skill of sailors and soldiers alike at Dunkirk, "Wars are not won by evacuations." For both the RAF and the Luftwaffe, the aerial fighting over the beaches was costly: the British lost 177 fighters; the Germans, 240 bombers and fighters.

With France defeated and Great Britain standing alone, Churchill went about the task of rallying his countrymen to face the greatest challenge in the long history of the British Isles. Toward that end, he gave the best speeches of his long and famous political career, speeches that should be ranked among the outstanding pieces of literature of the twentieth century. The greatest of those speeches came on June 18, 1940, the day after the French had signed an armistice with the Germans:

What General Weygand called the Battle of France is over. I expect that the Battle of Britain is about to begin. Upon this battle depends the survival of Christian civilization. . . . The whole fury and might of the enemy must very soon be turned upon us. . . . But if we fail, then the whole world, including the United States, including all that we have known and cared for, will sink into the abyss of a new Dark Age, made more sinister, and perhaps more protracted, by the lights of perverted science. Let us therefore brace ourselves to our duties, and so bear ourselves, that if the British Empire and its Commonwealth last for a thousand years, men will say, "This was their finest hour."

Fighter Command had indeed suffered heavy losses during the six weeks of fighting over northern France and the Low Countries. Ten Hurricane fighter squadrons (nearly two hundred aircraft) had been lost in the campaign, although a number of Hurricane pilots escaped the debacle in France to return to the United Kingdom and fight again. From the British point of view, the six-week period of relative calm that followed the collapse of France was a godsend. During the last two weeks of June and most of July, Dowding was able to refit and reequip a number of squadrons. Altogether, by the beginning of August, Fighter Command possessed 296 Spitfires and 460 Hurricanes, of which at any given time somewhere between 60 and 80 percent were in commission, depending on battle damage and the damage inflicted on field maintenance facilities. In terms of their fighters, the British possessed two major advantages. First, they had ramped up fighter production to a rate of approximately four hundred to five hundred aircraft per month. Second, the Americans began providing high-octane fuel additives to the British in June 1940, which signifi-

German bomber over London
National Archives, Still Pictures Division, Washington, D.C.

cantly boosted the performance of the RAF's fighters over the course of the battle.

But the greatest advantage the British possessed lay in the systemic approach to air defense they had developed over the past five years. Radar made an important technological contribution, but intelligence and the reports of radar and ground observers allowed the British to coordinate their responses to major German raids with maximum effectiveness. It also allowed Dowding to deploy his squadrons with one third on the forward airfields in southern England, while the remainder of Fighter Command deployed on bases in the center and northern portions of the British Isles. There they provided a reserve from which Dowding could draw fresh squadrons to replace those on the front line that the fighting burned out—and which, in the event the Germans actually attempted a landing, could move forward to attack. Moreover, the fighters deployed throughout the British Isles were in a position to defend the rest of the country. The key No. 11 Group RAF, commanded by Air Vice Marshal Keith Park, who had served as Dowding's trusted senior air staff officer, was responsible for the southeast quadrant of the country and would bear the brunt of the coming battle. Finally, early inroads the British were already making in cracking the high-level ciphers of the Luftwaffe had provided them with important intelligence, including the fact that the Germans were using radio waves to guide their bombers at night and in bad weather.

The Germans, on the other hand, faced a number of significant disadvantages, the most important of which was a deep-seated arrogance about their technological and combat superiority. In a strategic memorandum written on June 30, 1940, the head of the operations section of the Oberkommando der Wehrmacht (OKW, the German high command), General Alfred Jodl, noted that "the final victory of Germany over England is only a question of time." His boss, General Wilhelm Keitel, commented that surmounting the English Channel would represent nothing more than a large river crossing. For the last two weeks of June, the Führer himself went on vacation, revisiting the battlefields on which he had fought in the last war and paying a quick visit in the early morning hours to Paris. While he was away, planning and preparations for military operations against Great Britain remained on hold, partially because none of the German leaders, including Hitler, expected that the Reich would actually have to fight such a battle and partially because Hitler reserved for himself so much of German strategic decision making.

By early July, it was clear that the British were not going to quit, a reality that the Royal Navy's massive bombardment of the French fleet at Mers-el-Kébir on July 3 served to underline. As the Germans weighed their options for attacking the British Isles, they began to produce intelligence estimates and plans for potential military operations, amphibious as well as aerial. Jodl's memorandum set the tone for scenarios that displayed little comprehension of the difficulties that the upcoming battles against the British air and ground defenses might involve. The general suggested several possibilities should military operations become necessary. The first would involve direct attacks on the British Isles, the second a war on the periphery, especially in the Mediterranean. Jodl believed the first offered the best approach. It would encompass attacks on Britain's trade routes, terror attacks on British cities, and, as the final blow, if necessary, an amphibious landing on the British Isles themselves. Jodl clearly took as a given Luftwaffe air superiority over the RAF and Fighter Command.

One of the major weaknesses in the German approach to war lay in the incompetence of its intelligence services. Owing to the fact that those officers detailed for intelligence work were usually the most ineffectual, while those in the tactical and operational spheres tended to focus on their own capabilities, the Germans consistently underestimated their opponents, a proclivity reinforced by their ideological beliefs in their superiority. That self-inflicted vulnerability would mark the conduct of their strategy and operations right through to the end of the Second World War. Nothing better underlines the nature of German intelligence than the estimate of RAF capabilities the chief of Luftwaffe intelligence, General Joseph "Beppo" Schmid, produced in mid-July. Although his estimate of the number of British fighters available was relatively accurate, virtually everything else in his assessment was wrong. Among other howlers, he estimated that the Luftwaffe's twin-engine Messerschmitt Bf 110 fighter was equal to the Spitfire and superior to the Hurricane. He entirely missed the nature of the British air defense system, calculated that British industry could manufacture only half the number of fighters it could actu-

British Hurricanes scramble to intercept German attack
National Archives, Still Pictures Division, Washington, D.C.

ally produce, assumed the British would deploy their fighter strength forward along the English Channel, leaving the rest of the country unprotected, and made no mention of radar, much less its role in British air defense.

Not surprisingly, on the basis of such intelligence the Germans made a number of faulty assumptions for the upcoming campaign. The Luftwaffe's commander in chief, Hermann Göring, made clear German intentions in a directive he signed on June 30: "As long as the enemy air force is not destroyed, it is the basic principle of the conduct of air war to attack enemy air units at every possible favorable opportunity—by day and night, in the air, and on the ground—without regard to other missions." So the whole RAF was to be the Luftwaffe's main target, not just Fighter Command, a decision that reflected a desire to ensure that the British would retain no striking power should the cross-Channel invasion of Great Britain, codenamed Operation Sea Lion, prove necessary.

Overall, the Luftwaffe staff estimated that it would take four days to knock Fighter Command out of the air. Then a four-week period would suffice to destroy the remainder of the RAF as well as the factories required to regenerate its strength. Yet the one true air superiority fighter the Germans possessed, the Bf 109, had a range barely sufficient to reach London from bases along the French coast and stay over the British capital for a few minutes before having to turn back. Thus, to attack major British targets beyond London, literally four fifths of the country, German bombers would have to fly unescorted by protecting fighters, because the Bf 110s, ostensibly Germany's long-range escort fighters, proved incapable of standing up to Spitfires and Hurricanes in air-to-air combat. In addition, the Luftwaffe had suffered heavy losses of aircraft and pilots in its operations in Scandinavia and Western Europe—over 30 percent of its bombers, 30 percent of its twin-engine fighters, and approximately 20 percent of its Bf 109s in the six-week campaign against France and the Low Countries.

Before the Germans could begin their air campaign against the British, the Luftwaffe, with its support services, mounted a major effort to deploy its logistical structure to airfields in western France, most of which did not yet exist. Two great Luftflotten ("air fleets") controlled air operations: the Second Air Force, under Field Marshal "Smiling Albert" Kesselring, was deployed directly across from southeast England in the Pas-de-Calais, while the Third Air Force, under Field Marshal Hugo Sperrle, settled in Normandy, which placed a considerable strain on its Bf 109 squadrons, given their lack of range. Astonishingly, the Germans never thought of equipping the Bf 109s with drop tanks, although they had experimented with their use during the Spanish Civil War. The smaller Fifth Air Force, located in Norway and Denmark, equipped only with bombers and Bf 110s because of the Bf 109's lack of range, was to participate by attacking targets in northern England and Scotland, supposedly areas of the British Isles unprotected by fighter cover.

In early July, the Germans began extensive operations over the English Channel to shut down the convoys the Royal Navy was shepherding along England's southeast coast. Increasingly heavy fighting took place as Fighter Command strove to cover the convoys while the Germans attempted to draw the British out from their lairs. Both sides suffered relatively heavy losses, but Dowding called a halt to British interception efforts toward the end of the month, because he believed the game was not worth the candle. The Germans remained thoroughly optimistic. Kesselring and Sperrle believed that the fighting over the English Channel in July had reduced Fighter Command's strength to no more than 450 deployable Hurricanes and Spitfires, when in fact Dowding had over 750 fighters available.

In the long run, the British gained the most from these aerial skirmishes. The combat with German bombers and fighters allowed the British to improve their air-to-air tactics. Even more important was the fact that they were able to excise the bugs from the coordination procedures that fed radar reports through to controllers and eventually to the intercepting fighters. For example, on July 11, relying on ambiguous radar intercepts, controllers scrambled six Hurricanes to meet what they believed was a single German raider. The Hurricane pilots were less than happy when they ran into a major raid of forty German fighters and bombers over the English Channel. By the end of the month, such mistakes had almost entirely disappeared. What is clear from this opening phase of the battle is that the British learned much about Luftwaffe procedures and tactics, while the Germans had

British Spitfires on patrol
National Archives, Still Pictures Division, Washington, D.C.

learned little about the RAF and continued to consistently overestimate the numbers of losses they were inflicting on their opponents.

THE SECOND PHASE of the battle opened on August 12 as the Germans increased the pressure. The main attack was on Portsmouth, but they also targeted the radar site at Ventnor on the Isle of Wight. The raid heralded the start of the Luftwaffe's direct offensive against the British Isles and aimed at blinding Fighter Command. The German raiding force consisted of 100 Ju 88 Junker twin-engine bombers, covered by 120 Bf 110s and 25 Bf 109s. After some confusion, Air Vice Marshal Park's controllers scrambled 48 Hurricanes and 10 Spitfires to intercept the raiders. The Germans heavily bombed Portsmouth but inflicted the most serious damage on the Ventnor radar station, smashing up the site's infrastructure so thoroughly that it would take the British more than three days to get the station back in operation. However, other sites were able to cover the gap in the British defenses and the Germans never discovered how successful their strike had been.

"Eagle Day," code name for the subsequent all-out assault on the British Isles and scheduled to open on August 13, rested on an extraordinarily inadequate intelligence base. The most thorough history of the battle notes that of the targets listed for the attacks that day, "*none* . . . would have impaired Fighter Command's operations for one moment." The attack itself got off to a less than impressive start when doubtful weather forced the Luftwaffe high command to postpone the morning raids at the last minute, literally when a substantial number of the fighters and bombers were already in the air. The fighters received the recall order, but a significant number of bombers did not. Five British squadrons scrambled, but only one was able to inflict serious damage on the German attackers.

Major attacks then followed later in the afternoon. These attacks hammered a number of RAF airfields, the most severely damaged of which had nothing to do with Fighter Command, as well as several more of the radar sites along the coast. By afternoon, all of Park's fighter squadrons found themselves engaged in heavy fighting against the Germans, with most squadrons flying multiple sorties. The Hurricanes and Spitfires inflicted serious damage on the attackers, particularly the slow, vulnerable Stuka dive bombers, which were virtually defenseless against the British fighters. The Spitfires of 609 Squadron caught one squadron of Stukas, which had lost its covering force of Bf 109s, and shot down six out of the nine the Germans had launched, with another damaged. Overall, the Germans lost forty-five aircraft on August 13, Fighter Command only thirteen. Even more to the British advantage was the fact that of the British pilots shot down, three were killed but ten parachuted to safety, of whom six were uninjured, two were slightly wounded, and only two were badly injured. The six uninjured promptly returned to duty, and the two slightly wounded joined them before the battle's end.

Heavy aerial combat continued on the next day, further exhausting the defending squadrons, but Dowding, relying on the dispersed pattern with which he had deployed his command, pulled three of his more exhausted squadrons out of the fight and replaced them with fresh units. This proved to be an inspired move, because on August 15 the Germans launched a massive, all-out offensive. Luftwaffe intelligence continued its unbroken record of providing operational commanders with bad information when it reported that Dowding had deployed all of Fighter Command's strength forward to meet the thrusts of the Second and Third Air Forces across the English Channel. On that basis, the Fifth Air Force in Scandinavia launched sixty unescorted Ju 88s from bases in Denmark against targets in the area of Hull. Farther north, sixty-five He 111 Heinkel medium bombers escorted by twenty Bf 110s from Norway launched to strike targets near Newcastle upon Tyne. Spitfire and Hurricane squadrons, enjoying a period of relative rest in northern and central England but nearly all manned by veteran pilots, had a field day in attacking bombers unprotected by Bf 109s. By the time it was over, the Germans had lost nearly 20 percent of the attacking force, and the Fifth Air Force was entirely out of the daylight air operations for the rest of the battle.

In the south, however, Fighter Command found itself involved in a brutal fight for survival. Again the Germans targeted airfields and radar stations, and again Dowding and Park did a masterful job in allocating their scarce resources of fighter aircraft to where the German threat was the most severe. By now the Germans were better prepared to meet Fighter Command's counterattacks. Late in the afternoon, 88

Do 17 Dornier light bombers supported by 130 Bf 109s crossed the English Channel flying toward Deal, while another 60 Bf 109s struck into Kent. Against this force, the controller at Biggin Hill could launch only three squadrons of 24 Hurricanes and 12 Spitfires. Meanwhile, heavy raids struck to the west against Middle Wallop. Overall, the Germans lost 73 aircraft, while Fighter Command lost 30 aircraft, but with only thirteen pilots killed. The numbers belied the terrible pressure the Germans were imposing on the British defenses. Over the day's course, the Luftwaffe flew more than two thousand sorties, while Dowding's pilots flew nearly one thousand. Most of Fighter Command's sorties were in the south, and almost all the pilots in No. 11 Group flew three combat sorties that day.

August 18 saw the last attacks on the radar sites, which knocked the critical Poling radar site out of action until the end of the month. Even though the Germans lost twelve of their twenty-eight attacking Stuka dive bombers, they had achieved considerable success and from Fighter Command's point of view now posed a terrible threat. But Luftwaffe intelligence failed to discern how badly the attack had damaged the Poling site. Inexplicably from the British point of view, the German attacks on the radar sites halted, which was to prove a key advantage for Fighter Command.

In fact, the Luftwaffe leaders had undertaken a number of reassessments and decisions between August 15 and 18. The easiest decision for the Germans was to pull the slow, unmaneuverable, and virtually defenseless Ju 87 dive bombers out of the campaign, given the disastrous losses the Stuka squadrons were suffering—an unsupportable rate of somewhere between 10 and 20 percent on most missions and upward of 50 percent on some contested missions. Thus, the Germans lost their pinpoint bombing capability. The Spitfires and Hurricanes had had a field day with the Bf 110s as well. It was left to the Bf 109s to escort the bombers to and from their targets. If they were to survive, this limited the reach of German bombers in daylight raids to that of the Bf 109s, which could remain over London for only five minutes. Finally, in midmonth Göring ordered the Bf 109s to maintain proximity to the bombers they were escorting, which deprived his fighter pilots of the flexibility to attack targets of opportunity.

Most important, German leaders made the fateful decision to halt the attacks on the radar stations. Their technical intelligence reports indicated that the attacks, though accurate, had not seemed to destroy British radar coverage, while the cost of many of these attacks appeared prohibitive. The key factor in the miscalculation lay in how the Germans themselves were using radar technology—in effect, not as part of an air defense system, but in a ground control intercept mode in which each radar station acted independently in controlling a single or at most several aircraft. The Germans had no conception that British radar sites formed part of a systemic approach to air defense or that Dowding and Park were able to focus their Spitfires and Hurricanes on German raids in a fashion that maximized their potential. In effect, by stopping the attacks on radar sites, the Luftwaffe high command ceded to Fighter Command's controllers the advantage of discerning the buildup and then the probable targets at which the German bomber formations were going to strike.

FOR THE NEXT THREE WEEKS, from mid-August through the first week in September, a massive battle of attrition took place as the Luftwaffe attempted to destroy Fighter Command's infrastructure in southern England by applying constant pressure on its air bases. While the British were able to shoot down a significant percentage of attacking German bombers, which were the main targets of the Spitfires and Hurricanes, Fighter Command was also suffering a steady drain of pilots. The pressure on its fighter squadrons placed them in an increasingly dangerous situation. Nevertheless, Dowding possessed several strategic advantages. He was always in the position to pull back his fighter squadrons to the north of London—where, given the Bf 109's lack of range, the Luftwaffe could not get at them or their bases—should the pressure and peril become intolerable. Then, were the Germans actually to launch Sea Lion, British fighters could return to the fray. Second, Fighter Command had to survive only until the end of September, when the normal pattern of British weather would make the continuance of a daylight air campaign against the RAF impossible, while simultaneously thwarting any effort to carry out an amphibious landing on the coasts of southeast England.

An important aid in Fighter Command's fight for survival lay in the number of foreign-born pilots who flew for the RAF in the Battle of Britain: no fewer than 141 Poles, 129 New Zealanders, 90 Canadians, and 87 Czechs, among a host of other nationalities. Seven Americans also flew in Fighter Command during the battle, only one of whom would survive the war. The leading ace in the Battle of Britain was a Czech, Josef František, who had fled Czechoslovakia in March 1939 as the Germans marched into his country. He machine-gunned the Nazi columns as he flew out to Poland. In September 1939, he had flown for the Poles in their ill-fated campaign to hold off the German invasion; then, while interned in Romania after the collapse of Poland, he had escaped to Syria and joined the French air force, in which he participated in the Battle of France. By the time he arrived in Great Britain, he had already shot down eleven German aircraft. The Germans finally killed him on October 8, 1940, but by then he had become the leading ace in the Battle of Britain, with twenty-eight more German aircraft to his credit.

The loss rate among aircrew was appalling. In July, the British had lost 10 percent of their fighter pilots killed or injured on active operations—many of the wounded with horrific burns on their faces and hands, scarred for life by the propensity of the engine coolant of damaged Hurricanes and Spitfires to catch fire. German fighter pilot losses were almost equal, approximately 11 percent. In August, the British pilot losses amounted to 26 percent of the number of those on duty at the beginning of the month, while the Germans lost 15 percent of their operational fighter pilots. Luftwaffe bomber crew losses reached close to 30 percent, a loss rate that was simply not sustainable measured against their aircraft production rate and the availability of fully operational bomber crews. Consequently, both sides had to push minimally trained crews and pilots into frontline squadrons to maintain combat capabilities.

On both sides, most of those who flew fighters were mere youths, many still teenagers. Survival rates were terrifyingly slim. New pilots were easy meat for the more experienced in the deadly game of aerial combat, and only those who survived the first four or five missions had some hope. British pilots were often called upon to fly up to five ex-

Damage caused by the German Blitz
National Archives, Still Pictures Division, Washington, D.C.

hausting missions a day, making them all the more vulnerable. Only the young could withstand the physical and psychological strain of the battle, while the heroism displayed on both sides remained unrecorded in the loneliness of the skies. The most thoroughly researched work on the battle, Francis Mason's *Battle over Britain,* has a simple dedication: "To the Hurricane pilot who crawled back into his cockpit to prevent his blazing fighter from falling in a densely populated area." The pilot is unnamed and perhaps unknown, but innumerable such acts occurred over the battle's course. The only Victoria Cross awarded during the battle went to Flight Lieutenant James Nicolson. On August 16, in spite of the fact that his Hurricane was enveloped in flames, Nicolson continued his attack on a Bf 110 until he had shot down the German aircraft; only then did he abandon his aircraft, already suffering from severe burns, only to be hit with shotgun pellets fired by overeager soldiers on the ground, who took him for a German.

★ ★ ★

THROUGHOUT THESE THREE WEEKS, the German savaging of Fighter Command's airfields throughout southern England placed enormous pressure not only on Fighter Command's pilots, but on the ground crews as well—the maintenance and supply airmen, the armorers, and those responsible for repairing runways and hangars. The strain on the controllers and radar operators was equally great, as was the danger. Two Women's Auxiliary Air Force telephone operators remained at their posts after their building was badly damaged by a Luftwaffe bomb; a subsequent bomb killed them. Under unrelenting pressure, a number of airfields became unusable, but Park and his fighter squadrons weathered the storm, buttressed by fresh squadrons Dowding fed in from the north, as the fighting steadily burned out No. 11 Group's frontline units. Fighter Command's leadership positions were proving increasingly difficult to fill; thus far in the battle, the command had lost one in five of its squadron commanders and one in three of its flight commanders. By early September, Dowding had reached the point where he had no fresh squadrons to move into the battle. Thus, he was forced to send in individual replacements to keep up squadron strength in the embattled south—a break with his strategic approach to the battle.

It now became a matter of who would blink first. By the first week in September, Fighter Command appeared to be on the ropes, at least to its leaders. But the Luftwaffe was in no better shape. On September 3, Göring met with his air force commanders to decide whether to continue the attacks on Fighter Command's airfields or switch to massive attacks on London. Beppo Schmid's intelligence reports continued to prove woefully inaccurate; they indicated that the RAF was through as a combat force. Moreover, and of decisive importance, the Führer himself was urging a massive aerial assault on London to pay the British back for their outrageous bombing of Berlin over the night of August 24–25. "Smiling Albert" Kesselring, always delighted to agree with his superiors, fully supported the assumptions that Fighter Command was virtually finished. Sperrle, however, expressed considerable doubts about the proposition that the British were beaten and argued for a continuation of attacks on Fighter Command's structure. Not surprisingly, given Hitler's preferences, he found himself overruled.

Thus, late on the afternoon of September 7, as Göring and much of the air staff watched from Pas-de-Calais, a massive swarm of German bombers, altogether four hundred in number and protected by more than six hundred Bf 109s and Bf 110s, set off to attack the British capital. Fighter Command's controllers and commanders clearly expected a continuation of the Luftwaffe's attacks on airfields of southern England and were surprised by the mass raid on London. Thus, the British response to the raid was largely ineffective, which gave the Germans the sense that their opponent was indeed on its last legs. London itself took a pounding, with much of the East End as well as its docks destroyed. Continued bombing throughout the night added to ferocious fires that almost completely obliterated the area, with the huge warehouses of grain, chemicals, lumber, and other flammable materials along the docks feeding the flames. One of the fires was so large, the London fire service calculated that it took three hundred pumpers to extinguish it. Under horrendous conditions and in the greatest danger, the firemen of the city of London—also heroes in the Battle of Britain—fought the fires, rescued the trapped, and treated the injured.

Ironically, the great raid provided Fighter Command a much-needed respite to recover from the strain of the previous three weeks of almost constant dogfighting. Moreover, the Germans, also in need of rest, failed to launch another massive raid for more than a week. Not until September 15 did a second great blow come. That morning, German aircrews received word from their intelligence officers in the pre-raid briefings that the resistance of Fighter Command had finally collapsed and they would encounter little difficulty over London.

They were wrong. This time, Fighter Command was ready. The first raid of more than one hundred Do 17s ran into heavy resistance from Spitfires and Hurricanes scrambled by No. 11 Group's controllers well before they reached London. In the afternoon, the Germans launched a second force of nearly two hundred bombers, covered by over twice the number of Bf 109s. They were met by one hundred fifty of Park's fighters, which savaged the bombers. Just as the low-on-fuel Bf 109s began to withdraw, the massed squadrons of No. 12 Group—which controlled the fighter squadrons to the north of London and in the middle sections of the country—smashed into the

German bomber force. The fighter ace Douglas Bader, who had lost his legs in a crash in the 1930s, led the mass assault. Caught completely by surprise, German bomber crews broke; those the British did not shoot down dropped their loads and fled for the coast. To all intents and purposes, the German daylight offensive was over. The British had won, helped enormously by the arrogance and mistakes of their opponents.

ABOVE ALL, the advantage that the British enjoyed in the Battle of Britain lay in the performance of key individuals throughout the government and military. Churchill's greatest moments as a statesman came in the period between his assumption of the position of prime minister on May 10, 1940, and September 1940, when the German daylight offensive finally ground to a halt. He had fought off the craven efforts of those who advocated surrender to Nazi Germany. He had supported Dowding even when the air marshal had gone against his wishes. And he had courted the United States and its president shamelessly, because it was in Great Britain's interest. Perhaps as important, he had provided the stirring speeches that had rallied his countrymen.

There were others, too numerous to mention, except perhaps for that greatest air commander of the Second World War, Sir Hugh Dowding. It was Dowding who had foreseen the direction developing technologies were headed, had contracted for the advanced technological weapons, had incorporated the weapons and technologies into an effective system of air defense, and then had finally fought and won the Battle of Britain. No other military figure in the Second World War could claim such an impressive visionary record, which had moved from research and development to conceptualization through to the actual use of military forces in battle, a use that possessed enormous strategic and operational significance.

And, of course, there were the pilots of Fighter Command, whom Churchill so brilliantly and so simply eulogized before the House of Commons: "Never in the field of human conflict was so much owed by so many to so few." The dangers those pilots faced were extraordinary, not the least being the terrible trials by fire so many endured, their faces and hands burned severely as they desperately attempted to bail out of their stricken aircraft. Their indescribable suffering, psychological as well as physical, extended indefinitely, as plastic surgeons attempted to rebuild burned faces into something that resembled a human likeness, a process that often required an almost endless series of painful operations. As for the ground crews, they as well as the pilots are saluted in Mason's dedication to his preeminent history of the battle, which states laconically: "To three Fighter Command groundcrewmen crushed to death when a bomb blew a hangar door down upon them; they had left the shelter trench to save aircraft in the hangar."

One of the great ironies of the battle was the fact that Dowding and Park, the two men most responsible for the victory, would be removed from command in the fall: Dowding to permanent retirement, Park to assignments in the Mediterranean, including eventually the air defense of Malta, where he would perform as spectacularly as he had in defending southern England. Churchill would attempt to use Dowding later in the war, but obdurate and inexplicable opposi-

St. Paul's Cathedral, surrounded by ruin, stands defiant
National Archives, Still Pictures Division, Washington, D.C.

tion from the Air Ministry would keep him on the shelf, perhaps the only explanation being that he had thoroughly disproven the RAF's prewar doctrine that "the bomber would always get through." The three German commanders most responsible for the German defeat would find their careers not at all damaged and would move on to other major commands during the war, where each would make considerable contributions to the ultimate Allied victory.

Great Britain's victory in the Battle of Britain was more important for its political and strategic impact than for its military ramifications. Admittedly, Fighter Command had defeated the Luftwaffe and there would be no Operation Sea Lion. Still, this was a defensive rather than an offensive victory, one that prevented the Germans from bombing the British out of the war. Yet its political and strategic impact would be direct, immediate, and enormous. The fact that the RAF had won the daylight air battle provided Franklin D. Roosevelt with the proof he needed to justify to the American people the financial and economic help that Churchill and his countrymen so desperately needed. That assistance would turn the British Isles into a great fortress and base for future operations against Nazi-occupied Fortress Europe. From that fortress the British and their allies, including the Americans, would wage three great campaigns. The first was the Battle of the Atlantic, which would make all that followed possible. The second campaign, the Combined Bomber Offensive, a great bombing effort against the Nazi war economy, would begin to have a substantial effect in spring 1943 and would drastically curtail Germany's ability to support the Wehrmacht's effort, eventually winning Allied air superiority over the entire European Continent in spring 1944. Finally, the British Isles would provide the base from which British and American armies would launch Operation Overlord, the invasion of Normandy and the return to the European Continent. Without the political and strategic success that the Battle of Britain represented, the Western Allies would not have been able to wage any of those great campaigns.

For the Germans, the defeat in the Battle of Britain confirmed Hitler's instinctive strategic reading of the situation that the road to victory would lie on the ground in an invasion of the Soviet Union. He found his senior military leaders, including those of the Luftwaffe, enthusiastic supporters of that view. That service's chief of staff, General Hans Jeschonnek, would even exclaim at the beginning of the attack on the Soviets, "At last a proper war." Ironically, the Luftwaffe would enter into the Eastern campaign even less well prepared for sustained combat than it had been on May 10, 1940, when it had embarked on the war in the West against Great Britain and its allies. On June 22, 1941, it would possess two hundred fewer bombers than the previous year, while the constant pressure of combat against the British Isles had exhausted its crews. In fact, for the remainder of the war, the Luftwaffe would never fully recover from the exertions of the campaign against the British.

In the end, the Battle of Britain ensured that Great Britain would survive. That very survival in turn ensured that the British Isles provided the base on which the great Anglo-American partnership not only defeated Nazi Germany, but also developed into the great alliance that would hold Western Europe against the Soviet tyranny until Communism collapsed of its own economic and political ineptitude and incompetence. As Churchill so eloquently suggested in that high summer of 1940, when the world teetered on the brink "of a new dark age," the heroism with which the British people and the pilots of Fighter Command fought the Battle of Britain would continue to reverberate into future centuries.

MIDWAY

Imperial Japan Stopped

1942

AT MIDDAY ON APRIL 18, 1942, AS ASSORTED JAPANESE CIVILIANS AND military personnel watched, sixteen twin-engine bombers hurtled at low altitude across the landscape of the Japanese home islands. The aircraft came from the east out of the Pacific Ocean. Many of the Japanese waved; who could possibly doubt they were the emperor's aircraft? But in fact they were American B-25s, led by Lieutenant Colonel Jimmy Doolittle and flown off the U.S. Navy's carrier *Hornet*. Relative to the amount of effort expended by the Americans in preparing for this raid, the B-25s inflicted minimal physical damage to their targets in Tokyo and the other cities they attacked, but the raid provided the American people with a major psychological lift. In retrospect, the attack was a harbinger of the devastating blows American bombers would deal out to the Japanese three years later. But in April 1942, after five months of stunning victories during which Japanese arms had destroyed the American battle fleet at Pearl Harbor and humiliated the Americans in the Philippines, the British in Malaya and Burma, and the Dutch in the East Indies, the Doolittle raid was a direct challenge to Japan's military, a bold shot across the bow of imperial Japan and its militarists.

For the Imperial Japanese Navy, which had not focused on the central Pacific after the attack on Pearl Harbor and had dismissed the latent threat the American fleet represented, the raid was a jolting wake-up call. Moreover, the attack on the home islands had put the safety of the emperor in question, an act that demanded a response. The leaders of Japan's Combined Fleet were already considering Midway as a potential target, with Admiral Isoroku Yamamoto, its commander, pushing hard for such an operation. Midway's importance lay in the fact that it was the only island between Wake Island and the Hawaiian Islands. If the Japanese captured it, they would hold a crucial jumping-off position for an invasion of Hawaii. Nevertheless, the naval staff and navy minister had been less sure about such an operation. The Doolittle raid settled matters. Midway it would be, with the underlying assumption that such an attack would bring the American fleet out into the central Pacific, where the Imperial Japanese Navy could destroy it.

However, there were major operations already under way that the Imperial Japanese Navy first had to complete. At the time of the Doolittle raid, Admiral Chuichi Nagumo and his fleet of six large carriers—the *Kido Butai*—and four fast battleships were returning to the home islands from the devastating attacks they had executed in the Indian Ocean against the British. Nagumo's ships and pilots had been in constant action since the Pearl Harbor attack, and they needed time to refit and resupply before another major operation. Meanwhile, the Japanese had been on the brink of launching an amphibious strike against Port Moresby, the U.S.-Australian position on the southeast corner of New Guinea. The covering force for that operation consisted of the fast carriers *Shokaku* and *Zuikaku*.

In late April, American code breaking revealed the imminent Japanese move against Port Moresby. Alerted with time to act, Admiral Chester Nimitz, commander in chief of the United States Pacific Fleet, provided a hot reception for the imperial forces—namely, the fast carriers *Yorktown* and *Lexington*. The two fleets met in the inconclusive Battle of the Coral Sea, the first fleet engagement in history

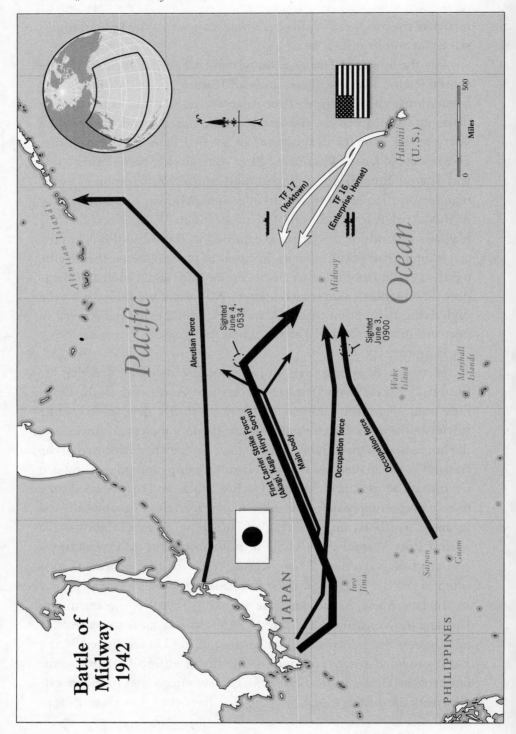

Battle of
Midway
1942

PHILIPPINES

JAPAN

PACIFIC

Pacific

Ocean

Aleutian Islands

Aleutian Force

First Carrier Strike Force
(Akagi, Kaga, Hiryu, Soryu)

Main body

Occupation force

Occupation force

Sighted
June 4,
0534

Sighted
June 3,
0900

Midway

*Wake
Island*

*Marshall
Islands*

*Iwo
Jima*

Saipan

Guam

*Hawaii
(U.S.)*

TF 17
(Yorktown)

TF 16
(Enterprise, Hornet)

Miles
0   500

where the opposing ships never saw one another. The Japanese gained a tactical victory, sinking the *Lexington* and damaging the *Yorktown*, while losing only a light carrier. But the battle was a strategic victory for the Americans. They had forced the invasion fleet to turn back, thereby saving Port Moresby. American carrier air also inflicted heavy damage on the *Shokaku* and such significant losses on the *Zuikaku*'s aircraft squadrons that neither carrier would participate in the Midway operation. Although the *Shokaku* had suffered serious damage, the *Zuikaku* was undamaged and could have participated in the operation, admittedly with a scratched-together air group, but the Japanese high command never considered that possibility, a sure sign of the "victory disease" infecting it.

While the Battle of the Coral Sea was under way, Japanese naval staffs were planning operations to seize Midway and destroy the American fleet. In retrospect, the Japanese planning for Midway ranks with German preparations for the invasion of the Soviet Union in terms of sloppy assumptions, underestimation of an opponent, and lack of clarity as to the main objective: Was it the American fleet? Or Midway? Would the Americans be able to mount an effective response? In a series of tabletop war games in early May, the Japanese examined the variables for the upcoming operation. One officer dared to suggest the Americans might be aware of Japanese intentions and deploy their carriers ahead of time to protect Midway. That idea received short shrift from senior officers, including Nagumo.

The chief umpire and controller for the games, Rear Admiral Matome Ugaki, chief of staff for the Combined Fleet, ensured that the games ran on an even keel and did not upset the Combined Fleet's rosy assumptions. In one of the games, the U.S. player broke through the Japanese screen and bombed Nagumo's carriers. The umpire for that portion of the game ruled that the American attacks had sunk the carriers *Kaga* and *Akagi*. However, Ugaki immediately overruled the umpire and judged the Americans had sunk only one carrier while slightly damaging the other.

The eventual plan, designed by Yamamoto and the naval staff, was a complex compromise that minimized the Combined Fleet's air and sea power. A task force of two light carriers, the *Ryujo* and the *Junyo,* and supporting vessels was to strike the Aleutians, while land-

Admiral Isoroku Yamamoto
National Archives,
Still Pictures Division,
Washington, D.C.

ing forces seized the completely useless islands of Attu and Kiska. What exactly the naval staff aimed to achieve by attacking the Aleutians and seizing those two islands is impossible to reconstruct. The excuse was that the attack on the Aleutians would serve as a decoy to draw the attention of the Americans away from the main attack on Midway. But since Japanese naval leaders timed the attack on the Aleutians almost concurrently with Midway, it is difficult to see what they expected the deception to achieve.

But it was the planning for the main operation against Midway that revealed the Japanese at their most careless. In effect, they determined to launch three separate forces against the island. From the south, Admiral Nobutake Kondo was to lead a group consisting of the landing force with a covering force of older battleships and a close-support force of four heavy cruisers. The opening move against Midway would come from a second force consisting of Nagumo's four fast carriers. A third force under Admiral Yamamoto, consisting of the newest battleships in the Japanese fleet, would follow three hundred miles behind the fast carriers to clean up the Americans, if they were to come out. Two of the more forward-thinking Japanese airmen, Lieutenant Commander Shigeharu Murata and Commander Mitsuo Fuchida, characterized the plan in the following terms:

Murata: "What a nonsens[ical] operation! The *Yamato* and the others are coming three hundred miles behind our task force! What the hell do they think they can do with those useless guns to the rear of our carrier force?"

Fuchida: "If those damned battleships were ahead of our force, those big guns would be of some use and also helpful for the operations of the task force. But otherwise, I can't help asking myself if they hardly have enough will to fight."

Although the Americans had broken into the highest ciphers of the Imperial Japanese Navy, they were decoding only a relatively few messages, given the flood of Japanese transmissions and the complexity of both the codes and the Japanese language. Nevertheless, Nimitz and his intelligence analysts were able to make educated guesses on the basis of incomplete information as to what Japanese intentions might be. On the basis of what these intercepts suggested, they believed Midway was the target for the upcoming operation but were not certain. On May 10, they had Midway send out a message en clair (in plain language), reporting that the island's desalinization plant was out of order and there was a shortage of water. Forty-eight hours later, American cryptologists deciphered a Japanese message reporting there were water shortages at the invasion target.

It is one thing to know one's opponents' intentions; it is another to ensure that one's own forces can take advantage of that information. Not surprisingly, the mood at Nimitz's Pacific Fleet command headquarters at Pearl Harbor was fraught with anxiety. Nimitz made a number of crucial decisions. First, on May 15 he recalled Admiral Bull Halsey and his Task Force 16, consisting of the *Enterprise* and the *Hornet,* from the South Pacific, where they had arrived too late to participate in the Battle of the Coral Sea. At the same time, he ordered Admiral Frank Fletcher with Task Force 17—with the loss of the *Lexington,* now consisting only of the *Yorktown,* damaged in the Coral Sea—to return as fast as possible. Nimitz also had at his disposal the battleships that had survived the Pearl Harbor attack, but he chose to leave them in San Francisco, since they were too slow to keep up with the carriers and hence represented a vulnerability rather than an asset. Moreover, Nimitz appears not to have had full confidence in their admiral, Vice Admiral William Pye, who had botched the effort to relieve the gallant garrison at Wake Island after Pearl Harbor. Halsey arrived in Pearl Harbor on May 26, but the strain of the past six months had temporarily broken his health, and he had to give up command of the task force. Admiral Raymond Spruance replaced him.

Immediately upon arrival at Pearl Harbor, the *Enterprise* and *Hornet* replenished their fuel tanks and ammunition magazines. Two days later, on May 28, they sortied under Spruance. Meanwhile, Fletcher and the *Yorktown* had arrived back at Pearl on May 27. Fletcher had estimated it would take two months to repair the damage three Japanese bombs had done to the carrier. As she entered the harbor, the *Yorktown* went straight into dry dock, and there, awaiting her, Nimitz

Admiral Raymond
Spruance
*National Archives, Still
Pictures Division,
Washington, D.C.*

had fourteen hundred dockyard workers ready to repair the damage. They swarmed over her and for the next forty-eight hours attempted to fix her injuries. They jury-rigged damaged bulkheads and in some cases made repairs by using wooden beams to strengthen and support damaged areas throughout the ship.

One day after Task Force 16 sortied, the *Yorktown* followed. The repair work had taken only two days. Admittedly, the *Yorktown* was capable of making only twenty-five knots, well under her maximum speed, but she was at sea, combat ready. Owing to the heavy losses of aircraft in the Coral Sea, the *Yorktown*'s air complement was little better than a hodgepodge of aircraft and units, including some aircrew with no experience at all. But even an air group cobbled together to provide a semblance of combat capabilities was good enough to level the odds, especially since the Japanese did not expect to encounter significant resistance in the air, much less American carriers, in the opening days of their invasion of Midway.

With respect to the correlation of forces, the Japanese held a significant advantage over their American opponents. They possessed four carriers, as opposed to three for the Americans. Moreover, the *Yorktown,* even with the desperate repairs made at Pearl after her arrival, was hardly in first-class shape. In battleships, the Japanese again held the advantage: they possessed five fast battleships (not counting the battleships delegated to the Aleutian operation), including the monster battleship *Yamato,* compared with none for the Americans. Only in heavy cruisers was there a rough parity: six for the Japanese and seven for the Americans. The Americans were also at a serious disadvantage in the air. The Mitsubishi A6M2 Zero was far and away the premier fighter aircraft of the first year of the Pacific war, while Japanese aircrews, in both training and combat experience, were superior to their American opponents in every respect.

Yet there were incalculable advantages on the American side. The most important, of course, was the American edge in code breaking and intelligence. The Americans also paid close attention to what the intelligence suggested: thus, they made a massive effort to turn Midway into a fortress, while concentrating their carriers in the Hawaiian Islands to meet the Japanese thrust. In the field of technology, they enjoyed a significant advantage in that their carriers and cruisers were equipped with up-to-date radars, which would enable them to pick up and prepare to meet incoming Japanese air attacks. In addition, Midway possessed two obsolete radar sets capable at least of warning its defenders of an impending attack. The American task forces also operated with short-range ship-to-ship and air-to-ship radios, which the Japanese could not intercept and which improved ship-to-ship communications.

On the other side, only two ships among the Japanese task forces possessed radar, and those were assigned to the Aleutian operation. Like their German allies, the Japanese were outstanding tacticians, but they were not particularly good at incorporating technology into their war-making capabilities. Nevertheless, despite their inability to read American messages, the vast increase in the message traffic issuing from Pearl Harbor in mid-May should have raised a clear warning that the Americans were up to something.

However, a comment in Admiral Ugaki's diary on May 28 underlines the overconfidence that would prove so lethal to Japanese fortunes in the battle: "[Radio interceptions] indicate that enemy planes and subs in the Aleutian Islands, Hawaiian Islands, and the mid-Pacific are engaged in brisk activities. Exchanges of urgent messages are at a very unusual rate. Certain indications make me suspect that they are taking countermeasures against our suspected movement rather than engaging in operations based on their own initiative." Nevertheless, Ugaki appears to have disregarded his own instinctive interpretation of the telltale American activity; he and his forces took no precautions.

The Americans enjoyed another major advantage: their leadership. Nimitz played his cards with exquisite calculation of the odds; he concentrated U.S. forces with dispatch and then provided his subordinates with the latitude to execute their missions. On the other side, Yamamoto squandered his advantages in force strength and experience by being too clever by half. The diversion to the Aleutians made no sense, especially given the congruence of the start times of the two attacks, nor did the separation of the Combined Fleet into two distinct attacking bodies make much sense.

The American leadership advantage extended into the lower levels of command, which would fight the battle. Nagumo was a cautious admiral. Despite his command of the fast carriers over the past six months, he had not distinguished himself. Above all, he failed to interpret his orders with the slightest amount of imagination. On the opposing side, Spruance, handpicked by Nimitz and Halsey to replace the latter in command of Task Force 16, would display the calculated coolness that was to make him the premier U.S. fleet commander of the Second World War. Spruance was not averse to taking calculated risks when the situation justified it. In retrospect, he was perhaps the most thoroughly educated student of naval warfare ever to make flag rank. The commander of Task Force 17, Admiral Frank Fletcher, stood less high in his contemporaries' judgment. One of Nimitz's staff officers would describe him a bit unfairly as "a big, nice, wonderful guy who didn't know his butt from third base."

ALMOST CONCURRENTLY with the American sortie from Pearl, the Japanese sortied from their bases in the western Pacific. On May 27, Nagumo's carriers upped anchor; on the next day, the battleship heart of the Combined Fleet departed the home islands under Admiral Yamamoto. Meanwhile, the transports and their accompanying heavy cruisers and destroyers were moving on Midway from Saipan, headed on a course to the northeast. Nagumo aimed to position his carriers northwest of Midway and from there launch the first strikes of the battle against the island, while using his scout planes to cover his flank to the east and northeast. Steadily over the last days of May and the first days of June, the two fleets drew closer, the Americans with an accurate picture of Japanese intentions, the Japanese with no clear idea as to the reception committee the Americans were preparing.

Nimitz's instructions to his two task force commanders were that "in carrying out the task assigned . . . you will be governed by the principle of calculated risk, which you shall interpret to mean the avoidance of exposure of your force to attack by superior enemy forces without good prospect of inflicting . . . greater damage on the enemy." For most military commanders such instructions could have proven inhibiting, but not for Spruance. He possessed a unique capacity to act aggressively with minimal risk to his forces. Although Fletcher outranked Spruance, the two agreed on their roles, which set the parameters of the coming action and granted the latter considerable freedom of action.

The American task forces would stand off to the northeast of Midway to catch Nagumo from an unexpected direction. While the American carriers positioned themselves, Nimitz completed a massive buildup of American ground and air forces on Midway itself. Thus, the Japanese were going to find themselves under attack from two different directions when they arrived off of the American base. In both cases, the Americans would catch the Japanese by surprise, in the case of the latter by the strength of the resistance on Midway and in the case of the former by the mere presence of the carriers.

On the other side, by positioning the Japanese carriers northwest of Midway, Yamamoto expected his operation to catch the Americans by surprise. That possibility disappeared at 9:00 A.M. on June 3, when an American long-range Catalina amphibian scout plane spied the Japanese landing force approaching Midway from the southwest. Slightly more than five hours later, nine B-17s flying off Midway's airfield made contact and bombed the landing and covering forces. They reported hitting two battleships or cruisers and two transports. In fact, they merely replicated the miserable failure of high-level bombing by B-17s against naval targets thus far in the war: the American bombers missed their targets entirely, at best killing a few fish. Still, Nagumo had no reason to expect that the Americans were aware his carriers were approaching from the northwest.

At 4:30 A.M. on June 4, both sides launched reconnaissance aircraft to locate their enemy. The Americans had the advantage in that they were able to launch their reconnaissance aircraft from two different positions, first from Midway and second from the *Yorktown* carrier deck. The Japanese, however, believing that they should devote maximum strength to the strike missions, failed to allocate sufficient resources to the search mission. Some of their reconnaissance aircraft took off from the carriers, some from the accompanying cruisers. But the Japanese allocated only one aircraft for each of the reconnaissance sectors. After all, according to Nagumo's estimate of the situation, "the enemy is not aware of our plans. . . . It is not believed that the enemy had any powerful unit, with carriers as its nucleus, in the vicinity. . . . After attacking Midway by air and destroying the enemy's shore based air strength . . . , we should be able to destroy any enemy task force which may choose to counterattack."

At this point, the first of those seemingly tiny incidents on which so much of history turns occurred. All of the Japanese reconnaissance aircraft succeeded in launching on time, except for the seaplane from the heavy cruiser *Tone*. Given Japanese overconfidence, there was no backup aircraft. Not until 5:00 A.M., half an hour later, was the *Tone* able to launch its single-float plane. Fortunately for the Americans, the search sector for the *Tone*'s seaplane was the sector in which their task forces were lying in wait. The Japanese were now about to experience the all-too-common phenomenon that Churchill, commenting on Great Britain's disastrous failure at Gallipoli peninsula in 1915, described as "the terrible ifs accumulate."

Nagumo was not even aware of the gap in the Japanese reconnaissance umbrella, although it is doubtful he would have changed anything had he known. Almost immediately after the reconnaissance aircraft had departed on their missions, the *Kido Butai* launched the initial attack on Midway: thirty-six Vals (dive bombers), thirty-six Kates (dual-rolled to drop torpedoes and regular bombs), and thirty-six Zeros. As soon as the last aircraft had departed, Nagumo, always cautious, ordered his carriers to bring additional Kates (all armed with torpedoes) up onto the flight deck, in case the unexpected was to occur and the Japanese search aircraft located an American task force.

The battle's pace now accelerated. At 5:20 A.M., an American Catalina, flying off Midway, spotted Nagumo's fleet; twenty-five minutes later, it made its first brief report. Ten minutes later, the radar on Midway picked up the incoming Japanese raid and the island launched all its aircraft. At 6:03, the Catalina reported the presence of Japanese carriers. Spruance with his two carriers proceeded southwesterly to attack the Japanese, while Fletcher's *Yorktown* recovered its search aircraft.

Between 6:35 and 6:50, Japanese aircraft plastered Midway. The accompanying Zeros slaughtered the obsolete American fighters defending the island. Out of twenty-six Buffalos and Wildcats, the Americans lost seventeen shot down, with seven more badly damaged. But the Japanese suffered heavily as well, losing approximately one third of the attacking force, most as a result of heavy antiaircraft fire. The Japanese commander of the raid radioed back to the carriers that the attack had been successful but that the carriers needed to launch a follow-up raid.

Nagumo had already come to the same conclusion. While his aircraft had been attacking Midway, the Japanese carriers had come under attack by four B-26s and ten marine torpedo bombers launched from Midway. At 7:15, Nagumo ordered his carrier commanders to replace the torpedoes and armor-piercing bombs on the ninety-three aircraft on the carrier decks with high-explosive bombs for a second raid on Midway. At almost the same time, Spruance, relatively sure of the Japanese carriers' location, ordered the air groups of the *Enterprise* and *Hornet* to launch. Altogether, Task Force 16 sent out sixty-seven dive bombers, twenty-nine torpedo bombers, and twenty fighters to strike the Japanese flattops.

At this point, Nagumo's day began to come apart. Thirteen minutes after ordering the weapons on the ninety-three aircraft on deck to be changed to conventional high-explosive bombs, he received a message from the *Tone*'s reconnaissance float plane that it had spotted ten enemy surface ships northeast of the Japanese carriers. For the next quarter of an hour, the Japanese admiral dithered as to what to do; meanwhile, the window closed on launching an attack on this mystery fleet. The survivors of the Midway raid would soon be returning, and the decks would have to be kept clear to recover, rearm, and refuel those aircraft. Thus, virtually the entire deckload of aircraft had to be moved down to the hangar deck.

What is astonishing about Nagumo's performance is that the only reasonable explanation for the presence of any U.S. surface vessels that far to the northwest of Hawaii had to be that there was a larger task force, including carriers, in the area. Yet the Japanese admiral failed to connect the dots until it was too late. Finally, at 7:45, he decided that he had better deal with this American force of indeterminate makeup and ordered a halt to the rearming with ground attack bombs of the Kates in the carrier hangar decks. But another thirty-five minutes passed before the *Tone*'s reconnaissance aircraft reported that it had at last identified a carrier as being present among the American surface vessels.

U.S. dive bombers prepare to attack
National Archives, Still Pictures Division, Washington, D.C.

Finally apprised of the presence of American carriers, Nagumo found himself caught in the vise of first having to recover the Midway raiders. The Japanese carriers could not strike at the American fleet until their maintenance people and armorers had repaired damage and refueled and rearmed the returning aircraft. As this process was ongoing, the carrier decks were littered with bombs, fuel bowsers, and torpedoes, while on the hangar decks one level down, the Kates were fully fueled and rearmed with torpedoes and ship-killing armor-piercing bombs. Even more dangerous, the high-explosive bombs with which they had initially been armed had yet to be returned to the carrier magazines.

Had Nagumo possessed any presence of mind, he might well have considered pulling out to the west to get matters sorted out, given the unexpected presence of U.S. carriers in the area. But such a move would have demanded imagination and initiative, and he was lacking in both. Caught on the horns of a dilemma, the Japanese admiral proved incapable of making a decision that took into account the radically unexpected situation he confronted.

As the Japanese drove their carriers toward the Americans, they encountered a series of uncoordinated and unsuccessful attacks from a steady flow of ineffective but fierce U.S. Navy and Army Air Force aircraft: at 7:55, sixteen U.S. Marine dive bombers from Midway attacked, no hits; at 8:15, fifteen B-17s at twenty thousand feet, no hits; at 8:20, eleven U.S. Marine aircraft from Midway, no hits; at 8:25, the submarine USS *Nautilus* launched torpedoes at one of Nagumo's battleships, no hits; at 9:25, *Hornet* torpedo bombers attacked, all aircraft lost, one survivor, Ensign George Gay, no hits; at 9:40, *Enterprise*'s torpedo bombers attacked, no survivors, no hits.

These prolonged attacks had a number of serious effects on the Japanese. First, they exacerbated the problem of recovering and then turning around the aircraft returning from the Midway strikes, as the carriers desperately maneuvered to escape their tormentors. Second, the series of uncoordinated torpedo bomber attacks had the unintended effect of pulling the Japanese combat air patrols (CAPs) down to sea level to protect the carriers, leaving nothing at higher altitudes to cover the possible arrival of American dive bombers. And that was precisely what happened. The Japanese, who had seen virtually every roll of the dice go their way over the previous six months, now saw chance, that element of war Carl von Clausewitz had emphasized so heavily in his writing, alter the game entirely.

As the Zeros splashed the last of the torpedo bombers, American dive bombers, almost out of fuel, picked up the wake of a destroyer the Japanese had detached to take care of the *Nautilus*. Lieutenant Commander Clarence McClusky, leading the *Enterprise*'s Dauntless dive bombers, decided the ship was attempting to catch up to Nagumo's carriers and turned his squadron to follow the destroyer's course. Minutes later, the dive bomber pilots spotted the Japanese fleet laid out just ahead of them. There was no CAP to contest them on arrival as they positioned their aircraft directly above the carriers, which had stopped taking evasive action after the destruction of the last torpedo bomber.

⋆ ⋆ ⋆

IF ANY BATTLE in history has a decisive moment, it is the Battle of Midway. As the last American torpedo bomber smashed into the sea shortly after 10:00 A.M., Nagumo ordered his carriers to turn into the wind and begin launching additional CAP Zeros. Soon the aircraft, refueled and rearmed with ship-killing bombs and torpedoes, would launch and be winging their way toward the American carriers. The strike never got airborne. Suddenly, one of the lookouts on the *Kaga* screamed, *"Hell diver!"* It was McClusky and his dive bombers arriving from the south.

As the southernmost of the carriers, the *Kaga* was the first one the Americans attacked, and not surprisingly it received the most attention. The first three bombs dropped by McClusky's group missed; the fourth, however, scored a direct hit on the flight deck near the aft elevator, pierced the wooden planking, and exploded in the hangar deck among a host of fueled and bombed-up aircraft. Three more bombs would hit the carrier minutes later, one striking the bridge directly and killing virtually the entire command element of the carrier. It did not matter, nor did the next three bombs that hit her make much difference, because the *Kaga* was already dying, one sympathetic explosion following another, turning the entire ship into a mass of flames. Horrendous blasts on the hangar deck followed in sequence as the torpedo aircraft, their torpedoes, and the bombs stacked carelessly for return to the magazine all exploded.

A recent study of the battle describes the catastrophe in the following terms: "The conditions in *Kaga*'s hangars immediately after the bombing were horrific beyond description. Bodies and pieces of bodies of *Kaga*'s armorers and mechanics lay strewn everywhere among the wreckage of her aircraft. . . . Mechanics, plane handlers, and armorers alike were slaughtered by the score—blown apart, immolated, crushed under the aircraft they had been servicing, or mown down by the shrapnel as they crouched on the bare metal deck, seeking shelter where there was none. . . . Taken together, the initial hits on *Kaga* probably killed or badly wounded every man in the upper hangar." To add to the explosive nature of what was on the hangar deck of the *Kaga,* there were approximately twenty torpedoes with their oxygen tanks as well as their warheads and some twenty-eight 1,280-pound bombs and forty 400-pound bombs. The follow-on explosions ignited by the American bomb hits literally blew the heart out of the ship.

Meanwhile, similar disasters hit the *Akagi* and the *Soryu*. The *Akagi* was a lucky hit for the Americans, because only three dive bombers attacked it. Lieutenant Richard Best had been about to join the attack on the *Kaga* but pulled out at the last moment when it was clear that more than enough aircraft were attacking that carrier. Only two aircraft followed him, and their bombs missed, but Best's bomb hit the *Akagi* behind the center elevator. The one-thousand-pound bomb exploded in the upper hangar deck, which was packed with fully fueled and bombed-up aircraft, and was more than sufficient to doom the carrier as sympathetic explosions spread throughout her hangar decks.

The *Soryu* was the northernmost of the Japanese carriers, and it was hit by an entirely different formation of American dive bombers off the *Yorktown,* which approached the Japanese from the northeast. The dive bombers hit the *Soryu* with three bombs, but again, only one

Ensign George Gay recovering after being shot down early in the battle
National Archives, Still Pictures Division, Washington, D.C.

was needed. Sympathetic explosions throughout her hangar deck doomed her in a matter of seconds after the first bomb exploded.

One individual with nothing to do—Ensign Gay, the sole survivor of the *Hornet*'s torpedo bomber squadron, who was treading water and hiding under an aircraft cushion, not daring to open his yellow life raft for fear the Japanese would pick him up—had a ringside seat to watch disaster strike the Japanese carriers. His recollections, given to U.S. Navy historians later and perhaps overdramatized, were vivid: "The carriers [dead in the water] during the day resembled a very large oil field fire, if you've ever seen one. The fire coming out of the forward and aft end of the [carrier] looked like a blow torch, just roaring white flame and the oil burning, the crude oil, boil up, I don't know how high and just billowing big red flames belched out of this black smoke. The dive bomber [pilots] told me they saw the smoke at 18,000 feet that day and [it] really did make a nice fire and they'd burn for a while and blow up for a while and I was . . . in the water hollering, 'Hooray, hooray.'" In fact, given the distances among the Japanese carriers, which had become widely separated during the earlier American attacks, Gay may have seen only one of the great ships explode, but he certainly would have seen the funeral pyres of the others.

For the Japanese, death came with dreadful suddenness. For those on the main and hangar decks, explosions and fire incinerated most before they could grasp what was happening. For those belowdecks in the engine rooms and the magazines, the massive explosions occurring above undoubtedly alerted them to their mortal peril. As the lighting failed, the lucky ones died of asphyxiation, carbon monoxide poisoning, or internal detonations that racked the flaming torches that had once been the spearheads of the *Kido Butai*'s drive across the Pacific. As the heat worked its way down into the bowels of the carriers, others were baked to death; finally, some were drowned as the carriers began to sink.

One Japanese carrier, the *Hiryu,* survived untouched because it had been in the middle of the carrier formation and therefore never received any attention from the attacking American dive bombers. The *Hiryu* now launched its aircraft to extract a measure of revenge. The first target its aircraft found was the most vulnerable of the Amer-

USS *Yorktown* under attack
National Archives, Still Pictures Division, Washington, D.C.

ican carriers, the *Yorktown*. Alerted by their radar, the Americans were ready; the Wildcat CAP was already at altitude. Eighteen Val dive bombers formed the strike package, protected by Zeros. The Wildcats shot down ten of the Vals, antiaircraft got another two, but six made it through. Three bombs hit the carrier, one damaging the flight deck, one hitting the funnel and extinguishing the boiler fires, and one punching its way through four decks to explode deep in the bowels of the ship.

Astonishingly, within an hour and a half the *Yorktown*'s damage control had repaired the flight deck and relit the boilers, so that the ship was able to reach twenty knots. The advantage the *Yorktown* enjoyed as opposed to the Japanese carriers was that she had been alerted by radar to the attack, so she had been able to get most of her aircraft airborne, while all the bombs and torpedoes were stored deep belowdecks. Within two hours, the *Yorktown* was able to resume flight operations. Three hours after the first attack, Japanese torpedo aircraft again found the *Yorktown;* such was her condition that they thought they were attacking an undamaged carrier. But the *Yorktown*'s luck had run its course. The attackers this time hit the carrier with two torpedoes, and their explosions inflicted mortal damage—breaching most of the fuel tanks on her port side, jamming the rudder, severing all power connections, and causing an immediate list of seventeen degrees that quickly increased to twenty-six degrees. The captain, fearing the carrier was about to capsize, ordered the crew to abandon ship at 3:00 P.M.

Two hours later, twenty-four Dauntless dive bombers from the *Enterprise*—ten of them *Yorktown* aircraft that had landed on the *Enterprise* after the Japanese had hit their carrier—struck the *Hiryu,* which they caught in virtually the same position in which the Americans had found her sister carriers seven hours earlier: with a deck full of fighters, bombers, and torpedo aircraft, an indication of the lack of radar capability on the most important ships in the Japanese fleet. Four bombs hit the carrier, with the results matching those inflicted on the other Japanese carriers. The Americans left the *Hiryu* a flaming torch, a fourth Japanese carrier with most of her aircrew scratched.

For all intents and purposes, the Battle of Midway was over. Spruance drew the two undamaged American carriers off to the east to ensure that any approaching Japanese surface vessels could not get at them. Yamamoto considered advancing with the Combined Fleet to compensate for the devastating defeat his carriers had suffered, then decided that discretion was the better part of valor. He too pulled back, as did the invasion fleet. In the battle's aftermath, U.S. aircraft sank a Japanese heavy cruiser and badly damaged another the next day, but there was no major resumption of the battle, so resounding had the American victory been.

IN TERMS of both its immediate and its long-term effects, the Battle of Midway had a major impact not only on the course of the Second World War, but on the Cold War that was to follow. The destruction of the heart of Japan's carrier fleet and the loss of the naval pilots from the carrier air groups opened up the opportunity for U.S. and Australian forces to undertake limited offensive operations in southeast New Guinea and at Guadalcanal. The Allies launched those operations on a shoestring. But the Japanese never mounted a concentrated effort with their naval and ground forces sufficient to defeat these limited

Allied offensives. Had the Combined Fleet sortied at full strength in late summer or early fall 1942, it might well have swamped Allied naval forces protecting Guadalcanal and set the conditions that would have allowed the Imperial Japanese Army to destroy the 1st Marine Division. It might also have severed the tenuous hold Allied forces had gained to keep the supply lines open to Australia from the United States. But the Japanese had been stung by their defeat at Midway and the losses they had suffered and failed to take such a gamble until 1944 in the Battles of the Philippine Sea and Leyte Gulf, when they had no hope of affecting the war's course.

The crucial factor in Japan's unwillingness to mount such a massive operation seems to have been a fear that Midway might be repeated in the dangerous seas that envelop eastern New Guinea and the Solomons. As a result, in the period from August 1942 through January 1943, they waged a lengthy battle of attrition in that area by committing their air and naval forces in fits and starts over the enormous distances between their bases at Truk and Rabaul and the battlefields

The *Hiryu* just before it sank
National Archives, Still Pictures Division, Washington, D.C.

on New Guinea and Guadalcanal. They were able to punish Allied forces severely, but in the end, over the course of that six-month battle of attrition, the Japanese suffered losses as heavy as those of their opponents. Those losses, particularly aircrew, were irreplaceable for the Japanese, while the great wave of American production and personnel began arriving in spring 1943. It was soon to overwhelm the Japanese and lead to the great island-hopping campaign that would bring the Americans to the doors of the Japanese home islands by early 1945.

In the short term, Midway also relieved the political pressure at home for the Roosevelt administration to devote greater resources to the Pacific theater. As a result, the president and his somewhat unhappy military advisers were able to order the commitment of U.S. troops to Operation Torch, the invasion of French North Africa, in November 1942, an operation that kept the focus of American efforts on a "Germany first" strategy. In that sense, the political ramification of Midway led to the almost concurrent defeat of Germany and Japan between May and August 1945.

Midway was also crucial in the long term. By ensuring that the war in the Pacific ended when it did, it allowed the Americans to exclude the Soviets from participating in the occupation of Japan. In August 1945, the Soviets were able to launch an invasion of Manchuria, but not the Japanese home islands. Without a presence on Japanese territory, they lacked the political prestige to demand an occupation zone. As a result, Japan would not find itself divided, as was the case with Germany; there would be no tyrannical Communist regime in northern Japan that would have undoubtedly resembled East Germany or, even more disastrous, North Korea. Instead, Japan would emerge from its devastating defeat as a democratic nation—one, moreover, that was to become the first economic powerhouse in the explosion of Asian economies that has come since the Second World War and fundamentally altered the world's political and economic map. Midway, indeed, cast a long shadow.

KURSK

The End of the Drang Nach Osten

1943

DESPITE GREAT BRITAIN'S CONTINUING DEFIANCE, IN 1941 HITLER turned the German army east. The titanic struggle with Soviet Bolshevism plunged Germany into a catastrophic two-front war and locked the two great continental powers in a death embrace that continued for four horrific years. From late June until December, it appeared that everything was going Germany's way, as its panzers rolled over Russian opposition. But by early December, the Germans were approaching the limits of their endurance, even as the Russians were mobilizing huge forces to their front. With the aid of Russia's greatest general—General Winter—the Germans were thrown back from Moscow, and their army escaped complete destruction only by the thinnest of margins.

By spring 1943, the war in Russia had already been raging for two years. The Soviet Union had just narrowly survived the Wehrmacht's two titanic assaults in 1941 and 1942. The first had foundered within sight of Moscow's church steeples. The second had collapsed in the orgy of death and destruction at Stalingrad. Here the Soviets came within a hairbreadth of breaking the back of the German army and did manage to annihilate Field Marshal Friedrich Paulus's mighty Sixth Army. But in the immediate aftermath of the surrender of the Sixth Army's remnants, the Red Army overreached itself and discovered the Wehrmacht still possessed a sting. Fresh from reducing "Fortress Stalingrad," as Hitler had grandly dubbed Paulus's trapped forces, Soviet armies raced for the Dnieper River, retaking Kharkov, Belgorod, and Kursk. In the process they laid themselves open for a hard counterpunch. On February 19, Field Marshal Erich von Manstein, arguably the best German operational commander of the war, delivered it.

In a brilliant counterstroke, Manstein bloodied the Soviet armies and sent them reeling backward. By mid-March, both Kharkov and Belgorod were back in German hands. But the Germans were exhausted and could go no farther. Despite Manstein's pleas to continue on to Kursk, where Soviet troops remained concentrated, Hitler dithered. And when Manstein went to Field Marshal Günther von Kluge, commander of Army Group Center, he was told that the troops needed a rest. Reluctantly, Manstein called a halt. The Russians had been thrown back, but a great bulge, with Kursk at its center, protruded from the Soviet lines into the German position like a giant fist, stretching at its base over 70 miles, with a total perimeter of more than 250 miles—an area that could easily fit the state of New Jersey twice. This giant bulge acted on Hitler's psyche like a magnet. What was obvious to Hitler, however, was just as obvious to Stavka, the Soviet high command.

Soon afterward, the *rasputitsa*—rain and mud—began, bringing all operations to an end until at least late spring. Taking advantage of the lull, the Germans poured troops and new tanks into the theater. Despite their efforts, however, there was nowhere near enough manpower available to make up the enormous losses of the previous year. Even after raiding vital industries for several hundred thousand recruits, the Wehrmacht remained approximately eight hundred thousand short of its target strength. Plans to bring the panzer divisions up to four hundred tanks apiece also fell well short. Still, by the time of the Kursk assault the panzer units were more powerful than at any time since early June 1941. Moreover, a number of panzer formations were equipped with the deadly Panther tanks, while a few of them

Latvia

★ **Moscow**

Poland

Area detail

• **Kursk**

• **Stalingrad**

Romania   *Black Sea*

Battle of Kursk 1943

Bryansk Front
(Popov)

Army Group Center
(Kluge)

NINTH ARMY

S O V I E T   U N I O N

Sosna River

• Olkhovatka

Central Front
(Rokossovsky)

Army Group South
(Manstein)

• **Kursk**

Seym River

Voronezh Front
(Vatutin)

• **Prokhorovka**

FOURTH PANZER ARMY

Steppe Front
(Konev)

Army Group South
(Manstein)

• **Kharkov**

0   10   20   30   40   50

Miles

were equipped with the ultra-powerful Tiger tanks. Hitler's insistence that the attack be postponed until these new-model tanks arrived at the front constituted a further dangerous delay.

As the German army recuperated, Hitler continued to fixate on the Kursk salient. This time, however, he was not thinking in grandiose terms. Previous dreams of destroying the Red Army and occupying all of European Russia were buried by the past two years' winter snows. Rather, Hitler and his generals aimed at a more limited attack, to pinch off the Kursk salient. Such an attack would restore German prestige among its allies, who were beginning to think they had backed the wrong horse. It could also shorten their defensive lines and degrade the Red Army's capability of launching its own summer offensive.

As German forces poured into the Kursk area, it became clear that the limited attack originally envisioned was rapidly turning into a winner-take-all roll of the dice. When Hitler postponed the attack planned for May 4 until June 12, General Heinz Guderian, inspector general of armored troops, asked him, "Do you believe, my führer, that anyone even knows where Kursk is? Why do you want to attack in the east, particularly this year?" Hitler replied, "You are quite right. The thought of this attack upsets my stomach." A queasy stomach, however, proved insufficient to call off the attack. Hitler was prepared to take the final gamble. It was a losing one. The disasters at Moscow and Stalingrad ensured Hitler would not win the war, but it was the Battle of Kursk that decided he would lose it.

None of the German preparations escaped Stalin's notice. Even before the Germans had completed retaking Kharkov, he had sent his fireman, Marshal Georgi Zhukov, to take over the entire Kursk region. Zhukov had been the mastermind behind the Red Army's success at Moscow in 1941 and at Stalingrad in 1942. Wherever the fighting promised to be long and desperate, Stalin sent Zhukov. After a quick survey of the situation, Zhukov determined that his first order of business was to convince Stalin to resist his urges to attack. Instead, he advised that the Red Army absorb the forthcoming German blow and then counterpunch.

The Kursk bulge was just as visible to Zhukov as it was to the Germans. It was equally clear that the Germans would do everything possible to reduce this threatening salient thrusting deep into their lines. When it came to divining German intentions, Stalin and Zhukov were hugely assisted by the British passing on of Ultra intercepts and from their still unidentified spy "Lucy," who kept them updated on the latest strategic decisions made by Hitler and the general staff. In response, the Red Army began moving reserves and fortifying the Kursk salient to an extraordinary degree. Although German frontline commanders became increasingly worried over Soviet defensive preparations, they had no clear grasp of the extent to which the Soviets were turning the Kursk salient into a giant killing ground.

Throughout the spring, the German army group commanders responsible for the attack were dismayed by the speed and extent of the Soviet buildup in the Kursk sector. Repeatedly they pleaded with Hitler for permission to attack immediately, before the Soviet defenses were made impregnable. Hitler, however, acting on the advice of Guderian, ordered another postponement until early July, so as to allow a few more Panther and Tiger tanks to arrive at the front.

By EARLY JULY, everything was in place. The German plan called for the bulge to be snipped off by attacks from both the north and the south. General Walter Model's Ninth Army, part of Kluge's Army Group Center, would spearhead the northern attack. To accomplish its mission, the Ninth Army had twenty-one German and three Hungarian divisions. Of these, six were panzer and one was a panzer grenadier division. The remaining fourteen were infantry divisions. In total, the Ninth Army numbered approximately 335,000 men, 590 tanks, and 424 assault guns. In the south, Manstein commanded General Hermann Hoth's Fourth Panzer Army and General Werner Kempf's ad hoc conglomeration of forces named Army Detachment Kempf. In total, Manstein had managed to collect twenty-two divisions, of which six were panzer and five were panzer grenadiers. The armored fist of this force consisted of 1,381 tanks and 245 assault guns, concentrated in the XLVIII Panzer Corps and the II SS Panzer Corps. Within the XLVIII Panzer Corps was the ultra-powerful Grossdeutschland Division, with over 500 tanks, including 200 Panthers in its 10th Panzer Brigade. The II SS Panzer Corps consisted of the infamous and feared Leibstandarte SS Adolf Hitler, Das Reich, and Totenkopf Divisions, which together had close to 500 tanks and assault guns. Supporting these two pincer movements were the 730 combat aircraft of the Sixth Air Fleet (for the north) and the 1,100 aircraft of the Fourth Air Fleet in the south.

To their front lay a Red Army that had taken full advantage of the lull. In three months they had turned the Kursk salient into a fortress. Throughout the lull, the Red Army toiled alongside three hundred thousand civilian laborers to create an unbreachable barrier, consisting of successive defensive belts reaching back over seventy miles, crisscrossed by more than three thousand miles of trenches and hundreds of miles of anti-tank obstacles. Hundreds of camouflaged blockhouses, and minefields that often numbered more than three thousand mines per kilometer, added to the defensive strength. This alone made the approaches to Kursk a deathtrap for any advancing army, but that was only the start. Throughout these defensive belts, the Soviets emplaced hundreds of anti-tank strongpoints bristling with thousands of anti-tank guns and often tanks. Moreover, every inch of these defensive lines was within range of thousands of artillery pieces, all registered on the most likely German approach routes.

Manning these defenses was the Red Army's Central Front, commanded by General Konstantin Rokossovsky in the north; in the south was the Voronezh Front, commanded by General Nikolai Vatutin. In reserve, Zhukov held General Ivan Konev's Steppe Front, which along with many other formations controlled the one thousand tanks within the powerful Fifth Guards Tank Army. In total, for the upcoming battle the Red Army possessed nearly two million men and over five thousand tanks, supported by approximately thirty-two thousand guns and mortars and thirty-five hundred combat aircraft. This gave the Soviets a numerical superiority in men of nearly 2.5 to 1 and almost 2 to 1 in tanks. As most doctrinal manuals specify that the attacker typically needs an advantage of at least 3 to 1 for success, the Germans were risking everything on their proven battlefield op-

Field Marshal Erich
von Manstein
*National Archives, Still
Pictures Division,
Washington, D.C.*

erational and tactical superiority. Unfortunately for the Germans, the Red Army had made impressive strides in both areas over the past two years of war.

THE NORTHERN PINCER

Forewarned by prisoners of the exact time of the German attacks, the Soviets launched a massive artillery barrage on known and suspected concentrations of German troops and artillery just hours before the German assault. Except for some exposed German artillery positions, the firing did little damage. It did, however, disrupt the final movements to attack jump-off points, forcing the Ninth Army to push back the attack by two and a half hours. More ominous, it told the Germans that the Russians knew they were coming and were ready to meet them. The Soviets also took the opportunity to launch a massive air attack, hoping to catch the Germans unprepared. But as the Russian planes approached, swarms of German fighters pounced on them, downing several hundred Russian aircraft and depriving the Soviets of effective air cover for most of the battle's first day.

At 4:30 A.M., the German artillery opened fire. An hour later, Model's Ninth Army advanced. It ran into a storm of fire. By midday, the German attack was slowing. By evening, it had ground to a halt, except in one narrow sector. Here the 20th Panzer, the only panzer division committed in the north on the first day, crushed the Red Army's 15th Division. By 9:00 A.M., the 20th Panzer was through most of the first defensive belt and the Soviets to their front were in disarray. The 20th Panzer advanced nearly five miles before being stopped by an avalanche of artillery fire. As one Russian reported:

> The sky blackened from smoke and heat. The acrid gasses from the exploding shells and mines blinded the eyes. The soldiers

Marshal Georgi Zhukov
National Archives,
Still Pictures Division,
Washington, D.C.

were deafened by the thunder of guns and mortars and the creaking of tracks. The motto became the words "Not a step back, stand to the death." . . . The infantry skillfully destroyed the tanks with grenades and bottles filled with mixtures of fuel. Under a hurricane of fire they stole up to the enemy vehicles, struck them with antitank grenades, set them on fire with incendiary bottles, and laid mines under them.

Ever so slowly, Model's Ninth Army ground its way forward. Repeatedly, battalions and regiments reported: "We're getting there! Not easily, and the battle has been bloody and costly. But we are getting there." For the Germans, the shock was that "nowhere had the enemy been taken by surprise. Nowhere had he been soft." Still, by the end of the first day, the 20th Panzer had punched through the first defensive belt at the juncture of the Soviet Seventieth and Thirteenth Armies. This was Model's chance. His troops had thrown the Soviets off balance. According to a German general on the scene: "If the tanks had rolled through, then we would have reached Kursk."

Whether he was right or not is a moot point, because there were no tanks available to exploit the breakthrough. The 20th Panzer was a spent force and needed time to recuperate. As for Model's other four panzer divisions and the panzer grenadiers, they were still sitting in their assembly areas and not yet committed to the fight. If the German offensive in the north ever had a moment when it could have succeeded, it was now. The initial breakthrough had occurred, but the armored fist was not ready.

Rokossovsky, however, was troubled by the breakthrough, although it did give him one inestimable advantage. He now knew the main axis of the German attack. From that, he surmised that Model would begin feeding the rest of his panzer divisions into the initial breakthrough the next morning. To counter this threat, he ordered all three corps of his Second Tank Army to move behind the shaken Thirteenth Army. The Soviet tanks were in place just before dawn and in heavy action soon after daybreak. Model, still unwilling to risk everything on a single daring thrust, refused to throw all of his armor into the attack. Instead, he continued to commit his panzers piecemeal, thereby giving up any chance of achieving a decisive breakthrough. By midmorning, the 2nd and 9th Panzer Divisions were in action under a sweltering sun. But instead of running into a demoralized and collapsing enemy, these divisions had to fight off dogged attacks by the Second Tank Army. By noon, each side had committed over five hundred tanks and assault guns on a front of less than five miles.

The German attacks focused on the town and ridge of Olkhovatka, which the Russians had turned into a veritable fortress in the months of waiting for the German assault. Repeatedly the German panzers attacked, were repulsed, re-formed, and attacked again. Although there was heavy fighting along much of the Ninth Army front, most notably within the villages of Maloarkhangelsk and Ponyri (a miniature Stalingrad), it was at Olkhovatka that the outcome of the northern contest would be decided.

Today, it is almost impossible to imagine the hellish realities of the Kursk battlefield. This was war on a truly industrial scale, where the entire plethora of modern killing hardware was unleashed on a tiny portion of ground without pause. Historians' attempts to bring order to the chaos of battle tend to sterilize the reality of fighting. Never is that more true than in describing the Battle of Kursk. At Kursk, there was nowhere to hide. At any moment, barrages of a thousand guns or more could fall on a single square mile, obliterating everything and everyone. At no time of the day or night did the shooting cease. Every second brought more gruesome deaths, as human flesh was shredded by machine guns, cannons, and mines. Moreover, the entire battle was being fought in the scalding heat of the open Russian steppes. The soldiers on both sides were suspended in a living hell where unrelenting German attacks were matched by Soviet counterattacks and death stalked their every move.

Each new German attack met a hurricane of fire, as the expertly concealed Soviets refused to reveal themselves until they had unsuspecting targets in their sights. Anti-tank guns waited patiently as the massive Tiger tanks passed and then struck at their vulnerable flanks and rear. Only German infantry could dislodge the Russian gunners and their supporting infantry, who took every opportunity to sneak up on the panzers and attack them with mines and Molotov cocktails. But the German infantry had gone to ground, as thousands of pieces of Soviet artillery blasting along the length of the battlefield made it suicidal for any infantryman to leave whatever hole he had crawled into.

The tanks went on alone. Soon, though, only the heaviest tanks could push through the hail of fire. Some of the Tigers had no machine guns, forcing them to fight off Russian infantry with their main gun—"shooting quail with a cannon." Even as Model's Ninth Army ground forward, the Soviets refused to break. Throughout the next four days, the Soviet Second Tank Army threw everything it had at the leading German formations. What was worse for the Germans was the fact that by July 7 the Soviet air force had recovered from its pummeling on the battle's first day. For the rest of the battle, the Soviets not only contested the airspace over Kursk, they often dominated it. German soldiers now spent as much time looking up as they did peering forward.

It was not until July 8 that Model finally committed the last of his panzers. He threw the fresh 4th Panzer Division into the assault on the Olkhovatka ridge. Time and again, German tanks supported by whatever infantry had the courage to brave the maelstrom of fire advanced on the ridge, only to be bloodily repulsed. A German observer noted:

> Within an hour all of the officers of the 5th Company, 112th Panzer Grenadier Regiment, had been killed or wounded. Nevertheless the grenadiers swept on through the cornfields, capturing trenches and encountering new ones. The battalions melted away. Companies became mere platoons.
>
> The famous battle of El Alamein, where Montgomery employed 1,000 guns to bring about the turning point of the war in Africa, was a modest operation by comparison. Even Stalingrad, in spite of its more apocalyptic and tragic aura, does not stand comparison. . . .

Finding a gap between two Soviet divisions, the 4th Panzer smashed into the open. But once again, before German forces could concentrate to exploit the gap, Rokossovsky plugged it with Red Army reserves. For several more days, both sides fed men and matériel into the fight, but the contest was no longer in doubt. By July 11, the Ninth Army was a spent force. Worse, Soviet armored formations had launched their own offensive north of Orel, threatening the Ninth Army's rear. With no reserves left, Model began withdrawing armored forces from the front to meet this new threat. The German northern pincer was finished, the back of the Ninth Army broken. At the battle's climax, it was no longer available to divert Soviet attention from the southern pincer, as it was too busy fighting for its own survival.

The Southern Pincer

At 2:30 A.M., General Nikolai Vatutin, Soviet commander in the southern portion of the Kursk salient, ordered six hundred guns to begin firing on known and suspected German positions. An hour later, the Germans joined in with a tremendous barrage of their own. Reportedly, the Germans fired more shells in this one barrage than they did in the entire Polish and French campaigns combined. To further help the German cause, the Luftwaffe made a maximum effort in the sector, launching more than two thousand sorties on the first day. By 4:00 A.M., General Hermann Hoth's Fourth Panzer Army was on the move along its entire front. Its two giant battering rams, the XLVIII Panzer Corps and II SS Panzer Corps, smashed into the Soviet's Sixth Guards Army with shattering force. But, as in the north, the Red Army was ready and waiting.

The XLVIII Panzer Corps attacked with three divisions abreast: the 3rd Panzer on the left, Grossdeutschland in the center, and the 11th Panzer on the right. On such a narrow and crowded front, there was no room for subtlety. The panzers went forward en masse, straight into a minefield. When they finally emerged from that obstacle, after heavy losses, they ran into a marsh. Through it all, Soviet artillery rained down a torrent of deadly steel, while dug-in Soviet infantry and anti-tank guns registered a steadily increasing toll on German men and machines. It was a repeat of the slaughter in the north, except on a far grander scale.

The advance of General Paul Hausser's II SS Panzer Corps, to the right of the XLVIII Panzer Corps, was swifter. Some of Hausser's success resulted from the greater élan of the SS troops, but his initial progress had much more to do with the concentration of firepower at the tip of the spear, along with the magnificent close support provided by the Luftwaffe in the early stages of the fight. By dusk, II SS Panzer Corps had penetrated over thirteen miles into the Soviet defensive positions, but only at a terrible cost. Each of the leading divisions had suffered more than six hundred killed and wounded, most of them in the spearhead battalions. Still, considering the defenses they had fought through, it was a good day's work.

It was not good enough, though. Hoth had counted on breaking through the entire Soviet line within forty-eight hours. Although he had driven a deep wedge into Red Army positions, his Fourth Army had barely cleared the first defensive belt, and while his troops had badly mauled the Soviets to their front—some of them losing over 30 percent of their strength—at no place did the Russian line collapse. The Russians were battered, but they were holding. Moreover, the Germans were far behind schedule and had failed to reach their first day's objective, the crossing of the Psel River south of Oboyan. Still, Hoth remained confident that the next day would bring a breakthrough, followed by a rapid drive on Kursk itself.

Vatutin had other ideas. As the troops in the second defensive belt, joined by those retreating out of the first, prepared for a renewal of the German assault, he ordered forward the First Tank Army, reinforced by the II Guards and V Guards Tank Corps. At first, Vatutin ordered them to counterattack and throw the Germans out of the first defensive belt. But when it became clear that the Sixth Army was not going to hold, he ordered the First Tank Army to occupy defensive positions within the second belt. Vatutin was not going to waste his precious armor until his forces had bled the German attackers white. Local commanders, however, could still launch counterattacks, and these attacks were often sharp and vicious. Even as the Soviet blocking positions blunted the powerful German assaults, other Red Army formations continually tore at their flanks.

On the right of the Fourth Panzer Army, Army Detachment Kempf made rapid initial progress, but then it also bogged down. Over successive days, the detachment would inch forward with its three panzer divisions, but it never cracked the reinforced Soviet line. Later, this failure had fateful consequences for the Germans. As Detachment Kempf was not able to protect the flank of the advancing Fourth Panzer Army, that force had to strip off significant forces to do the job itself. Moreover, at the climactic moment of the Red Army's main counterattack, Detachment Kempf was not in position to strike the flanks of the advancing Fifth Guards Tank Army. If it had been, the result of Kursk might have been hugely altered.

All the next day, July 6, the Fourth Panzer Army pounded at the Soviet defenses. Progress in the XLVIII Panzer Corps area was steady but slow. By nightfall, the corps had still not reached its objective on the Psel River. Things went somewhat better in the II SS Panzer Corps area. Advancing side by side, Das Reich and Leibstandarte annihilated the 51st Guards Rifle Division and raced forward over eight miles. An alarmed Vatutin threw the V Guards Tank Corps into a pell-mell counterattack, only to see it bloodily repulsed. When darkness fell, Hausser's II SS Panzer Corps had torn a significant hole through the Soviet defensive belt, and there were very few defenses to their front. But Hausser was unable to take advantage of the opportunities his soldiers' hard fighting had gained. Instead of collapsing, the shaken Soviet forces had maintained their order and moved onto his flanks, where they continued to strike at the exposed SS units. Because of Detachment Kempf's failure, and with his own infantry lagging far behind, Hausser had to continually bleed off armored units to guard his flanks. By the end of the second day, over a third of German tanks were fighting defensive battles on the flanks. On July 8, the situation worsened enough that Hausser was forced to leave the entire Totenkopf Division behind to guard his corps' right flank. Soon thereafter, Soviet attacks on the left flank of the XLVIII Panzer Corps forced its commander to send Grossdeutschland Division back to deal with them. For most of the next forty-eight hours, the forward momentum in this sector ceased, as the 11th and 3rd Panzer Divisions waited for the Grossdeutschland's return.

Incessant Red Army counterattacks, besides bleeding the Germans, also forced a change in the angle of the German assault. The initial objective had been Oboyan. But as resistance along that route stiffened, the German frontline commanders, acting on their own initiative, began angling their attacks toward the town of Prokhorovka. This change was to have fateful consequences. Unknown to the German commanders, Stavka had become so concerned about the II SS Panzer Corps penetration that it had ordered the strategic reserve, a large segment of the Steppe Front, under General Pavel Rotmistrov, to move toward Kursk. Soon after midnight on July 7, the mighty Fifth Guards Tank Army was on the road. It would assemble with powerful reinforcements by July 9 at Prokhorovka.

After another day of hard fighting on July 7, the II SS Panzer Corps broke through the second defensive belt and reached the Psel River. Large numbers of Soviets were surrendering, and for the Germans it looked as though the happy days of 1941 were returning. Soviet morale appeared to be cracking, and Vatutin and his political commissar, Nikita Khrushchev, were beginning to worry. At a meeting at First Tank Army headquarters that night, Khrushchev announced: "The next two or three days will be terrible. Either we hold out or the Germans take Kursk. They have staked everything on this one card. For them it is a matter of life or death. We must see to it that they break their necks!"

Encouraged by the knowledge that the Fifth Guards Tank Army was rushing to his aid, Vatutin threw all of his remaining reserves in front of the German juggernaut. For the remainder of July 8 and 9, the armored fists of XLVIII and II SS Panzer Corps hammered the Soviet's Sixth Guards Army and the First Tank Army. By the evening of July 9, the Germans had battered to within a dozen miles of Oboyan, but the reinforced Soviet line had yet to break. Worse, the attacks tearing at the German flanks were getting ever more ferocious and threatening. Despairing of cracking the Russian line in front of Oboyan, Hoth officially ordered the Fourth Panzer Army to change its axis of advance toward Prokhorovka, something that was already happening as units naturally took the line of least resistance.

On July 10, XLVIII Panzer Corps continued pounding the remnants of the two Soviet armies to its front. But Hausser had no faith they would achieve a breakthrough. Rather, they were to divert Soviet attention as II SS Panzer Corps disengaged from the front so that it could regroup before launching the hopefully decisive assault on Prokhorovka. Before pulling back to regroup, the Totenkopf Division, finally released from flank guard duties, had scored a success. On July 10, Totenkopf struck the battered Soviet First Tank Army, which by now was only a shadow of its original strength. In heavy fighting, Totenkopf established a bridgehead over the Psel, breaching the final Soviet defensive line. The following morning, Totenkopf's pontoon bridges arrived and the division's panzers began crossing into the bridgehead. Reinforced by an entire rifle corps, the Soviet First Tank Army regrouped its shaken formations and threw them at the Psel bridgehead. It was too late: Totenkopf was there to stay.

During the night of July 11, Hausser rested and resupplied his three SS panzer divisions. In the morning, he planned to launch them onto the open steppe behind the last belt of Soviet defenses. After almost a week of hard fighting and heavy losses, the breakthrough had been achieved. Victory was at hand.

Unfortunately for German hopes, a few miles to the north General Rotmistrov's Fifth Guards Tank Army, reinforced by two additional tank corps, was rolling into its assembly areas. His one thousand tanks would be ready for battle the next morning, when they would face the approximately five hundred tanks the Germans could still muster.

As the Fifth Guards Tank Army launched its headlong assault on the II SS Panzer Corps, Vatutin threw everything else in his arsenal at both the XLVIII Panzer Corps and Army Detachment Kempf. These attacks did not make much headway, but they ensured that neither of these two powerful German forces was available to either reinforce the II SS Panzer Corps or strike into the flanks of the onrushing Soviet Fifth Guards Tank Army. Without the contributions of these bloody attacks, which were pushed throughout the day with the utmost vigor, the result at Prokhorovka might have been very different.

Still, it was the fighting around Prokhorovka that decided the fate of the German offensive. Here, on July 12, the II SS Panzer Corps resumed its assault just after dawn. It was warm, humid, and cloudy. Throughout the day there were scattered rain showers, but they were not heavy enough to hinder operations. As the German panzers, finally clear of the minefields, obstacles, and anti-tank guns, began fanning out across the open steppe, a crushing barrage of artillery and rockets smothered them in fire, smoke, and dust. No sooner had the

Tiger and T-34 in battle
DIZ München GmbH, Süddeutsche Zeitung Photo/Alamy

firing ceased than General Rotmistrov shouted into his radio the code word that unleashed the mass of Soviet armor: *"Stal! Stal! Stal!"* ("Steel! Steel! Steel!") Hundreds of Soviet tank commanders battened down their turret hatches as their steel monsters lurched forward on a collision course with II SS Panzer Corps. Tiger Company Commander Rudolf von Ribbentrop, son of the German foreign minister, later noted, "What I saw left me speechless . . . in front of me appeared fifteen, then thirty, then forty tanks. Finally there were too many to count. The T-34s were rolling toward us at high speed, carrying mounted infantry."

All along the German line rose a wall of purple smoke—*tank warning.* The German panzers halted. Shock at the sight of so much massed armor lasted only a moment. The tank commanders and gunners of the II SS Panzer Corps were seasoned veterans, who knew their lives depended on what they did in the next few moments. They needed no orders. Everyone knew his role, and while leaders established respective zones of fire, gunners leveled their guns. In another moment, hundreds of high-volocity shells were screaming toward the

Soviets. The Soviets did all they could to close rapidly on the German tanks, knowing they could damage the Tiger tanks only if they got within five hundred meters. The veteran German tank crews did not panic. By the time the Soviets were within one thousand yards, every shot scored a direct hit.

Far from engulfing and then chewing up the II SS Panzer Corps, the avalanche of Soviet armor was being mauled as it approached. But the Soviets were nothing if not dogged. No matter the losses, they kept coming. The battle degenerated into a swirling, confused mass, as packs of tanks hunted one another in a murderous game of hide-and-seek. In the dust, an enemy was seen only for a fleeting moment. Training and skill counted for much, and in this regard the Germans held an advantage. Still, the Soviets were not far inferior, and often luck would take their side.

The battlefield was soon littered with burning hulks. The Germans congratulated themselves; they had seen off the worst the Red Army could throw at them. They had weathered the storm and were preparing to advance when Rotmistrov released his second wave. In a repeat of the first attack, the second of Rotmistrov's three corps rushed forward. The Germans, although heavily pressed throughout the sector, repulsed all assaults. Although Soviet losses were catastrophic, the Germans also paid a heavy cost. But by midafternoon, the II SS Panzer Corps was able to resume its advance toward Prokhorovka. With two of the Fifth Guards Tank Army's three corps wrecked, Rotmistrov had to commit his reserve corps. The fighting was desperate, but with their final ounce of strength the Soviets stopped the German advance. The II SS Panzer Corps and Manstein's Fourth Panzer Army had failed. Although the attack had not been "the death ride of the Fourth Panzer Army," as postwar myth maintained, it had greatly weakened Germany's operational forces in the East. From this point forward, the Russians would take and maintain the strategic offensive until their tanks finally entered Berlin in 1945.

It did not have to end this way. Manstein still had a reserve panzer corps with which to reinforce the exhausted Fourth Panzer Army, and he begged the German army high command and Hitler to release its units. He was sure the Soviets were used up and that one more powerful push would break their lines. He may have been correct, but it was too late. Concerned about the Allied landings in Sicily on July 10, Hitler was already eyeing the II SS Panzer Corps as a strategic reserve he could move west to combat the growing Anglo–American threat.

On July 13, Manstein, Kluge, and a number of other senior commanders were ordered to Hitler's headquarters in Prussia. Upon Manstein's arrival, Hitler informed him of his intention to call off the Kursk offensive. Manstein, convinced that victory was still within his grasp, persuaded Hitler to listen to his plan for eliminating the Soviet forces and regaining the operational initiative (Operation Roland). For a moment Hitler appeared intrigued, but upon confirmation that Model's Ninth Army could not assist in the attack, he reconfirmed his decision to end the fighting at Kursk. All Manstein could get was Hitler's approval to conduct minor attacks to damage the Soviets sufficiently for his panzer forces to more easily disengage. With that the great German offensive came to a sputtering conclusion.

Manstein later wrote, "And so the last German offensive in the east ended in fiasco, even though the enemy opposite the two attacking armies of Army Group South suffered four times their losses." True as this was, the Soviets could replace those losses, while the Germans could not. From Kursk forward, the Germans would never again be able to launch a major offensive in the East. In fact, by mid-July the II SS Panzer Corps was rushing south to contain a Soviet offensive along the Mius River. No sooner had its divisions completed that task than the exhausted corps had to rush north to fight the rebuilt First and Fifth Guards Tank Armies. By the end of the summer, Kharkov, Belgorod, and Orel were again in Soviet hands and the German army was reeling. It would not meet its final war-ending catastrophe until July 1944—Operation Bagration—when Soviet armies tore Army Group Center to shreds in a mere two weeks. But for all intents and purposes, the outcome of the war was decided on July 17, when the Kursk offensive ground to a halt.

WHAT WOULD HAVE HAPPENED if the Germans had won at Kursk? Although the Communist and Nazi systems would have remained hostile to each other, by mid-1943 both sides were exhausted and close to collapse. A German victory would have meant the loss of several of the Soviets' carefully husbanded reserve tank armies, as well as the entrapment and destruction of several more conventional armies along the front. Possibly the Soviets could have made good those losses, but doing so would have required a superhuman production effort from an industrial base that was already wheezing. On the other hand, even a decisive German victory would have come at a heavy cost. After reducing the Kursk salient, the Germans would not in all probability have retained sufficient strength to continue the offensive. In fact, they would have been lucky to hold on to what they had gained in the face of the forces the Soviets had massed to strike at Orel, just north of the Kursk bulge.

The most predictable outcome of a German victory would have been a prolonged stalemate leading to a shaky peace. Any such peace would likely have doomed the Allied cause in the West. As it was, the Normandy invasion was a near run thing. With the pressure off in the East, the Germans could have moved the bulk of their combat formations into France. Forced to face the rested, refitted, and rearmed panzer divisions from the eastern front, the American and British troops that stormed Normandy's beaches would not have lasted through the afternoon. It would have been a repeat of the 1942 Dieppe raid, on an unimagined scale. Of course, such an event may have had one terrible result for the German population, as it is likely the Reich would have moved ahead of Japan in the A-bomb sweepstakes.

Events at this point become impossible to even guess. What is certain is that a German victory at Kursk would have had immeasurable consequences for Europe and the world. Even if the eastern peace did not hold for more than a few years, one can only imagine the additional human devastation that Hitler and his henchmen would have brought about if they had been given even a bit more time to work their vileness.

Fortunately the Germans did not win, but one can forgive Eastern Europeans if they regarded the results of the Soviet victory almost as unpalatable. For the immediate result of Kursk was that Eastern Europe would find itself dominated by a Soviet Union ruled by Stalin, who demonstrated no inclination to cede to Hitler any claim to the title of history's most brutal tyrant. By destroying the carefully husbanded German armored reserves at Kursk, the Soviet victory made it impossible for the Germans to resist the titanic Soviet assault, Operation Bagration, in the summer of 1944 that annihilated the Wehrmacht's Army Group Center. With their panzer formations squandered at the Battle of Kursk and its immediate aftermath, the Germans were unable to stop the Soviet onslaught until it reached the outskirts of Warsaw and the Vistula River.

Victory at Kursk also made it possible for the Soviets to win the race for Berlin and earned them a European empire. The course of history over the next fifty years—the Cold War—was determined at Kursk. Because of Soviet economic mismanagement, the effects of this fallen empire still echo throughout the East today. Despite investment on a massive scale, Western Europe has been unable to completely integrate the former Soviet Empire into the wider European economy. Fully two decades after the breaching of the Berlin Wall, Eastern European standards of living remain well behind those of Western Europe. Finally, ethnic conflicts that were brought into the open and for the most part dealt with peacefully in the West simmered within those nations under Soviet rule. With Russia's post-1991 retreat from empire, these conflicts boiled over and continue to threaten the general peace of Europe.

The ultimate effects of the Battle of Kursk have yet to reveal themselves. But there is little doubt that Kursk had profound effects on the course of global affairs that continue to ripple forward in time.

NORMANDY

The Death Knell for Nazi Germany

1944

THE FALL OF FRANCE IN SPRING 1940 SEEMED TO HERALD THE TRIUMPH of Nazi Germany over all of Europe and perhaps the world. Throughout the 1930s, young Germans had enthusiastically sung, *"Heute Deutschland, Morgen die Welt"* ("Today Germany, tomorrow the world"). Only Winston Churchill's hard-nosed recognition that Nazi Germany represented not only a strategic but a moral threat to what Western civilization at its best had represented in its long and tumultuous history prevented the British from surrendering to what the prime minister characterized as the possibility of "a new Dark Age, made more sinister, and perhaps more protracted, by the lights of perverted science." As a great historian and strategist, Churchill recognized that the semi-alliance between Hitler and Stalin could not last and that the United States would eventually realize it could not allow Nazi Germany to dominate the European Continent. Great Britain had stood fast, battered by the relentless air and submarine assault the Germans mounted against it. Then in 1941 Hitler had made the mistakes of invading the Soviet Union and declaring war on the United States. Britain was no longer alone.

From the first, Churchill had understood that the British Army would have to return to the Continent for Great Britain to survive as a great power. In a speech to the French people in October 1940, he had promised: "Good night, then: sleep to gather strength for the morning. For the morning will come." Morning came on June 6, 1944, with the massive Allied invasion of Normandy, as British, American, Canadian, and French soldiers, sailors, and airmen smashed their way through the defenses on the Normandy coast and into Hitler's Fortress Europe.

For almost four long years there had been no western front, despite considerable public pressure for the United States and Great Britain to come to the aid of the hard-pressed Red Army. The Western Allies had contributed vast amounts of aid to the Soviets through Arctic convoys to Murmansk and shipments through Iran and Siberia. British as well as Australian and New Zealand Army Corps (ANZAC) soldiers had held the Axis forces at bay in North Africa, but it was only with Field Marshal Bernard Law Montgomery's victory at El Alamein in October 1942 that German hopes in that theater began to collapse. The Anglo-American landings in Morocco and Algeria in November of that year further secured the Allied position in the Mediterranean, while the landing in Sicily in July 1943 soon knocked Italy out of the war.

Certainly from Churchill's perspective, the Allied Combined Bomber Offensive, which was reducing German cities to ruins, represented a second front, but whatever the successes of bombing Germany, and they were considerable, the air offensive could not replace the political and military necessity of the Western powers attacking the Third Reich at its heart on the European Continent. Nothing could disguise the fact that it was the Soviet Union that was bearing the bloody burden of fighting the Wehrmacht to a standstill on the eastern front or mitigate the strategic need for a successful amphibious landing on the French coast.

And therein lay the rub, because there was no possibility for a successful landing on the European Continent until 1944. There were a number of reasons why that was so. First and foremost, until early 1944 America's mobilization would not create ground forces sufficient to achieve a lodgment on the European Continent with their British allies and to win the major battles that were sure to follow. Second, the Allied navies would not win the Battle of the Atlantic until May 1943, and until they had defeated the German U-boat menace, the required buildup of American ground forces in the United Kingdom could not begin. Third, a successful landing on the Continent would not be possible until Allied air forces had achieved general superiority in the skies over Europe, and that would not occur until spring 1944.

Finally, of all military operations conducted during the Second World War, none was more difficult to execute than a major amphibious operation, because of the specialized equipment required, the complexity of the joint interaction of air, naval, and ground forces, and the necessary landing of supplies and follow-on forces after the achievement of a successful lodgment. As early as the Casablanca Conference in January 1943, General George Marshall, architect of the American victory in Europe, had recognized that reality and admitted that the earliest such a landing could take place would be spring 1944.

As the Italian campaign ground its way into deadlock in fall 1943, British and American political and military leaders began to focus on the issues involved in the planning and execution for the amphibious landing on the French coast. An important influence over the choice of where to land was the defeat of British and Canadian forces at Dieppe in August 1942. The Dieppe raid had underlined that Allied forces would not be able to seize a major built-up area at the onset of a landing on the French coast because of the difficulties involved in fighting through urban terrain. Thus, the buildup of Allied forces in the initial days of the invasion was going to have to occur across the beaches of the lodgment, which added considerably to the logistical difficulties.

The most obvious place for a landing on the French coast was the Pas-de-Calais, directly across the white cliffs of Dover. That area offered the fewest obstacles to the Allies in terms of providing air cover and moving the attacking and follow-on forces across the English Channel. Moreover, it would offer Allied forces, once established, the clearest invasion route into the heart of Germany. However, there

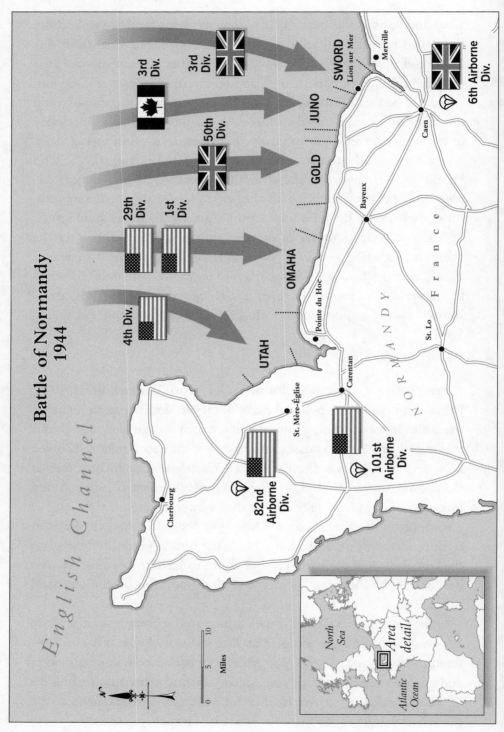

Battle of Normandy 1944

were three major difficulties. The Germans were not dumb and fully understood the operational advantages that a landing on the Pas-de-Calais would provide the Anglo-American allies. They had prepared the defenses in that area with Teutonic efficiency and thoroughness. Second, any lodgment on the Pas-de-Calais would be open to attack from three different directions, the northeast, the east, and the southeast. Finally, while the Pas-de-Calais offered an easy route into Germany, it also offered the Germans a direct route by which to rush reinforcements to the defenders and to launch counterattacks on the landing force.

So the decision in the Allied high command was for Normandy. A landing in Normandy presented some disadvantages. It was farther from Great Britain, making the crossing logistics and air cover more difficult. Moreover, both the area's limited road network and its distance from Germany would make the exploitation of a successful landing more difficult. But Normandy's advantages more than outweighed its disadvantages. It was going to be more difficult for the Germans to build up their forces once the landing had occurred; its defenses were less formidable than those of the Pas-de-Calais; and owing to the position of the Cotentin Peninsula, it could be difficult, if not impossible, for the Germans to launch a major counterattack from the west, while the swamps lying east of the Dives River would make German counterattacks from that direction impossible, provided the Allies managed to seize the valley through which the Dives ran. Thus, Allied forces would have to guard against German counterattacks coming only from the south.

Planning for the invasion swung into high gear in 1943 under British lieutenant general Frederick Morgan. The initial plans postulated a landing force of three divisions, supported by a single airborne division. But when the overall commander of the invasion, General Dwight Eisenhower, and the land force commander, General Bernard Montgomery, arrived from Italy in January 1944 to take control of the planning and the conduct of operations, both made it clear that a four-division force was completely inadequate to achieve a successful lodgment on the Continent. Instead, they demanded a landing force of five divisions along with a drop of three airborne divisions to protect the western and eastern flanks of the landing areas. In addition, by the time the landing occurred on June 6, the British had added three armored brigades to the three beaches on which they and the Canadians would land. This considerable expansion of the landing force required a mad scramble to build additional landing craft and then to train their crews in time for the invasion, which was one of the major reasons D-Day took place in early June rather than in May.

Meanwhile, the greatest air battle in history was occurring in the skies over Germany, one that would play a crucial role in the outcome of the landings. Beginning in February 1944, the United States Eighth Air Force launched a massive series of raids into Germany aimed at destroying the production facilities for the engines and aircraft on which the Luftwaffe depended. The American effort in the last half of 1943 had come close to defeat at the hands of German fighters because of the failure of American airmen to recognize that escort fighters were essential to the survival of long-range bombing formations. In fact, such fighters had remained low on the Eighth Air Force's priority list until the disastrous second raid on the ball-bearing center at Schweinfurt in October 1943 underscored that such protective aircraft were a necessity.

The great difference in the air battles of 1944 was the introduction of a long-range escort fighter, the extraordinary P-51. Its appearance had largely been a matter of luck, since it featured an American-designed air frame but a British Rolls-Royce engine. The not-made-here syndrome had beset both the U.S. Army Air Forces and the RAF in their unwillingness to accept the P-51 despite its outstanding capabilities. In the end, however, it had been produced, and not only was it the best piston-engine fighter of the Second World War, but because it could carry fuel in its fuselage, by March 1944 it was able to accompany B-17 bomber formations all the way to Berlin.

Thus, the Eighth Air Force was at last able to provide its bombers with fighter escorts to the essential targets deep in Germany. There were still not enough fighters in the first great raids, and the Luftwaffe put up tenacious resistance—from February through April 1944, the Americans were losing approximately 30 percent of their bomber crews and aircraft each month, a frightening rate of attrition. But the Luftwaffe, attacked by P-47s to the Rhine and P-51s on the eastern side of that river, was losing pilots and aircraft at a rate that it could not

[handwritten margin note:] MORE LIKE THE 2ND OR 3RD BEST AFTER THE C.V. F4U-4 CORSAIR AND THE RUSSIAN YAK-3

sustain, whereas the Americans with their great rate of production and ability to train new crews could support their heavy losses.

Between January 1 and May 31, 1944, the Luftwaffe's average of single-engine fighter pilots on duty each month was 2,283; during that same period, it lost 2,262 single-engine fighter pilots, killed, wounded, or missing. Admittedly, the Germans had managed to replace most of those pilots, but the majority of the new fliers were poorly trained, while an increasing number of the more experienced fighter pilots had died or been injured. Ultimately, the great air battles, beginning in February, broke the Luftwaffe's back by May and gave the Allies complete air superiority over Europe to conduct their operations.

In March, at the approach of the invasion, now code-named Overlord, a furious debate arose about the role that the Allied strategic bombing force with its increasing lethality should play in the assault on Fortress Europe. The main contestants were on one side those responsible for the invasion—namely, Eisenhower and his chief deputy, Air Marshal Arthur Tedder—and on the other the bomber barons, General Karl Spaatz, commander of U.S. Army Air Forces in Great Britain, and Air Marshal Arthur "Bomber" Harris, commander of the RAF's Bomber Command. Tedder, one of the most outstanding airmen of the war, had designed a plan to utilize the American and British strategic bombers to destroy the French transportation network, particularly its railroads, which would complicate German efforts to reinforce and resupply their forces along the coasts once the Overlord landings had occurred.

In the end, Eisenhower won a considerable degree of authority over the strategic bomber forces, sufficient to allow him to order a massive campaign against the French transportation network beginning on April 1, 1944. How successful was that campaign? A German report on June 3, three days before the Allied landings, read: "The rail network is to be completely wrecked. Local and through traffic is to be made impossible, and all efforts to restore the services is to be prevented. This aim has so successfully been achieved—locally, at any rate—that the Reichsbahn [the German railroad authority responsible for running the French railroads] authorities are seriously considering whether it is not useless to attempt further repair work." Thus, when the landings occurred the Germans found it exceedingly difficult to move their reserve divisions forward from their deployment areas scattered throughout the French countryside.

The Allied plan for Overlord was simple enough, although the details of coordinating its various elements raised a number of difficulties. There would be five main landing beaches, two for the Americans and three for the British. The British landings were to occur on the eastern side of the Allied lodgment between Ouistreham and Arromanches: on the far left, the British 6th Infantry Division would land at Sword Beach near Ouistreham; next in line to the west, the Canadian 3rd Division would land at Juno Beach; and then yet farther to the west, the 50th British Infantry Division would land on Gold Beach with its right flank on Arromanches. There, British engineers would emplace one of the great artificial Mulberry harbors that the Allies had prepared and which were supposed to ease the movement of supplies from ships to the shore and across the beach.

Montgomery placed the capture of Caen as the main objective of his Canadian and British troops on the first day. His rationale was that the capture of Caen would provide his armored forces with access to that city's road network and allow British and Canadian forces to use their armored strength on the more open terrain east of Normandy's capital. Montgomery's plan had the Americans playing a subsidiary role. They were to provide the logistical basis for the campaign to liberate France by seizing the Cotentin Peninsula with its great port of Cherbourg and then moving into Brittany to capture the Breton ports, including Brest.

Considerably farther to the west, the two great American landings were to take place. Closest to the British and Canadian landings would be Omaha Beach, with half of the 1st Infantry Division landing on the eastern portion of the beaches and half of the 29th Infantry Division landing to the west. The Omaha Beach landings, encompassing the most difficult terrain, presented the greatest challenge. Great cliffs, broken by a few easily defended draws, lay along Omaha's length, providing the Germans with ideal defensive terrain. But capturing that stretch of land was essential to the invasion's success, because it would provide the link between the British and American forces. Finally, across from Omaha Beach, the 4th Infantry Division would land on Utah Beach, on the southeastern part of the Cotentin Peninsula.

Naval support for the invasion was enormous, involving no fewer than 7,000 naval vessels: 138 warships, including 4 battleships, provided naval gunfire support for the invading troops, while 221 escort vessels prevented German U-boats from interfering with the cross-Channel movement of the invasion force; 287 minesweepers and 495 light coastal vessels also contributed to the massive amphibious undertaking. All told, it was the largest amphibious effort in history.

The Allied high command consisted of the first team, generals and admirals who had proven themselves in the Mediterranean or on other battlefronts. In that theater, Eisenhower and Tedder had provided the political and strategic common sense and vision that had sustained the coalition, which comprised a number of fractious senior officers. Montgomery brought considerable effectiveness as a trainer and battle-tested leader to his position as overall commander of the ground war, although his waspish personality consistently got in the way of his effectiveness. One prewar colleague had accurately described him as "that little shit." Nevertheless, whatever his personality failings, he was a consummate professional.

Admiral Bertram Ramsay was in overall command of Allied naval forces during both the initial landings and the buildup phases. Through his planning and conduct of the battle, he had been the naval hero of Dunkirk, which had enabled the British Expeditionary Force to escape the Continent in May and June 1940. He had then commanded the amphibious forces in the Sicilian and Italian campaigns. In every respect, he too was a consummate professional.

The one marked weakness among the top Allied officers lay in the commander of American ground forces, General Omar Bradley. Bradley was an unimaginative and uninspiring commander, who had already proven to possess a streak of jealousy for subordinates more competent than he was. In addition, he was an Anglophobe who exacerbated tensions with the British, which considering Montgomery's personality would have been strained anyway. In every respect, Patton would have been a far more effective commander of American ground forces. He was not only a more competent general, but he knew Normandy's terrain inside and out, having traveled extensively throughout the province after competing for the United States in the 1912 Olympics in Sweden. But Patton's appalling lack of self-discipline in slapping two enlisted soldiers in a hospital in Sicily had led to his being sidetracked in favor of Bradley.

The actual tactical planning for the amphibious landing drew largely from the Allied experiences in the Mediterranean as well as Dieppe. The major amphibious landings in the Mediterranean, particularly the experiences gained in Sicily and Salerno, reinforced for British commanders the crucial importance of naval gunfire support both before and during the initial stages of the landing. Thus, the German defensive positions along the beaches where the British and Canadians were to land received a sustained pasting from British battleships, cruisers, and destroyers, which extended an additional hour beyond the American bombardment of its sectors. As a result, the British landings took place a full hour later than those of the Americans.

Despite the fact that the Americans could have drawn useful lessons from their experiences in the Pacific as well as in the Mediterranean, their planning for Omaha and Utah showed far less recognition of the difficulties U.S. forces might encounter during the initial stages of the landings. Here the prime culprit was Bradley, who had not actively participated in the major landings on Sicily or at Salerno. Moreover, he displayed a distinct prejudice against the navy.

General George C. Marshall, U.S. Army chief of staff and one of the key figures in the American victory in World War II, had brought Major General Charles "Pete" Corlett back from the Pacific in early April 1944 explicitly to elicit lessons from that theater. Corlett had commanded the successful landing of the 7th Infantry Division on Kwajalein in the Marshall Islands in early 1944. After receiving a briefing from Corlett on the outstanding cooperation between the navy, army, and marines, Marshall shipped him off to the European theater of operations to share with Bradley and his planners the wisdom gleaned from opposed amphibious landings in the Pacific.

Perhaps the most crucial of these lessons was the importance of naval gunfire support. The two divisions landing on Kwajalein (the other being the 4th Marine Division) had received fire support from seven battleships and a large number of cruisers. In reviewing the plans for Overlord, Corlett pointed out that the landings were to receive the support of only two battleships and then for a period of less than half an hour. Instead of a naval bombardment, Bradley was counting on a major raid by the medium bombers of Ninth Air Force to destroy the German defensive positions. However, in the early morning hours of June 6, clouds would enshroud the beaches, and the American bomber crews, afraid of hitting landing craft, bombed long, where their ordnance killed a few cows and blew up a number of trees but had no impact on the German defenses.

Moreover, Bradley's disinterest in the experiences gained in the Pacific extended to an innovation that might have saved a considerable number of American lives: amphibious tractors, "amtracs," had first seen service in the American landings at Kwajalein in January and February 1944. There they had been employed in getting soldiers and marines across the killing zone of the beaches and into the Japanese defenses, playing a significant role in reducing American casualties. The navy had shipped three hundred amtracs to England by late May 1944, but since no one in Bradley's headquarters knew about the significant role they had played in the Kwajalein landings, they sat in a depot unused until October and November 1944, when the Canadians used them in clearing the Scheldt estuary that opened up the port of Antwerp.

THE ALLIES also benefited enormously in both operational and tactical spheres from German missteps. Up until November 1943, the Wehrmacht had used France largely as a training ground for new formations and the reconstitution of divisions burned out in the fighting in Russia, with the only divisions remaining in the country third-class formations made up of recovering wounded, the old, and the lame. Moreover, the vaunted Atlantic Wall was a sham, with only modest construction efforts on fortified positions having taken place. But in November 1943, Hitler decreed that France was no longer to be a rest camp for the Wehrmacht's battered divisions but was instead to receive top priority in order to meet a potential Allied invasion in spring 1944.

In December, Hitler asked the unemployed field marshal Erwin

Rommel to inspect the Atlantic Wall from Denmark to the Spanish border. The resulting report underlined how unprepared the Germans were in the West to meet an invasion. Hitler responded by appointing Rommel the commander of Army Group B, which controlled the most vulnerable sections of the Atlantic Wall. In that position, the field marshal, perhaps the premier tactical and operational commander of the Second World War, immediately instituted a massive program to build up the west wall with field fortifications, beach obstacles, mines, and inland defenses against paratrooper drops and glider-borne landings. He also applied his considerable store of energy to the training of units in the West to meet the coming invasion.

After the war, Rommel came in for considerable criticism by surviving German generals as an officer who was a good tactician but did not understand strategy. In fact, Rommel was the only one among the senior German staff with a real grasp of strategy. He argued that the Wehrmacht must defeat Allied forces on the beaches and prevent them from ever getting ashore. His reasoning rested on his hard-won experience in fighting Anglo-American forces in North Africa and observing the Sicilian and Italian campaigns. That experience indicated to Rommel that Allied air superiority, combined with the immense quantity and flow of matériel as well as Allied superiority in firepower, would allow Anglo-American forces to build up more quickly, once they had achieved a successful lodgment on the Continent, than the Germans could. The days after the successful Allied landings were to prove him correct.

The commander of all German forces in the West, the aged field marshal Gert von Rundstedt, pressed for a different approach. He believed it would be impossible to hold the beaches in sufficient strength to defeat the invasion. Rather, Rundstedt argued that the Germans should fight a mobile battle in which their greater tactical experience would allow them to defeat the Allied forces once they were ashore. However, as the Germans were to discover and Rommel had predicted, Allied air superiority, along with the fact that the Allied buildup of forces in Normandy proceeded far faster than that of the Wehrmacht, forced the Wehrmacht to fight a desperate defensive battle just to hold a crumbling front.

In the end, Hitler was the one who made the major decisions. He decided that while Rommel would be allowed to build up the German defenses along the coasts, the panzer and panzer grenadier formations would remain back from the beaches as a mobile counterattack reserve. Moreover, those divisions would not be under the command authority of either Rommel or Rundstedt; rather, they would be under the Führer's direct control to ensure that he and not his generals would command the effort to throw the Allies into the sea. Only Hitler could order the movement forward of the counterattack divisions against the invading Allied forces.

Two decisions by German commanders in May substantially determined Overlord's fate. In mid-May, Rommel requested permission to move the 12th SS Panzer Division, Hitler Jugend, from deep in eastern Normandy to Carentan, a position from which it would have been ideally placed to intervene in the battles to contain the Utah and Omaha landing forces. The Hitler Jugend officers and NCOs were among the toughest veterans of the eastern front, drawn mostly from the 1st SS Panzer Division, while its soldiers came from the ranks of the most fanatical members of the Hitler Youth.

Not surprisingly, given its title, the division received the best equipment German industry produced. Highly trained, the division proved not only a deadly, combat-effective force against the Canadians in the days after the landing, but a murderous one as well, shooting large numbers of Canadian POWs in cold blood and even in one case dragging a dead Canadian soldier behind their tank in replication, one supposes, of what Achilles had done with Hector's body in the Trojan War. But Hitler Jugend would not fight the Americans, because Hitler and Rundstedt overruled Rommel. The division remained where it was in eastern Normandy and not at Carentan, where it could have played a disastrous role in reinforcing the defenders of the Utah and Omaha Beaches, both landings crucial to Overlord's success.

The second decision had to do with the 352nd Infantry Division. After the war, a number of historians would ascribe the difficulties on Omaha Beach to the fact that Allied intelligence had not picked up the division's arrival in the area immediately before the invasion. In fact, the division had arrived in May. Rommel had inspected it in midmonth and criticized its commander, Major General Dietrich Kraiss, for the disposition of his battalions, all of them, with the exception of one, placed well back from the cliffs and draws overlooking the beaches of the future Omaha landing.

Rommel ordered Kraiss to move the division up to the beach defenses and then left. Kraiss, however, for unknown reasons, ignored the field marshal's instructions and kept his division back as a counterattack force, which accorded with German doctrine but not with Rommel's plans to defeat the invasion before it could establish a toehold. On June 6, only one battalion of the 352nd Infantry Division and one from the 716th Infantry Division occupied the pillboxes and other field fortifications commanding the draws along the beachfront of Omaha, while only a scattering of German troops were available to hold the cliffs overlooking the beaches.

For most of May, southern England and Normandy across the English Channel enjoyed wonderful spring weather. All of that changed in June, when a gale blew up the Channel out of the Atlantic. The period within which an Allied landing could take place was a relatively short interval between June 3 and 6, when low tide coincided with dawn. Landing during low tide would enable the landing force to avoid the vast array of booby traps and obstacles the Germans had placed in the flux area between low and high tide in the belief that the Allies would land at high tide. For anyone who has walked the beach at Omaha, where the shelf between high and low tide is over three hundred yards, the German supposition makes sense. But looking at the obstacles the Germans had emplaced in that zone, Allied planners decided the landing would have to take place at low tide and in the early hours of the morning.

With the winds howling through the English Channel and the troops already at sea, Eisenhower faced a terrible decision. If he called off the operation, the next acceptable date for the invasion would come nearly a month later, with heavy political costs, blows to overall morale, and the increasing chance that the Germans would learn the time and place of the landings, which the Allies had gone to extraordinary lengths to conceal. On June 4, he postponed, hoping against hope that the weather would mitigate. The next morning, his chief meteorologist reported that the storm would lessen the following day, and Eisenhower, in an afternoon meeting with the senior Allied commanders, announced that the invasion would go in on June 6. Ironically, the bad weather probably helped the Allies, because the Germans, with little meteorological data from the Atlantic available to them, calculated that the storm would not abate and that the Allies would not invade during this period. Rommel was so confident of that assessment that he returned to Germany to celebrate his wife's birthday.

It is easy now in reading carefully crafted and researched histories of the war to believe that Allied success was inevitable. That was not how those at the time saw matters. The Allied high command's decision to launch Overlord was taken in full knowledge that the invasion might fail. Eisenhower himself penned a brief note to be read should the invasion fail: "Our landings in the Cherbourg-Havre area have failed to gain a satisfactory foothold and I have had to withdraw the troops. My decision to attack at this time and place was based on the best information available. The troops, the air and the Navy did all that bravery and devotion to duty could do. If any blame or fault attaches to the attempt, it is mine alone."

Owing to the heroism of tens of thousands of Allied soldiers, sailors, and airmen, the attempt did not fail.

The Paratroopers and Rangers

Overlord began with one of the most successful special operations of the Second World War. British Horsa gliders, flown with extraordinary skill, landed almost on top of the bridges over the Caen Canal (Pegasus Bridge, named after the 6th Airborne Division's symbol) and the Orne River (Horsa Bridge) between Caen and Ouistreham, at sixteen minutes after midnight on June 6. The glider-borne troops, under the command of Major John Howard, caught the Germans completely by surprise, and both bridges were in British hands in a matter of minutes. By seizing the bridges, Howard's men ensured that the British could open communications with the remainder of the 6th Airborne, which had landed to the east of the Orne, and that reinforcements from the British beaches at Sword could quickly and easily join up with the lightly armed airborne troops.

The reinforcing troops were from the 1st Special Service Brigade, commanded by Lord Lovat. Paying no attention to the strictures of the War Office, which had forbidden commanders from having anything so esoteric as the skirl of bagpipes accompany their troops, Lovat had his personal bagpiper, Bill Millin, play as his brigade landed. Millin had objected that such actions had been proscribed by the War Office. Lovat, in the best Scottish tradition, had replied: "Ah, but that's the *English* War Office. You and I are both Scottish and that doesn't apply."

The British 6th Airborne Division's mission was to take out the major German batteries to the east of the Orne River to prevent them from bombarding Sword Beach and to protect the flank of British and Canadian forces from a potential German counterattack. The British drops were not quite as successful as the attack on the Orne River and Caen Canal bridges, with considerable scattering of the paratroopers and gliders. Nevertheless, the 3rd Parachute Brigade gathered sufficient soldiers to storm the German batteries at Ranville, and throughout the day the division received a steady stream of reinforcements by gliders, which nearly doubled its strength, while airdrops of ammunition and rations kept the paratroopers well supplied. The linkup by Lord Lovat provided additional reinforcements and a firm supply route.

The mission of the American paratroopers was similar to that of the British. In their case, they were to seize a number of key towns and road junctions to prevent the Germans from concentrating their forces to launch a major counterattack against Utah Beach. However, the drops of the 82nd Airborne and the 101st Airborne Divisions were not nearly as concentrated as the British drops, for several reasons. First, the crews flying the C-47 and C-46 transports were not as experienced, and their mission required them to fly over the Cotentin Peninsula, where they encountered flak thrown up by German 88s. Under the intense barrage, some crews panicked and dropped their sticks of paratroopers too soon. Second, the weather over the Cotentin Peninsula was much worse than over eastern Normandy where the British dropped, making navigation and identification of the drop zones difficult. In some cases, the inexperienced transport crews dropped paratroopers into the flooded areas the Germans had engineered throughout the peninsula, where the paratroopers, with their heavy loads, drowned. Nevertheless, the majority of the sticks were dropped on dry land and began the business of making life miserable for the German defenders.

The scattered drops may well have worked to the advantage of the Americans, because it was almost impossible for the Germans to determine the main objectives of the paratroopers. In addition, the Germans had so much difficulty in clearing up pockets of paratroopers that they failed to focus attention on the amphibious landing made by the 4th Infantry Division on Utah Beach. In spite of the widely scattered landings, sufficient numbers of paratroopers reached the important crossroad villages of Sainte-Marie-du-Mont and Sainte-Mère-Église to seize and hold them. In particular, paratroopers of the

General Dwight Eisenhower talks with 101st Airborne paratroopers just hours before they jump into Normandy
National Archives, Still Pictures Division, Washington, D.C.

101st rendered a crucial service to the Utah landings by taking out German artillery positions that covered the causeways from the beaches across the flooded terrain to the high ground. Lieutenant Richard Winters, one of the heroes in *Band of Brothers,* played a key role in eliminating one of the German batteries.

By midmorning, the paratroops and lead units of the 4th Division on Utah had linked up. As a result, American ground forces were able to begin moving inland over the causeways. Meanwhile, the Germans found themselves in so much difficulty sorting out what was happening and fending off American paratroopers that they were never able to concentrate sufficient forces to launch a major counterattack. On both the eastern and western extremities of the Overlord operation, the Anglo-American paratrooper drops had rendered yeoman service in covering the invasion's flanks.

The British Beaches

As suggested earlier, the British landings occurred considerably later than the American assaults because of Montgomery's call for a prolonged naval bombardment. The Royal Navy's shelling largely achieved its objective in suppressing the German defenses along the buildup area facing the beaches. There were, of course, some pockets of resistance that caused the British and Canadians considerable difficulty. But the major problem lay in getting their tanks, vehicles, and artillery over the seawalls, while the Normandy tide raced in with a speed that always astonishes those who are first-time visitors to its beaches. A massive traffic jam mushroomed on the beaches while engineers and others attempted either to knock holes in the seawall or to build up sand ramps to get the vehicles across. This added to the time required to gather formations and begin the crucial move inland.

The next major obstacles the British encountered in the move inland were the cleverly disguised defensive positions the Germans had established behind the beaches. The British 3rd Infantry Division was supposed to lead the drive to Caen from Sword Beach. But the ground behind Ouistreham and the beaches sloped gradually upward. Two German concrete strongpoints, Hillman and Morris, were ideally situated to stall the advance off the beaches. The maps of the area reflect none of the fact that those German positions totally dominated the terrain. From well-camouflaged sites, German machine gunners, with their deadly MG 42 light machine guns possessing a rate of fire of more than one thousand rounds a minute, gave notice that the Normandy campaign would be anything but easy for the Allies. It took much of the late morning and early afternoon for the British to clear out those positions before they could resume their advance on Caen. By the time evening fell, the strain of three days at sea in the English Channel, the wrenching anticipation of the landing, the fighting through the defenses, and then the attacks on the German strongpoints had exhausted the 3rd Infantry Division's infantry. The advance stalled four miles short of Caen; the British would not take the city for another forty-three days of ferocious fighting.

The landings at Juno Beach ran into less resistance, partially because there were fewer built-up areas. By the time evening fell, the Canadians had advanced seven miles inland. One battalion had a clear road open to Caen, but its commander deferred advancing farther to the brigade commander, who decided he was unwilling to take the initiative himself. So the Canadians failed to move into Caen—in retrospect, probably a good thing, because the murderous juvenile soldiers of the Hitler Jugend were already approaching the city from the northeast. On the next day, they would launch a furious counterattack that would rock the Canadians back on their heels.

The British at Sword and the Canadians at Juno failed to connect their beachheads over the course of the day. As a result, the one major counterattack that the Germans launched on June 6 managed to drive through that gap and almost reached the coast. Mark IV tanks of the 21st Panzer Division reached the outskirts of Lion-sur-Mer, but the German counterattack came late in the day when the British were ashore and fully deployed. British Sherman Fireflies (an improved Sherman tank with a high-velocity gun, instead of the American version's low-velocity weapon), anti-tank guns, and Typhoon fighter bombers slaughtered the attacking Germans. The 21st Panzer Division's commander reported that although he had had 120 tanks at the day's onset, his division had only 70 tanks at day's end.

On Gold Beach, the British 50th Division ran into considerably heavier resistance than its Canadian neighbors. The German positions around Le Hamel proved to be a particularly tough nut to crack. But the British had a number of advantages the Americans did not. Here the bombardment, both naval and air, proved less than successful, because most of the German positions were not facing out to sea but in enfilade positions facing down the beach. Nevertheless, British-specialized armor, flamethrowers, and "flail" tanks, which possessed great drums with huge chains in front of the tanks, proved particularly useful in clearing mines and barbed wire and German-fortified positions.

However tenacious the initial German resistance, the lack of reserves soon allowed the British to break the thin crust and work their way inland. The fate of the German battery at Mont Fleury underscored the inability of German artillery to interfere with the amphibious landings. Struck by bombers and twelve six-inch shells from HMS *Orion,* the gun crews bugged out. Anyone who has visited the site can understand in looking at the damage why the German gun crews abandoned the position. By the end of the day, the 50th Infantry Division was well inland and several of its units had almost reached Bayeux, which they would seize the next day against minimal resistance, preserving that beautiful medieval town as one of the few in Normandy not to be wrecked by the fighting. As we shall see, the British success here would also render an important service to the Americans fighting for their lives at Omaha.

The generally sluggish response by the Germans on June 6 was due to several factors. The inacurate weather forecasts undoubtedly lulled their senior commanders. The fact that the Seventh Army, which was responsible for the defense of Normandy, was holding a map exercise for its corps and division commanders suggests how unprepared for the invasion senior German commanders were. But the most important factor was Rommel's absence, away in Germany. Without the field marshal's presence as the initial reports of the Allied invasion began coming in, there was little spark in the headquarters of Army Group B. Adding to the lack of German response was the refusal of Hitler's staff to wake the Führer until the early afternoon. Without Hitler's permission, Rundstedt refused to order the main

German counterattack units forward toward the invasion beaches until 2:30 that day.

THE AMERICAN BEACHES

The one landing where the Overlord operation came close to foundering was the amphibious assault on Omaha Beach. Of all the beaches it was the most important, because its capture was essential to linking Utah in the far west on the Cotentin Peninsula with the British beaches to the east. Had the 352nd Infantry Division's commander obeyed Rommel's orders, the German defenses on Omaha would have been impregnable. Even with only two infantry battalions holding the draws, the Germans came close to turning the landing into a disastrous defeat. As at Gold, the Germans' defensive positions enfiladed the beaches, looking down on them rather than out to sea. The main killing zones onto which German MG 42 machine gunners sprayed their murderous, preset fire were thus in front of and to the flanks of the draws that led up to the cliffs overlooking the beaches. There was less intense fire farther down the beaches in front of the great cliffs.

Even before the landing began, everything that could go wrong for the Americans seemed to indeed have gone wrong. The bomber attack intended to pulverize the German defenses missed entirely; the perfunctory naval bombardment Bradley had decreed hardly damaged the enfilade fortifications; the naval officer in charge of dropping the amphibious tanks to churn ashore cravenly dropped them too far from the beach, where twenty-nine out of thirty-four were promptly swamped by the English Channel's choppy water, taking their crews to watery graves.

The landing units on Omaha consisted of regiments from the combat-experienced 1st Infantry Division and the inexperienced 29th Infantry Division, supported by various tank, engineer, artillery, and Ranger units. The sea was dangerously choppy, which undoubtedly contributed to the troubles of the amphibious tanks, but it also swamped ten landing craft and made it virtually impossible for the

Troops wade ashore on Omaha Beach
National Archives, Still Pictures Division, Washington, D.C.

DUKWs (amphibious vehicles) to bring the supporting artillery ashore.

Because the landing took place at low tide, the completely exposed and unprotected infantry had to run across approximately three hundred yards of tidal flats, one hundred yards of beach, and then fifty yards of rocky shingle to reach the cover of the dunes lying below the cliffs, all under the murderous fire of German machine guns. As one Ranger survivor recalled forty years later: "I was the first one out [of the boat]. The seventh man was the next one to get across the beach without being hit. Two were killed; three were injured. That's how lucky you had to be." Those few who survived that terrifying journey huddled behind the cover of the dunes as the dead, the wounded, and smashed-up burning vehicles accumulated behind them. Robert Capa, the great combat photographer, took more than one hundred pictures of the landing, but only a few survived after the developer overexposed most of the film. Those few remaining captured the hell endured by the Americans from the 29th and 1st Infantry Divisions and their accompanying support.

German officers on the scene reported the slaughter to their superiors and indicated their troops had repulsed the landing. That was sufficient for the 352nd Infantry Division's commander to redeploy most of his force to reinforce those contesting the British landings on Gold Beach. The German estimate of the situation was not that far off the mark, because the difficulties on Omaha Beach came close to persuading Bradley to call off the landing there and redirect the reinforcements scheduled to come ashore in following waves over to Utah. But the Germans began to suffer from their lack of reinforcements as well as the fact that their ammunition was running low. Moreover, the U.S. Navy provided crucial additional firepower, as destroyer captains brought their vessels so close inshore that some almost grounded on the shelf of the shoreline. In a navy where a captain who grounds his ship usually gets fired, that is saying a great deal. The destroyers' five-inch high-velocity guns were able to reach the concrete German firing positions with direct fire, which proved deadly.

Most important, a number of those Americans who had survived, mostly between the draws, began to work their way up the cliffs. At the top, they discovered relatively few Germans, and once a sufficient number of them had gathered, they were able to attack the German defenders in the rear. Typical of such efforts was the one led by Second Lieutenant John Spaulding, who with only three men managed to neutralize one of the German strongpoints by midday, capturing twenty-one Germans in the process. Innumerable such actions, most of them unrecorded, slowly but steadily unraveled the defenses that were preventing American troops from moving up the draws.

The opening up of the draws allowed the Americans to land more tanks and artillery and bring those supporting weapons to the battle on the high ground behind the cliffs. By evening, the Americans had established a tenuous lodgment on Omaha. They held the beaches, the draws, and a very small portion of territory inland. The few survivors were exhausted, short of ammunition, and desperately in need of reinforcements. Their losses had been as heavy as any American force has suffered in a single day with the exception of Antietam. Casualties on Omaha came close three thousand. The fact that only one hundred tons of the twenty-four hundred tons of supplies that were supposed to come ashore actually made it to the beach in usable condition suggests how close a run thing the Omaha operation had been.

Yet the Germans were certainly not in a position to counterattack Omaha, both because of the lack of reserves in the area and because their initial success in the first hours of the landing led them to discount the danger of an American buildup in the area. German reinforcements continued to flow toward the British beaches over the next several days, allowing the Americans to solidify their hold on the lodgment and to link up with the British to their east and eventually with the 5th Infantry Division and U.S. airborne forces to their west.

The American landing at Utah Beach unfolded as almost a mirror image of the landings across the bay at Omaha. Even where things went wrong, they worked to the advantage of the Americans. The initial landing force hit the beaches at the wrong spot, over two thousand yards south of where they were supposed to land. The assistant division commander, Theodore Roosevelt Jr., reportedly commented: "We'll start the war from right here." In fact, the beach where the 4th

General Dwight Eisenhower heads toward the beachhead
National Archives, Still Pictures Division, Washington, D.C.

Infantry Division was supposed to land was heavily defended. The stretch where they did land was lightly defended, discounted by the Germans, who were confident they could easily defend with artillery fire the few causeways across the flooded terrain behind the beaches.

But the Germans had not calculated on the large American paratrooper drops, which as noted earlier took out the infantry and artillery positions. Thus, the 4th Infantry Division found the move inland to link up with the paratroopers relatively easy to accomplish. The success at Utah provided the Americans with quick access to the Contentin Peninsula, which, along with the important port of Cherbourg, they would clear by the end of June.

On June 6, 1944, the Allied armies achieved their lodgment on the European Continent. Over the course of the day, the Allies landed 155,000 soldiers on French soil—75,215 across the British and Canadian beaches and 57,500 at Utah and Omaha, with 23,000 paratroopers and glider-borne infantry being dropped into the Norman countryside. In some respects, the landing was not as successful as Eisenhower and Montgomery had hoped. Nowhere had the Allies managed to push as deeply inland as they had planned. Yet, as the British official history notes, "The area held [by the Allies at the end of the day] was large enough for manoeuvre and safe enough for the build-up to proceed with confidence."

The British and Canadians had failed to capture Caen on the first day, as Montgomery had planned, and so had also not gained access to the more open terrain lying to the south and east. That may have been a blessing in disguise, because all too soon, at Villers-Bocage, where the German tank ace Michael Wittman destroyed an armored brigade with a few Tiger tanks, British armor would prove no match for German armor, in either training or equipment. But hunkered down to the north of Caen, the British were able to hammer the attacking panzer divisions and slowly force them back over ground that was not favorable to maneuver warfare, but that maximized British superiority in firepower.

The Americans had suffered a near catastrophe at Omaha, but the

General Dwight Eisenhower and Field Marshal Bernard Law Montgomery confer
National Archives, Still Pictures Division, Washington, D.C.

closeness of that struggle and the bare toehold the Americans gained led the Germans to reinforce other sectors. The result was that the American divisions pushed ashore over Omaha Beach and in the succeeding days were able to move inland and link up with the British 50th Infantry Division to the east and the 5th Infantry Division and the paratroopers of the 101st Airborne Division to the west at Carentan. The *bocage* country came as a great surprise to most Allied commanders, but again that may have been an unexpected blessing, because it forced the Germans to fight a battle of attrition, one that in every respect Allied manpower and superiority in equipment guaranteed they would lose. The only Allied commander who might have understood the difficulties of the *bocage* was Patton, and he would be on the shelf until late July.

For the Germans, the destruction of the French transportation network by the Allied air campaign made moving reinforcing troops and supplies to the Normandy battlefront a nightmare. The transfer of the 2nd SS Panzer Division from Limoges to Normandy was supposed to take two days. It took two weeks. In every respect, events bore out Rommel's assessment that the only chance the Germans had was to defeat the invasion at the outset on the beaches and that any sustained campaign in northern France would guarantee an Allied victory and Germany's final defeat.

On June 7, the battle of the buildup began. It was a battle the Germans had no hope of winning. Fresh Allied divisions flooded ashore, while the Germans made a desperate attempt to cobble together a counterattacking force. They were never able to do so under the constant pressure Allied forces applied to the German front. Nevertheless, the next two months proved frustrating for Allied commanders as their troops advanced at a snail's pace. But the fighting steadily ground the Germans down, and in late July their left flank facing the Americans collapsed. Within a month, British and American forces had liberated all of France and Belgium and had rolled up on the German frontier. The success on June 6, 1944, "the longest day," had made all of that possible.

The success of the Normandy landing had significant implications well beyond assuring the defeat and absolute destruction of Nazi Germany. Normandy reestablished British and American credibility on the Continent and enabled the British and Americans to project not only their military power, but their political influence into the heart of central Europe. What Churchill so eloquently and accurately termed the Iron Curtain fell over Europe in spring 1945. But the countries liberated by British and American armies—France, Italy, Belgium, Luxembourg, Holland—and the western portion of Germany provided the political and strategic base from which the United States and its allies were able to wage and win the Cold War.

DIEN BIEN PHU

Imperialism Defeated

1954

THE DISASTROUS COLLAPSE OF WESTERN MILITARY INSTITUTIONS IN
Southeast Asia before the onslaught of Japanese military forces in late
1941 and early 1942 put paid to the idea that the white man and his
regimes were inherently superior to the colonial subjects they ruled.
In quick order, Hong Kong, Malaya, Borneo, the Dutch East Indies,
and the Philippines fell to the Imperial Japanese Army. However, it
was a different story with the French colony of Cochin China, consisting of Vietnam, Cambodia, and Laos. Shortly after the collapse of
France in June 1940, the Japanese government demanded that the
new French government in Vichy allow its military forces to occupy
jointly with the French the northern half of Cochin China in order to
shut off the transportation of military goods to China, against whom
the Japanese were waging a ruthless, merciless war. Initially the French
governor refused, but his appeals for aid from Washington met stony
silence. Meanwhile, the Japanese bombarded French positions along
the Red River Delta. With no possibility of aid on the horizon, the
French caved in. One year later, the Japanese demanded that their
forces occupy the naval and air bases in southern Vietnam, and again

the French agreed. This time, however, the Americans reacted, considering that the Japanese now had bases from which they could threaten all of Southeast Asia. Along with the British and the Dutch, the Roosevelt administration not only froze Japanese assets, but embargoed the export to Japan of commodities, including oil. Thus, the Americans had set the road to Pearl Harbor.

While the other colonial regimes went down to stunningly swift defeat, the French regime in Cochin China remained on the sideline. Its time came in February 1945, when the Japanese in a sudden coup overthrew the French colonial regime and destroyed French forces throughout Vietnam. Desperate calls from the French for help went unanswered by the Americans, who were guided in their policies by Franklin Roosevelt's deep contempt for French colonialism. But Japan soon collapsed with the dropping of the atomic bombs on Hiroshima and Nagasaki. With the Japanese defeat, the question then arose as to what would be the fate of the European colonial regimes in Southeast Asia. For the most part, the British withdrew gracefully by granting independence to their colonies; the Dutch were less inclined in that direction, but they lacked the military and economic power to regain the Dutch East Indies, so they too withdrew in December 1949. With Cochin China, it was another matter. The government in Paris proved incapable of restraining its military, which was staffed by many officers resolved to wash away the double stain of the defeat of 1940 and the 1945 collapse in Cochin China. They arrived in Southeast Asia determined to reestablish French control over Vietnam, Laos, and Cambodia.

However, in fall 1945, as the French arrived to take over occupation duty from the British (in the southern half of Vietnam) and the Chinese nationalists (in the northern half), they found themselves confronting Ho Chi Minh and an indigenous group of Vietnamese nationalists who called themselves the Viet Minh and had no intention of allowing the French to reestablish their rule. The Viet Minh were deeply committed revolutionaries, while by any standard, Ho's record as a revolutionary was extraordinary. He was a founding member of the French Communist Party in 1920, a senior official in the Comintern in the Soviet Union in the 1920s, an adviser to the Chinese Communists, and the founder of the Vietnamese Communist

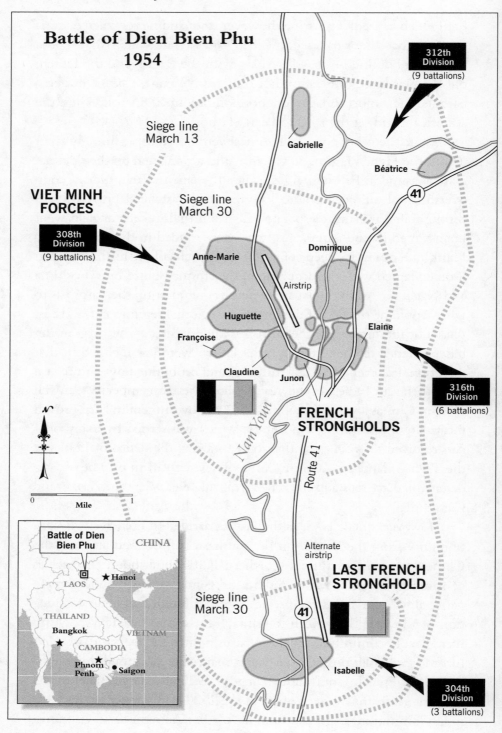

Battle of Dien Bien Phu 1954

VIET MINH FORCES

308th Division
(9 battalions)

312th Division
(9 battalions)

316th Division
(6 battalions)

304th Division
(3 battalions)

Siege line March 13

Siege line March 30

Siege line March 30

Gabrielle

Béatrice

Anne-Marie

Dominique

Airstrip

Huguette

Elaine

Françoise

Claudine

Junon

FRENCH STRONGHOLDS

Nam Youn

Route 41

Alternate airstrip

LAST FRENCH STRONGHOLD

Isabelle

41

41

N

0   Mile   1

Battle of Dien Bien Phu

CHINA

LAOS

★ Hanoi

THAILAND

Bangkok ★

VIETNAM

CAMBODIA

Phnom Penh ★

● Saigon

Party. Like a number of his senior advisers, including the great general Vo Nguyen Giap, Ho had attended the French lycée Quoc Hoc. There, he became imbued with the ideological fervor of the French Revolution. One of the great miscalculations of the French lay in their failure to understand that they were opposed by leaders who were not simply nationalists and Communists, but full-fledged revolutionaries along the lines of Robespierre and Saint-Just, both of whom had been spawned by France's own revolution. Ho's command and love of French was such that in 1922, while in Paris, he had written an article in a French sports magazine complaining about the adoption by French sportswriters of English words such as *le manager, le round,* and *le knockout.* Ho provided the extraordinary political leadership that kept the insurgency alive, but the former history teacher Giap provided the military savvy. Giap learned war by waging it. Without a day spent at a staff college or a war college, he was to prove a master of both guerrilla tactics and the use of conventional forces. In the end, he would humiliate not only the French on the battlefield, but the Americans.

Negotiations between the French and Ho broke down at the end of 1946, and conflict began throughout Vietnam, especially in the north. From the first, this was a war waged by the professional French military, with governments in Paris refusing to send draftees to Vietnam. As a result, units manned by long-term volunteers, members of the French Foreign Legion, and colonial regiments of Moroccans, Algerians, Africans, and eventually Vietnamese, bore the brunt of the fighting. Moreover, in the war's first year, the Americans with their hostility to colonial regimes refused to provide the French significant military help. It was a war France could not afford, and it was a war that quickly became unpopular, but as with the tar baby, the French discovered that once they were in, there appeared to be no exit.

At the outset of hostilities, French armored and infantry units pushed the Viet Minh insurgents out of the port of Haiphong and then out of Hanoi. In straight-up, conventional fights, the Viet Minh had no chance, but Giap, already proving that he possessed a first-class military mind, waged a hit-and-run war. His first target was control over the countryside, which the Viet Minh increasingly dominated, while the French held the cities and locations beyond the urban areas where they could deploy their troops. In 1949, the correlation of forces began to shift against the French. The collapse of Chiang Kai-shek's regime and the arrival of Mao Zedong's soldiers along the border allowed the Viet Minh to receive extensive military aid from the Chinese Communists. By late summer 1950, the Viet Minh's first well-trained and -equipped regiments handed the French a series of defeats along the border areas in capturing the forts of Cao Bang and Lang Son.

It appeared that France's days in Vietnam were numbered, but two important events intervened. Well to the north in East Asia, the Korean War exploded with Kim Il-sung's invasion of South Korea. The outbreak of that war changed American attitudes toward the war in Vietnam. Many in Washington quickly concluded the French were waging a war against the spread of Communism and that if the Viet Minh won, the rest of Southeast Asia would fall like a row of dominoes. The collapse of the North Korean invasion then forced the Chinese to intervene, which limited their ability to aid Ho and Giap. Nevertheless, Giap made the mistake of overestimating Viet Minh capabilities. At the beginning of 1951, believing his troops could take on the French in a straight-up, conventional battle, he launched three major attacks against French positions along the Red River Delta. But while Chinese aid to the Viet Minh had decreased, American aid to the beleaguered French forces had increased significantly.

Perhaps most important, General Jean de Lattre de Tassigny, one of the most competent French generals since the great Napoleon, had arrived in Vietnam as the commander of French forces. De Lattre had commented to his aides on arrival, "My presence is worth a division." To a considerable extent, he was right. In a short period of time, he rebuilt French morale. Using aircraft and other equipment provided by the Americans, de Lattre's forces savaged the attacking Viet Minh in three major battles, first in January, then in March, and finally in May 1951. But de Lattre's time in Vietnam was short. He died in January 1952, and the French generals who followed had little of his drive and none of his competence.

Meanwhile, the war continued. Giap recognized the fact that his forces were not yet capable of taking on the French in a stand-up, conventional fight. Thus, he focused on husbanding his forces, striking at isolated French garrisons, undermining French control of the countryside politically and militarily, especially in the Red River Delta, and responding to French offensive strikes that moved out from the defensive positions around the delta. These French attacks resembled efforts to punch a pillow, because the Viet Minh simply pulled back deeper into the jungle. Moreover, while the French found it relatively easy to reach their objectives in the heavily forested areas held by the Viet Minh, pulling back proved a more difficult matter, as Giap concentrated his reserves and forced the French to fight their way back to the delta. By 1953, the balance of forces in Vietnam had created a stalemate, but one that was sliding slowly in favor of the Viet Minh. Although the French continued to dominate the conventional arena, Giap's forces were gaining an increasing hold over the countryside. Admittedly the Americans were providing substantial aid, but that aid came at a price—namely, increasing pressure to create an independent Vietnam, precisely the political result against which the French were fighting. On the other hand, and perhaps most dangerous for French prospects, was the unpopularity of the war in France. Time was the ally of the Viet Minh.

The Decision to Fight at Dien Bien Phu

In May 1953, the French government appointed a new commander in chief for the war, General Henri Navarre. Navarre had considerable combat experience; he had fought on the western front in the First World War from 1917 through 1918, had two years fighting guerrillas in Morocco in the early 1920s, and had commanded a regiment in the advance into Germany in 1945. But during the interwar years and after the Second World War, he had served in intelligence and staff positions. Moreover, he had never served in Asia and knew almost nothing about the war in Vietnam. Astonishingly, that was why he was picked. Upon his arrival in the theater, Navarre did streamline the organization and coordination of the three French services, but he made relatively few personnel changes. The most important of these was to appoint Brigadier General (soon Major General) René Cogny to command the key northern region of Vietnam, in particular the

Red River Delta. The general was six feet four, handsome, definitely a ladies' man, possessed of impressive credentials—but also, as Navarre discovered, an intriguer who made considerable efforts to ensure that others would take the blame if things went wrong.

The basic strategic problem the French faced was that they were attempting to do too much with too little. Their opponents, however, had almost complete freedom of action to attack when it was in their interests. In June 1953, Cogny suggested that French forces launch a deep airborne attack on the provincial town of Dien Bien Phu in the northwestern hill country of Vietnam. He would later claim that his aim was to create a base from which the French could mount guerrilla operations using the indigenous population to attack the Viet Minh's rear areas and logistical system. Navarre liked the idea, but he viewed Dien Bien Phu as a blocking position to prevent further Viet Minh incursions into Laos and capable of withstanding a siege.

The two concepts addressed similar problems—namely, how to deprive the Viet Minh of their relative freedom of maneuver by threatening their base areas—but French decision making rested on two fatal assumptions: (1) Given the appalling terrain that surrounded Dien Bien Phu, Giap and the Viet Minh would lack the expertise and logistical capabilities to mount a prolonged siege; and (2) Such would be the superiority of French firepower, artillery, and airpower in Dien Bien Phu that, as had happened in the 1951 winter and spring battles, the French would slaughter attacking Viet Minh infantry and suppress whatever artillery Giap's troops dragged across the mountainous jungles of northwestern Vietnam. French leaders also hoped they could attract the Viet Minh into a meat grinder battle, in which they could inflict such heavy losses on their opponents that Ho would have to come to the peace table on their terms. The French picked Dien Bien Phu because they believed the valley in which it lay was sufficiently large, unlike the other valleys in the northeast of Vietnam, to allow the garrison to strike Viet Minh rear areas. The fact that major hills surrounded it on all sides, and thus provided excellent observation for Viet Minh artillery positions, failed to bother the French because they believed they would dominate the artillery battle.

What the French missed in their assessment was that Dien Bien Phu's location would make it an attractive target for Giap, because its

defenders would consist largely of light infantry with limited artillery and armor support, all of which an air bridge from Hanoi would have to support over a considerable distance. That distance would also affect the ability of bombers and fighters to provide close air support for the defenders. The French also failed to recognize that the Viet Minh, heirs of the French Revolution, would willingly pay an extraordinary price to move their forces and the required artillery to the hills surrounding the valley.

Navarre selected a dashing cavalryman, Colonel Christian Marie Ferdinand de Castries, to command the garrison at Dien Bien Phu once French paratroopers had seized the area. Castries had an outstanding combat record but lacked both the rank and the experience for the assignment. In fact, it was a paratrooper, Lieutenant Colonel Pierre Charles Langlais, who would assume combat command of defending Dien Bien Phu once the Viet Minh offensive began. The real weakness in Castries's assignment lay in the fact that as a mere colonel, he ran into considerable difficulty in getting Cogny and his staff in Hanoi to recognize the difficulties the garrison was confronting as well as its desperate need for resupply and particularly for more troops.

THE BUILDING OF THE FORTRESS

So the die was cast. On November 20, 1953, the first waves of C-47s took off from Hanoi's Bach Mai Airfield. The first paratroopers to drop were from the 6th Colonial Parachute Battalion (Bataillon de Parachutistes Coloniaux, BPC), under one of the legendary French soldiers to fight at Dien Bien Phu, Major Marcel Bigeard. Initially, the 6th BPC ran into significant opposition from the local Viet Minh, but by midday succeeding waves of paratroopers had gained control of the valley. By nightfall, three battalions of paratroopers had seized the area around the town and had solid control of the three drop zones. Overwhelmed by French numbers and firepower, Viet Minh Regiment 148 withdrew into the hills, leaving behind more than one hundred dead. Now the process of the buildup began. On the day after the first drops, the commander of French airborne forces in Vietnam, Brigadier General Jean Gilles, after carefully stowing his glass eye in the pocket of his parachute, jumped into the valley along with additional reinforcements. By November 22, the last of the paratroopers had arrived along with the airborne combat engineers to build the airfield on which the steadily increasing garrison would depend for survival. Yet there was a considerable gap between what it was possible for the engineers to accomplish and what would be required to make Dien Bien Phu defensible against a major Viet Minh attack. Simply put, they had too much to do in laying out not one but two landing fields and constructing roads and bridges with minimal troops and resources, so they devoted little or no effort to constructing fortified bunkers, trenches, and barbed-wire emplacements. The engineers were short approximately 30,000 tons of the minimal requirements to make Dien Bien Phu defensible. Through December and into January, with other heavy commitments throughout Vietnam, the airlift into Dien Bien Phu barely totaled 150 tons per day.

Thus, the effort to create defensive positions throughout the valley fell to the soldiers themselves. Here, there were other difficulties. Given that Navarre intended Dien Bien Phu to serve as a base from which French commandos and native guerrillas would strike at the Viet Minh, why expend major efforts at building strong defenses? The elite troops who formed much of the garrison were by their nature and training little disposed to spend time digging bunkers and trenches or emplacing barbed-wire entanglements. Only on strongpoint Gabrielle did the defenders, tough Algerians, fortify two complete defensive lines. All the other positions possessed only a single defensive line. To add to Dien Bien Phu's vulnerabilities, the garrison's soldiers quickly stripped most of the vegetation off their positions, partially to create fields of fire, but also for firewood. They also failed to camouflage their positions. The result was that when the Viet Minh struck in March, they could observe virtually everything that was happening in the valley, while the fortified zones that were supposed to protect the main positions were hardly imposing.

Exacerbating the whole problem of defending the valley was the fact that the French began serious work on constructing defensible positions only at the end of January, when it appeared the Viet Minh were about to attack. Although Giap's troops would not attack for another month and a half, it was already too late. Nevertheless, as early as mid-December, French patrols and raiding parties had run into significant Viet Minh forces, and by the end of the month, it was clear the garrison would not be able to conduct deep-penetration raids in the jungles north of Dien Bien Phu. In fact, by early January the Viet Minh ring was drawing ever closer around the garrison. By the end of the month, French intelligence had picked up the presence of three main Viet Minh divisions, the 308th, 316th, and 304th, north and northeast of the valley. It should have been clear to Cogny and his staff that they should either immediately pull out as much of the garrison as possible or heavily reinforce the defenders. They did neither, instead resembling a group of freshman psychology students watching the rats run around their cages. Navarre refused to consider a pullout, while Cogny committed much of his mobile reserves to other operations.

By mid-March, the correlation of forces was already strongly weighted against the French. By that point, Viet Minh logistics had managed to build up in the hills overlooking Dien Bien Phu a reserve supply of shells—3,000 120 mm, 15,000 105 mm, 21,000 81 mm, 5,000 75 mm, and 44,000 37 mm—for their howitzers, flak, and mortars. Altogether, Giap's soldiers transported and dragged through the jungle approximately 45 105 mm howitzers, 48 75 mm pack howitzers, 48 120 mm heavy mortars, and a bit more than 48 75 mm recoilless rifles of the 351st Heavy Division. They then dug these into caves on the forward slopes of the hills surrounding Dien Bien Phu, from which they could easily trundle their weapons out, fire, and quickly drag them back under cover before French counterbattery fire could reply. In addition, the Viet Minh brought twenty-eight infantry battalions, numbering some 37,000 soldiers; to that total, Giap would throw another 10,000 reserves into the battle, many half-trained.

Against these numbers, the French counted some 10,814 infantry, tankers, and artillery soldiers. Of these, 1,412 were from mainland France; 2,969 were soldiers of the Foreign Legion, including 2,607 North Africans and 247 Africans (nearly all gunners); and 3,579 were Vietnamese and mountain tribesmen. Nearly all the officers and the majority of the NCOs were French. The French and legionnaires were outstanding soldiers; the North Africans were as well, but the morale of many of them deteriorated toward the battle's end. The

Vietnamese paratroopers were at times outstanding, but at other times their morale proved shaky; the hill tribesmen, trained to fight as guerrillas, were hopeless. The paratroopers, including the Vietnamese, the legionnaires, and the specialist tankers and gunners, formed the heart of the garrison, and they would fight to the last. During the battle, 4,291 soldiers jumped into Dien Bien Phu as reinforcements; 680 of these were not jump qualified.

THE FIRST BATTLES

The French had laid out their defense of Dien Bien Phu in the following fashion, with the strongpoints supposedly named after Castries's various mistresses. The northernmost bastion, Gabrielle, lay approximately a mile and a half to the north of the runway on a hill that rose one thousand feet above the valley floor. The Algerians held Gabrielle, and they had made the most of their defensive preparations to hold the strongpoint. Southeast of Gabrielle was Beatrice, also separated from the main defensive positions by a considerable distance. Making its defense more difficult was the fact that the French had not removed the jungle directly to its north, which provided the Viet Minh with the cover to approach close to the strongpoint's defensive positions. Although Beatrice's garrison had not worked as hard at preparing its defensive positions as had the Algerians, its legionnaires were among the toughest troops in the garrison. Yet even before the fighting began, the Foreign Legion battalion holding Beatrice had lost nearly 30 percent of its men in keeping the road open to the main positions.

To the east of the Nam Yum River, which ran through the center of the valley and the garrison, lay strongpoints Dominique—to the southwest of Beatrice—and Elaine. The former contained several hillocks that made the position particularly important, because it overlooked the main airstrip from the east. Algerians and Moroccans defended these two positions. Here the leadership of French officers and NCOs was critical, because when it was weak or when leaders went down, the North Africans usually lost cohesion and discipline. Across the Nam Yum lay the heart of Dien Bien Phu: the airstrip, the ammunition and supply bunkers, the hospital, Castries's command center, and the main artillery positions. North of the runway was Anne-Marie, an area easily flooded during the monsoon and defended primarily by unreliable mountain tribesmen. To the west were the Huguette and Claudine positions, neither one of which was on recognizable geographic features, but portions of which became considerably important later in the battle. Finally, well to the south lay Isabelle, located over three miles from the main base in the midst of a fetid swamp. The French had sited Isabelle to provide supporting artillery fire for the main garrison, but its location as well as its drain on the strength of the main garrison made little sense.

On March 13, the French discovered how wrong they were. By this point, increasing Viet Minh shelling of the airstrip had rendered it almost unusable, thereby knocking out one of the basic assumptions on which the defense of Dien Bien Phu rested—namely, that immediate air support would be available from the aircraft on the garrison's airstrip. But that proved the least of French assumptions to go up in smoke on March 13. At 5:00 P.M., Viet Minh artillery opened up with a fierce bombardment of Beatrice, while interdiction fires hit most of Dien Bien Phu's other major positions. An hour and a half later, a shell took out Beatrice's command bunker as waves of Viet Minh infantry surged through its outer defenses. But worse followed. Two hours later, another shell killed Lieutenant Colonel Jean Gaucher, commander of the central sector, and most of his staff. Castries called Langlais (who was alive only because a Viet shell had failed to explode after piercing his bunker) to assume command of the fight.

By now the defense of Beatrice was nearly over. Despite the delivery of what is now called "danger close" artillery fire, the Viet Minh swarmed over the position, while only a few centers of resistance were still holding out. At 8:30 P.M., the company defending the strongpoint's northeast corner no longer answered efforts to contact it. Half an hour later, another company desperately reported: "Viets all over the place." Shortly after midnight, contact ended with the last group of defenders; a few survivors made it back to French lines the following morning. Perhaps even more depressing than Beatrice's fall was the fact that the garrison's artillery had used up a quarter of its ammunition supply over the night. Moreover, French counterbattery fire had achieved virtually no success in suppressing Giap's guns. By the next morning, Viet Minh artillery had made the airstrip largely unusable. Nevertheless, in midafternoon Major André Botella's 5th Vietnamese Parachute Battalion jumped into Dien Bien Phu to make up for some of the garrison's losses simply in keeping open the roads to Beatrice, Gabrielle, and Isabelle.

Gabrielle was obviously next, and its Algerian defenders steeled themselves for what they knew was coming. At 6:00 P.M. on the dot, the Viet Minh opened up with a massive bombardment that covered all of Gabrielle. The first wave of attackers came close to breaking through both defensive lines the Algerians had constructed, but intense French artillery fire—along with a timely counterattack led by a sergeant who had been the getaway driver for a gangster with the wonderful name of Pierrot-le-Fou ("Pierre the Crazy One") before joining the army to escape the long arms of French justice—drove the Viet Minh off Gabrielle. The success was short-lived. A second mass barrage began at 3:30 A.M. and took out the command post with the strongpoint's senior officers. A counterattack collapsed when the Viet Minh sprang an ambush on the tanks, legionnaires, and Vietnamese paratroopers. By morning it was over, although a few escaped. When an Algerian being led away to prison camp balked at walking on a wounded soldier, the Viet Minh officer casually commented: "You can step on him. He has done his duty for the People's Army."

The twin defeats on Beatrice and Gabrielle devastated the French. The garrison's artillery commander, Colonel Charles Piroth, who had lost an arm in Italy in 1943, retired to his bunker, pressed a hand grenade against his chest, and pulled its pin. Castries's chief of staff suffered a psychological collapse, while Hanoi sank into despair at the shattering of its illusions. The immediate question should have been, What to do now? There were only two answers: Allow the garrison to go down in defeat in the imminent future or massively reinforce the French forces still holding out. However, senior officers in Hanoi and Saigon dithered, quarreled, and refused to make a decision. Cogny assured his staff that with the monsoon season close at hand, the Viet Minh would have a more difficult time supplying their forces than the French. In fact, with a delicate air bridge supporting the garrison, the opposite was true. Troubles were also occurring within the garrison's command element. Shortly after the fall of Beatrice and Gabrielle, Langlais, a mere lieutenant colonel, assumed tactical command of the battle and a garrison that numbered ten thousand soldiers. Bernard Fall pointed out the situation's irony in his magnificent classic, *Hell in a Very Small Place:* "The opposing forces in the battle of Dien Bien Phu were finally led by a French lieutenant colonel who, in effect, commanded a whole division, and by a Vietnamese history professor who, in effect, commanded a whole army."

With Viet Minh control of Gabrielle, the enemy could now position his flak directly in the path of French aircraft attempting to land on the main airstrip. That ended the airstrip as a means of reinforcing the defenders. From this point, the French would have to drop by parachute everything required to keep the garrison fighting—reinforcements, food, ammunition, supplies, blood, and medicine. And as the area controlled by the French shrank and Viet Minh anti-aircraft fire became more proficient, aerial resupply became increasingly difficult. So serious did the problem become that Castries had to ask Bigeard to take out the Viet Minh's flak positions to the west of the airfield. In the early morning hours of March 28, Bigeard, a major commanding a battalion, orchestrated a combined-arms attack by the garrison's artillery, five of its elite battalions, and a portion of the garrison's small force of American Chaffee tanks. The attack caught the Communist infantry by surprise and smashed them. When it was over, the French had killed at least 350 Viet Minh and captured large amounts of weapons, including 20 mm antiaircraft guns. But despite that momentary victory, the French could not afford the losses. Cogny and his staff in Hanoi were refusing to feed the paratroop battalions at their disposal into Castries's diminishing ranks, while the airborne bureaucrats in Hanoi refused to allow anyone to jump into Dien Bien Phu who did not possess the mandatory five training jumps, despite a desperate situation and large numbers of volunteers willing to jump without training.

Langlais calculated that Giap's next target would be the small hills on the east bank of the Nam Yum. Thus the French made desperate attempts to strengthen the defenses of the strongpoints on Elaine and Dominique as well as to provide substantial numbers of paratroopers to buttress the units holding these key positions. In the early evening hours of March 30, the Viet Minh fired off another intensive artillery barrage. What the French termed "the fight for the five hills" had begun. Strongpoints Dominique 1 (D1) and D2 fell almost immediately to waves of Viet Minh infantry as the Algerians and mountain tribesmen collapsed. The paratroopers and French NCOs fought to the last and bought time for the other strongpoints on Dominique. It was now a matter of whether D3 could hold or not, because if Giap's troops captured the position, they would have a clear run into the unprotected heart of the Dien Bien fortress. While the Algerians on D3 were on the brink of collapse, the African gunners on the main artillery positions on the other side of the Nam Yum depressed their guns and at almost point-blank range, along with the garrison's quad-fifties, blasted the attacking Viet Minh.

The fight for the positions on Elaine was just as fierce: waves of Viet Minh infantry seized E1 as well as a portion of E2. French counterattacks supported by the Chaffees drove the Viet Minh back from the summit of E2, but E1 remained in Giap's hands the following morning. Unwilling to allow the Viet Minh to hold on to that position, Langlais ordered a counterattack that afternoon. The French retook what had been strongpoint D2, while Vietnamese paratroopers retook E1. Nevertheless, both positions were unrecognizable, with hundreds of the dead from both sides already moldering in the hot sun and humidity. Despite the French success, the cost of the two days of fighting had been extraordinarily heavy: nearly 20 percent of the garrison dead, wounded, or missing.

Langlais and Castries had mounted the counterattacks in the belief that the 2nd Battalion of the 1st Parachute Regiment would jump into Dien Bien Phu that night. It did not. Cogny had social engagements, and no one in his headquarters would make the decision to authorize a night drop of the whole battalion. On succeeding days, Cogny would refuse to authorize major drops into the garrison; yet at the same time, he continued to mount major operations around the Red River Delta. For his part, Navarre failed to intervene in the tactical decision making of his subordinate. In effect, the French high command had settled the garrison's fate. The battle now quieted down as the Viet Minh rebuilt their forces after the terrible losses they had suffered during the last two weeks of March. Nevertheless, Giap continued to nibble away at French positions. Thus the engagement turned into a battle of attrition, one the French had no hope of winning, especially considering Hanoi's unwillingness to allow significant reinforcements to jump into the valley. Despite the desperate situation, the commander of the airborne replacement force, Colonel Henri Sauvagnac, continued to demand that paratroopers drop into properly marked jump zones and that only those who had passed the full curriculum of jump qualifications be allowed to parachute into Dien Bien Phu.

By mid-April, the conditions under which the defenders and the Viet Minh were fighting had reached a point that resembled the worst one can imagine, a landscape of horror Hieronymus Bosch might have painted. The monsoon rains had turned everything into a morass of mud in which the disintegrating, maggot-infested dead of past battles were exposed; within a matter of hours, the recent killed were already rotting; the living had to relieve themselves in flooded trenches, the whole permeated by the combined stench of the smells of death and a sea of floating sewerage. The garrison's wounded suffered immensely in the fetid bunkers of what was supposed to be a hospital, while many lay in the open, awaiting death. Food was out of

French paratrooper reinforcements arrive   *Associated Press*

cans; by this point Viet Minh artillery had taken out the water puri-
fication plants, so troops had to drink water drawn from the fetid and
disease-ridden Nam Yum.

The French Defeat

Considering the heavy losses the Viet Minh had suffered, Giap pulled
back to a strategy of asphyxiation. As he noted after the battle, his approach aimed at "advanc[ing] our attack and encirclement lines . . . ;
progressively tighten[ing] our stranglehold so as to completely intercept reinforcements and supplies . . . utilizing trenches that have been
driven forward until they touch the enemy lines, the tactic of gnaw-
ing away at the enemy piecemeal." Yet Viet Minh losses continued to
mount, while French forces, including the Vietnamese paratroopers,
hung on. However, the unwillingness of Cogny to commit substantial reinforcements told against the French chances to hold out. Significantly, while French fighters and bombers inflicted serious losses
on the Viet Minh, weather and distance from Hanoi prevented the
kind of airpower success the French had expected initially.

By April 21, the Viet Minh had taken much of Huguette and the
northern portion of the airfield. With fewer paratroopers and legionnaires available, French counterattacks became less effective. The battle had by now settled into death by a thousand cuts. But the Viet
Minh suffered as heavily as the French. By April 24, Giap's soldiers
had taken the last of the Huguettes; the fighting over what a French
officer had derisively called a bunch of rice fields had cost the Viet
Minh three regiments and the French five hundred soldiers. But the
Viet Minh could afford those losses; the French could not. Nevertheless, dangerous signs of wavering from the revolutionary path were
appearing. As Giap later noted, "Our forces had not been able to avoid
decimation, which requires rapid reorganization and reinforcement. . . . Among our cadres and combatants there appear[ed] negative *rightist* tendencies, whose manifestations [were] the fear of having
many killed, the fear of suffering casualties, of facing up to fatigue,
difficulties and privations. . . ."

The end came over the first week of May. A series of Viet Minh attacks steadily consumed the ground the French held; desperate efforts to fend off the Viet Minh led the surviving artillery to fire its supply of shells at a rate that rapidly used up ammunition reserves; and the effect of masses of Viet Minh antiaircraft fire made it increasingly difficult for resupply aircraft to drop their loads within areas that the garrison's soldiers could reach. On the night of May 6, the Viet Minh blew up a massive mine under Elaine 2, which eliminated that position. The survivors held out until morning, when they were overwhelmed. Over the course of May 7, the remains of the garrison slowly disintegrated under the pressure of constant Viet Minh attacks. At 5:30 P.M., the radio operator in Castries's headquarters signed off. It was over.

While the French were going down to defeat, the administration of Dwight Eisenhower had wrung its hands as it attempted to decide what to do. The U.S. secretary of state, John Foster Dulles, and the chairman of the Joint Chiefs of Staff, Admiral Arthur Radford, had strongly favored intervention via American airpower. On the other hand, two of the leading American paratrooper generals of World War II, General Matthew Ridgway, now army chief of staff, and Lieutenant General James Gavin, both argued forcefully against the commitment of American airpower. They maintained that once in the war, the United States would find itself in an open-ended commitment. In their view, Vietnam would not be worth the resources that a war in that country would entail. In the end, Eisenhower agreed with them, and the United States refused to support the French struggle against Vietnamese nationalism, even if it was cloaked in Communism.

CONCLUSION

The defeat of French forces at Dien Bien Phu led to the fall of the government in Paris. A new government under Pierre Mendès-France then agreed to a settlement that divided Vietnam in half, with the Viet Minh to control the north and a separate government in the south. The latter soon came under the control of Ngo Dinh Diem, who although a committed nationalist was also strongly anti-Communist.

While the French quickly left Vietnam, the Americans just as quickly moved in to support what lower-ranking officials and military officers believed to be a crucial strategic element in preventing Southeast Asia from collapsing like a string of dominoes. Yet the Viet Minh's victory over the French at Dien Bien Phu was clearly the catalyst for the independence of not only the Communist regime in the north, but the regime in the south as well. In the broader sense, it marked the rise of a new kind of conflict and a new mode of warfare and balance of power that would reverberate into the twenty-first century.

By refusing to commit its forces to prevent a French defeat at the hands of the Vietnamese, the Eisenhower administration had determined that the defense of Vietnam did not merit the cost in American lives or treasure. Ten years later, another American regime calculated otherwise, despite what its strategic war games suggested. In 1964, Charles de Gaulle, recognizing that the administration of Lyndon Johnson was hell-bent on intervening in South Vietnam to crush an increasingly successful insurgency, dispatched to the Pentagon the French government's top-secret after-action report on the Dien Bien Phu defeat, its causes, the French mistakes, and the lessons learned. Not even bothering to translate the report into English, the bureaucrats in the U.S. Department of Defense sent the report over to the classified library at the National War College, where it remains to this day.

Perhaps even more depressing is the fact that after the debacle of 1972–1975, the American military decided that it was no longer worth studying insurgencies, including America's Vietnam War, in its staff and war colleges. Thus, having prepared almost exclusively to fight a conventional war, the American military in the "post-conflict" phase of Operation Iraqi Freedom managed to repeat not only virtually every mistake the French had made in Vietnam, but every mistake the United States had made as well. It was as if the two wars in Vietnam had never occurred. As that great American philosopher Yogi Berra once noted, it was "déjà vu all over again," but the price that was paid was in the lives of young Americans.

OBJECTIVE PEACH

The Drive for Baghdad

2003

CHINESE PREMIER ZHOU ENLAI, WHEN ASKED WHAT HE THOUGHT about the French Revolution, famously replied, "It is too soon to tell." Much the same can be said about the American invasion of Iraq almost a decade ago. The immediate effects are clear to see and are evident whenever one takes a moment to look at the news. As this book is being written, the Middle East is in upheaval, in a process of political destruction and rebuilding that will likely persist for multiple generations. Historians will surely argue for a century or more the exact impact the American invasion of Iraq had on the current upheavals, tentatively named "the Arab Spring." That it had an impact, probably as a catalyst, is already certain.

At a minimum, a dictator as brutal as Stalin or Hitler, even if on a reduced scale, was removed from power, and the first Arab democracy was given an opportunity to flourish. However, the jury remains out as to whether this democratic experiment will succeed. Without question, the invasion also destroyed the uneasy balance of power between Iraq and Iran that settled upon the region in the wake of their almost decade-long conflict in the 1980s. There is little doubt that without a

Sunni-led Iraqi military as a counterweight in the region, Iran appears emboldened to take steps toward securing its own regional hegemony. Still, an aggressive, and possibly soon to be nuclear-armed, Iran is creating significant turmoil already. As it continues to undermine shaky regional governments, violence is certain to rise. Moreover, the impact of fighting, instability, and institutional collapse in an area from which the world draws a significant percentage of its crucial energy supplies does not bode well for global economic or military security.

Thus, although the long-range impact of the American invasion remains unknowable, certain trend lines have already developed. The invasion of Iraq is even now demonstrating the hallmarks of a battle that will one day be seen as a tipping point in history. Whether it will represent the high-water mark of American power in what historians have already tag-lined as "the American Century" or an opportunity for the United States to recast its role in a rapidly changing global environment will be for others to judge. That the invasion has set the world on a new and radically altered course is as certain as the long-term effects of any of the other battles discussed in this book.

IN THE WAKE of the 9/11 attacks, American policy makers along with a small coalition of allies, decided that Saddam Hussein presented too great a threat to regional and global stability to remain in power. Whether the decision to invade Iraq was a correct one remains an emotionally charged and divisive issue. Little is gained by rehashing those debates here. Rather, it is the impact of that decision that concerns us.

Even as a separate war in Afghanistan was in its second year, the American military began rapidly concentrating significant power in the Gulf region. Despite the fact that the attack had much larger aims than the 1991 war with Iraq (Desert Storm), only a fraction of the force employed in that earlier fight was sent to the Gulf. Later, as the insurgency in Iraq took hold and spread, this lack of "boots on the ground" would appear to be one of the great mistakes of the war. For the purposes of defeating the Iraqi army and destroying the elite Republican Guard, however, it was sufficient. This was due mainly to

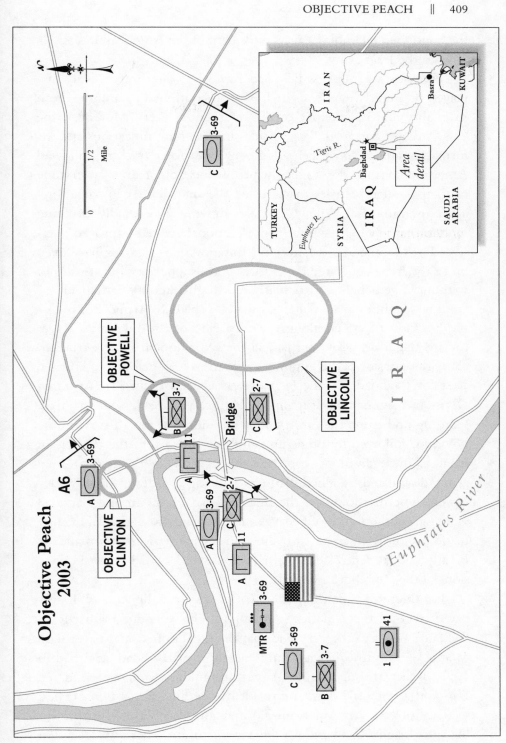

Objective Peach
2003

the continued technological advancement of the American forces relative to the Iraqi army.

Precision weapons, which Americans had seen impressively displayed on nightly newscasts in 1991, had continued to improve both in quality and in quantity in the intervening years. Moreover, the U.S. military had made large strides in the communications and information arenas. Such technologies as "blue force tracking" allowed American commanders to see the precise location of almost every one of their combat vehicles that crossed the Iraqi border in something approximating real time. On a fast-moving and rapidly evolving modern battlefield, this dominant situational awareness proved decisive. The so-called Revolution in Military Affairs may not have lived up to the hype generated by its most vocal supporters, but it was not without huge benefits, particularly on a high-intensity battlefield.

The Coalition plan of attack called for the U.S. Army's 3rd Infantry Division to attack along the west side of the Euphrates River toward Baghdad, while the 1st Marine Expeditionary Force attacked along the east side of the Euphrates toward Al Kut, before it too turned west for Baghdad. To the far east was Great Britain's 1st Armored Division, assigned to capture and hold the Basra area in southern Iraq. Coming up behind the 3rd Infantry Division was the 101st Airborne Division, followed by other units as they rolled into the theater. In front of these divisions stood several divisions of the regular Iraqi army, designated by allied planners as being of inferior quality. Between these divisions and the final defensive lines around Baghdad were tens of thousands of Fedayeen irregulars, whose suicidal bravery made a significant impact on the minds of American commanders. Finally, Saddam entrusted the final defense of Baghdad to the six divisions of the Republican Guard.

For the most part, the Iraqi defenses were misaligned and ill prepared to resist the American onslaught. This was due primarily to Saddam's belief to the very end that the Coalition would never dare to attack—and if it did, it would halt short of Baghdad, as it had in 1991. In fact, throughout the American buildup, Saddam considered Iran and a potential domestic revolt by the Shia as his two greatest security threats. An American-led invasion placed a distant third in his calculations. Saddam also fell victim to an American deception plan that convinced him the main Coalition attack would come from Jordan and not Kuwait. Owing to this erroneous belief, Saddam ordered the movement of several Republican Guard divisions to the west side of Baghdad, a decision that had a grievous effect on his defense. He never accepted that the main American attack would come from the southern desert until the 3rd Infantry Division began tearing apart his much vaunted Republican Guard divisions.

ON MARCH 19, 2003, the 3rd Infantry Division (3ID) blasted across the Iraq–Kuwait border. Initially, only the Iraqi 11th Infantry Division stood in its way, but it soon dissolved under 3ID's first hammer blows. As the American forces raced across the Iraqi desert, they expected a joyous welcome from the majority population in the Shia-dominated south. There was no love lost between the Shia and the Sunni-dominated Saddam government. In fact, in the wake of the 1991 war the Shia had revolted. That revolt came within a hairbreadth of toppling the regime and was put down only by mass slaughter. Saddam's Republican Guards killed an estimated one hundred thousand Shia as they battled to retake the region. Nevertheless, American hopes of Shia welcoming parades and celebrations in honor of their deliverers were soon quashed. Having endured years of persecution, the Shia were a defeated people. They simply were not going to take overt steps until they were absolutely sure Saddam was dead.

As the lead elements of 3ID entered the city of Samawah, revelers were nowhere in sight. Instead the Americans were set upon by hundreds and later thousands of Fedayeen irregulars. These troops were not well trained, were poorly led, and were usually equipped only with light arms. However, they were fanatically loyal to the regime and possessed suicidal courage. Over the succeeding days, 3ID soldiers were awed and, in the early going, a bit unnerved by the Fedayeen's willingness to press assaults through murderous American fire. Some attacks were broken up only at the edges of the American line, while one brigade commander was even forced to shoot a Fedayeen who had climbed aboard his tank. In the end, though, it was all in vain. Fedayeen fanaticism proved inferior to walls of armor belching out thousands of rounds a minute. The Fedayeen put a scare into some senior leaders and caught the attention of the press, but after the initial contacts they rarely made an impression on the 3ID soldiers. The Fedayeen would come out en masse again at Najaf and Karbala and to contest the final "Thunder Runs" into Baghdad itself. The fighting was always fierce, but the result was the same. Thousands of Fedayeen were sacrificed in futile attempts to slow the pace of 3ID's advance.

Outside of Najaf, however, 3ID was halted. This was mostly a result of massive sandstorms and the fact that the armored formations had outrun their logistics. A few days were needed to rest, rearm, and refuel before the next push. However, by now the Fedayeen had captured the public's imagination, and the media presented the halt to the American people as a natural result of the unexpectedly high levels of Iraqi resistance. An air of pessimism was pervasive everywhere except among the American combat leaders, who were convinced they were on the edge of victory. As the commander of 3ID's 2nd Brigade Combat Team (2BCT), Colonel David Perkins, said when asked about the Fedayeen, "I did not expect this many of them, but all that means is that I have to use more ammunition . . . and I have plenty of that." When told that *Time* magazine was planning a cover story titled "Why Are We Losing?" he was reported to have said: "Today my brigade leaves Najaf and heads north. Tomorrow we rest, rearm and refuel. The next day I attack to annihilate the Medina Division. The day after that I will be in Baghdad." But before Perkins could lead his 2BCT into Baghdad, 3ID's 1st Brigade Combat Team (1BCT), commanded by Colonel William Grimsley, would have to secure the narrow Karbala Gap and seize a crossing on the Euphrates River.

THE KARBALA GAP was the one place in Iraq the soldiers of the 3rd Infantry Division feared. It was the narrowest choke point along their route from Kuwait to Baghdad, and everyone from private to general was sure that this was where Saddam would hit them with chemical weapons. However, by early morning on April 1, Grimsley's 1BCT had moved unmolested through the gap and was consolidating on the far side. But the tedious passage coupled with the incredible tension of expecting at any moment to be hit by chemical weapons left everyone exhausted and looking forward to a planned twelve-hour rest before

Third Infantry Division tanks on the move to Baghdad   *Military History Institute*

the lunge for the critical Euphrates bridges that would open the door to Baghdad.

Determined to take advantage of the rapid advance through the Karbala Gap, the division commander, General Buff Blount, was already forming new plans. He considered the lack of Iraqi resistance in the Karbala Gap to be evidence that the Americans had rocked the Iraqis back on their heels and was not inclined to give the enemy time to recover. He called Grimsley and ordered him to have his brigade moving forward before noon. Despite the troops' exhaustion, Grimsley had Lieutenant Colonel Rock Marcone's 3-69 Armored Battalion refueled and roaring toward the Euphrates bridge—Objective Peach—by 11:00 A.M.

Objective Peach (the al-Qaʿid Bridge) was a dual-span bridge over the Euphrates River and the final obstacle before Baghdad. It presented the last chance the Iraqis would have to slow the American onslaught. The Iraqi II Republican Corps commander, Lieutenant General Raad Hamdani, had long recognized the importance of the bridge, which he termed "the Iraqi Remagen." Almost two weeks before, he had put a company on the bridge under the command of one of his best junior officers and ordered him to blow up the bridge if he even suspected the Americans were approaching. A week later, he sent his chief of staff to the bridge to make sure the defenses were ready and the demolitions were in place. However, this officer took it upon himself to countermand Hamdani's order, telling the bridge commander that Saddam had ordered that no bridges be destroyed and that if he blew up this bridge, Hamdani would be executed. Though one span of the bridge was damaged in an unexplained explosion, the officer charged with the duty of blowing up the bridge refused to carry out Hamdani's orders as 3ID tanks approached. Hamdani later said, "Both men acted out of personal loyalty to me, but it was a big mistake. It cost us the war."

Knowing the bridge was still standing, but not for how long, Rock Marcone's combat-tested 3-69 Armored Battalion set a furious pace as it led the 1BCT's drive to Peach. Along the way, Marcone's troops met sporadic resistance, which only two weeks earlier would have caused the attacking columns to deploy and take precious time developing the situation. But something had happened to Marcone and the rest of the 3ID soldiers in the two weeks since invading Iraq—they had become veterans.

Now, encountering the enemy on the line of march was almost routine. Only the most determined resistance called for a halt. For Marcone's veterans, enemy contacts merited only a quick radio report as his armored battalion destroyed everything it encountered and continued its advance. Radio traffic became a litany of targets spotted, engaged, and destroyed. Only at one point did the enemy make a serious stand, when two hundred Iraqis fired from behind fortified positions into the flanks of the onrushing armored column. Marcone's Alpha Company veered out of the advancing column and annihilated the position, then rejoined the battalion fifteen minutes later. What Marcone's troops were reporting as light and sporadic contact was actually the entire 14th Brigade of the Republican Guard's Medina Division being ground out of existence. One Iraqi general later said, with this attack in mind, "The American soldiers are very disciplined. They fight like robots and engage and kill everything on the battlefield. The Americans did not even seem to react to our defensive plans. They simply fought their way through anything that stood in their path."

Worried about reports that the Americans were through the Karbala Gap and that his front was collapsing, Hamdani rushed to the Medina Division's headquarters north of Karbala. While being briefed by the Medina Division's commander, Hamdani proudly watched the 1st Regiment of the 14th Brigade form up to launch a counterattack. A regiment in attack formation, however, was a lucrative and rarely found target, and U.S. sensors spotted it almost immediately after it formed. Before the regiment could move forward, American jets pounced. As Hamdani looked on, the regiment was annihilated in an instant of blast and flame.

Shortly after 1:00 P.M., Hamdani was called back to Baghdad for the most incredible meeting of the war. All he could do for the Medina's commander was to tell him to hold on and that he would send whatever reinforcements were available. It was a comment of despair, because by that time Marcone's leading tanks had already covered half the distance from Karbala to Objective Peach and the Medina's 14th Brigade no longer existed.

When Marcone's troops were only a few miles from the bridge, Grimsley ordered the execution of a sustained multibattery artillery barrage, followed by a series of pinpoint joint direct attack munition (JDAM) strikes on each of the buildings in the bridge's immediate vicinity, designed to wipe out any local defenders. If there was an Iraqi sitting on the other side ready to push a plunger and blow the bridge as American tanks began crossing, Grimsley wanted him dead. Just as

Objective Peach
Military History Institute

the soldiers of the 3-69 Armored Battalion closed on the bridge, the far side erupted into balls of dust and flame. Despite the intensity of this preemptive bombardment, Marcone could not be sure that the bridge would not blow up as soon as he started crossing. He therefore decided to take the bridge with a river assault.

He ordered Captain Todd Kelly's C/2-7 infantry company to move to the edge of the Euphrates and provide covering fire for the engineers who would assault the bridge. At the same time, Captain Dan Hibner had a company of engineers three hundred yards behind Kelly's line, preparing for the most audacious action of the war: a daylight river assault in small rubber boats.

Hibner originally planned a four-boat assault, but it would be some time before his men could muscle all the boats forward. With Iraqi artillery already beginning to fall and fearing the Iraqis might blow the bridge at any moment, Hibner ordered the first boat to cross the river. As one sergeant remembered, "We started paddling as fast as we could, but the infantry guys with us did not know how to do it. We were out in the open, being shot at in a paddle boat that had a big leak, and had to stop to show the infantry how to paddle. We were also slowly drifting directly towards the building we were receiving fire from. Of course everyone was very pissed off."

Marcone had every weapon he could bring to bear plastering the buildings on the far side of the river to give the men in the boats some protection. After the war, he said, "Putting those guys in boats was the hardest thing I ever did. It really bothered me because I expected we might lose a lot of them. I just didn't want to have any of my soldiers' bodies in the Euphrates." At the time, he did not know that every soldier at the river's edge volunteered to go over in the first boat and the squad selected considered itself lucky.

By the time the first boat was halfway across, Hibner had his second boat in the water. After what seemed to Hibner an interminably long time, both boats made it across and began expanding their toehold at the base of the bridge. Job one, cutting the wires, fell to the engineers, while the infantry began clearing Iraqis out of nearby buildings. By the time Hibner crossed in the third boat, his men were already hard at work.

Hibner started to direct the wire-cutting activities and ordered

Marcone's armored battalion in the assault   *Military History Institute*

the exposed wires shunted off so that stray radio waves could not set off the explosives. He also let the infantry continue clearing the nearby buildings, until they stumbled on a manned and intact bunker complex, at which point he ordered them to pull back and set up defensive positions. Hibner knew he did not have enough men to take on bunkers and wanted his men ready to repel a counterattack. Once the position was secure, and he was sure every wire leading to the bridge had been cut, Hibner called Marcone, who immediately sent his tanks across. Hibner, later awarded the Silver Star for leading this action, said, "It was a good feeling to hear the rumbling of the tanks on the bridge. It was much to our joy, as it meant the demise of the Iraqis who were still shooting at us."

Captain Jared Robbins led his C/3-69 armored company across the bridge and secured the far side. As soon as that was done, Captain Dave Benton, commanding the B/3-7 infantry, led his company through Robbins's troops and began making his way through the smoke and debris toward the canal bridge on the far side of the objective area. His mission was to occupy a position where he could cover the bridge with fire and not allow the Iraqis to cross it. Navigating proved tricky, and it took Benton some time to find a narrow dirt road on which his Bradley Fighting Vehicles could move. Finding the road too restricted for tanks, Benton left his tank platoon in an over-watch position on a hill and went forward with his Bradleys.

Two hundred yards past the bridge, Benton's Bradley ran into a dug-in Iraqi BMP (a Soviet-made armored personnel carrier) that he had failed to see in the smoke. Immediately backing up fifty meters, Benton fired high-explosive 25 mm rounds into it until the turret blew off. His vehicle was then hit by a missile from a second BMP, which he also quickly dispatched with 25 mm fire. By this time, Benton was receiving heavy fire from entrenched Iraqis, and his strung-out unit could not find enough maneuver room to add their additional firepower to the growing fight. With no other choice, Benton ordered his infantry out of the Bradleys and told them to start clearing the enemy entrenchments. As the infantry assault began, Benton continued to attack down the road with his Bradley. He destroyed four more BMPs before his 25 mm gun malfunctioned. Still, Benton continued to move forward until he found a spot where he could pull over and let the other Bradleys swing past him and move toward the canal bridge. They destroyed two more BMPs as they advanced.

Within moments, Benton's Bradleys dominated the objective, and he sensed the fight had gone out of the remaining Iraqis. Afterward, Benton said he could not understand their fighting methods. "They really didn't establish good engagement areas, and as far as I could see, the infantry stayed in their holes. As my infantry would go through, they would throw grenades in and kill five or ten of them and then spray the hole to make sure there were no survivors to surprise them as they moved to the next hole. . . . They should have surrendered." Benton's company had run into the reconnaissance company from the Medina's 10th Brigade. It was an indication that the rest of the brigade could not be far behind.

By 5:00 P.M., Marcone had his entire 3-69 Armored Battalion across the bridge and in defensive positions. They met intermittent resistance, but before dark Marcone had five companies of mixed armor and infantry tied into a single defensive front, waiting for an expected major Iraqi counterattack. However, for the next several hours the Iraqis made only sporadic platoon- and company-sized attacks on the bridgehead. Marcone assumed they were incapable of mounting any major threat. He was wrong. The Iraqi attacks were merely the probes designed to find weak points in his line. Even as the Americans repelled every assault, the Iraqi 10th Armored Brigade was forming up for the most powerful Iraqi counterattack of the war.

While Marcone's men fought their way to and across Objective Peach, Hamdani returned to Baghdad to meet with Saddam's son Qusay, along with the minister of defense and other senior military commanders. It was to be one of the more bizarre meetings in the history of a regime that had a penchant for holding such meetings. As Hamdani relates:

> The Minister of Defense had a message from Saddam. The message was an order for immediate execution. He said that Saddam would not be able to meet during the next two days, but that he [Qusay] had just met with Saddam and the plan was explained to him. The minister went on to explain that what had happened over the last two weeks was a "strategic" trick by the Americans. He told us American forces were going to come from the direc-

Captain Dan Hibner leads river assault   *Military History Institute*

tion of Jordan, through Al Ramadi, and into northern Baghdad. Emergency procedures were to go into effect at 0500 the next morning. The Al Nida was supposed to shift to the northwest of Baghdad under the Republican Guard I Corps. Minefields were to be immediately established to the west and northwest of Baghdad. The talk of establishing minefields made me think that they thought we were fighting Iran again or something.

At this point, Hamdani strenuously objected, telling them that they were wrong and that he was facing the main American attack and the attack out of Jordan was the trick. The minister of defense replied that he was only the messenger and that discussions were of no further use since Saddam had spoken. Qusay at least allowed Hamdani to explain his view of the situation:

> I said that a minor attack was moving up the Tigris along the line from An Nasiriyah to Al Kut [the U.S. Marines 1st Regimental Combat Team]. This attack was actually somewhat of a surprise to me given the tight roads and poor armor terrain in the area. Another minor attack was pushing up the middle ground from As Samawah to Ad Diwaniyah. However, the main attack was on the west side of the Euphrates River through Karbala and into the southwest side of Baghdad. The U.S. 4th Infantry Division would soon join in the main thrust. I said that the Americans would own Karbala by that night, and they would move quickly to take the bridge [Objective Peach].

After Hamdani finished his presentation, Qusay turned back to the minister of defense and Republican Guard chief of staff to ask for their opinions. The former could suggest only that whether Hamdani was right or wrong, the plans should still be carried out as President Hussein had ordered. According to Hamdani:

> He said that we should execute the plan as Saddam directed. The Republican Guard chief of staff at first did not answer either way. He repeated over and over, "We must fight." The regular army

chief of staff said that he did not agree with my theory and that Saddam was right. He said, "We must all be 100 percent with Saddam." The Republican Guard chief of staff then said that I had never executed the plan and that I moved forces without permission. He said that I was to blame for all these casualties.

Qusay remained unsure of what to do but finally ordered that the Al Nida Republican Guard Division and the 16th Regular Army Division move to support the Republican Guard I Corps, which was tasked to defend Iraq from the supposed American thrust coming from northern Jordan. According to Hamdani, "He also directed a withdrawal from Karbala and that all units move to the east side of the Euphrates."

Hamdani, realizing the argument was lost, tried to salvage something and asked for permission to destroy the strategic al-Qa`id Bridge on the Euphrates (Objective Peach). He received Qusay's permission and then went to talk privately to the chief of staff. Hamdani was speaking to him for only a moment when he received a call informing him that the al-Qa`id Bridge had fallen. As he recalls, the officer reporting indicated that columns of enemy armor were moving from Jaraf al-Sakhr toward the bridge. "I gave the report to those present, but they did not believe it." After the war, he wrote about the moment:

They all wanted me to change my comment. They now saw me as their "adversary." I could not stay for one more second. To the president's son I said, "Sir, the disastrous fate of Baghdad will happen within the next forty-eight hours. I hope to be wrong in the opinion that we have chosen to follow the wrong decision. Please allow me to return to my headquarters." He dropped his head down for a moment, and then he raised it so he was looking at me with a sad expression, or it was a strange expression I couldn't read, and he said, "As you wish. Go ahead." I said my good-byes to him and left sadly. I looked at my watch, which told me it was 1540, and I did not know that I had just seen Qusay for the last time.

Hamdani later commented on the dismal scene, saying, "It was the kind of argument that I imagine took place in Hitler's bunker in Berlin. Were all these men on drugs?" In a mood of utter disbelief, he left the meeting to go back to the real fight, while the generals, Saddam, and his sons dealt with their "imaginary universe."

HAMDANI RETURNED to the front to discover that the bridge was still standing and that the Americans were across the Euphrates in strength. He ordered limited counterattacks with available troops and newly arriving special forces regiments. At the same time, he sent for the Medina Division's 10th Armored Brigade and other forces from the recently arrived Nebuchadnezzar Division, intending to build a new defensive line north of the American bridgehead. Before he could put those orders into effect, the Republican Guard chief of staff arrived and refused to entertain any thoughts of building a new defensive line. He emphatically demanded Hamdani order a major counterattack to retake the bridge, and Hamdani had no choice but to oblige.

By 3:00 A.M., Hamdani had assembled a substantial force around the 10th Armored Brigade, and he ordered the advance on the bridge.

> The attack moved forward slowly because we did not have nightvision. . . . The Medina Division's commander and I followed the 10th Armored Brigade with our communications groups. . . . At 0200 American jets attacked our force as we moved down the road. We were hit by many missiles. Most of the Medina Division's staff were killed. My corps communications staff was also killed. When we reached the area near the bridge where the special forces battalion had set up a headquarters, we immediately came under heavy fire. Based on the volume of fire, I estimated at least sixty armored vehicles.

At this point, Hamdani knew all was lost. But because he was being pushed by his superiors in Baghdad, he ordered one final assault. He personally briefed the commander of the armored battalion that would make the final push.

The tank battalion commander was astounded when I told him his mission and how dangerous it was. He saluted me and said, "I am a martyr and I promise I will not return without accomplishing my mission." Within a half hour, he fell as a martyr.

By daybreak, Hamdani had managed to get several hundred special forces soldiers within a few hundred yards of the bridge. They had some trucks filled with explosives that were to join them in a final rush and then be exploded on the bridge. Just as Hamdani was about to give the order for a final suicidal charge, disaster struck.

At that moment, a huge number of American aircraft and combat helicopters launched a series of intense attacks. When they were done, I did not have a single tank or other transport left to me. They were so accurate. I could not believe how they hit targets. All around me were columns of smoke from burning vehicles. At this point, I lost hope and ordered a withdrawal.

For Marcone's men, the Iraqi counterattack was a shock. After hours of fighting off small, hastily gathered bands, they assumed that this was the best the Iraqis could do. However, Marcone had not left much to chance. After crossing the bridge, he had coordinated a linear artillery target area and a close air support kill-box along what he considered the most likely avenue of approach for an Iraqi counterattack. He guessed right. When the counterattack came, the 10th Brigade drove right through both the preplanned artillery coordinates and the kill-box. They met a storm of steel.

Bravely, the battered survivors continued to come on, directly into Marcone's tankers. First Lieutenant Jim Temple's platoon story will have to suffice to tell what twenty-two other platoons also faced that night:

At three o'clock in the morning, we noticed another big push. This time, they were definitely using modern tactics. They were using three- to five-second rushes and low crawls. We thought this must be something a little bigger than the militia or Fedayeen coming at us. More trucks started coming at us. We had several trucks with crew-served weapons in the back. Then came the big-money targets.

At the time, there was no illumination. We thought these were BMPs, but were not sure. When we fired them up, we fired sabot at first, and that had negative effect. It looked like it just went right through them. So we broke out the HE [high explosive], and we fired at approximately three tanks. I didn't know it at the time, but later we discovered we killed two with one shot. They were in a line and the round went through both and blew their turrets right off. They went a good three hundred meters in the air. In fact, from my position almost a kilometer down the road, we had shrapnel coming down on us.

We continued to fight. Steel 6 [Marcone] continued to direct air support for us. You could tell there was mass confusion. People were falling out of vehicles. They were running back and forth. We just kept raining fire on them until the column stopped.

At daylight we drove up the road. There were body parts all over the place and bodies everywhere, a sea of body parts. We did a lot of damage to them. A lot of hurt.

The fight for Objective Peach was over. Colonel Marcone's 3–69 Armored Battalion had first ground the 14th Brigade out of existence in getting to Peach and then had annihilated the 10th Armored Brigade when they tried to take it back. By morning, Marcone's supporting artillery was out of ammunition and his own vehicles had used up their 25 mm HE and most of their machine-gun ammunition. Marcone later said, "If they'd thrown another brigade at us, we would have gone zero on ammo and it would have been hand-to-hand for the bridge." The Iraqis had attacked bravely and at times ferociously, but they were nowhere near a match for what they ran into. In an interview long after the war, Marcone recalled:

The way they attacked unnerved me. They kept coming, rolling over their own dead. They should have learned. Fighting for us was easy. Killing at close range, though, is very hard and unforgettable. I am still dealing with having to kill so many people. Destroying the 10th Brigade still bothers me.

After the 10th Brigade's counterattack was smashed, Grimsley called Perkins and told him to take his brigade through. Soon afterward, Perkins's 2BCT pushed through Marcone's exhausted troops and rushed for Baghdad. Thrown off balance, the Iraqis were never again able to offer coherent resistance. Individual units still often fought hard, but 3ID had little problem sweeping resistance aside, and seventy-two hours after Peach was declared secured, Perkins was leading his brigade on the first of two "Thunder Runs" that collapsed Saddam's murderous regime.

ACKNOWLEDGMENTS

NO BOOK IS EVER PUBLISHED WITHOUT A STRONG SUPPORTING CAST who are willing to take up the slack as the authors lock themselves to their desk and begin writing. In this regard, both of us are blessed to have the strong and loving support of our wives, who were not only a source of constant encouragement, but also invaluable as early readers of the original manuscript. It is difficult to see how this book could have been finished without their willingness to take on more of the daily burdens. Thank you.

Professionally, we would first like to thank our agent, Eric Lupfer of William Morris Entertainment. Eric was the original inspiration for this book and an aggressive supporter throughout its production.

A particular note of thanks is due to our wonderful editor at Bantam, Tracy Devine. Throughout the entire process she has been at our side, motivating us, encouraging us, and most important making the final manuscript far superior to what we originally handed her. Tracy, you have been wonderful to work with, and whatever praise this book garners is mostly a reflection of your tireless work.

The authors also want to thank Wendy Palitz, who did a fantastic job coordinating and overseeing the photo selection and map production.

We owe thanks, too, to the superb team at Ballantine Bantam Dell, who championed *Moment of Battle* from the start: Libby McGuire, Jennifer Hershey, Kim Hovey, Jennifer Tung, Richard Callison, Kristin Fassler, Matt Schwartz, Quinne Rogers, and Susan Corcoran. Lisa Barnes and Steven Boriack have been tireless in their efforts on the publicity front, as have Angela Polidoro and Sarah Murphy in all matters of editorial coordination. The brilliant managing editorial and production staff took our raw materials and made magic. We are deeply grateful to associate copy chief Dennis Ambrose, managing editor Benjamin Dreyer, copyeditor Sona Vogel, production director Maggie Hart, senior designer Susan Turner, and art director Carlos Beltrán.

NOTES

INTRODUCTION

xii **"There are some battles"** Edward S. Creasy, *Fifteen Decisive Battles of the World: From Marathon to Waterloo* (New York: Harper & Brothers, 1851), p. viii.

MARATHON *Athens Saves Western Civilization*

4 **"Took a bow"** Herodotus, 5:105. There is no way to determine the veracity of this passage, but it is unlikely that the Zoroastrian Darius would have prayed to Zeus. Herodotus may have inserted the name of a god that would be familiar to his Greek audience.

5 **Many submitted and sent back earth and water** Herodotus, 7:133. The Athenians threw the envoys into a pit reserved for condemned prisoners. Sparta threw the envoys into a well and told them to gather earth and water from it.

7 **No doubt Hippias expected** Herodotus states that the prime reason the Persians selected Marathon was that it provided excellent ground for cavalry options. However, this is true of many possible landing sites on the Attic coast. Possibly Hippias used Marathon's horse-friendly location as part of the reasons he presented to the Persians for selecting the site.

7 **There was only one exit** Of course, Datis could have viewed this as an advantage, as once he had posted it with good troops, it would be impossible for the Athenians to march down on his landing site.

7 **Moreover, rather than seizing that exit** A number of historians have declared that given the Persians' overwhelming numbers, they landed near Eretria at the same time. They suggest that Datis waited at Marathon because he was expecting the other half of the army to finish off Eretria and join him for a joint march on Athens. If this is accepted, then the reason the Athenians attacked before the Spartans arrived is that after the fall of Eretria they had to attack before the forces joined up. I, however, discount this entire theory, as there is zero evidence for it and its originators never presented any analysis of why it was possible, other than they wished it that

way. (See F. Maurice, "The Campaign of Marathon," *Journal of Hellenic Studies* 52, part 1 [1932]: 13–24.) Besides, it breaks a tenet of warfare that no ancient general would violate without good cause: Never split your army in the presence of the enemy!

7 The most likely reason the Persians At the very least, the Marathoni (residents of the deme of Marathon) would probably have been in the area, and there were at least several hundred hoplites in this group. This would be one of the groups that Hippias would have expected to come over to him. To find them strongly outposted at the exit of the Marathon plain and unalterably opposed to his return better accounts for his pessimism on the beachhead than the reason Herodotus presents (a quaint story of him coughing up a tooth, which he uses to interpret a dream that predicts his failure to return to power).

7 At the same time the main Athenian army I will not enter into the debate on whether Herodotus meant Pheidippides and not Philippides. Athens employed a contingent of professional runners to deliver messages who were famous for their ability to run all day.

8 Taken as a whole The location of the Grove of Herakles was a matter of great dispute for a number of years but has now been definitively located by Eugene Vanderpool in the southeast corner of the Marathon plain. See Eugene Vanderpool, "The Deme of Marathon and the Herakleion," *American Journal of Archaeology* 70, no. 4 (October 1966): 319–23.

9 As far as he was concerned I am not going to discuss my reasons for disbelieving Herodotus's account of the command arrangements at Marathon, as I have argued my point in some detail in my earlier book *The First Clash* (New York: Bantam Books, 2011). Although this debate may be of some interest to professional historians, it is not crucial to this narration. For the purposes of this book, Callimachus commanded at Marathon, with Miltiades probably his second in command and a dominant personality on any war council.

9 Herodotus relates the dispute Herodotus, 6:109.

9 "It is now up to you" Ibid.

9 Miltiades accepted the extra command days Herodotus, 6:110.

10 They sent out spies There is a weak tradition that states that spies in the Persian camp (possibly Ionians) approached the Greek camp and signaled that the cavalry was away. Unfortunately, the source (*The Suda,* authored by Suidas) is a Byzantine text written over fifteen hundred years after the event, and it gives no reference for this information.

12 Today he would fight bravely There are several reconstructions of the order of the Greek line as it formed to meet the Persians. I have accepted that of Raubitschek, as it is listed by Sekunda (Marathon, 490 B.C.).

15 Callimachus, seeing the Persian left routed I imagine the pursuit could not have halted on its own and would require a signal. Bugle calls were common in Greek armies, and only a bugle could be heard over the din of the battle.

16 To keep the pressure on Philip Sabin has presented a new viewpoint for what ancient battle must have looked like at the level of the individual soldiers. I have found his reconstruction convincing and believe that the battle in the center probably played out in approximation to what Sabin suggests. Given the evidence presented by Herodotus, I do not believe his reconstruction of ancient battles applies to what took place on the flanks during the Battle of Marathon. See Philip Sabin, "The Face of Roman Battle," *Journal of Roman Studies* 90 (2000): 1–17.

18 **When the Athenian generals took stock** This probably counts only Athenian hoplites and excludes Plataean losses as well as slaves and light troops.

18 **With the victory won** This is the historical legend on which today's marathon races are based. Interestingly, Herodotus does not mention any messenger being sent from the battlefield and does not credit Pheidippides with the run. The first mention of any runner in the historical record is given by Plutarch approximately six hundred years later. It is not mentioned again for almost another hundred years, until Lucian. Plutarch says the runner's name was either Therisippos or Eukles, while Lucian credits Pheidippides and has him exclaim, "Joy, we win!" as he drops dead. As both writers are further away from the Battle of Marathon than present readers are from the Spanish Armada, some historians doubt the run ever took place. It is inconceivable, though, that after winning such a glorious victory, the Athenian hoplites would have failed to relay the news home. Back in Athens, the women, old men, and children were waiting for news. The Athenian commander surely did not keep them guessing one minute longer than necessary. So although the true details of the story are lost in the mists of time, I believe it can be judged a certainty that someone was sent with the message from Marathon. As Athens had a corps of professional runners for just this purpose, it is also likely that the messenger ran the entire distance. So there almost certainly was a first Marathon run, although it was a bit less than the modern 26.2 miles. Who made that run remains anyone's guess. However, by the time the Battle of Marathon was won, Pheidippides had had time to recover from his run to Sparta and back, and it is possible that he may have been given the honor of carrying the news of the great victory to a waiting Athens. As for whether the runner used his last gasp to announce a victory, we will never know for sure.

GAUGAMELA *Alexander Creates a New World*

22 **As one noted historian stated, Aeschylus** Norman Davies, *Europe: A History* (New York: HarperPerennial, 1998), p. 103.

22 **Aristotle wrote** Aristotle, *Politics* 7:7.

24 **In his *Laws*, Plato noted** Plato, *Laws* 3:695a–b.

25 **Alexander's word was law in Greece** The year before Alexander's departure for Asia, Athens and Thebes both revolted against his rule. Alexander, making an example of Thebes, reduced the city to ashes and distributed its territory to surrounding cities. The annihilation of once powerful Thebes sufficiently cowed Athens, which made a hasty peace.

25 In a hard-fought contest While leading a cavalry charge, Alexander was struck by an ax wielded by the Persian satrap Spithridates. Before he could dispatch Alexander with a second blow, Spithridates was killed by Cleitus, one of Alexander's Companions.

25 In his haste to reach safety Approximately three thousand talents (about half as much as the entire Athenian treasury at the start of the Peloponnesian War and enough to pay Alexander's army for about six months). An unreported but much larger amount was seized by Alexander's top general, Parmenio, at Damascus soon after the battle.

26 "The horses which were harnessed to the yoke" Diodorus, *World History,* 17:34.2–3.

26 "Around Darius' chariot lay his most famous generals" Quintus Curtius Rufus, *The History of Alexander* (New York: Penguin Classics, 1984), book III.

27 Here, a worried Darius This reconstruction is based on a carefully considered merging of the accounts presented by Arrian, Plutarch, Quintus Curtius Rufus, and Diodorus Siculus. See Quintus Curtius Rufus, *The History of Alexander;* Plutarch, *The Age of Alexander* (New York: Penguin Classics, 1973); Arrian, *The Campaigns of Alexander* (New York: Penguin Classics, 1971); and Diodorus Siculus, *Library of History,* vol. 8 (Cambridge, MA: Loeb Classical Library, 1963), book XVII. For an excellent essay examining the quality of the ancient sources in reference to the Battle of Gaugamela, see "Alexander the Great: The Good Sources" at www.livius .org/aj-al/alexander/alexander_z1b.html. It must be noted that reconstructing any ancient battle is fraught with difficulties; first and foremost among these is the limited number of primary sources. Many other historians have taken a hand in reconstructing the Battle of Gaugamela, with varying degrees of success. We have used the best of these to help frame our own interpretation. Although we believe our reconstruction is on the whole the most accurate to date, serious historians of the battle will want to review other interpretations of the evidence. They should take particular note of the following: E. W. Marsden, *The Campaign of Gaugamela* (Liverpool: Liverpool University Press, 1964); J.F.C. Fuller, *The Generalship of Alexander the Great* (Piscataway, NJ: Rutgers University Press, 1960); A. M. Devine, "Grand Tactics at Gaugamela," *Phoenix* 29, no. 4 (Winter 1975): 374–85; G. T. Griffith, "Alexander's Generalship at Gaugamela," *Journal of Hellenic Studies* 67 (1947): 77–89; and A. R. Burn, "The Generalship of Alexander," *Greece and Rome* 12, no. 2 (October 1965): 140–54.

28 Alexander had already rejected a suggestion We have to be very careful in making judgments on Parmenio's capacity and bravery. Later, in the invasion of the Persian Empire, Parmenio's son Philotas was condemned to death by the army for plotting against Alexander. Believing it dangerous to kill the son while leaving the father alive, particularly as the father commanded an army located close to his treasury and athwart his supply line, Alexander sent three assassins to stab Parmenio to death. Then, realizing there was no evidence of Parmenio's involvement in the plot, Alexander likely ordered history rewritten so as to minimize his contributions to Macedonian success. Although we include the story, as it admirably shows Alexander's frame of mind, there is good reason to have serious doubts as to whether Parmenio ever suggested a night attack.

28 Noting the bemusement of his officers Dio claims that Alexander spent most of the night in trepidation of what the next morn might bring and finally gave in to exhaustion just before morning. This is not corroborated in any other account and appears to be entirely out of keeping with what is known of Alexander's character.

28 Exactly how many of the enemy they saw No historian has presented a definitive answer for the number of Persians at Gaugamela, with estimates ranging as low as forty-eight thousand and as high as a million. Most historians now accept a number in the range of eighty thousand to one hundred thousand. Given the population and resources of the Persian Empire, I believe this estimate is much too low. There is good evidence that cohesive ancient empires could maintain about 2 percent of their population under arms for indefinite periods and could mobilize much more in an emergency. And if ever the Persian Empire faced a true emergency, this was it. Moreover, given the vast hordes of bullion Alexander later found in Susa, Persepolis, and Babylon, the empire was far from constrained financially and could afford to hire every available fighting man. Even if we lowball the population at forty million, King Darius could easily muster, arm, and pay for four hundred thousand men (a mere 1 percent of its population). Of course, a substantial number of them would be needed for other duties (manning garrisons, guarding the borders). And although the nearby Royal Road and the recently harvested Tigris-Euphrates grain crop greatly eased logistics, there was still a limit to how long a large army could be supported in one location. Allowing that logistical difficulties would cut Darius's potential force by half, the Persians could still easily muster two hundred thousand men for one great effort. And in this, the contest that would decide the fate of the Persian Empire, there can be little doubt that Darius strained every resource to assemble an overwhelming force. A detailed analysis of the available military strength of the Persian Empire can be found in the author's (Lacey's) earlier book *The First Clash*. The figures found in that work, although significant, would be even larger in the time of Alexander, after approximately 150 years of stable and mostly peaceful government. For anyone wishing to undertake a serious study of the size of the opposing forces, the best starting place is E. W. Marsden's *The Campaign of Gaugamela*, pp. 24–39. Although I am far from convinced his final estimates are correct, Marsden presents an analysis that cannot be ignored.

29 The left flank of the Persian army He would later murder Darius and claim the empire for himself. On the approach of Alexander's army, his own people turned against him and turned him over to Alexander, who had his nose and ears cut off. The sources disagree as to how he died. He was either crucified where Darius was murdered, decapitated at Ecbatana, or torn apart in Bactria.

29 On the Persian right flank stood Mazaeus Syrians, Mesopotamians, Medes, Parthians and Sacae, Tapurians, and Albanians.

29 Although Bessus controlled the army's best cavalry After the battle, Mazaeus retreated into Babylon. He soon surrendered the city after Alexander promised it would not be plundered. In return for this and other services, Alexander appointed him satrap of Babylon, the first Persian to be given a high office within Alexander's domains.

30 Against this immense force This number comes directly from Arrian's account. It has been analyzed, disputed, and argued about by generations of historians. Now, however, there is a consensus that Arrian's figures are substantially correct. Moreover, Arrian states that a copy of the Persian order of battle (unfortunately, it appears not to have included numbers) was captured by Alexander's forces. It is therefore relatively safe to assume that Arrian is almost as well-informed about the Persian situation as he is of the Macedonian army.

30 Rather, it was a well-integrated, combined-arms force The Macedonian war machine would not meet its match until it faced the legions of Rome, but by that time it was a mere caricature of the army led by Alexander.

34 As Plutarch relates Plutarch, *Age of Alexander,* p. 291.

35 Likewise, Darius's own phalanx Philip and Alexander had armed their phalanx with pikes (*sarissa*) several feet longer than the typical Greek phalanx (fifteen to eighteen feet). This length advantage gave the Macedonian phalanx a decisive advantage in any frontal encounter. However, if the phalanx was taken in flank or broken, the unwieldy *sarissa,* which took two hands to handle properly, became a serious impediment.

35 When a Macedonian spear impaled his charioteer This interpretation is drawn from Greek sources, who would have possessed little inclination to show Darius in a favorable light. Some historians have made a convincing case that just as at the Battle of Issus, Darius did not run off in a blind panic. Even the Greek evidence shows that he remained on the field and directing the battle until the last possible moment. All of the evidence indicates that he did not turn to depart until his bodyguard was cut down at his feet. The sources say that the limbs of the dead were intertwined with his chariot. As at Issus, Darius did flee, but only just before his own capture or death. Although some may say that is not how a hero would have comported himself, a more sensible view is that with Darius dead, the war was over. If he lived, there was still hope of raising another army, as he did after Issus, and once more returning to the fray. The only surviving account from the Persian side claims that Darius did not flee the battle. Rather, he was deserted by his own troops: "Opposite each other they fought and a heavy defeat of the troops of the king [Darius] he [Alexander] inflicted. The king [Darius], his troops deserted him and to their cities they went. They fled to the east" (*ahû* tablet 29 of *Enûma Anu Enlil;* obv. 59–61).

37 Parmenio sent a messenger to Alexander As was mentioned in an earlier note, there is good reason to doubt many of the sources when it comes to the actions of Parmenio. That a message was sent to Alexander is probably beyond question, as too many sources attest to it. However, Parmenio was an old and steady soldier. The idea of him panicking when the fight was still winnable is hard to fathom. Moreover, the battlefield was not so large that Parmenio could not see the broad outline of what was going on elsewhere. He surely must have been aware of the Companions' charge. He also knew that when Alexander broke through, he would have a choice to make. He could roll up the Persians either to his right or to his left. Parmenio's message may have been intended to help Alexander decide to go to his left and ride to his relief.

37 If Alexander had any doubts After the charge of the Companions, the fight on the Macedonian right flank is not well covered by the sources. What I have reconstructed here is inferred from two known facts: that the Persian left flank did collapse and Bessus led the survivors off to Babylon; and that Menidas was killed in the next phase of the battle fighting alongside Alexander.

37 Knowing that his right was secure The sources present various versions of what happened at this point. However, most historians have accepted Arrian's account that Alexander was in full pursuit of Darius and was angry when news from Parmenio forced him to break off the chase and return to assist his threatened left flank. We find Arrian's account highly unlikely for several reasons. First, Alexander was the finest military commander of the era. As valuable as the capture of Darius was to his cause, he would not have left the battlefield while the issue was still in doubt. Next, if Alexander was in headlong pursuit, there was little chance that any messenger Parmenio sent would catch up to him in time to do any good. Finally, by the time the first histories of the campaign were collected, Parmenio was in disrepute and his past deeds were clearly being recorded in the worst possible light.

38 Alexander and the Companions first encountered Inexplicably, many historians have interpreted this passage as an indication that the Persians and Indians returning from their raid on the baggage train were the strongest and finest cavalry in the Persian army. We believe that Arrian was referring to two separate formations. The returning raiders were by no means the best the Persians had, nor were they organized to attack in squadrons, as Arrian later says they did. This passage reflects the superbly trained units to the right of Darius, but not yet engaged with Parmenio, who were now turning to make a breakout attempt.

38 "For the barbarians, posted many rows deep" James Romm, *The Landmark Arrian: The Campaigns of Alexander* (New York: Pantheon Books, 2010), p. 123.

38 But here the Thessalians Ibid.

39 Crucially, it was a Western conqueror This domination was more pronounced along the Aegean and Mediterranean coast and receded the farther inland one went. Still, although Persia itself held on to much of its Eastern character (rising again as the Sassanid Empire, which was to give Rome much trouble), Greek cultural influences still managed to penetrate the heart of the former Persian Empire.

39 If Alexander had lost at Gaugamela Of course, it is possible that some segment would have cut its way through in a manner similar to the way the Greeks were let out of Persia by Xenophon after the Battle of Cunaxa in 401 B.C.; see Xenophon, *The Persian Expedition,* trans. Rex Warner (New York: Penguin Classics, 1950).

ZAMA *An Empire in the Balance*

41 Rome became accustomed to the long-term commitment This point is made by Adrian Goldsworthy, and his book on the Punic Wars provides a first-rate history of the struggle as well as a thorough discussion of the war's legacy. See Adrian Goldsworthy, *The Fall of Carthage* (London: Cassell, 2000), pp. 357–68.

42 Hannibal's failure to march Other elements that bear consideration were the state of Hannibal's own forces after the bloody battle and his lack of a siege train capable of investing and breaching Rome's walls.

44 Rome overcame its naval deficiencies Because they could not defeat the Carthaginians in a typical naval engagement, where the primary tactic was ramming, the Romans invented an assault bridge called the *corvus,* which was attached to all Roman warships. This hinged bridge swiveled around the mast and could face in any direction. When a Carthaginian ship approached, a rope would be cut and the bridge would fall, impaling the opposing deck with a large metal spike. Legionnaires would then storm across and massacre all who opposed them. The Romans had found a way to turn naval battles into the kind of infantry contest in which they excelled.

46 This led one of his senior officers Livy, 22:51.

48 Every year, the Senate ignored their petition Although a number of ancient sources address the Second Punic War and the Battle of Zama, this chapter is derived mostly from the works of Livy and Polybius (whom Livy used as one of his sources). Polybius, who is often credited with an objective approach to his historical writings, must be read carefully, as his commentary may be colored by his close association with the Scipio family. However, he is the only source on this battle who actually interviewed many veterans of the fight. He also had access to a great deal of archival material that was not available to other ancient historians and is lost to us.

51 As the talks progressed, the centurion-slaves As told by Livy (30:4): "Whilst the envoys were in conference these men strolled about the camp noting all the adits and exits, the general arrangement of the camp, the positions of the Carthaginians and Numidians, respectively, and the distance between Hasdrubal's camp and that of Syphax. They also watched the methods adopted in posting the watches and guards, to see whether a surprise attack would be better made by night or by day. [3] The conferences were pretty frequent, and different men were purposely sent each time in order that these details might become known to a larger number."

51 **Unobserved, Scipio's two columns** The ancient sources give various interpretations of these events. Appian says nothing about any negotiations or reconnaissance of the enemy camp. Rather, he claims that the attack was the result of a sudden decision by Scipio to move to the offensive. Others indicate that the Carthaginians were planning an attack for the following night, which Masinissa learned of. When he informed Scipio of the impending attack, the Roman decided to preempt with an immediate attack of his own. Dio claims that the events listed above took place but were not a ploy. In his version, Scipio broke off negotiations and attacked after a failed attempt to murder Masinissa.

52 **"Thinking that it was a mere accidental conflagration"** Polybius, 14:4.

52 **As for the remainder** Ibid., 14:5.

52 **Thrown into a state of confused panic** Appian gives a different version of this fight. He outlines the battle that proceeded as presented here, but in reverse, stating that Scipio attacked first. Once again, Dio is in general agreement with Appian's account.

52 **Men, horses, and beasts of burden** Polybius, 14:5.

55 **All of Numidia was not conquered** For the final campaign, the Carthaginians were able to recruit two thousand Numidian cavalry under a chieftain named Tychaeus, who feared for his life owing to the ambitions of Masinissa.

55 **Sophonisba, equally unwilling to serve as a Roman pawn** Syphax, along with other prisoners, was taken to Italy, where he was imprisoned in Alba. He later died in prison at Tibur.

56 **Scipio, claiming a violation of the truce** Polybius claims there was a final peace treaty agreed upon between Rome and Carthaginian ambassadors. However, Livy claims the negotiations had broken down and that no final agreement was reached.

56 **This was the Roman way of war** Tacitus, *The Life of Canaeus Julius Agricola*, c. A.D. 98.

56 **These scouts, totally unaware of the pending arrival of Masinissa** Livy reports that Masinissa's reinforcements came in before the scouts departed and that their report to Hannibal greatly distressed the Carthaginian commander.

57 **As Livy recounts** Livy, 30:31.

57 **In the first were the elements of Hannibal's late brother Mago's army** Mago, a brother of Hannibal, was defeated by Scipio in Spain (Battle of Illipa). Afterward he landed up in Cádiz and the Balearics, where he raised a new army with which he invaded northwestern Italy (Liguria). With fifteen thousand men, he took Genoa and Savone in 205 B.C. and occupied it for the next three years. In 203 B.C., this force moved south, and Mago was seriously wounded in a drawn battle. A summons from

Carthage forced him to bring his army, now about ten thousand to twelve thousand men, to North Africa, where it joined Hannibal. It did so without its commander, who died of his wounds during the journey.

58 To add menace to his formation Some sources state that there was a force of several thousand allied Macedonian troops in the second line, but most historians discount this, as Polybius was unlikely to have failed to mention them.

59 He made only one point Polybius, 15:10.

61 "The space between the two armies was full of blood" Ibid., 15:14.

61 For some minutes, the issue was in doubt Ibid.

62 As Polybius says Here Polybius is quoting an unknown author, although some scholars believe it to be from a lost work written by Theognis.

62 "And this we might say was the case with Hannibal" Polybius, 15:16.

62 Moreover, Carthage had to pay an indemnity of ten thousand talents To put that ten thousand talents into perspective, one talent would pay all the costs of keeping a trireme at sea for approximately a month or pay twenty mercenaries for a year.

TEUTOBURGER WALD *The Division of Europe*

65 Augustus's supposed final warning to his successors Cassius Dio, 56:33.

66 Whether or not Augustus actually bequeathed such policy advice For an excellent outline of the debate, see Josiah Ober, "Tiberius and the Political Testament of Augustus," *Historia: Zeitschrift für Alte Geschichte* 31, no. 3 (Third Quarter 1982): 306–28. It is more recently discussed in David J. Breeze, *The Frontiers of Imperial Rome* (Barnsley, UK: Pen & Sword Books, 2011), pp. 14–19.

66 Certainly Augustus himself never followed such a policy Modern historians have followed P. A. Brunt's lead, and it is now generally accepted that the ancient historian Dio created a fiction that Augustus was always oriented toward peaceful solutions. Dio, who was opposed to expansion, was perfectly willing to create a pacific Augustus as an exemplar for future emperors. See P. A. Brunt, *Roman Imperial Themes* (Oxford: Oxford University Press, 1990), pp. 96–109.

66 Augustus saw himself as conqueror Alison Cooley, *Res Gestae Divi Augusti: Text, Translation, and Commentary* (Cambridge, UK: Cambridge University Press, 2009).

66 In fact, some historians believe that Augustus Brunt, *Roman Imperial Themes*. Although the authors have argued that the Romans had a very good idea of the geography of the empire and beyond the frontier for several hundred miles (well over one thousand miles in the Eastern Roman Empire). Augustus may not, however, have had any idea how much farther the world extended beyond that zone, making it feasible that he and other contemporaries believed that with one great push beyond the existing frontiers, they could occupy the world.

66 In keeping with his tradition of delegating crucial matters The one major exception to this rule was Augustus's trusted boyhood companion and one of Rome's greatest generals, Agrippa. This narrative of Drusus's campaigns is drawn mostly from Cassius Dio (54:32–55:2) and Florus (2:30.26), who are both accepted as reasonably reliable on this topic.

67 **"For the enemy harassed him everywhere by ambuscades"** Dio, 54:32.

67 **In his final campaign** Dio states that he was deterred by a dream, when after he tried to cross the Elbe, a woman of superhuman size came to him and said, "Whither, pray, art thou hastening, insatiable Drusus? It is not fated that thou shalt look upon all these lands. But depart; for the end alike of thy labors and of thy life is already at hand" (Dio, 55:1.3).

67 **During his return march, Drusus** Possibly he suffered a broken leg when he fell off his horse, and it later became gangrenous.

68 **Swift Roman marches through Germania** Velleius Paterculus, 2:97.4.

68 **The reality of the matter was that Drusus's** Syme, *Cambridge Ancient History,* vol. 10, p. 363.

68 **As a result, Augustus relieved Ahenobarbus** Velleius Paterculus, 2:104.2.

68 **In A.D. 4, Tiberius returned to command the Rhine legions** After leaving the German legions, in 6 B.C., Tiberius opted to exit the political arena and retire to Rhodes. However, with the death of Augustus's grandsons Lucius and Gaius, who were being groomed as future emperors of the Roman Empire, Tiberius was called back to duty in A.D. 4. From this point forward, Tiberius was Augustus's heir apparent.

69 **"Soldiers burst into joy at the sight of him"** Velleius Paterculus, 2:104.

69 **During the first year** Adrian Murdoch, *Rome's Greatest Defeat* (London: History Press, 2006), p. 43.

69 **According to the historian and Tiberius's staff officer** Velleius Paterculus, 2:108.1.

69 **Over the past two millennia** He was first married to the daughter of Augustus's most trusted adviser, Agrippa, and later to Augustus's grandniece Claudia Pulchra.

70 **"Varus Quinctilius, descended from a famous"** Velleius Paterculus, 2:117.

70 **This was one of the most important governorships in the empire** During Augustus's reign, there were two types of provinces: those with legions that Augustus personally controlled and those settled provinces that no longer needed the permanent presence of troops to pacify or defend them. These latter provinces, Augustus allowed the Senate to control.

70 **It was a significant operation** Varus's actions made enough of an impression on the Jewish people that the entire period after Herod's death is still known as "Varus's War" in the Talmud. It is worth noting that Jesus was probably a young teacher, and as he lived just outside Sepphoris, he would likely have had a close-up look at the results of a Roman army on the rampage.

71 **As the ancient Roman historian Florus writes** Florus, 2:30.

71 **As far as can be determined from the sources** Ibid., 2:31.

71 **As Dio notes** Dio, 56:18.3 and 56:18.4.

71 **Because of these close family ties** Flavius remained loyal to Rome throughout this period.

72 **"There appeared a young man of noble birth"** Velleius Paterculus, 2:118.

72 Well schooled in what was needed The following reconstruction is the author's own. It is based on evidence provided by ancient writers and recent archaeological excavations of the Teutoburger Wald battle site. See Cassius Dio, 56:18–24; Velleius Paterculus, 2:117–120; Tacitus, *The Annals,* 1:60–62; and Florus, *Epitome of Titus Livy,* 2:30. This reconstruction was also informed by two recent works; see Adrian Murdoch, *Rome's Greatest Defeat,* and Peter S. Wells, *The Battle That Stopped Rome* (New York: W. W. Norton, 2003). Of these, Velleius's history must be given the highest credit. Although it was written twenty years after the battle, he was the only ancient source who actually talked to survivors. Moreover, he was a Roman general with extensive combat experience in Germania. For an excellent discussion of the sources and their credibility, see www .livius.org/te-tg/teutoburg/teutoburg02.html.

74 Bordered by a high hill to the south The pass was in reality about a mile wide, but men and beasts could move along the edges only because of the high-water table.

75 The Germans repulsed most of these legionnaires Archaeological digs show evidence of dead Romans on the German side of the wall.

76 "In the plain between were bleaching" Tacitus, 1:60–61.

76 In the succeeding weeks after the destruction of Varus's army Only a small force based at Aliso, near modern Haltern, commanded by Cadencies (an experienced veteran and likely the *primus pilus*—commander of a legion's first cohort—of the XIX Legion) managed to cut its way through enemy territory back to the safety of Gaul.

77 Distraught over the collapse of his strategy Suetonius, *The Twelve Caesars,* trans. Robert Graves (New York: Penguin Books, 1957); rev. ed. with introduction by Michael Grant (New York: Penguin Books, 1979); paperback ed. (New York: Penguin Classics, 1989).

77 There is no profit to be had by a minute examination of Germanicus's invasions For those interested in a more detailed treatment of Germanicus and his military career, see Adrian Goldsworthy, *In the Name of Rome: The Men Who Won the Roman Empire* (London: Weidenfeld & Nicolson, 2003), pp. 237–62.

77 During Rome's relentless drive of conquest One possible exception was the defeat of Crassus's army at the Battle of Carrhae (53 B.C.), where the Parthians placed a temporary halt on Roman expansion to the East.

78 This inexorable process ended on the east bank of the Rhine Some may quibble and say that the Parthian Empire also checked the power of Rome. There is some truth to this, but almost up to the fall of the Roman Empire, Caesars continued to lead armies into the East in a vain attempt to conquer Parthia.

78 But after the Varian disaster at Teutoburger Wald Some quibble that Germanicus's invasion in the immediate aftermath of the Varian disaster was meant to conquer the region. This surmise is at best debatable, but in any event, the emperor Tiberius saw soon enough that Germany was not worth the cost and so brought an end to Germanicus's operations.

78 **What is certain is that Rome's fall** For more than a generation, many historians have accepted a paradigm established by their German colleagues that portrayed the German invasions as a mere transition in political leadership. In this construct, the barbarian invasions of the fifth century were remarkably nonviolent and mostly reflected the migratory resettlements of the displaced.

79 **Rome's failure to conquer Germany** The Slavic divide was made much worse than the Teutonic divide by its adoption of the Cyrillic alphabet, which put it outside the continuum of Latin learning and goes a long way to explaining the slowness of Eastern intellectual growth as compared with the rapid speed of learning and development in the West, particularly after the Reformation.

79 **As with the East–West divide brought about by the Battle of Marathon** Many would argue, with a great deal of supporting evidence, that Germany would have been just as dangerous to its neighbors in preceding centuries if not for the fact that it spent most of the previous two millennia politically fragmented.

ADRIANOPLE *The End of Roman Supremacy*

82 **"And indeed, if anyone does but attend to the other parts"** Flavius Josephus, *The Great Roman-Jewish War: A.D. 66–70,* ed. William R. Farmer (New York: Harper Torchbooks, 1960), p. 121.

89 **"The moment that"** Ammianus Marcellinus, *Roman History,* trans. C. D. Yonge (London: Bohn, 1862), bk. 31, p. 599.

93 **"The fatal obstinacy of the emperor"** Ibid., p. 609.

94 **"[The Goths] designedly delayed"** Ibid., pp. 610–11.

96 **Nevertheless, they "yielded on their march"** Ibid., p. 611.

96 **At the moment the *scutarii* and the *sagittarii* collapsed** Ibid.

97 **"who were emaciated by hunger"** Ibid., p. 614.

98 **"The ground, covered with streams of blood, made their feet slip"** Ibid., p. 613.

YARMUK *The Islamic Conquest Begins*

101 **In 629, the prophet Muhammad** The Truce of Hudaybiyyah (628) was scheduled to last for ten years. But hostilities between those tribes that had accepted Islam and the Meccan-based Quraysh erupted again in less than two years. In 630, Muhammad led a force of ten thousand warriors into Mecca and accepted the surrender and conversion of the Quraysh.

101 **"Peace be upon him, he who follows the right path"** Majid Ali Khan, *Muhammad the Final Messenger* (Karachi: Kutub Khana Ishaat, 2010), pp. 250–51; and Martin Lings, *Muhammad: His Life Based on the Earliest Sources* (Rochester, VT: Inner Traditions, 2006), p. 260.

102 **The death of Justinian the Great in A.D. 565** One cannot, however, relieve Justinian from substantial blame over the empire's plight in the decades after his death. His obsession with re-creating the Roman Empire at its height led him to undertake a series of draining wars in Italy and Africa.

As he was wasting the best troops in the empire on a hopeless dream, the Avars and other barbarian tribes were making gains in the Balkans, while the Persians were again starting to push at the empire's Eastern frontiers.

102 **Taking advantage of political turmoil** Khosrau II is referred to in some histories as Chosroes II.

106 **That job was completed by his successor** The Ridda Wars were also known as the Wars of Apostasy, as they were aimed mostly at tribes that had accepted Islam while Muhammad was alive but reverted to paganism upon his death.

106 **The prelude to the Battle of Yarmuk** Nothing about the Battle of Yarmuk or its prelude is known with certainty. The scant Christian sources spend most of their effort trying to explain the Byzantine defeat without putting any of the responsibility on Heraclius. To say they are unreliable is to grossly understate the truth. There are more Arab sources, and their accounts are typically used by historians trying to narrate the course of the battle. As a result, much is unknown. For instance, it is generally accepted that the battle lasted six days, but some sources tell us it was over in a single day's combat. We are informed about some of the major movements of the battle, but not who directed them or where and what the various commanders were doing during crucial stages of the battle. Finally, we have no idea how many soldiers fought for each side. Historians are relatively certain that, for once, the Byzantines outnumbered their opponent, but by how much remains uncertain. Given the exhausted condition of the empire and the Byzantine army, we would be reluctant to state that Heraclius could field more than thirty thousand men and that any figures much above that are wildly exaggerated. Given that Wahlid entered Syria with fewer than eight hundred men and that this was considered a significant reinforcement to the Arab armies already present, one would be hard-pressed to estimate their number much above twenty thousand to twenty-five thousand men. In other words, the contestants were more evenly matched than historians typically credit. To create this reconstruction, I have made extensive use of the following sources (all of them written decades after the events chronicled): Jabir al-Biladuri's *The Origins of the Islamic State,* as translated by Philip Khuri Hitti (this 1916 translation was reprinted in 2010 by Cosimo Classics); and Ibn Jarir al-Tabari's *History of the Prophets of Kings,* in particular volume 11 (*The Challenge to the Empires,* translated by Khalid Yahya Blankinship) of the translations published by SUNY Press, Albany, New York. A. I. Akram's *The Sword of Allah: Khalid bin al Waleed, His Life and Campaigns* (Karachi: National Publishing House, 1970) is also valuable, if a little too trusting of the original sources. Copies of this work may be found on the Internet: http://ibnayyub.files.wordpress.com/2008/03/sword-of-allah-khalif-ibn-al-walid.pdf (accessed August 22, 2012). This work was also informed by two excellent master's theses: David E. Kunselman, *Arab-Byzantine War, A.D. 629–644,* www.dtic.mil/cgi-bin/GetTRDoc?AD=ADA494014 (accessed August 22, 2012); and Ibrahim, Raymond Reda,

The Battle of Yarmuk: An Assessment of the Immediate Factors Behind the Islamic Conquest, www.worldcat.org/title/battle-of-yarmuk-an-assessment-of
-the-immediate-factors-behind-the-islamic-conquests/oclc/051165482
(accessed August 22, 2012). By far the best single work on this period,
which includes an excellent analysis of the sources, is James Howard
Johnston, Witness to a World Crisis: Historians and Histories of the Middle East
in the Seventh Century (Oxford, UK: Oxford University Press, 2010).

108 **Among these reinforcements were six thousand Yemenis** Akram, Sword of
Allah, chap. 34, p. 5.

108 **According to a description given the historian by A. I. Akram** Ibid., p. 6.

108 **Battle began on August 15, 636** Although there are some good reasons to
doubt this battle lasted longer than a day or at most two, this reconstruction will follow the accepted historical reconstruction and place it over a
six-day period.

109 **Others claim that the infantry extended along the entire front** Some of the
sources discuss "An Army of Chains," claiming that three thousand Byzantine soldiers, after swearing to fight to the death, had chained themselves together (possibly in ten-man units). It is doubtful this ever took
place, although a chain, if one existed, would have made a handy device
for halting a cavalry charge.

109 **"'Take tent poles in your hands'"** Akram, Sword of Allah, chap. 34, p. 8.

110 **"This was more than the proud warriors"** Ibid., chap. 35, p. 3.

110 **Abu Sufyan had experienced his wife's violent temper** Ibid., p. 3.

111 **As one Muslim soldier exclaimed** Ibid., p. 5.

112 **This calamity is still referred to in Arab lore as "the Day of the Lost Eyes"**
Ibid., p. 8.

113 **Once the Byzantines were pinned in place** This was a maneuver the Ghassanid cavalry would have stopped had it not withdrawn from the battle
the day before. That the Byzantine commander did nothing to compensate for this loss is a display of inexcusable neglect.

HASTINGS The Remaking of Europe

116 **For historians, the year 1066** Historians in search of a quick payday learned
long ago that there is always a market for a new book on Waterloo, Gettysburg, and Hastings. Because of this, there is no shortage of interpretations of the Battle of Hastings for any interested party to consult. All of
these works have been built upon a very limited number of primary
sources of varying and still hotly disputed reliability. The best recent anal-
yses of this primary source material have been undertaken by Stephen
Morillo and M. K. Lawson. See Stephen Morillo, The Battle of Hastings:
Sources and Interpretations (Rochester, NY: Boydell Press, 1999); and M. K.
Lawson, The Battle of Hastings (Gloucestershire, UK: Tempus Publishing,
2002). This reconstruction is the author's own interpretation of these
sources, informed by a number of the more thoughtful works dealing
with the battle or its participants. The primary sources used for this work
are William of Jumièges and Oderic Vitalis, Deeds of the Dukes of the Nor-

mans; William of Poitiers, *Deeds of Duke William; Anglo-Saxon Chronicle,* versions C, D, and E; *The Chronicle of John of Worcester;* Eadmer of Canterbury, *History of Recent Events;* Henry of Huntingdon, *History of the English People;* William of Malmesbury, *Deeds of the Kings of the English;* Robert Wace, *Roman de Rou;* and the *Carmen de Hastingae Proelio.* The last of these is the most problematic, as its provenance has lately been questioned. It has been attributed to Guy, bishop of Amiens, and was supposedly written in 1068. As such, it is a valuable primary source and one of the few that presents events if not from an Anglo-Saxon perspective, at least with a more balanced view. Some claim that it was written by an unknown person many years later and is filled with unreliable traditions. This work, in keeping with the position of most historians who have examined the matter in detail, accepts its authenticity.

117 In 1066, the Normans, under William The authors understand that a sizable part of the Norman army was descended from Vikings and that therefore the Conquest of 1066 can be viewed as another successful Viking assault on the island. We contend that the Normans had been in France long enough to establish themselves as a unique culture.

117 What marked the Norman invasion as unique We are using a bit of historian's discretion here. For instance, we do not count the Glorious Revolution as a successful invasion. A few historians, using different interpretations of events, might disagree on this and a few other lesser examples over the past nine hundred years. They will no doubt write their own books.

117 From the time of the Conquest The authors are aware that a French army landed as early as the reign of King John to help the nobility overthrow the crown and that there were other armies that took part in pseudo-invasions of the British Isles over the centuries. They do not negate our general principle. Nor do we count periodic squabbles with the Welsh and Scots. We consider those fights to be intramural or family affairs. As before, those who disagree are free to take pen to paper and establish a contrary record.

117 The infusion of Norman energy This Norman energy manifested itself in the conquest not only of England, but throughout significant areas of Western Europe. This is most clearly apparent in southern Italy and Sicily, which were under Norman assault for almost two hundred years before being mostly conquered by 1091. Within a decade afterward, this same impulse to action and conquest was a primary factor in the assembly and dispatch of the first Crusader armies.

117 While a later era of massed armies The authors use the word *England* when referring to that country prior to the year 1707. Under the reign of Queen Anne, the Act of Union was signed, uniting the crowns of England and Scotland. For any period after that, we use "Great Britain."

118 Arguably, it was also one of the most militarily powerful states There has been a large amount of scholarship on Anglo-Saxon England in recent decades (taking us far beyond the great nineteenth-century debates of E. A. Freeman and J. H. Round). For those interested, the best starting point is Sir Frank M. Stenton's *Anglo-Saxon England* (Oxford, UK: Oxford University Press, 2001).

120 **Unfortunately, these gains were reversed** There was a short break in his reign from 1013 to 1014, when Viking inroads caused him to flee to the Continent. Also, the term *unready* is a mistranslation of Old English *unræd,* which means "bad counsel." This was a twist on the name "Æthelred," which means "noble counsel."

121 **The evidence indicates that Cnut** One is tempted to call him an early believer in trickle-down economics and a Keynesian spender a thousand years before his time.

121 **With no other acceptable choice available** Given that he spent thirty years of his life in Normandy, many historians consider Edward the Confessor's reign to be the "first" Norman invasion. It was definitely true that he had little in common with his subjects, and throughout his reign he was constantly bringing over Norman officials and priests to occupy the highest positions and bishoprics in the realm.

122 **By way of comparison, the two next strongest families** Frank McLynn, *1066: The Year of Three Battles* (New York: Random House, 1998), p. 133.

122 **At some point during his stay** Whether this ever happened has been a matter of dispute for nine hundred years. All of the contemporary Norman chronicles testify that it took place, while contemporary Anglo-Saxon chronicles are either silent or state that Harold was free to swear oaths, without being specific about what oaths he swore. The first Saxon writer to state that it never took place was Eadmer some forty years later. This debate will likely go on for another nine hundred years. However, the preponderance of the evidence is on the side of William, even after allowing for a substantial amount of Norman propaganda.

123 **By then Normandy was firmly within his grasp** In 1062, William invaded Maine, taking that region from the weak Count of Anjou. In 1065, he led a punitive expedition into Brittany, where he was joined by Harold.

124 **Assisting him was a small group of a dozen nobles** It was Odo who commissioned the Bayeux Tapestry, which tells the story of the Conquest and is still on display in Bayeux.

124 **"Bursting with confidence, [who] could make and take jokes"** David Carpenter, *The Struggle for Mastery: Britain 1066–1284* (Oxford, UK: Oxford University Press, 2003), p. 71.

124 **As a first step he sought the support of Pope Alexander II** William was a major supporter of the church reform that was emanating from Rome throughout the middle of the eleventh century. As such, he had the early favor of the church. Harold, on the other hand, was consecrated king by Stigand, the archbishop of Canterbury (one source states he was consecrated by Ealdred, bishop of York), who had been deposed by several popes in succession. England was resistant to papal reforms, and Alexander likely welcomed the opportunity to put William, a strong supporter of canonical reform, on the throne.

124 **The army encamped near Dives-sur-Mer** The size of this fleet is still dis-

puted. One chronicler (Wace) places the number of ships at 696, while a near contemporary ship list places the total at 776. Assuming the lower number and that only 500 were available to carry men or horses (the rest carried supplies, siege equipment, and the makings of a mobile fort), this still provides enough space for an army of at least twelve thousand men and a thousand horses (400 ships carrying thirty men each and 100 ships carrying ten horses each). Although the numbers that fought at Hastings are still disputed, we believe that many of the most recent estimates are far too low. New evidence demonstrates that early medieval economies were likely two or three times as wealthy as previously assumed. Given this strong economic underpinning, one can safely say that Normandy and England could both easily afford to support armies well in excess of ten thousand men, at least for a limited period.

124 William waited for over a month for the winds to turn Many historians claim he was well-informed about Harold's preparations across the English Channel and was waiting until the formidable Anglo-Saxon army broke up for want of supplies. William was definitely clever enough to conceive of such a plan. Still, he just barely held his army together during the waiting period, and it seems rash that he would hazard its disintegration or loss through disease when England beckoned. Moreover, William had only one hope of victory—to win a decisive battle early. By allowing the English force to scatter, he risked that such a battle might not take place until the following summer. By then, his army would likely have withered to a mere shadow of its former self.

125 Repulsed by the two northern earls Hardrada is Norse for "stern counsel" or "hard ruler," neither of which was an insult among the Vikings.

125 Hardrada, who had been fighting since his teenage years In fact, a collection of sagas detailing his life and martial exploits, the *Heimskringla,* is still available.

125 All summer the fleet and probably at least a quarter of the *fyrd* Estimates for the size of the *fyrd* vary, but it is probably safe to say that Harold kept approximately twelve thousand men under arms all summer. The debate over the fighting quality of the *fyrd* still rages. Although many historians believe it was a purely amateur force of doubtful ability, more recent evidence is beginning to overturn that view. This essay accepts that England was rich enough and took war seriously enough to ensure that those selected for the *fyrd* (probably less than 5 percent of the total male population) were well armed, trained, and in many cases battle tested.

126 At first the English had the upper hand The sources for this battle are few. Only the author of Norse sagas, Snorri, has left anything near a full account, and that is of doubtful reliability.

129 Harold himself, surrounded by handpicked housecarls The spot is easy to find today, as it is marked by the foundational remains of a high altar, which was part of a church constructed on the site of the battle by William as repentance for the great slaughter he had precipitated.

132 It was during this fighting that Harold's brothers Gyrth and Leofwine fell

There had been much speculation that the death of both brothers indi-cates this attack may actually have been an organized counterattack and of far wider scope than is indicated by a portion of the Saxon line chasing after the fleeing Bretons. If so, then Harold's immobility in the center is doubly puzzling. All that can be said is that there is no strong evidence for a coordinated Saxon assault. It is only speculation, but what is more likely is that the two Saxon commanders, seeing that their own right flank was being cut to ribbons, had moved to the point of greatest danger, as any good commander would, so as to restore some semblance of order. There is a tradition that Gyrth was slain by William himself; however, the evi-dence for this is not overly convincing.

133 **By attacking and then retreating** The long dispute among historians about whether the Normans conducted a number of feigned retreats or were even capable of such will not be resolved here. The author believes that the Normans were trained to a high enough degree to pull off such a tactic and had proven so on other battlefields. But for the purposes of understanding the battle, whether they were feigned or actual retreats is of little importance. The size of the battlefield made it near impossible to employ the entire Norman cavalry force at the same time. At any point in the fight, many hundreds of cavalry had to be resting or re-forming for a renewed charge. These forces, properly led, would have been available to smash any Saxon advance. So whether the retreats were feigned or actual localized panics, the outcome would have remained the same.

134 **There, the king of England was found dead** This is another long-standing debate among historians that will not be resolved here. See Frank McLynn's *1066: The Year of Three Battles,* p. 226, for an alternative version of Harold's death.

135 **It was the centuries-long fusion of these two cultures** For the serious his-torians of this period, my points here harken back to the great interpreta-tive debates between E. A. Freeman and J. H. Round and their supporters in the late nineteenth century. That debate will not be settled here. For the most part, modern historians lean toward Round's arguments. I, however, find much to recommend Freeman's interpretations, although Round points out a number of serious flaws in his reconstruction of the actual battle. For the best scholarship dealing with all of the historical debates on the Conquest and its effects, see Marjorie Chibnall, *The Debate on the Norman Conquest* (Manchester, UK: Manchester University Press, 1999).

THE SPANISH ARMADA *Miracle at Sea*

136 **Toward the middle of the sixteenth century** The Ottomans' final large-scale assault on the West was finally halted at Vienna in 1683.

139 **Upon ascending the Spanish throne** Mary had earned her sobriquet through the execution of 283 Protestants, most by burning, in her failed attempt to bring England back to the Catholicism of Rome.

139 **For some time, despite his religious differences** Early in Elizabeth's reign, Philip even offered marriage.

142 **However, preparations were slow** A small number of these ships (thirty-eight) were later used to send reinforcements to the Spanish army in Flanders.

142 **In less than two months, one of Europe's great powers ceased to exist** In reality, the final conquest of Portugal was not secured until the Azores were captured and the last pretender to the throne, Dom António, was removed from the scene.

143 **With the addition of nearly a dozen sturdily built and heavily gunned Portuguese galleons** For an excellent synopsis of this period, see Colin Martin and Geoffrey Parker's *The Spanish Armada* (New York: Penguin Books, 1989), pp. 57–81. This work and Neil Hanson's *The Confident Hope of a Miracle: The True History of the Spanish Armada* (New York: Random House, 2006) are the two best recent histories of the Spanish Armada.

144 **Philip, unwilling to see France ruled by a Protestant** It was not until February 1594, six years after the Spanish Armada sailed, that Henry IV was crowned king. To secure his position and the loyalty of his overwhelmingly Catholic subjects, he had converted to Catholicism, supposedly stating, "Paris is well worth a Mass."

144 **For almost two weeks Drake raided the coast** Martin and Parker place the damages at three hundred thousand crowns and twenty-six ships, which Drake took back to England as prizes.

146 **To ensure sufficient troops were on hand for a successful invasion** The Spanish Road was a 620-mile route, through mostly neutral territory, from Milan to Flanders. For further details, see Geoffrey Parker, *The Army of Flanders and the Spanish Road 1567–1659: The Logistics of Spanish Victory and Defeat in the Low Countries' Wars* (Cambridge, UK: Cambridge University Press, 2004).

146 **Just how the fleet would coordinate its arrival with Parma's army** Hanson, *Confident Hope of a Miracle,* p. 116.

146 **On April 29, 1587, Drake led sixteen warships and seven pinnaces into Cádiz** Pinnaces were smaller sailing vessels, often used as tenders to larger ships and for scouting, commerce raiding (piracy), and communications. In many ways, they served the same functions as sloops and frigates would a century later in support of ships of the line that dominated the battle fleets of Europe's great powers.

148 **Although only a fifth of the English fleet consisted of royal warships** The remaking of the English warships was directly overseen by John Hawkins. Of the twenty-one royal vessels, only four (the *Revenge,* the *Vanguard,* the *Rainbow,* and the *Ark Royal*) were built in the past decade. The remainder were older and closely resembled the design of the Spanish ships. Hawkins's genius was displayed by not wasting England's limited shipbuilding capacity on a line of new warships, which would have provided

three or four additional ships. Rather, he had all of the older royal warships brought into dry dock and rebuilt in accordance with the new racer
design.

149 **"Unless God helps us by a miracle the English"** Garrett Mattingly, *The Defeat of the Spanish Armada* (London: Jonathan Cape, 1959), p. 223.

152 **As Lord Howard wrote in a letter to Walsingham that evening** Letter from Lord Howard Effingham to Sir Francis Walsingham, July 21, 1588, in John Knox Laughton, ed., *State Papers Relating to the Defeat of the Spanish Armada,* vol. 1 (London: Navy Records Society, 1894), pp. 288–89. A copy of this letter is available at www.luminarium.org/encyclopedia/effinghamwalsingham.htm.

154 **Recalde, alone once again and facing an entire British squadron, was incensed** As quoted in Martin and Parker, *The Spanish Armada,* p. 155.

156 **There a swift current** Some accounts state that there was no Spanish panic and that the fleet vacated Calais in an orderly manner. In this interpretation, the winds, currents, and inability to anchor were the key causes of the ensuing disaster.

156 **Morning found only five Spanish galleons** The other three galleons were the *San Marcos,* the *San Mateo,* and the *San Juan Bautista.*

158 **As one witness later wrote** Letter from Henry White to Walsingham, Au-
gust 8, 1588. See Laughton, ed., *State Papers Relating to the Defeat of the Spanish Armada,* vol. 2, p. 64.

BREITENFELD *The Creation of Modern War*

179 **As the great historian of Gustavus's reign, Michael Roberts, has noted** Michael Roberts, *Gustavus Adolphus and the Rise of Sweden* (London: Hod-
der Arnold, 1973), p. 143.

ANNUS MIRABILIS *The Rise of British Supremacy*

186 **As Pitt accurately forecast** Quoted in Arthur Herman, *To Rule the Waves: How the British Navy Shaped the Modern World* (New York: HarperCollins, 2004), p. 279.

188 **The great historian of the campaign has described Wolfe** Fred Anderson, *Crucible of War: The Seven Years' War and the Fate of Empire in British North America, 1754–1766* (New York: Alfred A. Knopf, 2000), p. 311.

191 **It was during the following frustrating period** Quoted in Nigel Bagnall, *The Peloponnesian War: Athens, Sparta, and the Struggle for Greece* (New York: Thomas Dunne Books, 2006), p. 250.

191 **"My antagonist has wisely shut himself up"** Anderson, *Crucible of War,* p. 349.

194 **One of the officers present recorded the event** Ibid., p. 361.

197 **Therein lay the rub** Alfred Thayer Mahan, *The Influence of Sea Power upon the French Revolution and Empire,* vol. 2 (Boston: Little, Brown & Company, 1894), p. 118.

198 **"At about half past eight"** Quoted in Herman, *To Rule the Waves,* p. 287.

199 **"Black Dick" Howe** Ibid., p. 288.

199 **He ordered the ship's captain** Ibid.

200 **As one of the French officers exclaimed** Anderson, *Crucible of War,* p. 395.

SARATOGA *The Victory of Amateurs*

205 **"Three thousand miles of ocean"** Richard M. Ketchum, *Saratoga: Turning Point of America's Revolutionary War* (New York: Henry Holt, 1997), p. 70.

208 **"I have but to give"** Quoted in Robert Middlekauff, *The Glorious Cause: The American Revolution, 1763–1789* (Oxford, UK: Oxford University Press, 1982), p. 372.

211 **"The commander [whom Burgoyne] chose was a brave German dragoon"** Piers Mackesy, *The War for America, 1775–1783* (Lincoln: University of Nebraska Press, 1992), p. 134.

213 **As the weather cleared on August 16** Quoted in Ketchum, *Saratoga,* p. 305.

221 **That officer, however, was unwilling to catch Arnold** Ibid., p. 399.

TRAFALGAR *Napoleon's Plans Thwarted*

225 **But the peace was only a pause** Robert Goetz, *1805: Austerlitz: Napoleon and the Destruction of the Third Coalition* (Barnsley, UK: Greenhill Books, 2005), p. 22.

225 **Britain did not hesitate to pick it up** Ibid., p. 23.

226 **Instead of pursuing a policy of accommodation within Europe** Ibid., p. 27.

226 **He was so certain, in fact** The Army of England (Armée de l'Angleterre) was also known as the Army of the Ocean Coasts (Armée des côtes de l'Océan).

226 **To some of his generals** Herman, *To Rule the Waves,* p. 371.

226 **To transport them, he had collected over 1,400 boats** Ibid., p. 372.

230 **As a midshipman on the *Bellerophon* said** Roy Adkins, *Nelson's Trafalgar: The Battle That Changed the World* (New York: Penguin Books, 2005), p. 61.

230 **"Your memorialist has been in four actions with the fleets of the enemy"** G. Lathom Browne: *Nelson; The Public and Private Life of Horatio, Viscount Nelson* (London: T. Fisher Unwin, 1891), p. 171.

233 **As he was passing the ship's commanding officer** Brian Lavery, *Nelson's Fleet at Trafalgar* (Annapolis: Naval Institute Press, 2004), p. 162.

235 **One French captain complained after the battle** N.A.M. Rodger, *The Command of the Ocean: A Naval History of Britain, 1649–1815* (New York: W. W. Norton, 2004), p. 540.

236 **Collingwood grumbled, "I wish Nelson"** Herman, *To Rule the Waves,* p. 388.

238 **As he fell, Nelson exclaimed** Some versions of this story state that Nelson said, "They are done for me at last."

239 **"Our fire was so hot that we soon drove them from the lower decks"** Lavery, *Nelson's Fleet at Trafalgar,* p. 162.

VICKSBURG *Breaking the Confederacy*

243 **Braxton Bragg's Army of Tennessee** Reflecting the often parochial nomenclatures of the Civil War, Braxton Bragg's (Confederate) Army of Tennessee was named after the state of Tennessee, whereas the name of Grant's Union Army of *the* Tennessee, perhaps better thought of as the "Army of Western Tennessee," referred to the Tennessee River.

244 **"My heart resumed its place"** U. S. Grant, *Personal Memoirs of U. S. Grant,* vol. 1 (New York: Charles L. Webster & Company, 1885), p. 250.

246 **For one of the few times in his memoirs** Ibid., p. 434.

246 **To Confederate civilians** Ibid., p. 170.

246 **As he noted in his memoirs** Ibid.

247 **As he noted in his memoirs: "Up to the battle of Shiloh"** Grant, *Personal Memoirs of U. S. Grant,* p. 143.

250 **Grant let the work continue through to the end of March** Ibid., p. 176.

250 **"I, myself, never felt great confidence"** Ibid., p. 174.

251 **Grant held firm** James R. Arnold, *Grant Wins the War: Decision at Vicksburg* (New York: John Wiley & Sons, 1997), p. 74.

253 **Grant crossed with the leading troops** Grant, *Personal Memoirs of U. S. Grant,* p. 189.

256 **At that point, Grant records** Ibid., p. 200.

258 **Jauntily, Grant called out to one of McPherson's regimental commanders** Arnold, *Grant Wins the War,* p. 155.

258 **As he commented to a staff officer** Ibid., p. 180.

259 **An observer noted** Ibid., p. 183.

261 **As Lee had assured Seddon** Shelby Foote, *The Civil War: A Narrative,* vol. 2 (New York: Vintage Books, 1986), p. 450.

THE MARNE *The End of Old Europe*

270 **As one historian has noted** Martin Van Creveld, *Supplying War: Logistics from Wallenstein to Patton* (Cambridge, UK: Cambridge University Press, 1977), p. 140.

270 **Therefore, they believed the two most powerful German armies** The Liège Gap is a valley that cuts through the hills and forested terrain that lie between German and Belgian territory. As a result, the major rail lines from Germany into Belgium run through this gap.

271 **Above all, he was a reliable supporter of the Republic** The most famous of these troubles had been the Dreyfus affair, during which a Jewish captain in the French general staff had been falsely accused of treason, found guilty on the basis of manufactured evidence, and then exiled to Devil's Island.

274 **As Winston Churchill commented in his brilliant if self-serving memoirs** Winston S. Churchill, *The World Crisis, 1911–1918* (Toronto: Macmillan Company of Canada, 1930), p. 6.

278 **As he replied to reports of a German deployment into Belgium** Barbara Tuchman, *The Guns of August* (New York: Random House, 1962), p. 211.

279 **A British corporal noted that** Holger H. Herwig, *The Marne, 1914: The Opening of World War I and the Battle That Changed the World* (New York: Random House, 2009), p. 154.

282 **What Joffre was unable to achieve with Field Marshal Sir John French** Ibid., p. 193.

283 **Admittedly the enemy was retreating** Ibid., p. 290.

286 **Warned of the French threat** Ibid., p. 243.

287 **Moltke closed with a foreboding comment** Ibid., p. 276.

THE BATTLE OF BRITAIN *The Nazis Stopped*

293 **Winston Churchill reportedly responded** Churchill's quote is presented in William Manchester's *The Last Lion,* vol. 2 (Boston: Little, Brown & Company, 2012), p. 334. But it may be a combination of two quotes. For a discussion of the quote's reliability, see www.winstonchurchill.org/learn/speeches/quotations/quotes-falsely-attributed.

296 **"Dowding was indisputably the pivotal military figure"** Alan Beyerchen, "From Radio to Radar," in Williamson Murray and Allan R. Millett, *Military Innovation in the Interwar Period* (Cambridge, UK: Cambridge University Press, 1996), p. 282.

298 **"that if an adequate fighter"** Richard Hough and Denis Richards, *The Battle of Britain: The Greatest Air Battle of World War II* (New York: W. W. Norton, 1982), p. 89.

299 **But as Churchill warned the House of Commons** Hansard, June 4, 1940.

299 **"What General Weygand called the Battle of France is over"** Winston S. Churchill, *The Second World War,* vol. 2, *Their Finest Hour* (New York: Houghton Mifflin, 1949), pp. 225–26.

301 **Alfred Jodl, noted that** Chef WFA, 30.6.40, "Die Weiterführung des Krieges gegen England," International Military Tribunal, *Trial of Major War Criminals,* vol. 28, pp. 301–03, http://www.loc.gov/rr/frd/Military_Law/NT_major-war-criminals.html.

303 **The Luftwaffe's commander in chief** Bundesarchiv/Militärarchiv, BA/MA RL 2II/27, "Allgemeine Weisung für den Kampf der Luftwaffe gegen England," ObdL Führungsstab Ia Nr. 5835/40, 30.6.40.

306 **The most thorough history of the battle** Francis K. Mason, *Battle over Britain: A History of the German Air Assaults on Great Britain, 1917–18 and July–December 1940, and of the Development of Britain's Air Defenses Between the World Wars* (London: McWhirter Twins Ltd., 1969), p. 237.

311 **The most thoroughly researched work on the battle** Ibid., p. 7.

315 **As for the ground crews** Ibid.

MIDWAY *Imperial Japan Stopped*

318 **But in fact they were American B-25s** Within two years Doolittle would rise to the rank of lieutenant general and command the Eighth Air Force, its bombers, and its fighters in the great American daylight offensive against Nazi Germany.

323 **"What a nonsens[ical] operation!"** Quoted in Gordon W. Prange, with

Donald M. Goldstein and Katherine V. Dillon, *Miracle at Midway* (New York: Penguin Books, 1982), p. 37.

325 **In battleships, the Japanese again held the advantage** The *Yamato* was 72,400 tons with a main armament of nine 18.1-inch guns; the American equivalents, the *Iowa* class, were 45,000 tons with a main armament of nine 16-inch guns.

326 **"[Radio interceptions] indicate that enemy"** Matome Ugaki, *Fading Victory: The Diary of Admiral Matome Ugaki, 1941–1945*, trans. Masataka Chihaya (Pittsburgh: University of Pittsburgh Press, 1992), p. 131.

327 **One of Nimitz's staff officers would describe him** Prange, *Miracle at Midway*, p. 97.

327 **Nimitz's instructions to his two task force commanders** Samuel Eliot Morison, *History of United States Naval Operations in World War II*, vol. 4, *Coral Sea, Midway, and Submarine Actions, May 1942–August 1942* (Boston: Little, Brown & Company, 1964), p. 84.

328 **After all, according to Nagumo's estimate** Prange, *Miracle at Midway*, p. 182.

333 **A recent study of the battle describes the catastrophe** Jonathan Parshall and Anthony Tully, *Shattered Sword: The Untold Story of the Battle of Midway* (Washington, DC: Potomac Books, 2005), p. 248.

335 **"The carriers [dead in the water]"** Naval Historical Center, "Oral History, Battle of Midway," recollections of Lieutenant George Gay, USNR, sole survivor of Torpedo Squadron Eight, box 11 of World War II interviews.

KURSK *The End of the* Drang Nach Osten

344 **When it came to divining German intentions** Speculation has never ceased as to Lucy's identity, but whoever it was was remarkably well-informed. Still, Lucy's silence in early 1943 had allowed the Soviets to be surprised by Manstein's counterattack. Moreover, all through the spring of 1943, Lucy provided a series of incorrect reports, reflecting the uncertainty and plan changes within the German high command. Still, Lucy provided the Soviets with the exact date of the German assault within twenty-four hours after Hitler announced his final decision.

344 **Of these, six were panzer and one was a panzer grenadier division** The panzer divisions were the 2nd, 4th, 9th, 12th, 18th, and 20th. The panzer grenadier was the 10th.

344 **In total, the Ninth Army numbered approximately 335,000 men** All numbers for German and Soviet forces are taken from works by David Glantz. See David M. Glantz and Jonathan M. House, *The Battle of Kursk* (Lawrence: University Press of Kansas, 1999).

347 **"The sky blackened from smoke and heat"** Ibid., p. 89.

348 **Repeatedly, battalions and regiments reported** Ibid., p. 90.

348 **For the Germans, the shock was that** Ibid., p. 91.

348 **According to a German general on the scene** Mark Healy, *Zitadelle: The German Offensive Against the Kursk Salient 4–17 July 1943* (London: Spellmount Press, 2010), p. 229.

350 **Some of the Tigers had no machine guns** Lloyd Clark, *The Battle of the Tanks: Kursk, 1943* (New York: Atlantic Monthly Press, 2011), p. 254.

350 **"Within an hour all of the officers of the 5th Company"** Paul Carell, *Scorched Earth: The Russian-German War 1943–1944* (New York: Ballantine Books, 1971), p. 46.

350 **Finding a gap between two Soviet divisions** The Soviet divisions were the 175th and 70th Guards Rifle Divisions.

351 **Reportedly, the Germans fired more shells** Mark Healy, *Kursk 1943: The Tide Turns in the East* (Oxford, UK: Osprey Publishing, 1992), p. 37.

352 **As the troops in the second defensive belt** Soviet unit designations often get confusing here. The most important thing to remember is not to confuse the Fifth Guards Tank Corps with the Fifth Guards Tank Army, which arrived later in the battle. The latter was about four to five times as powerful as the corps.

354 **At a meeting at First Tank Army headquarters that night** Healy, *Kursk 1943*, p. 65.

355 **His one thousand tanks would be ready for battle the next morning** The number of tanks that fought at Prokhorovka has been a matter of argument driven by myth since the end of the war. Moreover, the scale of the individual fights and of both sides' respective tank losses has for most of the past fifty years been largely myth also. The Soviets, whom most historians have taken at their word, hugely inflated the number of German tanks destroyed while simultaneously reducing their own horrendous losses. As historian Robert Citino states on his military history blog: ". . . we have to look to the writings of General Pavel Rotmistrov, commander of the Soviet 5th Guards Tank Army. Tasked to launch a counterstroke to halt the drive of Army Group South (and its spearhead, II SS Panzer Corps), he did so *con brio*, as it were, launching a massive frontal assault into the teeth of the advancing Germans. Mixing it up close-range with Panthers and Tigers almost always had deleterious consequences. His losses were stupendous, and only recently have post-Soviet archives been telling the tale. The XXIX Tank Corps, for example, lost 95 of its 122 T-34 tanks, 36 of its 70 light T-70s, and 19 of its 20 assault guns. It didn't have to be this way. Soviet formations fighting alongside Rotmistrov fought with less boldness, perhaps, but with more wisdom, and brought the Germans to a halt without such mind-boggling losses. So Rotmistrov had some explaining to do, and explain he did. In his memoirs, he painted what became the received version of Prokhorovka, owning up to his own losses, yes, but claiming to have destroyed 400 tanks and broken the back of the SS Panzer Corps that day. Now, that really would have been an achievement, since there were only 267 tanks in the entire corps at Prokhorovka. Indeed, German losses for all of Army Group South in the entire twelve days of the Kursk offensive amounted to just 161. He also claimed to have destroyed 70 Tigers. The actual number of Tigers lost at Prokhorovka? 0." (See www.historynet.com/creating-kursk-general -rotmistrov's-portrait.htm.) The initial research into German tank

strength and daily losses was undertaken by George M. Nipe, who published his startling findings in *World War II* magazine in February 1998 (see www.historynet.com/kursk-february-98-world-war-ii-feature.htm, accessed August 22, 2012).

356 **Tiger Company commander Rudolf von Ribbentrop** Glantz and House, *Battle of Kursk,* p. 185.

358 **With that the great German offensive came to a sputtering conclusion** Mungo Melvin, *Manstein: Hitler's Greatest General* (London: Weidenfeld & Nicolson, 2010), pp. 375–78.

358 **Manstein later wrote** Lloyd Clark, "The Battle of Kursk: Clash of the Tanks," *World War II* magazine (December 2010). This article is available at www .historynet.com/the-battle-of-kursk-clash-of-the-tanks.htm.

NORMANDY *The Death Knell for Nazi Germany*

362 **In a speech to the French people in October 1940** Winston S. Churchill, *Blood, Sweat, and Tears* (Toronto: McClelland & Stewart, 1941), p. 403.

367 **"The rail network is to be completely wrecked"** RAF Air Historical Branch, "Air Attacks Against German Rail Systems During 1944," Luftwaffe Operations Staff/Intelligence, no. 2512/44, "Air Operations Against the German Rail Transport System During March, April, May 1944," 3.6.44.

382 **As one Ranger survivor recalled forty years later** Captain Robert Merill, quoted in *Newsweek,* May 1, 1984.

385 **Yet, as the British official history notes** Major L. F. Ellis, *Victory in the West,* vol. 1, *The Battle of Normandy* (Uckfield, UK: Naval & Military Press, 1962), p. 216.

DIEN BIEN PHU *Imperialism Defeated*

392 **De Lattre had commented to his aides on arrival** Quoted in Ted Morgan, *Valley of Death: The Tragedy at Dien Bien Phu That Led America into the Vietnam War* (New York: Random House, 2010), p. 115.

399 **Half an hour later, another company desperately reported** Bernard Fall, *Hell in a Very Small Place* (New York: Da Capo Press, 1965), p. 141.

400 **When an Algerian being led away to prison camp balked** Ibid., p. 152.

401 **Bernard Fall pointed out the situation's irony** Ibid., p. 179.

404 **As he noted after the battle** Quoted in ibid., p. 225.

404 **As Giap later noted** Ibid., p. 278.

OBJECTIVE PEACH *The Drive for Baghdad*

410 **In fact, throughout the American buildup** For a thorough analysis of these statements, see Kevin Woods, Williamson Murray, Mark Stout, and James Lacey, *The Iraqi Prospective Report* (Annapolis: USNI, 2006). This study, based on captured Iraqi documents and extensive postwar interviews with senior Iraqi commanders, presents a comprehensive picture of the Iraqi side of the war. Most of the Iraqi viewpoint found in this chapter is drawn from that work and from the papers gathered for the study.

411 As the lead elements of 3ID entered the city of Samawah Saddam became infatuated with the effectiveness of irregular troops after seeing what they did to American forces in Somalia (Black Hawk Down) and subsequently formed these units in 1994. Thousands of these loyalists were transported to southern Iraq to ensure the Shia would never rise again. They were poorly trained and only lightly armed. On the other hand, they often displayed fanatical bravery and were completely loyal to the regime.

413 The Iraqi II Republican Corps commander The Remagen Bridge spanned the Rhine River and was captured intact by advancing American tanks during the Second World War. It allowed the Americans to cross the Rhine into Germany without incurring the heavy losses that would have resulted by a boat crossing under fire.

414 However, this officer took it upon himself Saddam's order is a direct result of his firmly held conviction that the Americans, if they invaded at all, would stop short of Baghdad and that he would need all available bridges to rush his own armor south in the event of another Shia uprising.

INDEX

Note: *Italicized* page numbers refer to illustrations

ABOUT THE AUTHORS

JAMES LACEY is the author of *The First Clash: The Miraculous Greek Victory at Marathon and Its Impact on Western Civilization, Moment of Battle: The Twenty Clashes That Changed the World,* and many other works on military history. He is a widely published defense analyst who has written extensively on the war in Iraq and on the global war on terrorism. Having served more than a dozen years on active duty as an infantry officer, he recently retired from the Army Reserves. Lacey traveled with the 101st Airborne Division during the Iraq invasion as an embedded journalist for *Time* magazine, and his work has also appeared in *National Review, Foreign Affairs,* the *Journal of Military History,* and many other publications. He currently teaches at the Marine Corps War College and Georgetown University.

WILLIAMSON MURRAY is the author of a wide selection of articles and books, including, with Allan R. Millett, the acclaimed *A War to Be Won,* an operational history of World War II. He is professor emeritus of history from Ohio State, served for five years as an officer in the United States Air Force, and has taught at the Air War College and the United States Military Academy. He has also served as a Secretary of the Navy Fellow at the Naval War College, the Centennial Visiting Professor at the London School of Economics, the Matthew C. Horner Professor of Military Theory at the Marine Corps University, the Charles Lindbergh Chair at the Smithsonian National Air and Space Museum, the Harold K. Johnson Professor of Military History at the Army War College, and has just completed two years as the Distinguished Visiting Professor of Naval Heritage and History at the U.S. Naval Academy at Annapolis. He is presently a defense analyst at the Potomac Institute for Policy Studies and teaches at the Naval War College.

31901051994988